T0395034

# Praise

'A rich and distinctive collection of related essays by an erudite comparatist who moves with ease between classics and contemporaries. Miller is in a far better position than most to elucidate and critique modern theoretical, critical, and philological engagements of (mainly) the powerful French theorists from the 1960s to today with the likes of Plato and Cicero. With acuity, verve, and wit, Miller explores the precarious boundaries of philosophy, literature, rhetoric in and through what got to be called theory. The performance of Miller's text is a compelling, embodied argument of and for the impertinence of such boundaries.'

*Ian G. Balfour, Professor Emeritus of English and*
*of Social & Political Thought, York University, Canada.*

'Paul Allen has changed the Humanities by unconventionally bringing together antiquity and modernity, by illustrating not only the deep engagement of postmodern thinkers with the classical past but also how ancient philosophy and poetry preview and enact before our eyes the concerns and ideas of postmodernism. What he has accomplished in his career is prodigious. In the essays gathered here, both rigorous and magnificently adventurous, he integrates the philosophical and the literary in surprising ways, brilliantly demonstrating the political power of critical theoretical thinking in our times.'

*Mario Telò, Department of Comparative Literature,*
*University of California, USA.*

'In twelve essays of dazzling erudition, intellectual sophistication, and argumentative panache, Paul Allen Miller makes a timely defense of the humanities as fields of study that investigate the possibility of meaning and of the meaning of truth. Theory does not exist as a bounded space of reflection, but as open-ended dialogues between historically and culturally nuanced discourses that shape both our self-awareness and a truly democratic ethos.'

*Zina Giannopoulou, Associate Professor, Classics |*
*European Languages and Studies | Religious Studies, University of California, Irvine, USA.*

'Paul Allen Miller has long been a leading scholar on the relation between literature and theory. *Theory Does Not Exist: Comparative Ancient and Modern Explorations in Psychoanalysis, Deconstruction, and Rhetoric* brings together some of the key questions impacting the humanities today. Whereas a current wing of the humanities is keen on blaming "Theory" for the demise of literary studies (killing the love of literature, instrumentalizing the aesthetic for political reason, and so on), Miller asks us to pause and think, meticulously unpacking the meaning(s) of theory, and putting it in critical dialogue with ancient voices. From Plato to Derrida, theory persists and there is no better scholar than Miller to articulate its afterlives.'

*Zahi Zalloua, Whitman University, USA.*

'Paul Allen Miller argues that the instabilities of language are crucial to the very possibility of meaning. Postmodern thinkers did not produce static "theories," but were engaged in a dialogue "that constitutes the movement of truth in time." His essays brilliantly evoke and reaffirm the dynamism of the humanities.'

*David Konstan, Professor of Classics, New York University, USA.*

'Like the ghost of Patroclus that appears to Achilles in the *Iliad*, Miller's brilliant and compassionate book shows theory's paradoxical ability to move us beyond the present, however discouraging and grief-ridden it may seem, and to send us forth into the world to come.'

*Charles Platter, Professor of Classics, University of Georgia, USA.*

'*Theory Does Not Exist* proves that, in ancient and modern worlds, the rhetoric of theory is ever-present. Rather than treating theory as an object or tool of recent or long-standing influence, this illuminating book analyzes and thinks through theory's shaping, lively power. As such, Paul Allen Miller clarifies how the interpretive practices of the humanities pervades psychoanalysis, deconstruction, and rhetorical studies. *Theory Does Not Exist* thereby refreshes and expands the idea of the human dimension connecting ancient thinking and contemporary studies. In its light, we can envision a truly liberated world culture of human thought and free expression to come. This book puts the lie to the triumphalism of AI, with a warm smile on its face.'

*Daniel O'Hara, Temple University, USA.*

'In *Theory Does Not Exist*, one of our most eminent theorists, Paul Allen Miller, tells us that theory does not exist. Theory does not exist because it is never an isolated or positive entity. Instead, it is always an intimate other to discourses that have been central to the history of Western thought, whether these are termed philosophy, rhetoric, or science. In insisting on the dimension of rhetoric within any truth claim, while still affirming the importance of truth, Miller articulates a future for the humanities, one in which the quantitative must always be complicated and enriched by the qualitative.'

*Christopher Breu, College of Arts & Sciences, Illinois State University, Illinois State, USA.*

# Theory Does Not Exist

# Theory Does Not Exist

## Comparative Ancient and Modern Explorations in Psychoanalysis, Deconstruction, and Rhetoric

Paul Allen Miller

ANTHEM PRESS

Anthem Press
An imprint of Wimbledon Publishing Company
*www.anthempress.com*

This edition first published in UK and USA 2024
by ANTHEM PRESS
75–76 Blackfriars Road, London SE1 8HA, UK
or PO Box 9779, London SW19 7ZG, UK
and
244 Madison Ave #116, New York, NY 10016, USA

© Paul Allen Miller 2024

The author asserts the moral right to be identified as the author of this work.

All rights reserved. Without limiting the rights under copyright reserved above,
no part of this publication may be reproduced, stored or introduced into
a retrieval system, or transmitted, in any form or by any means
(electronic, mechanical, photocopying, recording or otherwise),
without the prior written permission of both the copyright
owner and the above publisher of this book.

*British Library Cataloguing-in-Publication Data*
A catalogue record for this book is available from the British Library.

*Library of Congress Cataloging-in-Publication Data*
A catalog record for this book has been requested.
2023952081

ISBN-13: 978-1-83999-085-4 (Hbk)
ISBN-10: 1-83999-085-6 (Hbk)

This title is also available as an e-book.

For Ann, as always.

# CONTENTS

| | | |
|---|---|---|
| *Acknowledgments* | | xi |
| *Theory Does Not Exist: An Introduction* | | xiii |
| Chapter 1 | Debits and Credits or Accounting for My Life: A Defense of Reading and Humanistic Education | 1 |
| Chapter 2 | The Trouble with Theory: A Comparatist Manifesto | 13 |
| Chapter 3 | Placing the Self in the Field of Truth: Irony and Self-Fashioning in Ancient and Postmodern Rhetorical Theory | 25 |
| Chapter 4 | Rhetoric and Deconstruction: Plato, the Sophists, and Philosophy | 41 |
| Chapter 5 | The Platonic Remainder: Derrida's *Khôra* and the *Corpus Platonicum* | 55 |
| Chapter 6 | Cicero Reads Derrida Reading Cicero: A Politics and a Friendship to Come | 71 |
| Chapter 7 | On Borders, Race, and Infinite Hospitality: Foucault, Derrida, and Camus | 89 |
| Chapter 8 | Sartre, Politics, and Psychoanalysis: It Don't Mean a Thing If It Aint Got *Das Ding* | 105 |
| Chapter 9 | Enjoyment beyond the Pleasure Principle: *Antigone*, Julian of Norwich, and the *Use of Pleasures* | 123 |
| Chapter 10 | Lacan le con: Luce Tells Jacques Off | 137 |
| Chapter 11 | The Repeatable and the Unrepeatable: Žižek and the Future of the Humanities, or Assessing Socrates | 149 |
| Chapter 12 | Theory Does Not Exist | 165 |
| *Index* | | 181 |

# ACKNOWLEDGMENTS

With the exception of the introduction, all of these essays have appeared in a variety of venues over the last two decades. I am grateful for the opportunity to update and revise them. A book written over this expanse of time has many debts. More than I can repay. As I look back though, I realize that over the years, I have been lucky enough to develop what in Buddhism they call a *sangha*, a spiritual community of fellow seekers, what in Greek we would call *philosophoi*. I want to take this opportunity to thank you all, to bow to you, and to say these essays would not exist in their current form without you. First, there is Chuck Platter. We have been on a long journey together of thought, seeking, and friendship. So much began that year we spent in Paris (1985–86). It is hard even to calculate. Sharon Nell, the years we spent reading Bakhtin, Lacan, Cixous, Kristeva, and Irigaray have left an indelible mark. The seminars we taught together at Texas Tech are some of my most precious memories. David Larmour, on the dusty plains of Lubbock, we dreamed of a new Classics. If you had not had faith in me and convinced your colleagues to hire me at Texas Tech, I would have never had a career. Micaela Janan, when I first read *The Lamp Is Shattered*, it changed my scholarly life. It was a revelation. I remember going to the basement of the library at Texas Tech to send you one of the very first emails I ever wrote. We have exchanged so many since. Jake Blevins, although you began as my student in Lubbock, you have long since become a valued friend and interlocutor. I wish we saw each other more often. Our conversations on irony, Lacan, and Catullus over the years have meant so much. Pierre Zoberman, the hike you led in Tübingen at the Institute for the Classical Tradition began a wonderful story and fruitful collaboration. Your hospitality in Paris, your patience in correcting my French, and your inviting me to speak at one of the first queer theory conferences in France have all been milestones in my life. Jeffrey Di Leo and Zahi Zalloua, when we met at the SCLA in Knoxville in 1999, we started a friendship and a dialogue that continues to this day and has broadened to include an expanding circle of friends and interlocutors: especially Nicole Simek and Brian O'Keefe. Jill Frank, the years we spent reading Plato together in Columbia touched so many of these essays, I cannot even begin to say. I look forward to every chance we get to renew that dialogue. Richard Armstrong, your work on Freud and your infectious love of learning is amazing. You are the only person I know who reads Homer in Ladino! I'm so happy we have become friends and collaborators. Mario Telò, the man who has read everything, you challenge me not to be complacent and you push me to find new sources of inspiration. My students and I dare not list you for fear of missing someone, you are a constant spur to creativity and a call to responsibility. My teachers, especially

Kevin Herbert, Barbara Gold, Carl Rubino, Wayne Rebhorn, and Leonard Schultze, I hope I have meant half as much to my students as you have meant to me.

"Lacan le con: Luce Tells Jacques off" is published with permission from the University of Nebraska Press. Paul Allen Miller © 2005. "The Trouble with Theory: A Comparativist Manifesto" is published with permission from the University of Nebraska Press. Paul Allen Miller © 2003. "The Repeatable and the Unrepeatable: Žižek and the Future of the Humanities, or Assessing Socrates" is published with permission from the University of Nebraska Press. Paul Allen Miller © 2010. "The Platonic Remainder: *Khora* and the *Corpus Platonicum*" is published with permission from Oxford University Press. Paul Allen Miller © 2010. "Enjoyment beyond the Pleasure Principle: Antigone, Julian of Norwich, and the Use of Pleasures" in *The Comparatist*, Volume 39. Copyright © 2015 by the Southern Comparative Literature Association. Used by permission of the University of North Carolina Press. "Placing the Self in the Field of Truth: Irony and Self-Fashioning in Ancient and Postmodern Rhetorical Theory." Copyright © 2015, Johns Hopkins University Press. This article first appeared in *Arethusa*, Volume 48, Number 3, Fall 2015. Published with permission by Johns Hopkins University Press. "Rhetoric and Deconstruction: Plato, the Sophists, and Philosophy" is published with permission from Oxford University Press. Paul Allen Miller © 2017. "Theory Does Not Exist" is published with permission from Bloomsbury Publishing Plc. Paul Allen Miller © 2019. "Debits and Credits or Accounting for My Life: A Defense of the Humanities" in *The Comparatist*, Volume 44. Copyright © 2020 by the Southern Comparative Literature Association. Used by permission of the University of North Carolina Press.

# THEORY DOES NOT EXIST:
# AN INTRODUCTION

We would need to think life starting from heritage, and not the opposite. We would need to start from this apparent formal contradiction between the passivity of reception and the decision to say "yes," then to select, to filter, to interpret, thus, to transform, not to leave intact, undamaged, not to leave *untouched* even what one respects before all. And after all. Not to leave untouched: to preserve, perhaps, still, for some time, but without any illusion about ultimate salvation. (Derrida in Derrida and Roudinesco 2001: 16, emphasis his)

Example: if one morning Socrates had spoken for Plato, if to Plato its recipient he had addressed some message, it's also that p. would have been able to receive, to await, to desire, would have in a certain sense called for what S. will have said to him; and therefore what S., under this dictation, has the appearance of inventing—he writes it. p. sent himself a post card (legend + image), he sent it from himself, or even, he sent himself S. (Derrida 1980: 35)

To entitle a book on deconstruction, psychoanalysis, and rhetoric, *Theory Does not Exist*, may seem perverse. A glance at the table of contents would lead many a reader and perhaps many a humanities scholar to say this book is filled with nothing but "theory." One need only look at the names mentioned or alluded to in the titles: Derrida, Foucault, Freud, Irigaray, Lacan, Sartre, and Žižek. They have become bywords for "theory," whether as an academic specialty, an intellectual talisman, or an anathema hurled at cultural adversaries.

At the same time, however, there is another set of names in these titles: Sophocles, Socrates, Plato, the Sophists, and Cicero. These are not simply target texts. They are not the textual or literary objects to which various theories are applied to produce "readings" or "interpretations." They are rather interlocutors and inspirations. They are where the "heritage" we sometimes call "theory" begins (insofar as it has a beginning). In a simpler, less self-aware (and hence more problematic, monologic, and oppressive) time, these ancient texts, all by Western men, designated what we called "Classics."

Within the essays themselves, we find a variety of other names, Catullus, Juvenal, Julian of Norwich, Dogen, Hegel, Kierkegaard, Mallarmé, Camus, Kristeva, and more. And this is very much the point. What we call theory is not a simple object that can be either accepted or rejected. It is a complex conversation that reaches back to our earliest recorded moments of asking: what is meaning; how do we communicate it to others; how does that communication create and exercise power; how does the possibility of meaning create and limit our desires; and how else can we create meaningful existences for ourselves and others except through narratives, except through the possibility of offering a variety of stories that we then receive, modify, and make our own?[1] This complex conversation is never linear. It is ramified and recursive, sometimes broken, always going back to different beginnings to create new futures, new traditions.

In the "Garden of Forking Paths" that constitutes the set of theoretical inheritances through which we interpret our received narratives and proffer new ones, each point of reception is a decision point that rewrites the past and makes possible the still to come. Individual paths branch off and intersect. They meet up with others that are possessed of radically different histories, and those meetings cause both themselves and their others to be rewritten.

Such rewriting in fact is the work of meaning. It is what we do in the humanities. We make and investigate the possibility of meaning, and thus the foundation of truth. If theory is this conversation, then there is no world outside of theory, outside the world's constitution in and through meaning. And thus, theory as a discrete thing in the world, one which can be either accepted or rejected, does not, indeed cannot, exist. It has no discrete being because the questions it asks, and the roots they have in our philosophical, rhetorical, literary, spiritual, and artistic traditions, constitute the ontological conditions of meaning being in the world. Outside these conversations, meaning can only be either an empty abstraction or a predetermined *logos* existing in the mind of God (or computational linguistics).

In the end, it all depends on what we mean by existence. Can something *exist* that has no clearly discernible beginning and end, when we cannot definitively describe what lies inside it or outside it? How would such an existence be rigorously distinguished from nonexistence? To define something is to give it borders (*fines*). The opposite of the defined and hence the definite is not so much the void as the infinite, not so much nothing as *no* thing. In saying theory does not exist, we are not saying (as some have) that postmodern or critical thought is somehow a hoax, that it is responsible for our post-truth society (Calcutt 2016; Iling 2019), or that people are deluded when they say they study theory. We are saying something closer to Gertrude Stein, when she said of Oakland, "there is no there there." That is to say, theory is less a defined place (*topos*), with a clear inside and outside, an identity, a geometrically demarcated location, than an opening or clearing where space (*khōra*) can be made (see chapter 5).

Theory as such may not exist, but there is a real sense in which we only exist *in and through* theory. It is only through concepts, metaphors, and images—received from the vast discursive universe into which we are thrown—that we come to define ourselves *as* subjects, that we come to define our communities *as* cities, states, and peoples, and that we body forth our understandings and thus performances of the good, the true, and the beautiful, of gender, genre, and genius. It is only through a moment of self-reflective abstraction, within our dialogically constituted universe, that we can begin to

---

1  I consider this endeavor very much in harmony with Mowitt's "Introduction" in *Offering Theory*. My time frame is larger than his, but we are both committed to moving beyond a reification of theory and to an insistence that a theoretical form of inquiry in the broad sense is central to what I term "the work of meaning" and to resisting the neoliberal university (2020).

# AN INTRODUCTION

articulate who we are and the objects we desire, that we can therefore come to care for both ourselves and others, and hence that we can start to understand what is the proper (*decus*), what are the specific *properties* of our objects, and what is my property versus yours (see chapters 1, 3, and 11).

If the ontology of theory, the humanities, and ultimately of our selves is something like what I have just outlined, then their proper study can only be comparative (see chapter 2). Such comparative study must not only be lateral—comparing different contemporary discourses and traditions—but also historical, examining the genealogy of the present, how it came to be. We must avoid what T. S. Eliot once termed a "provincialism, not of space, but of time; one for which history is merely the chronicle of human devices" (1945: 30). It is for this reason that the following collection of essays, are subtitled, *Comparative Ancient and Modern Explorations in Psychoanalysis, Deconstruction, and Rhetoric*. What they, at every turn, seek to examine is the ontology of the present as constituted through the past (Foucault 2008: 22), what Derrida labels the "hauntology" of our discourse (Derrida 1993: 69, 89; Derrida 2002: 57–58, 83–89).

From this comparative perspective, psychoanalysis, deconstruction, and rhetoric are less topics to be taken up serially, than aspects of the same enterprise: the insistence of the letter in the practice of life. While we often tend to think of psychoanalysis as a clinical practice and lump it with psychology or psychiatry, it works on a fundamentally different substance and in a fundamentally different way. As Lacan says in his Second Seminar:

> We cannot grasp being from a scientific point of view because it is not of the scientific order. But psychoanalysis is however an experience that designates, so to speak, its line of flight. It underlines that the human being is not an object, but a being in the process of trying to realize itself. (1978: 147)

The talking cure works on and through the process of signification, on and through the production and examination of dreams, jokes, parapraxes, associative chains, and other texts in order to determine and address the structures of our suffering and desire. It is closer to a humanistic or hermeneutic practice than a social-scientific one.

This is not what psychology does. When one looks at psychology departments in universities, much of the research done is focused on the evolution and adaptation of the brain. It is neuro- and cognitive science. When one examines what is taught in clinical psychology in those same departments, the objects of study are largely behavioral and adaptive practices, forms of operant conditioning, and self-assessment or self-monitoring. Such techniques make patients aware of patterns in their emotional lives and family dynamics. They can be useful in dealing with anxiety or in coping with cognitive differences, addictions, or other "disorders."

Psychological science presupposes in every case that there are stable entities in our mental and behavioral activities that can be defined, controlled, and modified, according to certain social norms, standard functions, or operational goals. The entities defined and studied can be either structures of the brain, measurable behaviors, or other forms of adaptation. In short, the behavioral sciences must posit that there are "things" in or determinative of our psyches or brains that we can define, measure, and hence universalize (all normal people do or have x). This process of universalizing anatomical structures or cognitive and behavioral patterns is what makes possible their scientific study, and hence the production of repeatable, testable data, as well as the derivation from that data of psychic norms and deviations, with all their attendant utilities for patient-, client-, and worker-management as well as dangers (one need only think of the history of the word *deviant*; Foucault 1999).

Psychiatric science works in an analogous fashion. It has a closer focus on how chemical modifications of the brain produce alterations in those same behaviors and functionalities and hence on the use of antidepressants, antianxiety medications, and antipsychotics to manage patient care. Psychiatry and psychology have beyond doubt brought many people, including in my own family, measurable and welcome relief. Nonetheless, they can only do so by abstracting from individual experience and hence from the processes and practices by which we make meaning in and for our individual existences. They must operate in the name of a set of ontological and epistemic presuppositions that, by definition, bracket the individual and exclude the unrepeatable: the moments that make our lives more than a mechanical repetition of universal patterns, and hence give them meaning and purpose (see chapter 11). They are in their essence reifying and normalizing, even when beneficial.

American Ego Psychology, which is what largely became of psychoanalysis when it reached North America, shares many of these same assumptions, reducing the psyche to a set of reified operations and entities. It is focused on the reduction of resistances and the producing of strong normative egos adapted to their social and economic contexts. It aspires to being a testable science but can always and only fail in that ambition because each analysand brings their own dreams, symptoms, and associations. It rejects the meta-psychological speculations of the late Freud in favor of what it hopes will be a Popperian science (Lacan 1973: 14–15; Lacan 1975a: 13, 259, 300; Lacan 1978: 22; Ragland-Sullivan 1986: 158; Julien 1990: 143; Gherovici 2000: 97; Liu 2000: 129–30; Armstrong 2005: 133–34).

Actual Freudian psychoanalysis works in a very different way, with very different presuppositions. Its domain is "the truth of the subject" and "the search for [that] truth is not completely reducible to objective research" (Lacan 1975b: 37). If we turn to *The Interpretation of Dreams*, at the beginning of the chapter on the Dream-Work Freud compares the text of a dream to a rebus: a puzzle that presents words and images in a seemingly random order, which must be deciphered if the message is to be understood. Typically, the immediate import of the depicted objects to one another is unclear. They lack appropriate scale, causal connections, and logical relations. Nonetheless, they can be made to yield a sensible solution.

> Suppose I have a picture-puzzle, a rebus, in front of me, It depicts a house with a boat on its roof, a single letter of the alphabet, the figure of a running man whose head has been conjured away, and so on. Now I might be misled into raising objections and declaring that the picture as a whole and its component parts are nonsensical.[...] But obviously we can only form a proper judgment of the rebus if we put aside criticisms such as these of the whole composition and its parts and if, instead, we try to replace each separate element by a syllable or word that can be represented by that element in some other way. (Freud 1965: 312)

# AN INTRODUCTION

xvii

Neuroscientists question whether dreams have meaning, seeing them as expressions of physical processes. Yet, from a psychoanalytic perspective, this is beside the point. Whatever their somatic origins, these images are not random. They pertain to us as their dreamers (my dreams are not exchangeable with yours). We must therefore assume something like the rhetoric of the rebus to be operative if the relation between dream and dreamer is to be discerned. The key problem is determining not simply the relation between parts and wholes within the dream-text, but also that to which they may point. What are those objects? Psychoanalysis is the study of the production of meanings, of the travails of signification, and those travails are always prior to the constitution of the discrete objects they attempt to name (Schneiderman 1983: 168).

Freud continues: in the traditional rebus, once commonly found in newspapers, the convention was that each puzzle had a single solution and that the relation between parts and whole was univalent. Such is not the case in Freud's dreams, however. The relation between parts and whole, between dream-work and dream-thoughts, is subject to "overdetermination." As he writes in his examination of the "Dream of the Botanical Monograph":

> The elements "botanical" and "monograph" found their way into the content of the dream because they possessed copious contacts with the majority of dream-thoughts, because, that is to say, they constituted "nodal-points" upon which a great number of the dream-thoughts converged, and because they have had several meanings in connection with the interpretation of the dream. The explanation of this fundamental fact can also be put in another way: each of the elements of the dream's content turns out to have been "overdetermined." (1965: 317–18)

Dreams are for Freud, ultimately, less like puzzles than complex texts whose meanings are beyond final specification. "The dream-thoughts to which we are led by interpretation cannot, from the nature of things have any definite endings; they are bound to branch out in every direction into the infinite network of our world of thought" (Freud 1965: 564).

The term "rhetoric," then, for the dream-work is used advisedly. I am far from the first to observe that Freud's use of terms like "condensation" and "displacement" mimics tropes such as metaphor and metonymy. Freud himself deploys artistic examples throughout his oeuvre, most famously perhaps *Oedipus Rex* and *Hamlet* in the *Traumdeutung* (1965: 294–300). There is a rhetoric and poetics to the dream-work that cannot be separated from rhetoric and poetics *tout court*, from the way signs are deployed in complex fashions to create layers of meaning and resonance. The unconscious, according to Lacan, is structured like a language (Lacan 1973: 167; Lacan 1986: 42; Kristeva 1996; 66–67). This rhetorical language is in evidence whether we are examining dreams, jokes, or parapraxes: a word or image, which in a quotidian setting might have one signification, through juxtaposition or substitution is revealed to have another more ramified set of meanings extending throughout the phenomenon in question, knitting together latent associations, drives, and desires.

For Freud, dreams are first and foremost a means of wish fulfillment (Freud 1965: 155–56). But he also observes that many of our dreams are less easily parsed. Their narratives are fragmented. Parts are missing, and one thing is substituted for another.

Freud resists the notion that there is a universal key to all dreams, arguing that each dream must assume its place in the associative chain produced by the analysand (1965: 130n.1, 274, 311–14, 552–53, 561–62). Nonetheless, one of the traits common to many dreams is that they express desires to which it would be forbidden to give voice in our waking hours. Freud argues, moreover, that many of these desires would be too disturbing in their unvarnished form even for our dreams and would wake us from our slumbers: hence the rhetorical devices of the dreamwork (Freud 1965: 175–76, 508–9). Thus, what often appears innocent in dreams can have a sexual meaning.

Freudian psychoanalysis works then not simply at the level of constituted subjects and objects, and hence at the level of a post-Newtonian science, but also at the level on which subjects and object are constituted. To put it in the language of the Freud of *Beyond the Pleasure Principle*, psychology and most forms of social science work from the economic standpoint, according to which objects are assigned positive and negative values, and the rational subject then chooses between them based on a calculation of pleasure and pain. Psychoanalysis sees that dialectic as dependent on a prior set of operations and figures (primary repression, the mirror stage, the Oedipus complex) which make possible those objects' constitution as *objects* rather than as the infinite continuity of the Real or of the Imaginary maternal body (Freud 1961; Derrida 1967: 295). It is, moreover, this set of prior operations and figures that enables those now defined entities, those *things*, to assume the guise of objects of our desire and for us to be constituted as desiring subjects.

The realm or moment of these operations is by definition beyond or before our subjective constitution and so beyond or before the constitution of the object world. It is also what makes possible the historicizing of that world and its subjects as entities whose boundaries (*fines*) are contingent and hence open to negotiation. This realm therefore is precisely what lies beyond the pleasure principle: a space or moment that Freud calls death and Lacan *jouissance*, because the drive (*Trieb*) toward it is a drive toward the ecstatic annihilation of the object world as given and of our subjective investments in it (Lacan 1975a: 70–71; Ragland-Sullivan 1986: 81; Derrida 1996: 146; Valdré 2019: 23–24; Braunstein 2020: 20–23, 56–57, 90, 125–27). Such a vision can only be anathema to the epistemic and ontological assumptions of psychology, psychiatry, and American Ego Psychology, but it is well at home in our poetic, narrative, and musical traditions.

Deconstruction has a long running engagement with both psychoanalysis and rhetoric. And while Derrida has offered a variety of definitions and descriptions of how he understands deconstruction over the years, we could do worse than if we start from the perception that the world as constituted by our categories of understanding consists of a series of binary judgements—everything can only be A to the extent that it is differentiated from the not A. If this is so, then every moment of division is provisional, in so far as it is dependent on a vast array of simultaneous divisions. A is only A to the extent that all other things are not A's (B, C, D, etc.), and all those not A's, in turn, are only what they are to the extent that they too can be divided from their others, and so on. This moment of division happens both in space and time. It is mobile. There is always a before and after of any moment of division, a moment in which boundaries (*fines*) are drawn and objects defined, even as that moment of

AN INTRODUCTION

division also only exists in the context of a simultaneous series of lateral movements and divisions. It is this ever-moving moment of division and specification, which makes knowledge possible and renders it provisional, that Derrida names *différance*. In the final analysis (and the final moment never comes), this moment of division is always arbitrary (divisions can be and are made other ways). It represents a decision. Nonetheless, the play of *différance* is, in fact, what makes meaning possible (Derrida 1972: 38–39; Derrida 1996: 48). Without it, the difference between signifier and signified, between names and things, but also between different signifiers and names would be impossible. Without it, therefore, description and redescription would be impossible, and hence both statements and their verification (and thus truth) would also be impossible.

By definition, *différance* itself can never have an origin and an end. There is no intelligible moment of the undifferentiated or a moment of homogeneity restored that is not synonymous with nonexistence and death. This *is* in fact Freud's death drive, what Plato in the *Philebus* terms the *apeiron* (Derrida 1980: 425). The attempt to impose an *archē* and/or a *telos*, then, to arrest this moving moment or differentiation, through positing a master signifier—God, the *logos*, the phallus, history—that organizes and subordinates all other divisions to it, without itself being affected by them is what Derrida terms variously logocentrism, phallogocentrism, or the closure of metaphysics: that is to say, an ideal finality of discourse, a center that structures all its effects but is not structured by them (Derrida 1967: 409–11; Derrida 1972: 30; Derrida 1996: 41–42; Lewis 2008: 121). Hence, as described in *Positions* and elsewhere, the archetypical deconstructive reading or act is the identification of what appears to be a foundational opposition—writing and speech, *muthos* and *logos*, man and woman, human and animal—and demonstrating that the moment of absolute division between these terms is always to some extent arbitrary, that there is always a certain degree of cross-contamination between these seemingly opposed categories, that in fact the not A always already inheres in A (as demonstrated in Hegel's logic, *Encylopedia* §73), and therefore any hierarchy based on that opposition is ultimately arbitrary (in the sense that it has no ultimate foundation) and hence open to reversal (Derrida 1972: 56–57: Lewis 2008: 111, 115). But in fact deconstruction in its Derridean guise never stops simply at this act of reversal or at the declaration that the world is logically constituted not as an identity but as an endless series of differences, as dissemination. Deconstruction is an act or gesture to point at what lies beyond these divisions and the economy they represent, what lies beyond this system of exchanges and substitutions, a finger pointing at the moon (Derrida 1986: 135; Derrida 1992: 260–61; Lewis 2008: 3–5, 238–39; Courtine 2008: 26). That beyond, of course, can itself only be specified through the movement of *différance*, but in that brief moment of the opening, in the beyond of the closure of the present, the possibility of a different set of structures can be envisioned, a different constitution of the world, and this in turn is the moment of political struggle, the moment of potential revolution, when the specter of the divisions of the past becomes visible as the hauntology of the present, offering a moment of decision and the possibility of a world to come (Derrida 1980: 536; Derrida 1993:102, 151; Derrida 1994: 128; Jameson 2007: 152–53).

Finally, if discourse is not a set of rigid designations that maps a preexisting world of discrete entities for a serene, self-present consciousness, but is instead a mobile system of differences and determinations, a vast and yet situated set of dialogic interactions, moving in time, then the categories that make up our world and qualify our perceptions to produce what we call experience, as a complex synthetic movement, can never be a univocal suite of logical divisions that of its own volition organizes the world as a *res extensa* laid out before a Cartesian *cogito*. Instead, the very fabric of our experience, insofar as it is meaningful and not simply a disaggregated welter of sensation, must always be implicated in systems of signification, must always be determined by and determining of the phenomenal world. In ways that can never be centered within a unified subject, our experience of the world must always be haunted by the specter of past, present, and future divisions and determinations, by other possible articulations and voices, and hence by the history of our own and others' desires and divisions. If, as Lacan said, the unconscious is the discourse of the other (1975b: 376; 1978: 127), locating it not as a throbbing pit of instinct within but as the moment of our self-constitution, the moment when the speaking and reasoning subject is demarcated from the other, what Freud calls castration (Kristeva 1979: 11; Ragland-Sullivan 1986: 57; Žižek 1992: 171; Braunstein 2020: 77), then the deconstructive understanding of the subject's relation to meaning and experience will always cast *différance* as a vector not simply of reason and signification but also of the unconscious, political and otherwise, and hence also of conflict and power (Derrida 1967: 314; Derrida 1996: 23–24; Zuckert 1996: 213–14; Lewis 2008: 120). In the end, we all have our differences.

And this realization brings us (back) to rhetoric. One of the recurring themes in these essays is the opposition between rhetoric and philosophy as a precursor to that between "theory" and philosophy or even theory and science (see chapters 3, 4, and 12). If our discourse or our conceptual universe were (or could be made to be) a set of rigid designations of things that exist in the world—and here a fuller discussion would require a parenthesis on the multiplicity of languages and possibilities of translation— then the rhetorical would be a distortion of the world, a sophistic focus on words rather than things, on power rather than truth, on enjoyment rather than rationality.[2] But if instead discourse is always a provisional and mobile set of situated distinctions, one that bears the smell and taste of its users, their irreducible particularities, their positions within overlapping networks of power and signification, then the rhetorical always already inheres in the moment of truth. Even the mathematicization of the universe never completely elides the moment of our experience, never completely reduces the concrete particularity of reference to the cypher of the universal. Rather we are in every truth claim exercising and/or resisting power. We are attempting to convince others of the rightness of our position, deploying means and mechanisms that are external to and yet determinative of that claim as a moment of pure meaning (Foucault 2012: 51, 74).

---

2  See Foucault's lecture on Aristotle's exclusion of sophistics (*sophistikē*) from philosophy in *Metaphysics* Gamma 2 and Aristotle's contention that the formal cause of philosophy is "a certain relation to truth" (2011: 32–33).

AN INTRODUCTION

Different conventions of rhetoric are applicable in different contexts: who can address which bodies (*ethos*), under what circumstances (*pathos*), and using what means (*logos*). These are all necessary determinations of power and persuasion that are profoundly familiar to anyone who works at a university, who is a member of a professional society, or who has served as a referee or reader for a learned journal or has worked in a laboratory.[3] Indeed, these conventions, despite their externality, are not impediments or obstacles to truth, they are what makes true statements and their ratification possible. The rhetorical is not the opposite of the philosophical and the referential, but their prerequisite. The fictive, in the sense of the made (*fingo, fingere, fictum*), is not the opposite of the true. Rather every statement refers both to a world beyond itself, to an object toward which it gestures, and to its own constructed and situated nature, to the factors that make its construction and reception possible. Every statement is always already a poetic (*poein*, "to make" or "do") act.

Recognizing that the rhetorical inheres in the referential is not an artifact of "theory" per se: of deconstruction, psychoanalysis, or any one of its other 31 flavors. It is not in particular postmodern. As these essays argue repeatedly, such insights are as old as philosophy and the systematic search for truth itself. Plato's *Gorgias*, arguably the first encounter between a body of discourse termed *rhētorikē* and an alternative, *philosophia*, ends not with a set of syllogisms, nor with the clipped back and forth of Socratic questioning, but with a story, a myth. By the same token, for Cicero, the philosopher, the orator, and the politician are not opposed but complimentary positions (see chapters 3, 4, and 6).

It is rather our assumption that the work of truth must be shorn of the provisional, the rhetorical, and the experiential that is anomalous.[4] The truth for Cicero is not a disembodied or unsituated relation between individual propositions or systematic philosophies and a virgin reality to which they refer. The premise of his masterful *De Oratore, On the Perfect Orator*, is not that there is no such thing as truth, nor that there is no distinction between persuasion and reason, but rather that there is no truth that is not contested and bound up with contingency and particularity, that there is no philosophy untouched by rhetoric, and that truly eloquent speakers can only be so to the extent they practice philosophy.

Far from being a nihilism, a sophistry, or a pantextualism, I would argue that such a position reveals the danger and emptiness behind many of our modern, conventional notions of truth: that it is completely objective; that it is separate from our experience; that it exists outside the materiality and hence sensuality of the language and institutions in which it is articulated. Not only is such a proposition nonsensical, but it also denies the status of truth to anything that has meaning in our lives, to the textured quality of our existence, to anything that is not quantifiable and hence commodifiable. Values in such a universe become articles of faith that are impervious to reasoned examination, communal discourse, and mediation. The wildest fanaticisms and conspiracy theories become authorized because truth has no purchase on their worldly existence.

---

3  Compare Foucault (2009: 62–65) and Miller (2021: chapter 5).

4  See Foucault (2001: 19–30), Hadot (1995: 20–21, 269–71, 395–96, 412), Hadot (2002: 20–33, 61; 272–73, 278 373–75), McGushin (2016), and Miller (2021: 88–91).

The rhetorical tradition offers us resources, ways to think about truth without abstracting it from our lives. Ciceronian philosophy, like what we denominate theory, operates in a middle space between the absolute ideality that would give us access to a realm of truth freed from contingency, from the messy space of the world, and a ruthless cynicism that sees only manipulation, only an immediate contest for domination (see chapter 6). In this context, it is worth reminding ourselves that "truth" is not the referent, that to which a true proposition, perception, or feeling corresponds, but the confirmation of a statement. The real exceeds every discourse. Every set of true propositions exists on top of, in addition to, and beside the real, as both part of and in addition to the real. Otherwise, there could be no discoveries. If the "truth" were coterminous with the real, then there would be no need for *truth* at all. It would simply be the world. As Foucault brilliantly summed up, "we have to ask ourselves about the fact that there are, in addition to things, discourses, to pose the problem: why in addition to the real is there the true?" (2014: 40).

The following essays were written over the last twenty years. They have been edited and updated. I was surprised to see how well they hung together when I reread them. I begin with an autobiographical reflection, about the stakes we face in the humanities. If the current political and neoliberal attacks on the value of reflection, of narrative, and of attention to language and the texture of our experience continue, I argue in "Debits and Credits or Accounting for My Life: A Defense of the Humanities," we will lose more than our careers, or a set of traditions, or even culture itself. We will lose the survival of a life that is not crushed beneath the demands of capital, conformity, and coercive enjoyment.

When we talk about debt in higher education, we too often speak of an abstraction. We speak only on the level of exchange. I understand that we cannot ignore our student's legitimate needs to ensure their material security. But an account that focuses on money alone is fundamentally impoverished in the narratives of existence it grants our students and ourselves. It confines the arts to the privileged, to those who can afford them, to those who make that "consumer choice." Every day, however, lives are lost to despair and anomie when access to richer, more imaginative accounts of existence is denied through poverty, ignorance, and grinding cynicism. Only when we touch upon what cannot be assessed in purely operational terms, on that for which there is no accounting, on what cannot be figured as debits and credits, as a balance between the pleasure and the reality principles, can we begin to talk about what we ought and what we owe.

In chapter 2, "The Trouble with Theory: A Comparatist Manifesto," I argue against the reification of theory as a set of models, applications, or protocols of reading. Instead, I contend we must recontextualize what we call theory as an ongoing conversation between historically and culturally embedded sets of discourses that seek to address basic questions about literature, meaning, and existence. The fact is that most of today's theory derives in origin if not in its latest incarnations from continental thinkers who write in languages and from cultural perspectives that are quite literally foreign to their American expositors. Looking at the examples of Derrida, Lacan, Foucault, and Kristeva, I argue that their texts are only truly understandable in terms of the complex dialogue that took place between them. That dialogue, moreover, forms part of the

AN INTRODUCTION                                                                    xxiii

larger cultural context in which these thinkers are situated and assumes a detailed literary and philosophical knowledge.

Having made the argument for a historically textured and comparative account of the work of theory, I expand the focus to questions of truth, rhetoric, and philosophy in chapter 3, "Placing the Self in the Field of Truth: Irony and Self-Fashioning in Ancient and Postmodern Rhetorical Theory." How does the speaker of truth, who also seeks to persuade and convince his auditors, navigate this difficult terrain? Ancient rhetorical theory and ancient philosophic rhetoric as found in Plato, Aristotle, Xenophon, Cicero, and Quintilian provide startlingly (post)modern responses. Frankness or *libertas*, they tell us, is only made possible through stylization. We come to be perceived as people who take up an intelligible relation to truth, not primarily through our asservations, but as ironists. The ironist is not the speaker with the air of truth, but the one who performs the gap between themselves and an impossible sincerity. The ironist is not the speaker who calls a spade a spade, but the one who plays a speaker who calls a spade a spade, and in so doing calls our attention to both the play and the spade.

Continuing this line of inquiry, in chapter 4, "Rhetoric and Deconstruction: Plato, the Sophists, and Philosophy," I turn to Derrida's reading of Plato's classic dialogue on truth, love, and rhetoric, *Phaedrus*. In "Plato's Pharmacy," Derrida demonstrates the way in which the ambivalent signifier *pharmakon*, meaning both poison and medicine, deconstructs the opposition between speech and writing that subtends the *Phaedrus*. That opposition, in turn, is based upon an even more fundamental one between internality and externality. Speech is the reflection of truth because it emanates from the inside and is directly present to consciousness. Writing is secondary and derivative, existing as an externalization of a prior moment of interiority, i.e., thought as silent speech. The deconstruction of the priority of speech over writing, through the latter being characterized as a *pharmakon* and hence as both a salutary healing agent and a foreign noxious other, is itself a deconstruction of the priority of truth over its external and derivative manipulation through formalized practices of speech and writing: i.e., rhetoric. Rhetoric as a practice is associated throughout the Platonic corpus with the sophists and is generally opposed to philosophy defined as the pursuit of truth. Derrida in his deconstructive reading of the opposition between speech and writing in the *Phaedrus* demonstrates that, in effect, Plato himself deconstructs the opposition between rhetoric and philosophy through the deployment of philosophy's initial, constitutive trope, Socratic irony, as figured by the duplicitous *pharmakon*. The result is that rather than philosophy and sophistry being mutually exclusive alternatives, each becomes a moment within the other, which can never be fully sublimated. Philosophy on this view, I contend, is less a policing of the borders of discourse than a series of persuasive interventions in the ongoing dialogue that constitutes the movement of truth in time.

Chapter 5, "The Platonic Remainder: Derrida's *Khôra* and the *Corpus Platonicum*," pursues this line of thought by examining Derrida's *Khôra*. In this book, Derrida pursues a moment in Plato that appears to be beyond the oppositions of appearance and reality, becoming and being, or *muthos* and *logos*, the *khôra* in one of Plato's most atypical dialogues, the *Timaeus*. As everyone from McCabe to Rivaud recognizes, the *Timaeus* comes to us surrounded by hermeneutic cautions. Timaeus's speech is anything but a dogmatic set of metaphysical assertions that we are invited simply to accept. It is rather a story that self-consciously labels itself as concerned with the world of appearance. None of this means that we should not take it seriously. Timaeus's tale is far too long, far too elaborate, and far too technically based in the scientific and mathematical speculations of the day to be dismissed. The cosmology of the *Timaeus* must be taken both literally and figuratively: as a parody of its own dogmatic pretensions that also demands to be seriously considered. Into this bottomless discourse, this *mise-en-abîme* of endless reflection, Derrida steps. The *Timaeus* is an unfinalizable dialogue in which each moment of positing is also a moment of irony and interrogation, of simultaneous acceptance and active separation.

In chapter 6, "Cicero Reads Derrida Reading Cicero: A Politics and a Friendship to Come," we move from questions of rhetoric and truth in metaphysics to questions of politics and friendship in the work of arguably antiquity's greatest rhetorician, a practicing politician, and the inventor of Roman philosophy, Cicero. This chapter examines Derrida's reading of Cicero's *De Amicitia* in the larger context of Derrida's work. In 1994, Derrida published the *Politics of Friendship*, a major work that followed 1993's *Specters of Marx* and *Khôra*. The *Politics of Friendship* is a book about the history of the concept of friendship from Plato to Blanchot by way of Cicero. It is also a book about the inseparability of politics from a concept of both the friend and the enemy. The true friend is portrayed in Cicero as a second self, as the other of myself who reflects my self to myself. But insofar as my friend remains other, he or she, as my second self, also has the potential to call the integrity, the sufficiency, of my self into question. There is a potential violence in friendship: a violence that recalls the passion of love. Thus, Derrida notes, Cicero observes that *amicitia* receives its name from love (*amor*) and that each sets the soul aflame. Yet, the flames of passion only too easily become those of hatred.

If politics and friendship are deeply interimplicated and can easily turn into violence and hatred, then the question of how we embrace the other without either denying them their autonomy or sacrificing our integrity becomes all the more pressing. In chapter 7, "On Borders, Race, and Infinite Hospitality: Foucault, Derrida, and Camus," I argue that concepts of race are integral to the way we understand national borders, and that inherent in concepts of borders and race are fear, aggression, and violence. After a brief opening that sets out the stakes of its argument, this chapter attempts to denaturalize and historicize our concepts of race and race war through a reading of Foucault. It then turns to Derrida's concept of infinite hospitality as an alternative way of conceptualizing identity in political space. It culminates in a reading of Camus's "L'hôte," which problematizes hospitality, race, and freedom in the French colonial context.

What, then, might an open and critical humanities look like? I offer one possible answer in chapter 8, "Sartre, Politics, and Psychoanalysis: It Don't Mean a Thing if It Aint Got *Das Ding*." In *Qu'est-ce que la littérature*, Sartre argues that literature is neither an exercise in pure aesthetics nor a mere reflection of preexisting conditions but always an intentional act directed toward a specific audience. He challenges the writer to take responsibility for both the act and the audience to which it is addressed. In this way, Sartre proposes that we produce a literature that is both engaged and authentic. For Sartre, the author simultaneously creates and unveils an object that calls upon

AN INTRODUCTION

the reader to make possible a unique moment of unveiling. In this essay, I take up Sartre's challenge of asking "what is literature," but I propose to move beyond the Marxian and existential terms in which he framed the question toward a more expansive, post-Freudian definition founded on the works of Žižek, Kristeva, and Lacan.

Any psychoanalytic account of cultural phenomena must of course come to terms with Foucault's critique of the repressive hypothesis and his larger genealogical project in the *History of Sexuality*. In chapter 9, "Enjoyment beyond the Pleasure Principle: *Antigone*, Julian of Norwich, and the *Use of Pleasures*," we examine the tensions between Foucault and psychoanalysis, working to understand both the salience of his critique and what a post-Foucauldian psychoanalysis might look like. Indeed, according to received wisdom, there is an irreducible antagonism between Foucauldian and psychoanalytic approaches to the history of sexuality and hence between a phallic queer theory and a more maternal feminist discourse. This paper argues that the received wisdom, however, is wrong: (a) that Foucault's work is not opposed to psychoanalysis per se but rather offers a historicization of it; (b) that insofar as it offers a historicization, it represents a critique of its normalizing tendencies; and (c) that the psychoanalytic response to a Foucauldian model of bodies and pleasures cannot be found in the refusal of its own history, or in the assertion of sexual norms, but precisely in terms of what lies beyond Foucault's model of reciprocity, of an exchange of pleasures. This beyond of the pleasure principle, which Freud names the death drive, I argue is represented in two examples of a discourse that cannot be reduced to the normative: Antigone's "no" and Julian of Norwich's feminized body of Christ. Lastly (d), the chapter observes that this beyond of the pleasure principle, which Foucault's *History* finds difficult to articulate, is in both the figures of Antigone and of Julian associated with the feminine, maternal body.

Chapter 10, "Lacan le con: Luce Tells Jacques Off," continues our examination of psychoanalytic feminism with a reading of Luce Irigaray's classic send up of Lacan, "Cosi fan tutti." The paper begins with the paradox that French feminism from the 1970s to the present constitutes itself both in reaction to and in the tradition of Lacanian psychoanalytic theory. Irigaray is exemplary in this regard. A member of Lacan's École Freudienne until her expulsion in 1974, she is both grounded in the Lacanian theory of the subject's sexualization in language and deeply critical of it. Of the many places in which this ambivalent and all but oedipal relation between teacher and student is played out, it is perhaps best seen in "Cosi fan tutti." The essay is a true tour de force. In it, Irigaray revisits Lacan's *Séminaire XX, Encore*, on female sexuality, and through a strategy of extensive quotation, commentary, and parody presents the discourse of the master in the guise of a Mozartian comedy of seduction, only with the genders reversed (Mozart's title was "Cosi fan tutte"). In "Cosi fan tutti," we see the subject presumed to know travestied by the other.

Each of these essays, either directly or indirectly, seeks to offer or to lay the groundwork for a vigorous defense of the humanities: that is to say of the tradition of the study of art, music, literature, history, philosophy, and rhetoric as something more than merely information, vocational training, or another consumer good. Chapter 11, "The Repeatable and the Unrepeatable: Žižek and the Future of the Humanities, or Assessing Socrates," argues that one of the gravest and most persistent threats to these studies is the assessment movement as launched by the US Department of Education in the presidency of George W. Bush. The emphasis on quantification and commodification in assessment necessarily reduces the object of study to a set of information, that is to a series of repeatable data points whether we are assessing the learning outcomes of a seminar on Kant, a lecture course on mythology, or a standard introduction to management.

Beginning with the founding figure of Western philosophy, I argue that Socrates according to these criteria would be considered a failure. As we learn in the *Apology*, all he knows is that he knows nothing. Given that he started in ignorance and ended there as well, his measurable progress would be negligible at best. This objection is more than a mere joke. The ideal of repeatability as expressed within a certain social scientific model that is currently hegemonic and underlies the concept of "testability" is that of functional identity, i.e., of the ability of each data point to substitute for another of the same value. Yet that is exactly what is under scrutiny in Socratic dialogue. The arc of Socratic inquiry, from ignorance to its self-conscious recognition, leads back to its point of inception, but with a difference. And it is precisely this irreducible difference of self-conscious critical reflection in its unresolved dialectic with the repeatable that is foundational to humanities education as traditionally understood.

To counter these arguments for knowledge and learning as information, I turn to a text by the Slovenian psychoanalytic philosopher, Slavoj Žižek, *The Parallax View*. It offers a series of arguments for grounding our reflection in what would traditionally fall under the categories of theology and metaphysics, cognitive science and philosophy of mind, and ethics and politics. It seeks the ground for those categories not in their content, but in the constitutive moment of excess or difference that makes them possible yet can never be fully subsumed within and hence accounted for by them. This work with all its manifest eccentricities, its Socratic *atopia*, offers decisive arguments for rejecting a model of knowledge as the repeatable, the reproducible commodity of an industry, and in favor of the Socratic moment of the unrepeatable as epitomized in the *Theaetetus*.

Chapter 12, "Theory Does Not Exist," brings us back to where we began. It argues that Theory, as such, does not exist, contending that what is commonly called "Theory" is in fact part of a complex set of dialogues. Civilization, it argues, is a delicate web that depends on long conversations extending over great expanses of time, and we should not fool ourselves about how easily its thread is snapped. Rome fell. The Third Reich, ISIS, and Donald Trump arose. As Achebe taught us, "things fall apart." Basic questions about meaning, truth, justice, and ethics, about the importance of reading, thinking, writing, and reflecting, about the nature of the beautiful, the abject, and the sublime can only be posed in terms of the history of their previous usages, predications, and definitions. The capacity to interrogate our present condition, to imagine alternatives to it, and to persuade others to join us in trying to realize those alternatives—as well as the conceptual quality and texture of those alternatives— is dependent on the continuity and context of this conversation. The inability of the next generations to continue it or to understand the complex nature of its genealogy and the subtle determinations that differentiate it from calculations of pure utility or

# AN INTRODUCTION

economic rationality is a real possibility. War, ecological disaster, educational mediocrity, and the unwillingness to recognize or support what cannot be subjected to a brutal immediate use all threaten to snap the threads that weave the text of this conversation. This chapter examines "Theory" as part of this larger conversation, rendering it at once less unique, and at the same contending that questions we call "Theory" are an integral part of the fragile conversation that constitutes the history of civilization(s).

## Works Cited

Armstrong, Richard. 2005. *A Compulsion for Antiquity: Freud and the Ancient World*. Ithaca: Cornell University Press.

Braunstein, Nestor. 2020. *Jouissance: A Lacanian Concept*. Trans. Silvia Rosman. Albany: SUNY Press.

Calcutt, Andrew. 2016. "The Surprising Origins of 'Post-Truth'—and How It Was Spawned by the Liberal Left." *The Conversation*. https://theconversation.com/the-surprising-origins-of-post-truth-and-how-it-was-spawned-by-the-liberal-left-68929.

Courtine, Jean-François. 2008. "L'ABC de la déconstruction." *Derrida, la tradition de la philosophie*. Eds. Marc Crépon and Frédéric Worms. Paris: Galilée. 11–26.

Derrida, Jacques. 1967. *Écriture et différence*. Paris: Seuil.

———. 1972. *Positions*. Paris: Minuit.

———. 1980. *La carte postale: de Socrate à Freud et au-delà*. Paris: Flammarion.

———. 1986. *Memoires for Paul de Man. The Wellek Library Lectures at University of California Irvine*. Trans. Cecile Lindsay, Jonathan Culler, and Eduardo Cadava. New York: Columbia University Press.

———. 1992. "Nous autres Grecs." *Nos Grecs et leurs modernes: les stratégies contemporaines d'appropriation de l'antiquité*. Ed. Barbara Cassin. Paris: Seuil. 251–77.

———. 1993. *Spectres de Marx*. Paris: Galilée.

———. 1994. *Politiques de l'amitié, suivi de l'oreille de Heidegger*. Paris: Galilée.

———. 1996. *Résistances de la psychanalyse*. Paris: Galilée.

———. 2002. *Marx & Sons*. Paris: Presses Universitaire de France/Galilée.

Derrida, Jacques and Elizabeth Roudinesco. 2001. *De quoi demain … Dialogue*. Paris: Fayard/Galilée.

Eliot, T. S. 1945. *What Is a Classic? An Address Delivered before the Virgil Society on the 16th of October, 1944*. London: Faber and Faber.

Foucault, Michel. 1999. *Les anormaux. Cours au Collège de France. 1974–1975*. Eds. Valerio Marchetti and Antonella Salomoni. Paris: Gallimard/Seuil.

———. 2001. *L'herméneutique du sujet. Cours au Collège de France, 1982–1983*. Ed. Frédéric Gros. Paris: Hautes Études/Gallimard/Seuil.

———. 2008. *Le gouvernement de soi et des autres. Cours au Collège de France, 1982–1983*. Ed. Frédéric Gros. Paris: Hautes Études/Gallimard/Seuil.

———. 2009. *Le courage de la vérité: Le gouvernement de soi et des autres II. Cours au Collège de France, 1984*. Ed. Frédéric Gros. Paris: Hautes Études/Gallimard/Seuil.

———. 2011. *Leçons sur la volonté de savoir. Cours au Collège de France, 1970–1971. Suivi de Le Savoir d'Oedipe*. Ed. Daniel Defert. Paris: Hautes Études/Gallimard/Seuil.

———. 2012. *Du gouvernement des vivants. Cours au Collège de France, 1979–1980*. Ed. Michel Senellart. Paris: EHESS, Gallimard, Seuil.

———. 2014. *Subjectivité et vérité. Cours au Collège de France, 1980–1981*. Ed. Frédéric Gros. Paris: Hautes Études/Gallimard/Seuil.

Freud, Sigmund. 1965. *The Interpretation of Dreams*. Trans. James Strachey. New York: Avon.

Gherovici, Patricia. 2000. "Psychoanalysis: Resistible and Irresistible." *Lacan in America*. Ed. Jean-Michel Rabaté. New York: Other Press. 93–105.

Hadot, Pierre. 1995. *Qu'est-ce que la philosophie antique?* Paris: Gallimard.

———. 2002. *Exercices spirituels et philosophie antique*. Rev. ed. Paris: Albin Michel.

Iling, Sean. 2019. "The Post-Truth Prophets: Postmodernism Predicted Our Post-Truth Hellscape. Everyone Still Hates It." Vox. https://www.vox.com/features/2019/11/11/18273141/postmodernism-donald-trump-lyotard-baudrillard.

Jameson, Fredric. 2007. "Interview with Sarah Danius and Stefan Jonson." *Jameson on Jameson: Conversations on Cultural Marxism*. Ed. Ian Buchanan. Durham: Duke University Press. 151–70.

Julien, Phillipe. 1990. *Pour Lire Jacques Lacan*. 2nd ed. Paris: E. P. E. L.

Kristeva, Julia. 1979. "Le temps des femmes." Cahiers de recherche de. S. T. D. Paris VII: 5–19.

———. 1996. *Sens et non-sens de la révolte: Pouvoirs et limites de la psychanalyse I*. Paris: Fayard.

Lacan, Jacques. 1973. *Le séminaire livre XI: Les quatre concepts fondamentaux de la psychanalyse*. Ed. Jacques-Alain Miller. Paris: Seuil.

———. 1975a. *Le séminaire livre XX: Encore*. Ed. Jacques-Alain Miller. Paris: Seuil.

———. 1975b. *Le séminaire livre I: Les écrits techniques de Freud*. Ed. Jacques-Alain Miller. Paris: Seuil.

———. 1978. *Le séminaire livre II: Le moi dans la théorie de Freud et dans la technique de la psychanalyse*. Ed. Jacques-Alain Miller. Paris: Seuil.

———. 1986. *Le séminaire livre VII: L'éthique de la psychanalyse*. Ed. Jacques-Alain Miller. Paris: Seuil.

Lewis, Michael. 2008. *Derrida and Lacan: Another Writing*. Edinburgh: Edinburgh University Press.

Liu, Catherine. 2000. "Lacanian Reception." *Lacan in America*. Ed. Jean-Michel Rabaté. New York: Other Press. 107–37.

McGushin, Edward. 2016. "Deconstruction, Care of the Self, Spirituality: Putting Foucault and Derrida to the Test." *Between Foucault and Derrida*. Eds. Yubraj Aryal, Vernon W. Cisney, Nicolae Morar, and Christopher Penfield. Edinburgh: Edinburgh University Press. 104–22.

Miller, Paul Allen. 2021. *Foucault's Seminars on Antiquity: Learning to Speak the Truth*. London: Bloomsbury.

Mowitt, John. 2020. *Offering Theory: Reading in Sociography*. London: Anthem Press.

Ragland-Sullivan, Ellie. 1986. *Jacques Lacan and the Philosophy of Psychoanalysis*. Urbana: University of Illinois Press.

Schneiderman, Stuart. 1983. *Jacques Lacan: The Death of an Intellectual Hero*. Cambridge: Harvard University Press.

Valdrè, Rosella. 2019. *Psychoanalytic Reflections on the Freudian Death Drive: In Theory, the Clinic, and Art*. London: Routledge.

Žižek, Slavoj. 1992. *Enjoy Your Symptom: Jacques Lacan in Hollywood and Out*. New York: Routledge.

Zuckert, Catherine H. 1996. *Postmodern Platos: Nietzsche, Heidegger, Gadamer, Strauss, Derrida*. Chicago: University of Chicago Press.

# Chapter 1

# DEBITS AND CREDITS OR ACCOUNTING FOR MY LIFE: A DEFENSE OF READING AND HUMANISTIC EDUCATION

The temporality of debt is complex and always points in two directions. What I ought to do is based on what I owe, but what I owe is based on what has been entrusted to me (*creditum*) and what I therefore must pay back/forward to bring the scales of justice into balance, in a very real sense to account for my life, to give it a meaning, a shape, a *logos*, a word that simultaneously means rational discourse, the accounting presented by each official to democratic Athens at the end of his term of office, and the rational structure of the universe. In the beginning was the word.

Every step forward in any such account projects a simultaneous recursive step backward. The future (re)writes my past on a tablet bequeathed to it by Plato, Socrates, Hegel, Freud, Marx, and the other assessors of our collective and individual balance sheets, of what we owe and what is owed to us by traditions of discourse that stretch back three thousand years. When we enter into discourse, when we take up the conversation, there is created a space and frame of memory, a *chora* of inscription, that organizes our pasts into different possible futures. This is how we come to articulate what we ought to do. This is how our debts are to be credited: not through some primal scream or a moment of revelation, certainly not through self-ex-pression, but through coming to formulate new possibilities from within the discursive field into which we are thrown, possibilities which are bequeathed to us, and which we make new in relation to a past that never fully existed before the moment of its articulation. This same magic tablet of discourse, which is also the discourse of the other, the unconscious, is ever overwritten by the language of experience but is never completely fading. It is not just a product of philosophical majesty, but it is equally bequeathed to us by Proust and Bergson, by Horace and Catullus, by Bronte and Beauvoir: those most acute accountants of our souls, of the multiple futures and pasts that any present produces. We owe them all—I owe them—so much. And yet, in a very real sense, we are their predecessors, as every down payment we make creates a debt to a past that we create even as we inherit.

So begins a Derridian tale, the tale I imagined I would tell when Jeffrey Di Leo first asked me to write on debt, the tale on account of which I received his generous invitation. I am endebted to him, as I am endebted to many of my friends more than I can ever tell, more than I can account for, and yet this debt is not one I will fully repay, not today at any rate. There is a deeper debt I owe: an older debt that I feel I must repay; one that is at once deeply personal, but also one that I believe strongly—one that I credit—both with saving my life (in the quite literal sense) and with making my life worthy of interest, making it a creditable existence. It is that personal, autobiographical debt, that I shall try to expose to you, as I strive to stand naked before you, but more importantly to stand naked before myself, so that I can see what is owed, what has been entrusted, what I ought to do. There must be a reckoning.

Why should you care? If it were only a matter of my own ethical accounting, you should not. My life, in so far as it is *my* life, is simply not that worthy of interest. But many of my readers will be students or professors at universities: institutions that are increasingly powered by debt, institutions that are increasingly asked to render an account of themselves. Most are scholars of the humanities: a field increasingly seen as a source, a cause of debt. Many are here scholars of literature, students of poetry, lovers of wisdom and beauty. And we are being called to account every day, by parents, politicians, provosts, and plutocrats. Are historians employable? What is the value added of reading Wordsworth or Neruda? Why should we pay for this? How much money will my son or daughter make as an English major, a philosophy major, a student of Latin? What ought they owe and to whom?

I have an answer, but it is not one that can be expressed in terms of profit and loss or learning outcomes. It will require patience and forbearance. It will be awkward and embarrassing. I am here to tell you that I owe these arts, these disciplines, these institutions my life, as do many others—I meet them every day—and that every day lives are lost when access to them is denied through poverty, through ignorance, through the grinding cynicism of a world that sees only profit and loss, seeks only a return on its investment, and seems unwilling to pay what is owed. I am here to tell you that only when we touch upon that which cannot be assessed in operational terms, that for which there is no accounting, that which cannot be figured as debits and credits, as a balance between the pleasure and the reality principles, can we really begin to talk about what we ought and what we owe. Only then can we have a serious conversation about debt. I am here to tell you a story, to give an account.

What on earth do I mean? And who am I to talk. I was the vice provost of a major research university. I hold an endowed professorship in Classics and Comparative Literature. I am a white, male, protestant by birth, American by nationality, and over sixty. I am the symbol of elite and effete privilege. I have a pool and a house in France. Easy for me to talk about what we owe art, the humanities, literature, philosophy, and music. Easy for me to blather on about "saving people's lives" and other first world problems: what do I know about real suffering, about the dead in Gaza, the children fleeing Honduras, about anger, humiliation, despair? Not a lot. I should stick to explicating Derrida.

I certainly did not grow up in poverty. I grew up in the suburbs of Kansas City, surrounded by malls, lawns, and a seemingly infinite sea of Anglo-Saxon whiteness. There was one black kid in my high school of over 2,000 students. The only Jew I ever met was my allergist. My parents played bridge. My mother belonged to the DAR. My dad became the local president of the National Association of Accountants. Who am I to talk?

I certainly had friends who had it worse. The middle-class veneer of our Midwestern suburban lives was often frightfully thin. The violence lurked just below the surface.

# DEBITS AND CREDITS OR ACCOUNTING FOR MY LIFE

My father never went to prison. He never raped one of my siblings. I love you Lea-Anne. I wish you peace. He also did not sit and drink beer every night till he threw up, talking about what he saw in World War 2 until he would get out the billy club he used as a member of the naval MPs and begin to terrorize the household. That was not my dad. Those were my friend's dads. Empty, angry people, trapped between a world that recognized only profit and loss—the world they worked in every single day—and a world that sought redemption, that sought to give their lives meaning through the assertion of absolute values: god, masculinity as moral and physical domination, the refusal to acknowledge pain, terror. I will never forget my friend Steve's dad as he worked his way through a case of Falstaff and a carton of Chesterfields, from five to midnight every night, fiddling with his radio to pull in a station from New Orleans that played the big band music of the forties, finding a brief respite in the music, in memory, in a form of utopian imagination before the rage and depression would catch up with him. I remember even as a boy of ten noticing how sad he seemed, and how ever so briefly when the music would start he had a smile and a moment of beatitude before the demons would escape. What do I owe him? What do I owe my best friend Steve, whom I lost track of for many year after college, who became a carrier then an airline pilot, whom I later found on Facebook, his dad dead, his first marriage ended, a bundle of hate and resentment, of aggressive masculinity, who defriended me for supporting the Affordable Care Act? A person lost in the barely sublimated aggression of the calculable, of the pound of flesh always sought but never payable. A university graduate, he did not go into debt, he was employable, he was a measurable success; but did he learn what he needed to have a good life, a sustainable life, a life of reflection? How do we assess his education, the discourse he learned, the world he learned to create? What account could he give (*logos*)? His education failed him. I love you Steve. I wish you peace.

No, my dad was none of these people. I loved my dad. I used to see him every week. We had lunch or dinner. Often my mom, whom I love and who has darkened into dementia, came too. My dad whose ribs I broke the last time he tried to hit me. My mom who in the throes of mental illness chased me at the age of fifteen with a steak knife and would have killed me if she could. I am the child of white suburban privilege.

Many of my friends in academe, their parents and grandparents were professors, scientists, doctors, lawyers, teachers. They were educated people who valued education. They went to private high schools. They went to universities before the GI Bill. And many of them had little sense of the marvelous gift that had been trusted to them, of their fiduciary responsibility, of what they owed the very possibility of being engaged in the kinds of discourse they took too much for granted. They were good people who did not recognize the fragility of civilization, the veil of *Até* that Lacan speaks of in *Antigone*, the thin line that separates the law from madness and yet also makes possible the life beyond accounting, that makes possible a good beyond goods.

I am not naïve about our humanistic inheritance. I know there were Nazi commandants who read Goethe in the shadows of the ovens. I know you can read Proust and be a prick. We all know lots of these people. Some are our colleagues. I know that our traditions are Eurocentric, misogynistic, and capable of genocide. But a world without Goethe and Proust, without Shakespeare and Sophocles, without Cicero,

4 THEORY DOES NOT EXIST

Cervantes, and Césaire is a world in which the total number of possible accounts has been drastically limited. The kinds of existence you can fashion for yourself and that you can imagine for others become truncated in such a world, a world where there is only profit and loss, a world founded on debt. We need more accounts not less. We need to owe more.

My dad was the first member of his family to graduate from college. He received a degree in accounting from Southwest Missouri State Teacher's College. He went through high school and college, having only to read a single book: *Ivanhoe* in high school English. He learned how to make money. He did not learn to think, to imagine, to create. How could he? Who would have taught him? He graduated with one goal in mind: someday, if he worked hard and was smart, he might make $10,000 a year, own a house, and a car. His parents had been tenant farmers in southwest Missouri, in the wheat fields of Nebraska, and in the rice bogs of Arkansas. Neither got past the eighth grade. There was the raw struggle for existence, there was church, and there were moments of transient joy when a favorite meal was made of biscuits with sausage or some bacon, when an outhouse was tipped over on Halloween. My aunt said she only saw her father, my grandfather, Frank, cry once. In 1930 they had moved to Arkansas in the depth of the depression to work in the rice fields. The mosquitoes were everywhere. Frank got the yellow fever. My dad who was only a baby was sent to stay with relatives. Months later when Frank had recovered sufficiently for my dad to return, my grandfather wept when Joe did not recognize him. They soon returned to Missouri. Frank never fully recovered, and in 1952 at the age of 53 his weakened heart stopped. He pitched forward dead on the steering wheel of his pick-up.

I never met my grandfather. I am told he was a hard-working man. I am told he was a brutal man. When my father would misbehave, he would be taken behind the shed and beaten with a belt or a sapling. When my grandmother had saved for a year the money she made selling eggs so she could buy a coat, he took it and gave it to another relative whom he thought needed it more. He did not drink. He did not dance. He was not unfaithful to my grandmother. After my aunt got married, she left her husband, who was a brutal man even by the standards of the time, and came home, Frank sent her back and told to do her duty. My father learned his parenting skills from this man. I know my father loved him, but I never heard him say it.

My uncle Lorne, Franks' brother, was generally thought to be the nicest of the brothers. I knew Lorne. He farmed, drove a truck, did other odd jobs. He could tell a good joke. People liked him. When the sparrows ate the corn that fell to the ground in the field and competed with the quail that my uncle liked to hunt, he built a trap out of chicken wire. The sparrows would light on a trap door covered with corn and fall into the cage. About once a day, Lorne would go out and reach in the cage. He would pull out one bird at a time and break its neck. He would make sure that he could hunt quail. He tried to teach me one time how to break a sparrow's neck. I got scared and let the bird go when it squirmed. I was a disappointment. When Lorne's hunting dogs would misbehave, he would hit them with a wrench. Lorne never read a book. He loved to watch *Hee Haw* every Sunday night. He loved a good joke and a soda pop.

It may sound like I am blaming or condemning these people. I am not. They are the people who made me who I am today. As my brother reminds me, they are my roots. They had hard lives. I owe them a debt that cannot, that must not, be repaid. But I also refuse to romanticize them. Dick Cheney can go on his hunting trips and so can Justice Scalia, but my dad hunted for food and he trapped small animals to sell their pelts in depression Missouri, pelts that went to make the gloves and coats of wealthy people in St Louis and points further east. Life in the good old days so beloved by conservative nostalgia was often nasty, mean, brutish, and short. I loathe the sugar-coated images of rural poverty marketed by the likes of Crackerbarrel. I detest the people who play at poverty and ignorance in the name of a lost sense of authenticity with their pick-up trucks, cowboy hats, pork rinds, mega churches, and stock portfolios.

But to condemn the likes of my uncle Lorne, my grandfather Frank, or even my dad, is to assume they had a meaningful choice. This is not to say there was no joy to their existence. Lorne loved to hunt, but he also hunted to eat. Aunt Doris made fried quail for breakfast. It was delicious. I can still taste it with black coffee and biscuits, homemade cherry preserves. But it was not a consumer decision. It was not Coke versus Pepsi. What we owe them, what we owe ourselves, what we owe our children is the possibility of a real choice. Not some abstract Milton Friedman notion of free choice, of maximizing utility, of rational choice, but precisely the ability to imagine worlds not yet thought of, to construct discourses of reflection that open possibilities of thought never yet experienced, to produce moments of imaginary identification with those one has never encountered. How are you supposed to fashion an existence beyond the brute arithmetic of domination and acquisition if you have never learned to think in any other way? My father, who was a very intelligent man, who made a million dollars by the time he was fifty, who retired at fifty-two and read *Candide* for the first time, thought it was a true story.

We in the humanities underestimate the power of what we do. We underestimate the lives it changes, the lives it makes possible, when we reduce it to accounting, when we reduce it to the problem of student debt. What we owe in fact is unaccountable, but only when we truly confront what its loss would mean. I'm not saying the problems of student debt aren't real. I am saying our means of accounting are impoverished.

My mother's family was more prosperous. My Mom was born in Kansas City. Her mother graduated high school. When the depression came, they returned to Southwest Missouri. The bank in which her grandparents had deposited the proceeds from the sale of their large farm collapsed. They were poor but they had seen a bit more. Their world was a bit larger than that of my father's family. My mother was a music major at Southwest Missouri State, even if she never graduated. She participated in drama. When I was a boy, she took me to the Nelson Art Gallery in Kansas City once. I still remember the first time I saw one of the Dutch Masters' paintings. There was a vase of flowers with a perfectly painted fly next to a perfectly painted dewdrop on a perfectly painted petal. I had never seen anything like it. I can see it still. I could not have been more than five. Mom when I was young played Bach on the piano and baked the most amazing cakes, pies, and cookies. No wonder my dad fell in love with her. Even though she was from Jasper Missouri too, the daughter of a barber who never went to high school, she had been exposed, however briefly, to a world my dad had never seen. Heck, she had been to California when her father briefly worked repairing juke boxes before being drafted for the war, juke boxes that played the same music Steve's dad would tune into every night for a brief moment of beatitude before the violence took hold.

My maternal grandmother was a recluse, who never lived more than a block away from her mother. She suffered from acute anxiety and depression. She was condemned to the state mental hospital in Nevada. She received shock treatment. She was profoundly phobic. The bathtub burned her skin. Strangers could not be trusted. Nobody ever talked about it. What could they have said? Who in Jasper Missouri knew how to talk about such things? It was not only shame, it was ignorance. They literally did not know.

It was not long before my mom began to suffer. Maybe she always did, and I was just too young to notice. She would be possessed by fits of uncontrollable rage. I have a very strong memory of hiding at the bottom of the basement stairwell with my brother watching as my Mom threw plates at my dad. He dodged. She screamed. He never hit her. He would whip us with the belt at the slightest provocation, often for crying. I remember running in terror down the hallway trying to escape the belt on the back of my bare legs. I couldn't have been more than three or four. The grandparents were visiting. Nobody thought a thing about it. It was normal. It's what his dad did. But no matter how violent my mother's rages would become, he never did more than restrain her. The next to the last time my father beat me, my elder brother held me for him. Years later my brother apologized. The last time he tried to beat me, I was sitting on the kitchen counter. I was probably sixteen. He came at me, reaching for his belt. I reared back with both feet and kicked him as hard as I could in the chest. I had waited my whole life for the chance. He reeled back and never touched me again. Years later I learned I had broken his ribs. He had grown up in a world of violent domination, a world in which reason was not the giving of an account but only accounting. When he ceased to have a monopoly of violence, the violence ceased. It would be many years before our account was settled, but debt is a world without forgiveness and without forgiveness you are always owed, always in arrears, always at a loss. I never hit my son.

During my teen years, my mother's struggle with what was variously diagnosed as acute depression, manic-depression, bipolar rapid cycling, personality disorder, etc. worsened. There was always the rage. Blind dissociative rage. Rage at my father, rage at my brother, rage at me. In high school, she once jumped me from behind because I forgot and wore my shoes in the house: screaming and scratching at my face. She then called my father at work saying I had attacked her for no reason, and he came home, and the rage continued. This was the period of the suicide attempts. Always pills. I don't recall how many times we loaded her into the car and drove to the emergency room to get her stomach pumped. These incidents were normally followed by brief stays in the psych ward. How do you process this without a structured discourse? I remember being questioned by the police in the emergency room: it was a potential drug crime; I was a witness. "Tell us what you saw." I hated them. We never talked about it. It was never to be talked about. My father never once asked me how I was doing. Never asked me how I felt. I was supposed to stop provoking my mother. I was supposed to be quiet and be good. There was no understanding of mental illness. My brother, who by this time was away at college, for years afterwards said "she was just trying to get attention." His rage, his anger, haunted him.

But how was my dad supposed to be able to talk about this? Who had taught him? Where was this *logos* supposed to come from? What was the framework? What was the balance sheet? *Ivanhoe* could only take you so far. The same for my brother. He had followed in my dad's footsteps. He too had become an accountant, getting a business school education at the University of Missouri. He had one required humanities course: art history. He bought a print. Where were the resources for a more comprehensive and compassionate understanding supposed to come from? Yet by every operational measure not only had he and my dad been educated, they had been successfully educated. They were not in debt, they were employable, they clearly had mastered the skills they had been taught. They owed no one a thing and were profoundly personally impoverished as a result.

My father after retirement, slowly began to read more. He began to travel. He even, at the prompting of my mom, when she was properly medicated and after the calming effects of several rounds of electroshock therapy, began to go to the opera. By the time he was seventy his world was beginning to open up. My brother, on the other hand, turned to the answers of fundamentalist Christianity. There was a clear moral calculus, a profit and loss statement that made clear distinctions between good and evil and reproduced on the level of the eternal the paternalistic domination in which he had been thrust on the level of the terrestrial. He was a frequently angry and unhappy man, who gets his news from right wing websites, and once expressed the conviction that the Muslims in Michigan will soon be taking over and sweeping south.[1]

Jesus Christ, Allen, could you be any more depressing? Well, actually, yes. But the good part is coming soon. I hope by this point I have established some credibility when I talk about the debt I owe a humanities education. It is certainly not the case that for me at least the study of Latin, Greek and French, of Plato, Cicero, and Sartre, of Foucault, Derrida, and Kristeva, represented some kind of inherited elite status, an assumed birthright, or even just a general notion of culture or civilization. Early on in life, I discovered reading. And pretty quickly I realized that I was smart. I did well on standardized tests and many routine tasks at school were pretty easy for me to accomplish. But the point of it all completely escaped me. None of us had ever met a writer, a poet, a professor, a psychoanalyst. "Professional students" were figures of mockery. Everybody had jobs. Everybody lived in the suburbs. Everybody went to church. Everybody was white. Everybody wanted to acquire stuff. Everybody thought if you did what everybody else did you would wind up like everybody else, which was good, and when you died you would go to heaven like everybody else. Other people did other things and looked different. They did not have jobs. They did not have as much stuff. They did not go to heaven.

I don't remember when exactly the vapidity of it all hit me. I do remember being very puzzled that my parents scolded me when at age eight I applauded the assassination

---

1 I should note, that since the time this was first written, almost ten years ago, my brother has come to a certain awakening. His political views have softened and he has begun writing.

of Martin Luther King Jr. They had always said he was very bad man. It didn't add up. I was confused. Then somehow my Mom made the mistake of ordering *Bury My Heart at Wounded Knee* from the Book of the Month of Club for me, because I always liked reading cowboy and indian stories. Reading the history of the Sand Creek massacre after living through the race riots, after seeing armed soldiers on the streets of Kansas City, after watching the Vietnam war every night on TV for most of my young life, gave a new frame for viewing American history, one very different from what was being taught in school. Then of course there was the yawning gap between the appearance of our middle-class lives, the neat suburban home, bridge parties, DAR meetings, and the reality of mental illness, repression, and violence. A yawning gap that existed not just in my own home, but in the homes of many if not most of my friends. I quickly became an alienated youth.

There were a limited number of outlets for my anger and alienation. Most of all, there was drugs. I did a lot of drugs. I mean a lot of drugs. We used to play this game in high school. See who could do the most speed, go into the cafeteria, and not lose it. It's harder than you think. When the cafeteria pizza starts breathing on the tray, it will fuck you up. Dropping acid and talking to the vice principle was another challenge not to be underestimated.

I had a shirt with a large pocket in the back. I kept a variety of controlled substances in that pocket. The deal was, take one, leave one. People would come up to me in school, drop a pill or a joint or a tab of acid in and take something out. You never quite knew what you were taking. It was exciting. It sure as hell beat school and even more it beat home. Those people were fucking hypocrites. School was pointless. We were all just going to get meaningless jobs anyway. Drugs and music, that offered an escape, that offered access to another dimension, to a brief moment when experience was meaningful in itself, not just another means to another end, which was not only predetermined but normally prepackaged. I think it is important not to downplay the utopian element of a lot of 1970s drug culture if you want to understand what happened. For many of us there was a hunger for experience that could not be answered by the blight and sterility of suburban white America. It felt like a form of death. We did a lot of LSD and it was great, till it wasn't. To this day, I think there were moments of genuine insight. But there was also terror, a trip to the hospital, miraculously missed fatal car crashes, close calls with the police. The rampant use of inhalants—we were more partial to aerosols or amyl nitrate than glue—undoubtedly shaved off more than a few IQ points along the way.

To pay for the drugs and for my girlfriend's drugs, I needed a job. I found one at Happytime Entertainment. Happytime was a professional fundraising company. They contracted with the Jaycees, the Firefighters, the Sheriff's department, the Police Benevolent Society. What could be more respectable? These upstanding members of the community would hire Happytime and Happytime would put on a circus. The circus was for the "handicapped youngsters." A ten-dollar ticket meant ten handicapped youngsters could go to the show. We called people on the phone. We were doing a public service. I was good at this. Man, I sold the shit out of those tickets. "M'am, for some of these kids it may be their first circus and, well, for others it may be

# DEBITS AND CREDITS OR ACCOUNTING FOR MY LIFE

their last." I was good. There was a room full of drug-fueled hippies calling people on the phone all night long, doing the Lord's work.

At first, I had no idea it was scam and I was making good money, which meant I had a real measure of freedom from home and I could buy drugs. No one could fuck with me. At a certain point, I noticed that we were selling more than a 100,000 tickets per promotion. There were not 100,000 handicapped youngsters in the entire area. I may have been young, stupid, drug addled, but I could do the math. "Sir, you know we still have several hundred handicapped youngsters who need tickets to the circus." Really? But you said it. It worked. Then I actually saw the show. It was in a tent. There were a couple of flea-bitten dogs doing tricks, a few overweight acrobats in tights twirling on ropes from the top of the ceiling, a horse, and some clowns. There were maybe 200 spectators at most. The whole thing was a farce. The supposed benevolent associations for whom we raised money asked no questions and happily took ten per cent for doing nothing. Happytime Shows cleared ninety per cent. We were all paid in cash. I was made manager at age 17 and given my own phone room. My prospects were bright.

Here was a young man who clearly had vice provost and distinguished professor of Classics and Comparative Literature written all over him. It was predestined. Good breeding, excellent education, a high level of general culture. What could go wrong? Many years later I ran into one of my former high school teachers. She asked me what I was doing. I said I was a professor at the University of South Carolina. She replied, "I thought you would be in jail by now." I didn't say it, but it could have been true.

So, what happened? I had always read. When I was in ninth grade, I picked up *Catch 22* in a local bookstore. Later, I started reading Vonnegut, Brautigan. I tried Tolkein, but quickly got bored of the rings. I had little musical talent, but I listened to music constantly. I read books about Freud. I read *I'm Ok You're Ok*. I read a lot. It just had very little to do with school. I never made the connection. School was about obedience. School was about fitting in. School was about learning to get a job. I hated fitting in, and I already had a job. Reading, thinking, arguing, speculating, art, music that was something different. It certainly had nothing to do with school.

I had heard there was a class my senior year called "Introduction to Literature." It was a college prep class. I hadn't really thought about going to college. I didn't want to be an accountant. I already knew how to sell stuff. What was the point? One of the high school counselors told one of my friends that I should take to the ACT so I did. But that was about as far as I had thought about it. But this course was different. It had some interesting books. I wanted to take it. I went and spoke to the teacher, Rita Vonn. I did not have the grades to get in. I was a C student. The people in the Honors Society: they were either cheerleaders or nerds. But this was interesting. Miss Vonn must have seen something. Perhaps it was the first time anybody had ever asked to get into one of her classes. I got in and suddenly there was something I was good at. Suddenly school became a place of freedom.

About this time, I started writing. I wanted to be Kurt Vonnegut. I wanted to be a poet. I wrote all the time. I made poetry books and surreptitiously copied them on the school mimeograph machine. I have never stopped writing. The possibility of constructing worlds, of thinking differently, of developing a life that was not based merely on acquisition, on barely sublimated violence (if sublimated at all), on repression, created for me a debt that I can never repay, a debt that I can only service by keeping this possibility open for others.

Sometime in the middle of my senior year I quit the phone room. I couldn't do it anymore. I decided to go to college. Somebody told me I could go and study literature. I could be an English or creative writing major. I firmly believe this saved my life. If I had not died young or wound up in jail, I would have wasted my life. Years later I tried to find Miss Vonn and thank her. But she had disappeared. I will try again. I just sent a Facebook request. I owe her so much. By the last semester of my senior year I made all A's for the first time in my life. I never made a B again. Of course, it's not about the grades. But my life had changed.

In reality, this is all too linear and all too neat. It didn't happen this way. It didn't happen this way at all. How could it? All such intentional fictions leave out more than they include: they shape the facts, mold the story. But every *thing* I have told you is true. It did happen.

I got to college. My dad, of course, wanted to make me major in Business. He wanted me to get a job, to be employable. But I kept making good grades. And my mom intervened on my behalf, the woman who had taken me to the Nelson, who played Bach briefly reemerged. My life in many ways continued to be a mess. I transferred schools. I made bad decisions about girlfriends. I made bad decisions about drugs and alcohol. But I continued to read and write. I started taking language classes. I had decided that if I wanted to be a poet, I needed to learn everything possible about T.S. Eliot. If I wanted to understand Eliot, I needed to know Latin. So, the summer after my freshman year I took Latin in St. Louis, where my girlfriend lived. I started French shortly thereafter when a Professor told me that if I did Latin, I had to do French. A couple of years later I started Greek. My drug and alcohol use began to decline. I had no great moral revelation. I did not entrust myself to a higher power. I simply, for the first time in my life, had better things to do. Things I wanted to do. The world had ceased to be a small, enclosed place. It became as large as the conversation I was able to hold. I could construct my own world or at least a place within it. I could think and be differently. It was no longer a world from which I had to escape.

When I was a sophomore at Washington University, I took Kevin Herbert's Catullus class. Dr. Herbert had snow-white hair cut in a crew cut with steely blue eyes. He had a way of raising one eyebrow when you made a translation error that caused you to melt into your seat. He was an Irish Catholic and a war veteran. I was a longhaired kid who wore a "question authority" button. We had nothing in common. But he saw something in me and took me under his wing. His office was filled with books I had never heard of. His life was unlike any I had ever seen. It did not fit into any of my preconceived categories.

We read Catullus and I was bowled over. Who was this foul-mouthed young man, whose poetry contained obscenities I could not even translate? Who was this elegant young man who fashioned meticulous verse in which every poem was a perfect little miniature world, the opposite of the ragged free verse confessions that were supposed to betoken authenticity? Who was this young provincial from Verona in Rome, an outsider looking in on a social world he longed to be part of, and yet never could quite be? Who was this passionate young man who wrote of a love beyond counting, with an ache, and a wry rebelliousness that seemed to speak directly to me and yet was clearly so foreign:

> Let us live and love my Lesbia dear
> And count the ravings of the crabbed old men
> As lacking the worth of one red cent.
> The sun in the sky may rise and fall,
> But once our brief light is spent
> There is night, there is sleep, and that is all.
> Give me, then, a thousand kisses.
> Then a hundred, then a thousand.
> Then another hundred, another thousand.
> And with their number ever still mounting
> Let us destroy all means of accounting.
> So, love's number may in secret lie
> And nobody cast an evil eye.

This was a translation of Catullus 5 that I did as part of my Honors Thesis at Washington University. I can still quote it from memory, a memory whose structure and function had been fundamentally altered, a consciousness that had been fundamentally changed, a moment of inscription on a magic writing pad that had fundamentally reorganized all the marks and traces that lay beneath. How can I account for what I owe? What is my debt and to whom? How should I assess what I have learned, its outcomes, the return on my parent's investment? Was I more employable than five years before? What is this worth? I love you Kevin.

When we talk about debt in higher education, we too often speak of an abstraction. We speak solely on the level of exchange value, of calculation. I understand that we have to do this. I spent a good part of every day in the Provost's office working to make sure that my university was financially solvent and to produce student outcomes that were acceptable to all our various stakeholders. I get it. We have to keep the doors open. But I also know how fundamentally impoverished any such account is. I know this not because of any allegiance to a philosophical idealism, a religious faith, a committed aestheticism, or the right of inherited privilege. I know it in a real existential sense that I cannot communicate in any other way than through the kind of story I have just told. I owe a debt that can never be repaid, a down payment on which can only be made through offering this debt to others. I want to "owe it forward," because higher education without this debt, is merely another function of exchange, and so ultimately bankrupt.

# Chapter 2

# THE TROUBLE WITH THEORY: A COMPARATIST MANIFESTO

The trouble with contemporary theory can be summed up by a single symptomatic fact: theory has become the property of English Departments. This is not a slur on the competence of my colleagues who study Anglophone texts. They deploy abstract concepts as well or better than most comparatists. Nonetheless, the fact is that most of today's theory derives, in origin if not in its latest incarnations, from continental thinkers who write in languages and from cultural perspectives that are quite literally foreign to their American expositors. Thus, as we shall see below, the works of theorists such as Derrida, Lacan, Foucault, and Kristeva, are often only truly understandable in terms of the complex dialogue that exists between these writers. That dialogue, moreover, forms part of the larger cultural context in which these thinkers are situated, a context that assumes detailed knowledge of a tradition of literary and philosophical understanding unavailable to most monolingual scholars.

Unfortunately, theory in most American universities is taught as critical methodology. It is taught as "theory":[1] that is, as a body of abstract concepts that students can use to produce "readings" of texts. The result is a series of ahistorical abstractions that are directly "applied" to texts to which they have no articulated discursive or dialogic relation. We receive a Bakhtinian reading of Thackeray, a Jaussian response to Keats, a Derridean—followed by a de Manian—deconstruction of Sidney, and an Irigarayan interpretation of Sterne. In this fashion, concrete historical interventions into specific critical and philosophical debates become metaphysical truths.[2] The result is a perversion of these theorists' intentions since postmodern theory in general and poststructuralist theory in particular aims to critique precisely the kind of transhistorical metanarratives into which their works have been transformed (Lyotard 1984). The deconstruction of the closure of western metaphysics thus becomes the absolutization of *différance* as a textual property (Derrida 1980: 536). The critique of patriarchy's specular subject comes to function as an abstract universal fully as phallic as the Symbolic structures it was designed to fight (Irigaray 1974: 173, 178; Ragland-Sullivan 1986: 273; Weed 1994: 101–02). Finally, the corollary of this reification of concrete thought into abstract methodology has been a flight from theory toward historicism and "weak theory"

---

1 For the analogous fate of Lacan's reception by the American psychoanalytic and psychological establishment as "theory – not as the articulation of a clinical praxis," see Malone (2000: 6).
2 See Voloshinov's distinction between meaning and theme or abstract and contextual meaning (1986: 101) and Morson and Emerson (1990: 127).

(Tally 2023). In place of theory, in too many recent dissertations, we are offered the reduction of the text to the document, a move that threatens not only the specificity of literary reading but also its very rationale.[3]

The problem of course is that "theory" does not exist. It is a disciplinary fiction. Having begun life in the American university system as "literary theory," it represented an attempt to come terms with the rapid developments in linguistics, philosophy, psychoanalysis, the social sciences, and the formal study of literary and rhetorical technique that were known as structuralism and poststructuralism. In turn, these theoretical interventions, mostly centered in France, but drawing on traditions of linguistic and literary scholarship that originated in the former Soviet Union, Czechoslovakia, and Denmark, were often combined with the Hegelian Marxism of Frankfurt School critical theory, Georg Lukács, and Bertold Brecht.[4] The result, in the late sixties and early seventies, was a heady mixture of diverse traditions and focused debates. Comparative and general literature programs were at the center of this intellectual ferment in the United States. They combined a traditional interest in the definitional problems of literary form with the cosmopolitan and multilingual perspective necessary to engage these issues. At the same time, philosophy departments in the United States remained tied for the most part to a tradition of Anglo-American logical positivism and scientific empiricism that left little room for the speculatory flights of their continental confrères.

By the early 1980's when I was a graduate student at the University of Texas at Austin, my Comparative Literature classes were often filled with English and philosophy students coming to study what they could not read in their own departments. Yet, by this point, the change had already begun. Jonathan Culler's *Structuralist Poetics* (1975) had translated the difficult insights of Barthes, Saussure, and Derrida into a utilitarian American idiom that made these abstruse works approachable and appropriable. As Frank Lentricchia chronicled in *After the New Criticism* (1980), the potentially radical insights of Derrida, Lacan, and Barthes were during this same period rendered in terms that were cognate with the legacy of American New Criticism by the likes of Hillis Miller, Geoffrey Hartman, and, to a lesser extent, Harold Bloom and Paul de Man. By the end of the eighties, one no longer needed to know French to read Derrida, nor even know much about French intellectual history: the role of Kojève in the dissemination of Hegel; the concrete contributions of Sartre, surrealism, Bataille and Blanchot to French philosophy; or the traditions of French classicism.[5]

Derrida's readings of Plato, Saussure, Freud, and Rousseau were so many examples of deconstruction, which could be reduced to a method. All discourse is structured around binary oppositions, we were told. These oppositions are hierarchical. The deconstructive reader demonstrates the reversibility and hence contingent nature of that opposition: *et voilà*, an article, a seminar paper, and in some cases even a career

---

3   For a critique of this trend in recent literary studies, see Aviram (2001).
4   See Jameson (1971, 1972), Kristeva (1969), as well as collections such as Lucid (1977).
5   I am painting with a broad brush here, but see Stoekl (1992), Butler (1999), and Miller (1999) *inter alia*.

is born.[6] Of course, Derrida advocates nothing of the sort and is at pains to distance himself from precisely such facile appropriations (1980: 48; 1993: 141, 151). The problem is that once literary theory has been reduced to a method, such appropriations are not only natural but necessary.

The next step was the revocation of literature's license as a specific academic domain. In many ways, this was a positive development. The growth of Marxist literary criticism in the English speaking world had made us all aware of the class basis of many cultural institutions including the canon. This insight was echoed by the cognate insights of feminism, queer theory, and post-colonial studies (Eagleton 1996). At the same time, deconstructive formalism carried to its logical end overturned the opposition between the literary and the popular and that between high and low culture. The result was that literary theory became theory *tout court*, and the methods of reading it taught became all the more deracinated as they were applied without discrimination to greeting cards, slave narratives, and Dickens, often without the requisite ability to distinguish between these very different types of texts.[7]

What I am arguing for in this paper is not a return to a time before theory, but a recognition of what theory is. It is not a set of truths that can be simply applied to texts to produce results, preferably publishable. Rather theory per se does not exist—or at least it is of very recent and somewhat suspect vintage. What we call theory is a series of ongoing debates about the nature of meaning, texts, knowledge, and subjectivity that extend from the Platonic dialogues, through Aristotle to Cicero, Seneca, Augustine, Aquinas, Dante, and so on to the present. It is an ongoing set of conversations that can be entered at a variety of points. There are huge discontinuities, lacunae, and ruptures. Threads are dropped, picked back up, snapped, and woven into tapestries their founders could have never anticipated. They are relativized by encounters with the warps and wefts of alien traditions and concepts. Nonetheless, each entry point in that conversation only has meaning to the extent that it is a response to a set of ongoing dialogues (Voloshinov 1986: 11–12; Morson and Emerson 1990: 309; Holquist 1990: 167) and the moment we take a segment of that conversation out of context and elevate it to a timeless conceptual truth, the moment we crown it as "theory," we have robbed it of what makes it most authentic.

Obviously, I am not saying that we cannot offer a Derridian, Bakhtinian, or Lacanian reading of a given text. I have been guilty of this on numerous occasions and will no doubt recidivate. What I am saying is that when we do so or when we teach our students to do so, we must act in full cognizance of the context of the conversation we have entered. We do not only apply a theory, we re-ply to it and to its interlocutors.

---

6 An example of this kind of one size fits all deconstructive approach can be found in Hillis Miller (1981), in which Aristotle, Sophocles, Crabbe are reduced to "difference." A similar move can be seen in Hubbard (1984). After a sensitive reading of Catullus 68, Hubbard feels forced to make a series of statements on the self-deconstructing nature of all literary texts leaving the reader with the sense it matters little whether she has been reading Catullus, Sylvia Plath, or Lao Tsu.

7 On the transformation of "literary theory" into "theory," see Moi (2002: 171–85).

16 THEORY DOES NOT EXIST

To do so implies not only a knowledge of its intellectual presuppositions, but also of its historical and linguistic specificity: in short it demands the perspective of the trained comparatist.

Take a text such as Julia Kristeva's *Tales of Love* (1987). If we merely extract from her readings of Plato, Plotinus, the *Song of Songs, Romeo and Juliet*, Baudelaire and Bataille a general theory of love that we can then apply willy-nilly to other texts, we do this rich book a vast disservice. We completely miss that her reading of the *Symposium* not only complements Lacan's own (*Séminaire VIII*), but also includes direct replies to Derrida's reading of the *Phaedrus* as well as to Foucault's final volumes of the *History of Sexuality*, which featured its own interpretation of these same texts (67–69).[8] By the same token, her choice to include a substantial reading of Plotinus is a clear answer to Irigaray's *Speculum*, which also in the context of a psychoanalytically grounded feminist critique of occidental philosophies of the subject, offers both a substantial engagement with Plotinus and a lengthy reading of Plato. To do justice to the Kristevan text, it must be taught and interpreted then not only in terms of its own theoretical assumptions but also in terms of how it positions itself relative to the larger debates in psychoanalysis, feminism, and philosophy then underway in France. At the same time, it demands of the reader a detailed knowledge of the Platonic and neo-Platonic tradition and of their central importance in modern French intellectual life.

Indeed, the classical subtext of these debates has often gone all but unappreciated. This is in part because of a fundamental division in Anglophone culture. In the United States, the concerns of academic philosophy and philology have had little in common. This is due, in part, to analytic philosophy's self-confinement to technical questions of epistemology, speech act theory, and philosophy of science. As such, it has had little to say about the relation between antique and contemporary modes of thought. There have been, it is true, attempts to read Plato from an analytic perspective in which the Platonic text is reduced to its propositional content, but not to read Platonic philosophy as a critique of modernity or as a moment in the construction of the very reason that makes analytic thought possible. Rare is the philosophy department in the Anglophone world where continental thinkers are taken seriously, and rarer still those where contemporary French readings of ancient texts would be considered matters worthy of serious philosophical consideration.

It is also due to Anglo-American philology's own parochial instincts. Ensconced within a nineteenth-century German model of *Altertumswissenschaft* that continues to exercise a surprisingly strong influence, few classicists have made forays into philosophical, psychoanalytic, and other speculative modes of inquiry. The result has been that postmodern French thought has largely been the province, neither of philosophers nor philologists, but of English professors. These thinkers have produced some important readings of contemporary French thought. Unfortunately, however, they lack the training or the interest necessary to appreciate what is at stake in these thinkers' engagement with the philosophy and literature of Greco-Roman Antiquity.

---

8 The French original of *Tales of Love* was published before the last two volumes of the *History of Sexuality*, but Foucault was already lecturing on this material at the Collège de France (1994).

THE TROUBLE WITH THEORY

The kind of general culture that makes a figure like the great Comparative Indo-European scholar, Georges Dumézil, easily cited and appreciated by figures as diverse as Foucault, Derrida, and Kristeva is simply not available to most Anglophone scholars. The notion of Richard Rorty or Hillis Miller having the same easy familiarity with the analogous works of Calvert Watkins or Jaan Puhvel is all but inconceivable. Thus, a whole dimension of thought, which these thinkers simply assume, often goes unnoticed by even their most ardent enthusiasts.

Consequently, if theory is to be saved from the twin curses of reduction to an abstract methodology and being frozen in ahistorical presentism, a double contextualization is necessary. On the one hand, the immediate dialogic context of a particular theoretical intervention needs to be preserved and problematized. On the other, the larger intellectual context in which those discussions took place needs not only to be accounted for but directly engaged. In the case of continental and particularly French theory, this will often assume a detailed knowledge of the texts of antiquity. I will close this paper with an example of the type work I am proposing.

In *La Carte Postale*, Derrida argues that Freud's *Beyond the Pleasure Principle* owes an unacknowledged debt to Plato's *Philebus*. More specifically, he argues that Plato establishes the centrality of the concept of limit to the calculus of pleasure, and so also makes possible the envisioning, or the positing, of a beyond of that limit (1980: 425). In the same book, Derrida also contends that Lacan's reading of Poe's "Purloined Letter" founders on the psychoanalyst's logocentric claim that the "letter" is both material and ultimately indivisible (Lacan 1966a: 23–24). In this final section, I will claim that the *Philebus*' complex meditation on the relations between pleasure and limit as well as between the good life and the dialectical method of collection and division is central to understanding Derrida's arguments. I shall also offer the subsidiary thesis that the *Philebus* has the potential to mediate between Derrida and Lacan through its own overdetermined vision of the relation between the competing claims of the dialectic and of practical ethical life.

In *La Carte postale*, it is precisely the formation of the subject and the questions of origins, address, and identity that are at stake. In this text, Derrida interrogates Freud's debt to Platonic reason and Plato's debt to Freud in terms of both writing and a set of relays and mediations that he ironically dubs the "postal system" (1980: 190–91). A crucial passage in understanding Derrida's Platonic critique of psychoanalysis is the following:

> Toute l'histoire de la *tekhnè* postale tend à river la destination à de l'identité. Arriver serait à un sujet, arriver à <<moi>>. Or une marque, quelle qu'elle soit, se code pour faire empreinte, fût-elle un parfum. Dès lors elle se divise, elle vaut plusieurs fois en une fois: plus de destinaire unique. C'est pourquoi, en raison de cette divisibilité (l'orgine de la raison, l'origine folle de la raison et du principe d'identité), la *tekhnè* n'arrive pas à la langue—à ce que pour toi je chante. (1980: 207, his emphasis)

> Any history of postal *tekhnè* tends to join destination with identity. For a subject to arrive is to arrive at a self. Now a mark, whatever it may be, is coded to make an impression, be it only a scent. As soon as it is split, it is the equivalent of several instances in any one

instance: thus, no more unique destination. That's why, on account of this divisibility (the origin of reason, the mad origin of reason and of the principle of identity), the *tekhnè* does not arrive at language—at that which I sing for you.[9]

The "techniques" of the postal system join destination with identity in a system of transmission and mediation. However, every mark, every letter, to the extent that it is capable of being addressed to a specific identity, must be able to be reproduced, and hence to be divided from its originary unity: a fact that of necessity undermines that letter's relation to a unique destination. This divisibility is the origin of reason as demonstrated in the *Philebus*' exposition of the "divine method" of collection and division as the foundation of philosophical dialectic. It is also the origin of writing itself. As Plato points out, it was only by analyzing words into their component sounds, their ultimately meaningless phonemes, that the Egyptian god Theuth was able to develop the art of writing (17a–b, 18b–d).[10]

Division is also the origin of madness: for there must be a limit to divisibility if reason is to produce intelligible language, if the letter is to arrive at its destination. Yet that limit cannot be stated as principle separate from the process of division per se, outside of the categories of thought that division itself makes possible. Sense then depends on that very institution of difference or nonsense, and hence potential plurivocity, that Lacan labeled the insistence of the letter and origin of the Freudian unconscious (1966c). The very mark of division that makes transmission, mediation, meaning, and transference possible, is also that which necessarily derails it and subjective identity. This is what Derrida means when he speaks of Freud's (and hence Lacan's) unacknowledged debt to Plato (1980: 36, 70, 180–81; Zuckert 1996: 233).[11]

The addresser and addressee of communication in Derrida's postal system represent positions in an infinitely disseminated web of significations, whose very constitution under the images of law and limit was first elaborated in the Platonic corpus that also envisioned its beyond (1980: 60). The *Philebus*, inasmuch as it founds true knowledge on the dialectic of collection and division (14B–20A), and inasmuch as the burden of Socrates' argument is to demonstrate the superiority of knowledge to pleasure—but ultimately he shows knowledge to be a superior kind of pleasure, or more properly part of a mixed entity in which knowledge brings pleasure (20B–23B)—it must also posit a world beyond limit, beyond all division, and hence beyond all meaning, mixture, and exchange. The unlimited, *apeiron*, is that which does not contain any quantity, that which can never be reduced to a unity and hence to a unit that might be measured against another (24a–d).[12] The limit then is the marker of division that makes the delimitation of discrete logical or material entities possible and thus opens the possibility of exchange and classification, and hence of knowledge and

---

9 All translations are my own unless otherwise indicated.

10 Theuth plays a similar role in Plato's *Phaedrus* and features in "Plato's Pharmacy" (Derrida 1972).

11 Derrida, far from dismissing Lacan's basic reading of *Beyond the Pleasure Principle*, acknowledges it as "le plus intéressant et le plus spectaculaire" (1980: 402–03).

12 See Frede's helpful introduction and notes (1993).

culture (Lacan 1973: 169). Logical categories and rational entities are predicated then on the concept of limit (25a). The conjunction of limit and the unlimited, of continuity and its determinate negation, makes possible rhythm, music, and signification. This is the realm of the mixed (26a).

The pleasure principle in Freud, inasmuch as it represents the pursuit of the object of desire as delimited by the reality principle, which is itself a reflex of the pleasure principle and not its beyond, always operates within the realm of the mixed, of entities defined by limit (Freud, 1961a: 4; Lacan 1986: 29; Zuckert 1996: 233). It is for this reason that the Law, substitution, and transference are possible. The division of the subject instituted by its submission to the realm of law and language are founding moments of its desire, as recognized by both Aristophanes' speech in Plato's *Symposium* and by Lacan himself. This division is also the object of Derrida's own inquiry (1980: 36, 60; Ragland-Sullivan 1986: 270; Julien 1990: 151–52, 176, 231):

> La <<détermination>> c'est la limite—et d'abord du plaisir (du *Philèbe* à *Au-delà*…), ce qui lie l'énergie; elle identifie, elle décide, elle définit, elle marque les contours, et puis c'est la destination (*Bestimmung*, si on veut s'appeler comme ça), et la loi et la guêpe[13] (Sp) quand elle est pas folle, qu'elle veut savoir de qui de quoi: et moi donc qu'est-ce que je deviens dans cette affaire, faudrait encore que ça me fasse un peu retour, que la lettre revienne à sa destination, etc. (1980: 65)

> "Determination" is the limit—and first of all of pleasure (from the *Philebus* to *Beyond* [*the Pleasure Principle*]), it is what binds energy: it identifies, it defines, it marks the contours, and finally it's the destination (*Bestimmung*, if you want to call it that), it's both the law and the gap/Wasp, when it's not mad, that wants to know of whom and of what: and for me then, whatever I become in this affair, it will still be necessary that there be some small return for me, that the letter comes back to its destination, etc.

Deconstruction, as Derrida defines his own project, seeks to touch upon the same space beyond the limit, beyond the pleasure principle, as Freud in his Phileban investigation of the pleasure and reality principles as relative goods. It does not seek to destroy this initial opposition between desire and knowledge, but to move beyond it to the indestructible, which as Freud showed was indistinguishable from death (1980: 249, 304–04, 425–27).

Freud's position, however, as psychoanalyst and scientist, rather than as Nietzschean philosopher, is not to embrace the beyond or death, but rather the realm of limit. In *Beyond the Pleasure Principle*, he struggles constantly to articulate even the most radical of his metapsychological insights within the realm of the Law. For, on the one hand, the Law, as he acknowledges in *Civilization and Its Discontents*,[14] is the ultimate cause of our unhappiness, but on the other, it also marks the ground on which the pleasure principle founds its erection. The institution of language and culture constitutes the fundamental delimitation of the subject and the signifier that makes transference, treatment, and psychoanalysis possible (Lacan 1966b: 412–18; Kristeva 1987: 21–38; Derrida 1980: 360–61, 409). It is this fundamentally dual structure of being both

---

13  An allusion to Aristophanes' *Wasps*, a satire on the law, and to the "gap."
14  See Lacan's reading (1986: 36, 44).

within and beyond the Law that accounts for what Derrida terms Freud's "athétique" style in *Beyond the Pleasure Principle*, his constant hesitation before the positing of a potential transgression of the very limits that enable his discourse (1980: 425), "Je relis *Au-delà*... d'une main tout y est merveilleusement hermétique, c'est-à-dire postal et traînant ... il ne nous dit RIEN, ne fait pas un pas qu'il ne retire au pas suivant ("I am rereading *Beyond [the Pleasure Principle]* on the one hand there is something marvelously hermetic, that is to say postal and drawn out ...he says to us NOTHING, he doesn't make one step forward that he doesn't take back with the next") (1980: 153, emphasis his). Freud, then, even as he searches to articulate its beyond, continues to work within the closure of western metaphysics and the bounded entities it discerns. The signifier as it moves from one post to the next in its infinite path of circulation and exchange traces the path of transferences, substitutions, and displacements that produce the talking cure.

Thus, psychoanalysis consists of a series of relays through which meaning passes. It operates within the field of divisibility and the unit, not in the unmarked realm of the limitless, which like Plato it must posit as its own beyond. Through the transfers of meaning, through the delimited places of desire, psychoanalysis continues to function within the postal system of western metaphysics. Through the repetition of the law of the limit, it insures that the possibility of meaning always remains, that the letter always arrives at its destination (1980: 50, 73, 190–91).

It is Lacan's decision to continue to operate within this system of meanings that constitutes the burden of Derrida's indictment of him in the now famous essay from the same book, "Le facteur de la verité," or "the postman of truth" (1980: 455). As Derrida observes, the notion that the letter always arrives at its destination, is predicated on its final indivisibility, on there being a limit to delimitation (Lacan 1966a: 23–24). There is always in the last analysis a moment when the address can be reconstructed, even if only after the fact, even if that address is the site of a lack, the constitutive moment of the speaking subject's desire (1980: 464–65, 469).

Nonetheless, it is precisely the limits of the dialectic, of the philosophic practice of collection and division, in relation to pleasure and to the question of the good life—that is to say, in relation to the desire of the analyst—that is the subject of the *Philebus*. The *Philebus* begins with Socrates advancing the thesis that knowledge is superior to pleasure. Philebus has been Socrates' eristic opponent but at the beginning of the dialogue Protarchus is asked to take over for him (11C). This much debated move seems designed to prepare for the shift from a binary opposition between these two perspectives to the more pragmatic mixed position adopted at the dialogue's end. Protarchus is asked by Socrates if he will grant that there are different kinds of pleasures (12D–13A). This immediately leads into a discussion of the relation of the many to the one and to the introduction of the "divine method" of collection and division. There follows a lengthy and somewhat dry exposition that points to the conclusion that in order to determine the unity of any given form or abstract universal, such as knowledge or pleasure, one would first need to follow the procedure of division till one reached the smallest possible constituent unit of that universal and from there proceed back through its many genera and subspecies in quest of the unlimited realm of its infinite form (16C–17E).

# THE TROUBLE WITH THEORY

The unlimited itself is used in two different senses in the dialogue. It is both that which is beyond the many and hence the infinitely large, as just described, and that which is not yet limited or below the threshold of the one, the realm of pure continuity, discussed earlier (Frede 1993: xxxiii–xxxiv).[15] In reality, however, and certainly from a psychoanalytic perspective, these are the same. The realms of what is before and of what is beyond the law of limit are both worlds of pure continuity in which the one, the many, and the mixed have either been transcended or not yet come to exist. In this realm, there is possible neither knowledge nor individual existence (Freud 1961a: 2; Bataille 1957: 20–27, 155n.1; Lacan 1991: 174–75; 1973: 159).

Protarchus, however, is not interested in such abstract generalities. His question is much more practical. The potentially infinite progression and regression involved in the practice of collection and division may be the only method on which true knowledge can be based. Yet how does it lead to a decision on which is the superior good: knowledge or pleasure?

> Pro: While it is a great thing for the wise man to know everything, the second best is not to be mistaken about *oneself* …. You Socrates have granted this meeting to all of us, and yourself to boot, to find out what is the best of all human possessions…. Since you … committed yourself to us, we therefore insist, like children, that there is no taking back a gift properly given. So, give up this way of turning against us the discussion here.
>
> Soc: What way are you talking about?
>
> Pro: Your way of plunging us into difficulties and repeating questions to which we have at present no proper answer to give you. But we should not take it that the aim of our meeting is universal confusion. (19C–20A, Frede 1993: 13)

The result is a sudden shift in direction. Socrates, unlike the philosopher but much like the psychoanalyst, responds to Protarchus's demand by recounting a dream: in it, Socrates had learned that neither pleasure nor knowledge was the highest good, but there was third unnamed thing. In this way, Socrates undoes the false binary of pleasure and knowledge and relativizes both to an unnamed third object to which each can stand in relation. By the same token, their rapport is now relational rather than oppositional so that pleasure and knowledge are no longer seen as pure unities but are now able to appear together in mixed entities (20B–23B). This last move allows the earlier discussion of the pure dialectic of collection and division to be transformed into the more pragmatic analysis of the unlimited, the limit and the mixed discussed above (23C–27C).

The rest of the dialogue consists, then, of an analysis and classification of the various forms of mixed pleasures and knowledges. It concludes with a series of recommendations on how a balanced life might be pursued. In short, while acknowledging the claims of the dialectic and the search for absolute knowledge, the *Philebus* also grants the existence of another realm of practical ethical action: the philosopher as therapist or the therapist as philosopher. True knowledge may be founded upon the method of collection

---

15  For an analogous structure determining pleasure in Freud, see Zuckert (1996: 233).

22 THEORY DOES NOT EXIST

and division, which provides the epistemological foundation for the late doctrine of the forms, but it is a foundation that simultaneously posits its own beyond, the *apeiron* or limitless world of pure continuity in which the law of limit, demarcation, property, and exchange makes its mark (1980: 379). It is to this latter world, that beyond the closure of western metaphysics, beyond the field in which unity and the unit can be envisioned, that Derrida seeks the indestructible (1980: 249). This, as he notes, is the same realm that Freud locates beyond the pleasure principle (1980: 304–05).

This is also the realm to which he gestures when he argues that Lacan remains within the logocentric realm when the latter contends that the letter is ultimately indivisible and that it thus always arrives at its destination. Therefore, while the Lacanian letter may signal nothing more than absence or lack, that lack never lacks place. It is always localizable. It always traces a path through discourse and so can be endowed with a meaning and a relation to a speaking subject, even if only in the form of a negation or lack (1980: 443, 472, 492–93). The letter always arrives at its destination (Lacan 1966a: 41). It is always decipherable, at least as the symptomatic presence of the indecipherable.

Yet, how can it be otherwise in psychoanalysis (Lacan 1973: 236, 276; Ragland-Sullivan 1986: 218; Žižek 1989: 72, 174–75; Julien 1990 147–48)? The philosopher may and even must pursue the foundations of knowledge to and beyond the limitless realm in which meaning dissolves. He may and must conceive of the possibility of radical non-meaning, of a pure contingency in which the letter may or may not arrive at its destination (1980: 133–35). The psychoanalyst, however, is still faced with Protarchus, lying there on the couch wanting to know the value of pleasure. Lacan was always very clear that he was not a philosopher or literary theorist, but an analyst whose writings and teachings were in the first instance aimed at forming other analysts. Derrida, in contrast, says that his goal is precisely to pose the philosopher's epistemological question to the psychoanalyst (1980: 261). Thus, he and Lacan represent two sides of the same postcard—the readable and the unreadable—that must always co-exist with and condition one another (1980: 88). The *Philebus* itself, in its very discontinuity between the dialectic and the calculus of pleasure, embodies this same double logic even as it offers the possibility of mediating between the needs of the philosopher and the demands of the analyst and his or her analysand.[16]

The burden of Derrida's argument with psychoanalysis and the entire system of postality and address he constructs both in his more philosophical texts and in the epistolary novel that opens the collection are incomprehensible except as part of a larger dialogue between Freud, Lacan, and Derrida on the one hand and these thinker's engagement with and debt to the Platonic tradition on the other. Derrida is not here offering a general theory of address, the subject, or the letter, but a concrete intervention in an ongoing debate that stretches back 2500 years. We can most authentically join that debate, not by seeing it as a conclusion, but by developing our own finely

---

16 The possibility of this mediation is signaled by Derrida's acknowledgement that some have argued that the Lacanian and Derridian positions are homologous. As both he and others have acknowledged, this is an oversimplification, but not one with no basis (1980: 163).

# THE TROUBLE WITH THEORY

nuanced response to these same texts, even as we bring to this conversation the concerns and texts that are our own.

This can of course be done in English departments as well as anywhere else. The problem is not one of institutional or even disciplinary location per se. But it can only be done if these texts are not reduced to being the exemplars of a theory or critical methodology to be applied, and only by scholars willing and able to engage the multiple contexts that constitute this ongoing dialogue. It can only be done by those embodying the cosmopolitan and open spirit that constitutes the heart of comparative literature.

## Works Cited

Aviram, Amittai. 2001. *Intertexts* 5. 61–86.

Bataille, Georges. 1957. *L'érotisme*. Paris: Minuit.

Butler, Judith. 1999. *Subjects of Desire: Hegelian Reflections in Twentieth-Century France*. 2nd ed. New York: Columbia University Press.

Culler, Jonathan. 1975 *Structuralist Poetics: Structuralism, Linguistics, and the Study of Literature*. Ithaca: Cornell University Press.

Derrida, Jacques. 1976. *Of Grammatology*. Trans. Gayatri Spivak. Baltimore: Johns Hopkins University Press.

———. 1972. "La pharmacie de Platon." *La dissémination*. Paris: Seuil. 74–97.

———. 1980. *La Carte Postale: de Socrate a Freud et au-delà*. Paris: Aubier-Flammarion.

———. 1993. *Spectres de Marx*. Paris: Galilée.

Eagleton, Terry. 1996. *Literary Theory: An Introduction*. 2nd ed. Minneapolis: University of Minnesota Press.

Foucault, Michel. 1994. "A propos de la généalogie de l'éthique: un aperçu du travail en cours." *Dits et écrits: 1954–1988*. Vol. 4. Eds. Daniel Defert and François Ewalt. Paris: Gallimard. 609–31.

———. 1986. *The Use of Pleasures. History of Sexuality, Vol. 2*. Trans. Robert Hurley. New York: Pantheon.

Frede, Dorothea, trans and ed. 1993. *Plato: Philebus*. Indianapolis: Hackett.

Freud, Sigmund. 1961a. *Beyond the Pleasure Principle*. Trans. James Strachey. The Standard Edition. New York: Norton.

———. 1961b. *Civilization and Its Discontents*. Trans. James Strachey. The Standard Edition. New York: Norton.

Holquist, Michael. 1990. *Dialogism: Bakhtin and His World*. London: Routledge.

Hubbard, Thomas K. 1984. "Catullus 68: The Text as Self-Demystification." *Arethusa* 17: 29–49.

Irigaray, Luce. 1974. *Speculum, De l'autre femme*. Paris: Minuit.

Jameson, Fredric. 1971. *Marxism and Form*. Princeton: Princeton University Press.

———. 1972. *Prisonhouse of Language: A Critical Account of Structuralism and Russian Formalism*. Princeton: Princeton University Press.

Kristeva, Julia. 1969. Σημιωτικὴ: *Recherches pour une sémanalyse*. Paris: Seuil.

———. 1987. *Tales of Love*. Trans. Leon S. Roudiez. New York: Columbia University Press.

Julien, Phillipe. 1990. *Pour lire Jacques Lacan*. 2nd ed. Paris: E. P. E. L.

Lacan, Jacques. 1966a "Le Séminaire sur <<La lettre volée.>>" *Ecrits*. Paris: Gallimard, 1966. 11–60.

———. 1966b. "La chose freudienne ou Sens du retour à Freud en psychanalyse." *Ecrits*. Paris: Gallimard. 401–36.

———. 1966c. "L'Instance de la lettre dans l'inconscient ou la raison depuis Freud." *Ecrits*. Paris: Gallimard. 493–528.

24 THEORY DOES NOT EXIST

———. 1986. *Le séminaire VII: L'éthique de la psychanalyse*. Ed. Jacques-Alain Miller. Paris: Seuil.

———. 1991. *Le séminaire VIII: Le transfert*. Ed. Jacques-Alain Miller. Paris: Seuil.

———. 1973. *Le séminaire livre XI: Les quatre concepts fondamentaux de la psychanalyse*. Ed. Jacques-Alain Miller. Paris: Seuil.

Lentricchia, Frank. 1980. *After the New Criticism*. Chicago: Chicago University Press.

Lucid, Daniel P., ed. and trans. 1997. *Soviet Semiotics*. Baltimore: Johns Hopkins University Press.

Lyotard, Jean-François. 1984. *The Postmodern Condition: A Report on Knowledge*. Trans. Geoff Bennington and Brian Massumi. Minneapolis: University of Minnesota Press.

Malone, Kareen Ror. 2000. "The Place of Lacanian Psychoanalysis in North American Psychology." *Lacan in America*. Ed. Jean-Michel Rabaté. New York: Other Press. 3–24.

Miller, J. Hillis. 1981. "The Ethics of Reading: Vast Gaps and Parting Hours." *American Criticism in the Poststructuralist Age*. Ed. Ira Konigsberg. Ann Arbor: University of Michigan Press. 19–41.

Miller, Paul Allen. 1999. "The Classical Roots of Poststructuralism: Lacan, Derrida, and Foucault." *International Journal of the Classical Tradition* 5: 204–25.

Moi, Toril. 2002. *Sexual/Textual Politics*. 2nd ed. New York: Routledge.

Morson, Gary Saul and Caryl Emerson. 1990. *Mikhail Bakhtin: Creation of a Prosaics*. Stanford: Stanford University Press.

Ragland-Sullivan, Ellie. 1986. *Jacques Lacan and the Philosophy of Psychoanalysis*. Urbana: University of Illinois Press, 1986.

Stoekl, Allan. 1992. *Agonies of the Intellectual: Commitment, Subjectivity, and the Performative in the Twentieth-Century French Tradition*. Lincoln: University of Nebraska Press.

Tally, Robert, Jr. 2023. "Rehabilitating Theory." *American Book Review* 44: 35–38.

Voloshinov, V. N. 1986. *Marxism and the Philosophy of Language*. Trans. Ladislav Matejka and I. R. Titunik. Cambridge, MA: Harvard University Press.

Weed, Elizabeth. 1994. "The Question of Style." *Engaging with Irigaray*. Eds. Carolyne Burke, Naomi Schor, and Margaret Whitford. New York: Columbia University Press. 79–109.

Žižek, Slavoj. 1989. *The Sublime Object of Ideology*. London: Verso.

Zuckert, Catherine H. 1996. *Postmodern Platos: Nietzsche, Heidegger, Gadamer, Strauss, Derrida*. Chicago: University of Chicago Press, 1996.

# Chapter 3

# PLACING THE SELF IN THE FIELD OF TRUTH: IRONY AND SELF-FASHIONING IN ANCIENT AND POSTMODERN RHETORICAL THEORY[1]

Curiously enough, it seems only in describing a mode of language which does not mean what it says that one can actually say what one means. (de Man 1983: 211)

The identification of speaking the truth and having seen the truth, this identification between the one who speaks, and the source, the origin, the root of truth: there is here, without a doubt, a many-sided and complex process that has had a capital importance for the history of truth in our societies. (Foucault 2012: 49)

You are standing in a field. There is a person in front of you and a tree to one side. To make a true statement about the tree to that person, you must use language to form a proposition that makes your experience of the tree intelligible to the person you are addressing. If you say "the tree is an oak" and Marcus perceives a birch, the statement will not be received as true, but if Marcus's perceptions can be brought under the same linguistic categories as your own, then your statement will be received as true, and, inasmuch it will now be able to be reproduced by other speakers having similar experiences and again received as true, then it will become "the truth." Such is the classic western referential understanding of truth, from Augustine's discussion of how children learn the names of things (*Confessions* 1.8) to Hegel's deconstruction of the empiricist postulate of sense-certainty (see below). A similar paradigm underlies many of our current notions of scientific method, particularly as deployed in the social sciences. This scenario, however, begs certain questions. How do we align Marcus's categories with our own? How do we agree on the nature of an oak, let alone beauty, justice, or national identity? What kind of force, suasion, or manipulation needs to

---

1  This paper was presented in a number of venues and benefited from the feedback of friends and interlocutors. It began as a series of discussions with my graduate students in a Comparative Literature seminar on "Truth and Irony" at the University of South Carolina. Versions were presented as a talk at "Cosmopolitan Topographies," a conference sponsored by the Classics Program at Texas Tech University, January 2011, as an invited lecture at Beijing Language and Cultural University, June 2012, and as a workshop for the Yale Classics Department, February 2012. Along the way, it was improved by responses, criticism, and support from David H. J. Larmour, Chris Whitmore, Erik Doxtader, Jeffrey Di Leo, Charles Stocking, and Kirk Freudenburg. It also benefited from the criticism and editorial judgment of *Arethusa*'s readers and editorial board.

be deployed for such truth to come into being, for experience to be understandable, and for place, a location on a grid of intelligibility, to take place? These are central questions for philosophy and rhetorical theory from antiquity to the present. This paper argues that only a concerted reading of the ancient texts in conversation with their modern and postmodern interlocutors can begin to help us form cogent answers to those questions—can permit us the historical depth and theoretical sophistication necessary to begin to understand our own conjuncture in the "history of truth."

Truth on the model outlined above is, in fact, the product of a rhetorical situation, that is to say on the relation between a speaker, his audience, and their pragmatic situation. The truth of the proposition is not dependent on whether the tree in question really is an oak, a birch, or a larch.[2] There is no larch, nor even any tree, until such time as the category that renders them intelligible has come into being. The prelinguistic "larch" is a nonsequitur. My perceptions, as the Stoics recognized, cannot have the status of truth, nor can referential truth exist, until the data that constitute those perceptions have been raised to the level of universalizing, and hence linguistic or "sayable," categories (Frede 1994: 110–11; Nussbaum 1994: 327; Hankinson 2003: 65). Moreover, if we are to be assured that those perceptions are not the products of a private delirium, they must be received as true by at least one other speaker who has correlated his or her own experience with those categories and therefore provided "confirmation."

None of this is to say that the experiences in question—our perceptions of the oak, the birch, or the larch—do not play a decisive role in the rhetorical constitution of truth, or that they are somehow unreal. We have *res* ("things") and we have *verba* ("words"; cf. Frede 1994: 116–17), and their nonidentity is the condition of the possibility of language itself. The fact that the "word" is not the "thing" is what allows words to refer to things. Thus, in classical rhetorical theory, the speaker's task is to match the one with the other, to make an accord. It is the possibility of such a correlation that makes both truth and persuasion possible. As Cicero has Crassus explain in Book 3 of the *De Oratore*:

> Omnis igitur oratio conficitur ex verbis. ... Utimur verbis aut eis, quae propria sunt et certa quasi vocabula rerum, paene una nata cum rebus ipsis; aut eis, quae transferuntur et quasi alieno in loco conlocantur; aut eis, quae novamus et facimus ipsi. In propriis igitur est verbis laus oratoris, ut abiecta atque obsoleta fugiat, lectis atque inlustribus utatur. (3.149)

> Therefore all speech is fashioned from words. ... We use either those words, which are proper and exact, as if they were the direct names of things, almost as if they were born with the things themselves, or those which are transferred, as if they have been relocated into a strange place, or those which we invent and coin ourselves. The praise of the orator is in the use of the right words, so that he may avoid the vulgar and the archaic and may use those that are elegant and give luster to his speech.[3]

---

2   While my example of the tree is to a certain extent arbitrary—we could just as easily be discussing the proverbial cat on the mat (see, for example, Noonan and Curtis 2014)—this image comes trailing its own set of intertexts. See Saussure's famous image of the tree in chapter 1 of the *Course on General Linguistics* (1959).

3   All translations are my own, unless otherwise stated. On this passage, see Mankin's 2011 commentary, May and Wisse's translation (2001), and Wilkinson (2002: ad loc).

Thus, *res* and *verba* either come into being simultaneously, or we borrow a pre-existing *verbum* to make clear or rename a *res*, or we may on occasion invent a neologism to bring a wholly new phenomenon into speech, and thus give it the possibility of truth. But the labor of finding the proper accord between *res* and *verba* is what constitutes the burden of the speaker who would convince us of the "truth," and consequently *res* and *verba* must be assumed to be separate.

Nonetheless, the fact that *res* and *verba* are nonidentical does not mean that they exist apart from one another, that we simply take a bunch of names and match them up with the things to which they belong. What would a *res* be that exists outside the categories that define it? Adam cannot name the beasts of the field before those beasts have been identified, before they have names. What would a *res* be that exists outside the categories that define it: the names, words, or signifying structures we use to refer to it? It would not be an identifiable "thing" that exists in reality, which is what Cicero means here by *res*, but it could only be the nameless extension of pure materiality, the mute Lacanian Real: a realm of incomprehension beyond language and imagination (Lacan 1975: 85; Ragland-Sullivan 1986: 190; Žižek 1989: 170; Žižek 1991: 36). Indeed, as Kant teaches us, the *res* in itself does not appear. It is not phenomenal, and so it cannot be an object of experience. The thing outside the categories of its intelligibility, beyond the *logos*, does not exist as a possible object of discourse and experience. *Res* and *verba*, for Cicero and for us, are, by definition, both not identical—otherwise we would all call the same things by the same names and would never disagree about either names or things—and inseparable.

It is not the case, then, that things are simply out there waiting to be named. There is no *experience*, in fact, of the unmediated. There is nothing that *really* is an "oak," a "birch," or a "larch," outside the universalizing conventions that constitute it both as an ideal object and, hence, as an object of our possible experience: the categories of intelligibility that we use to manipulate, frame, and criticize our experience are in the first and last instance signifying. They are coterminous with the *logos* (cf. Eco 1976: 66, 73, 79; Todorov 1984: 32; Bauman 1984: 43, *inter alia*). In the beginning was the word.

On one level, this observation is nothing new. It has been made again and again by a wide variety of thinkers, including Cicero and the Stoics just cited. As Plato recognized, there is no chair without a concept of being a chair or "chairness," and there is no chairness outside a set of definitions that fixes its bounds and outside an articulated system of categories and signs. This observation is not the province of any one school, text, or period of time. It recurs throughout the work of a wide variety of ancient, modern, and postmodern theorists of discourse, of communication, and of the pragmatics of truth.

And yet it is not clear that we have consistently and rigorously thought through the consequences of this observation. We all too often continue to operate in both our daily lives and in our scholarly undertakings as if facts spoke for themselves, as if the scientific and the philosophical realm of truth could be rigorously distinguished from the rhetorical and the literary realm of *poeisis* ("making"). Plato may have kicked the poets out of the *Republic* in Book 10 if they were unable to give a proper defense of their craft (608c–e), but he responded to this projected exile not with an exaltation of the realm of the factual or the dialectical but with the Myth of Er. The *Republic* ends with Socrates telling a story. As Paul de Man observes in "The Rhetoric of Temporality," a meditation on irony's relation to allegory from Quintilian to Rousseau to Schlegel cited at the beginning of this paper, "Curiously enough, it seems only in describing a mode of language which does not mean what it says that one can actually say what one means."

The present paper proposes to begin the labor, once again, of seriously considering the mutual implication of referentiality, sayability, and rhetoricity in the constitution of truth. It will argue that the truth can only be said ironically—can only be said by saying something more, other, and different from what you mean. In the final analysis, it will suggest that the rhetorical, the literary, and the philosophical derive from this common root. It will argue this thesis from both the perspective of ancient rhetorical reflection and postmodern philosophy and theory. In doing so, it will invoke a variety of theoretical and philosophical perspectives, deliberately avoiding representing any one school, theorist, or point of view as privileged. It will not propose a psychoanalytic, deconstructive, or Foucauldian reading of a given set of ancient texts (although it owes debts to all these forms of thought), nor will it examine in any linear way the postmodern reception of the ancient texts. Rather, it will seek to join a conversation that begins in antiquity and continues to the present about the relationship between language, categories, experience, and truth. It does not privilege either the ancient or the postmodern but seeks to treat all the texts it engages as existing on the same plane—as having no privilege one over the other but as co-constitutive of the discursive structures that make possible our present literary, philosophical, and theoretical conjuncture. It recognizes that this joining of the rhetorical and the philosophical is not new, and it contends that we may come to conceive of this joining most rigorously not only in the company of postmodern theorists but also in dialogue with the ancient philosophical and rhetorical thinkers who are their implicit, if not always explicit, interlocutors,[4] even if this labor involves reading certain of their texts carefully and perhaps just a bit against the grain of their normative reception.[5]

Such observations on the distinctions between *res* and *verba*, on the possibility of true statements, and on the possibility of meaningful experience are deeply rooted in the western philosophical and rhetorical tradition from Socrates to the Stoics, Cicero, Kant, Eco, Lacan, and Derrida. As Plato argued, the individual sensible element is only intelligible to the extent that it participates in a complex whole, a one which is both inconceivable outside the many that make it up and which makes the many *qua* many and hence *qua* objects of speech and intelligible experience, possible (*Philebus* 16c–18d; *Theaetetus* 205d–e; *Sophist* 253d–e, 259e; Hampton 1990: 92, Goldschmidt 2003: 92–93). The *res* only exists to the extent that it participates in a larger category of intelligibility, that it is definable within the *logos*, and that it is sayable by means of the word.

---

4　See Miller 2017 and Miller 2010b.

5　See Nehamas's discussion of Socratic versus Platonic irony (1998: 19–198) and Too on Isocrates (1995: 84–85).

## PLACING THE SELF IN THE FIELD OF TRUTH

The truth, then, is not that which exists apart from the word but is only that which enters the *logos* and which the speaker may articulate to an auditor, even if only herself. The *logos* makes possible and "account" of the world, but also creates the world as an account and one account out of many possible. Thus while Plato may argue in the *Phaedrus* that the true *rhetor* must be a philosopher, as Cicero acknowledges in his own strong reading of that dialogue, *De Oratore*, the best philosopher, the true philosopher, is always a rhetorician (1.47–49; 3.15, 60, 129, 142), and no one demonstrates this better than Socrates in the *Gorgias*.[6] As such, for both Plato and Cicero, the true philosopher is not he who maintains unwavering fidelity to the referent or singular event, but he who expresses the truth of that event by transmuting it into things sayable, and hence potentially confirmable, by others. To locate ourselves, the objects of our experience, and others on maps cognitive or otherwise—to be in a defined place, a *topos*[7]—is therefore always already to have submitted to the co-constitution of truth and rhetoric, experience and its articulation.

As can be seen now, the basic scenario of referential truth, which initially seemed so simple, is irremediably complex: for, on the most basic level of perception, cognition, and communication, referentiality necessitates a remaking of the particular (the brute *datum* of my senses) in terms of the universal (a recognizable *res*), as well as the intelligibility and receivability of my idiom (*verba*) by another. Thus, every moment of reference, every moment of truth, implies a double movement of turning, of tropological remaking, as the Stoic understanding of concept formation explicitly understood (Hankinson 2003: 263–64): the move from the irreducible particularity of my experience to the categories of the universal and the expression of those categories in a fashion likely to gain the assent of the other.

The necessity of this tropological movement implies, as Wittgenstein recognized (1973 ¶ 243), the impossibility of a private language. There is no reference that is not acknowledged by another, that does not occupy a fixed place in a language game that is recognized by the other (Rorty 1989: 18–19). There is no truth that is simply my own. Truth, as Bakhtin and his followers would aver, is always dialogically constituted (Bakhtin/Medvedev 1985: 14–17; Bakhtin 1981: 279; Frow 1986: 405).

This recognition has certain concrete implications. Inasmuch as my perceptions can only attain the status of truth to the extent that they are raised to the level of a set of potentially universalizing linguistic terms, which must of necessity pre-exist

---

6  The Stoics too see philosophy as an essentially rhetorical practice (Nussbaum 1994: 329–30).

7  *Topos*, as logically delimited space, is thus distinguished from *khōra*, the receptacle of the *Timaeus*. "*Khōra* names the 'place' that is no place (*atopia*) that allows place (defined logical space, *topos*) to take place (the possibility of its eventuality and thus of the event)," (Miller 2010b: 329). Socrates is frequently referred to as being *atopos*. In this context, the term on the one hand, indicates a certain outrageousness or even absurdity in Socrates' conduct as seen by his fellow citizens, and, on the other, his unclassifiability, his seeming "out of place" (Vlastos 1991: 1 n.1; Hadot 1995: 57). The corollary of his *atopia* is his ability to provoke *aporia* (*Theaetetus* 149a). Because he does not occupy a classifiable space in the logic of ancient Athens, he therefore provokes perplexity (*aporia*), that is, the loss of a "way out" or "means of passage" (*poros*) between the *topoi* of Athenian life. See Derrida (1993: 15–16, 94–95).

me and which I use to communicate my perceptions, then my perceptions themselves are no longer (and never were) simply my own (Voloshinov 1986: 12; Holquist 1990: 167; Parkhurst 1995: 48). The originating "I" of my experience does not exist as a singular locus of truth, but the very possibility of that experience depends on the voice of the other, and on an intrinsic self-ironization. There is an inherent moment of self-alienation that is constitutive of the speaking subject, and it is only through the labor of fabricating an ethos, a persona, as ancient rhetorical theory well understood, that the perceiver of the referent and the speaker of truth comes into being and is receivable as such by another (Too 1996: 1, 86–87; Habinek 2005: 43–44). The self whose experiences are fabricated within language is never a self that is wholly coincident with its position or its meaning. As Hegel observes in the opening chapter on "sense certainty" in the *Phenomenology of the Spirit*:

> [The defenders of a naïve empiricism] speak of the existence of *external* objects, which can be more precisely defined as *actual*, absolutely *singular, wholly personal, individual* things, each of them absolutely unlike anything else; this existence, they say has absolute certainty and truth. They *mean* "this" bit of paper on which I am writing—or rather have written—"this"; but what they mean is not what they say. If they actually wanted to *say* "this" bit of paper which they mean, if they wanted to *say* it, then this is impossible, because the sensuous This that is meant cannot be reached by language, which belongs to consciousness, i.e., to that which is inherently universal (1977: 66, emphasis his).

As soon as our perceptions of the object are raised to the status of language, and hence become the objects of thought and communication (and thus objects qua objects, as opposed to a sheer welter of sensory data), they become crowded with the experiences and intentions of others. Language has no other ontology than the history of its usage, than the totality of situations in which a given set of terms has been used before the current moment of thought or speech, the current moment of enunciation and thus we can never truly say what we mean except by speaking with and through the voice of the other (Bakhtin 1981: 276; Bakhtin 1986: 93; Todorov 1984: 39–40, 49, 56–57; Morson and Emerson 1990: 131, 139, 309). As Hegel continues:

> But if I want to help language—which has the divine nature of directly reversing the meaning of what is said, of making it into something else, and thus not letting what is meant *get into words* at all—by *pointing out* this bit of paper, experience teaches me what the truth of sense-certainty in fact is: I point it out as "Here," which is a Here of other Heres, or is in its own self a "simple togetherness of many Heres"; i.e. it is a universal. I take it up then as it is in truth, and instead of knowing something immediate I take the truth of it. (1977: 66)

Thus, the "here" of my "I see an oak here," in the moment of its enunciation becomes the "simple togetherness of many Heres." The possibility of location, which is intimately linked to the possibility of referential truth, is predicated on its own simultaneous negation, on a moment of turning in which this particular location only comes to exist in relation to the possibility of location itself and hence of all other "locations." Thus, the truth itself, a truth that is not its own negation, would be possible only as the negation of the negation, a double movement beyond the referential (Žižek 1993: 98, 122–24, 263; Miller 1998: 202). "Curiously enough, it seems only in describing a mode of language which does not mean what it says that one can actually say what one means" (de Man 1983: 211). The speaking subject is always made from the voices of others, and only insofar as she is this process of *poeisis* or fictionalization does she become the subject of speech and experience. This process of *poeisis* in turn is the common ground of philosophy, literature, and rhetoric (cf. Habinek 2005: 52–53). It is precisely, on this ground, that the humanities find their strongest defense, because truth, including scientific truth, is always in the last analysis a poetic process.

# II

> Theaetetus: It does seem probably true that when we say change and rest are, we do have
> a kind of omen of *that which is* as a third thing.
> Visitor: So *that which is* isn't both change and rest; it's something different from them instead.
> Theaetetus: It seems so.
> Visitor: Therefore, by its own nature *that which is* doesn't either rest or change.
> Theaetetus: I suppose it doesn't. (*Sophist* 250c; White 2003: 72, emphasis mine)

Our pristine field of truth with two simple speakers and a lone tree has become a crowded place. Everyone of us is a bustling forum trying to formalize the partial and inchoate nature of our perceptions and desires into an intelligible code, receivable by others, a code that bears the smell and taste of others' perceptions and desires, so that we can then persuade one or more of those others to accept that our encoding of our thoughts, feelings, and desires in the speech of those who came before should become their encoding of their thoughts, feelings, and desires in the speech of others. Where before we had a simple topographical space with a direct triangular relation—speaker, listener, referent—we now have a set of partially overlapping internally divided pluralities in which the location of same and other, the one and the many has become of necessity highly problematic. The speaker only exists as speaker to the extent that her innermost thoughts are disseminated across a broad temporal, spatial and social field that makes the locus of identity inherently plural. The referent only exists for that speaker to the extent that it can be formalized within that disseminated field. And the truth of that referent can only be received by the equally decentered listener in terms of that disseminated field (cf. Habinek 2005: 72–73).

What then is a speaker to do? How can she say what she means? How can she speak the truth and convince others of it? Is not every moment of truth also a moment of nontruth, every moment of sincerity a confection, every moment of persuasion a moment of force that calls the possibility of truth as a universalizable correspondence between language, perception, and world into question? This is precisely the field into which ancient rhetorical theory steps, and which with remarkable self-consciousness addresses the problem of irony, of saying what you don't mean in order to mean what you say, as both a condition of existence and a strategy. In such a world, not only is the truth never simply out there, but you are also never simply here, but always, also, elsewhere and other.

We could do worse than begin with Aristotle, who, as Crassus in the *De Oratore* concedes, others may call a philosopher, but he qualifies as an orator (3.142). As the producer of the first full-blown philosophical treatment of rhetoric in the classical world, Aristotle is an important witness to the co-constitution of rhetoric and philosophy in their moment of tropic turning, as formalizations of language. Yet what he is the most important witness of in the *Rhetoric* is his almost total neglect of irony as a topic of rhetorical theory. *Eironia* is, in fact, treated only in passing (1379b, 1420a) and never defined.

Indeed, his most significant observation in this regard—and the passage does not deal with irony specifically nor does the word ever appear—is his claim that the exact same topic can easily serve as a subject for praise as well as advice for improvement, and hence as implicit criticism (1367a–68b). In and of itself, the exact purport of any such statement is therefore undecidable. When I say the emperor is courageous and sage, does that mean he *is* or that he *should be* (cf. Quintilian 9.2.65–66)? And how can you tell the difference? In recent years, this problem has become a keen topic of dispute concerning works like Ovid's exilic poetry and erotic elegy, where one group of critics has seen certain passages as flattering the emperor Augustus and others have seen the same passages as ironic condemnation. I argue elsewhere that structurally these two interpretations are indistinguishable, inasmuch as both must be imagined as speech acts that join a constative statement with a secondary or alternative meaning by means of a performative act, or a moment of nonmeaning, a moment which is unassimilable to the signification of the statement itself (Miller 2004: chap, 8). Such a moment can be well illustrated by the supreme ancient ironist, Socrates, in Xenophon's *Symposium*. Socrates has been discussing Common and Heavenly Love, when he turns to his host Callias and states that the latter's love for Autolycus is clearly of the Heavenly variety since he has invited the boy's father to attend the party as well. Hermogenes then remarks that Socrates, in congratulating Callias, is in fact "teaching" him how he should act. In short, what is presented as description, and hence praise, is in fact prescription, and admonition if not outright criticism. Socrates' reply neither accepts nor denies Hermogenes' interpretation, but allows both readings to stand, "By Hera, I wish to testify to him how he may still be even happier, since the love of the soul is stronger than that of the body" (8.9–12). Thus, Aristotle in the brief passage from the *Rhetoric* cited above, and as further illustrated by Ovid and Xenophon, is among the first formally to recognize this mirroring relation between description and prescription, between factual statement, praise, and blame. And it is in so far as the same statement on one level can be seen as laudatory and on another as blaming that irony necessarily obtrudes.

Such an understanding of this basic speech act further complicates our initial diagram of the speaker's relation to the listener and the referent. How do we know whether a given statement is serious, and what does "serious" in this context mean? Is ironic didaxis "serious" or "playful"? In point of fact, the two attitudes are far from mutually exclusive. The pairing of the serious with the more frivolous or comic (σπουδαιογέλοιον) is a recurring motif among ancient Socratic writers (cf. *Memorabilia* 1.3.8), where Socrates' consistent use of irony can make the difference between the serious and the playful difficult to discern. The attitude of the listener becomes accordingly more wary and complex as our once simple referent now becomes capable, at least linguistically, of bearing fundamentally opposite qualifications. Under these conditions, what then would be the truth of the speaker's statement and to what extent is it a testimony either to the state of the referent, the intention of the speaker, or the attitude of the listener?

Aristotle's treatment of irony is more extensive in the *Nicomachean Ethics*, but there it concerns not a figure of speech but a form of self-fashioning. The focus is less on irony than the "ironist." He begins with an initial contrast between the *alazōn* and the *eirōn*, the "braggart" and the "self-deprecator." There is also a third term: the *alētheutikos*, or the "sincere man" as it is sometimes translated, but more accurately, the man whose self-relation points to truth. *Alētheutikos* is a rare term. It is never used in Classical Greek outside this passage. The *alētheutikos* is not so much the "truthful" man (*alēthēs, alēthinos*), as the man who is defined by his relation to truth. In this sense, the *alētheutikos* disrupts the binary of the *eirōn* and the *alazōn*, not by offering a simple mean that would sublimate the two into a stable unity, but by leaning distinctly toward the ironic, without collapsing into it (cf. Frank 2005: 7–8 on the mean). The ironist and the braggart may be opposites and each may be excessive in their relation to the truth, but the ironist is less to be blamed than the braggart (1127a–b). The ironist, or he who presents himself as less than what he is— who opens a gap between himself and the way he represents himself, a gap which gestures, however, to the truth—is like Socrates (1127b). The notion that if Socrates would just be sincere, then, we would know the truth cannot be what Aristotle means here. It would be ludicrous to think that Aristotle saw Socrates as some kind of simple liar. Rather the *alētheutikos* is a kind of one-off formulation that points to an impossible self-coincidence that is neither that of the ironist nor the braggart, but which as in Socrates' own fashioning of a specific and recognizable ethos points to the truth in a way the *alazōn* cannot. The ironist performs an act of self-stylization, an act of doubling, that self-consciously points to the gap between the two images, and in doing so performs an ethical act, an act that has the potential to qualify him as a speaker of truth.[8] At the same time, the ironic speaker introduces an irreducible difference into the world that makes the coincidence of speaker, auditor, and referent impossible to restore (de Man 1983: 222). When Socrates says he is the teacher of no man (*Apology* 33b2–8), what he means, what teaching is, and how we are to understand that statement, as the entire subsequent history of Platonic and Socratic studies testifies, can never be restored to a simple constative speech act observing a specified state of affairs. He can never simply be *alētheutikos* and yet that is the condition of him speaking the truth (Vlastos 1991: 31; Nehamas 1998: 46–98).

It is precisely this complex series of Aristotelian, Platonic, and Stoic meditations that Roman rhetorical theory inherits. Under such circumstances, and given such a complex self-consciousness of the situation, how does a speaker present herself as a purveyor of truth? Does this not require a certain stylization of the speaker, the fashioning of a receivable ethos? On what level is this stylization a mere matter of ornament, of verbal manipulation, and on what level is it a reformation of the self, an ethical act that changes the very nature and possibility of the truth? As Antonius reports

---

8  Compare Artaud on the function of "doubling" in the theater (1964: 75, 81–82).

34 THEORY DOES NOT EXIST

in Book 1 of *De Oratore* (87–88), the successful orator must both present a self designed to appeal to the selves of his auditors and, in so doing, must be able to fashion an appropriate life, while having the knowledge of what that life is and how it would be perceived by the lives of his auditors. Ethos demands both ethics and systematic psychology.[9]

There is, then, no act of persuasion without a speaking subject who is recognized as a credible speaker by an audience and without an at least posited referent, which that speaker can place in relation to himself and to the audience. But if every act of self-stylization, which is recognized as an act of stylization, is also an ironization— the introduction of a doubling, of an alternative set of relations between speaker, audience, and referent—then does the condition of the possibility of speaking a truth that will be received as the truth not always necessarily involve not saying what you mean, i.e., irony?

To take a concrete example, the icon of Roman *libertas* (Greek *parrhēsia*), of the freedom to say exactly what you mean without fear or favor, is Lucilius, the founder of Roman satire (Cicero, *Ad Familiares* 12.16; Horace, *Sermones* 1.4.1–10).[10] At the same time, he is the model of *urbanitas*, an all but indefinable elegance, that qualifies you as one to be heard and yet is anything but a spontaneous or unpolished direct expression of artless personality. Thus Crassus in the *De Oratore*, in the context of evoking Lucilius's at times discomfiting *libertas*, refers to him as *doctus* ("learned") and *perurbanus* ("very urbane, elegant") while also agreeing with the satirist's contention that no one could be considered an orator who was not *omnibus eis artibus, quae sunt libero dignae, perpolitus* ("completely polished in those arts worthy of a free man"; *De Oratore* 1.72, cf. 2.25; Tzounakas 2005: 567–69). To put it another way, the recognition of the *urbanitas* of the speaker, a carefully achieved condition (Fitzgerald 1995: 88–93), is also a recognition of that speaker's own self-ironization. Indeed, on a certain level irony and *urbanitas* are all but interchangeable. Thus, in *De Oratore* 2.269–70, we read:

> *Urbana* etiam *dissimulatio* est, cum alia dicuntur ac sentias … cum toto genere orationis severe ludas, cum aliter sentias ac loquare. … In hoc genere Fannius in annalibus suis Africanum hunc Aemilianum dicit fuisse egregium et Graeco eum verbo appellat *eirōna*; sed uti ei ferunt, qui melius haec norunt, Socratem opinor in hac *ironia dissimulantiaque* longe lepore et humanitate omnibus praestitisse. Genus est *perelegans* et cum gravitate salsum cumque oratoriis dictionibus tum *urbanis* sermonibus adcommodatum. (emphasis mine)

> Irony is also "urbane," when things are said otherwise than as you feel … when you play seriously[11] by means of the whole style of the speech, when you feel differently than you say. …. Fannius in his chronicle says this very Aemilianus Africanus to have been outstanding

---

9 Compare in this regard, Bakhtin (1986: 95–96).

10 See Freudenburg (2001: 3–4) and Miller 2005: "Introduction"). *Libertas* has political connotations as well, although the notion of speech is always present. See Davis (2010: 24–25), Freudenburg (1993: 72), Stampacchia (1982), Wirzsubski (1950: 3, 7, 16–17), and Syme (1939: 155).

11 Or "being mock serious" in May and Wisse's translation (2001). The question is whether you "play seriously," as Socrates does, or whether you "play at being serious." It is not clear on what basis you would choose between them based on linguistic grounds alone. In fact, the ironist does both. He is in earnest in his play, i.e., he is in pursuit of a serious goal, and frequently that play involves a pretense of gravity. See Leeman, Pinkster, and Rabie (1989: ad loc) on this passage.

## PLACING THE SELF IN THE FIELD OF TRUTH

> in this type of speech and refers to him using the Greek word, *eirōn*; but as those who are expert in this matter say, I believe, Socrates excelled by far all men in irony and dissembling by means of his elegance and refinement. This is a very elegant mode of speech, and its wit is as well accommodated to serious matter and formal speech as to urbane conversation.

Irony here is the virtual definition of urbanity, a mode of speech that, on the one hand, involves "dissimulation," or a visible (audible) difference between what you mean and what you say, and, on the other, a mode whose supreme exemplar is Socrates, the first father of philosophy, antagonist of those who are said to be *deinos legein* ("clever/frightful at speaking"), and the seeker of truth per se (*Apology* 17a4–b8).

In Ciceronian rhetorical theory, then, to be received as a speaker of truth requires the foregrounding of a moment of nonmeaning, of a gap between what is felt or perceived (*sentio*) and what is said (*dico, loquor*). In this way the speaker comes to be qualified as *urbanus*, and hence worthy to be listened to, as opposed to the boorish *rusticus* ("bumpkin"), who is of no account. To speak what one intends in a way that will be received as true and thus will be able to become the truth cannot simply be therefore to say what one means, to directly reflect the referent in speech, any more than Socrates means nothing more and nothing less than what he says, when, following the Delphic oracle, he declares himself the wisest of men because at least he knows that he knows nothing (*Apology* 23b2–b4).[12] This observation is true not only for the perfect orator but for that font of frank Roman speech, Lucilius himself.

Irony is this elegant and learned gap between what is said and what is meant, a gap that is the foundation of Lucilian *libertas*, and that Quintilian in turn will go on to theorize in a more systematic manner than Cicero himself. For Quintilian, irony is not self-depreciation, as it is for Aristotle, or shamming, as is often the case with Socrates, but a formal use of language by a speaker that depends on the audience's recognition of the difference between the *dictum* ("the said") and the *intellectum* ("the understood"; 6.2.15–16). That difference, moreover, is revealed, as we should now expect, by a certain performativity. It is a property, in fact, neither of the words themselves, nor of the objects to which they refer, nor even of the audience, but of a performative moment, a moment that in itself has no other sense than the foregrounding of the difference that constitutes irony. In the following passage, Quintilian is in the process of discussing allegory and specifies irony as one type:

> In eo vero genere, quo contraria ostenduntur, ironia est; illusionem vocant. Quae aut pronuntiatione intelligitur aut persona aut rei natura; nam si qua earum verbis dissentit, apparet diversam esse orationi voluntatem. (8.54)

> Irony is that type in which opposites are displayed. Some call this dissimulation. It is understood either by pronunciation, or the character assumed, or by the nature of the thing: for if any of these is different from the words, there appears to be a different intention in the speech.

---

12 "Yet if reality by itself were sufficiently effective in delivery, we would have no need for any art at all" (3.215, May and Wisse 2001).

36                                  THEORY DOES NOT EXIST

Likewise, Quintilian also records that for many theorists of the day, allegory of necessity contains an element of obscurity or nonmeaning. There is a gap between meaning one and meanings two, three, four, etc., which must be made explicit. The ironist, then, as a species of the allegorist, who says one thing but means another, is ultimately the master of nonmeaning, of the gap between meanings, which must be recognized if the irony is to be perceived.

Now in point of fact, Quintilian's treatment goes well beyond this brief outline. He crucially distinguishes between two kinds of irony: irony as trope and as figure (9.1.3; cf. Clark 1957: 90–91). Tropic irony is in essence an ornament of language, in which a speech act that would be appropriate in one context is carried over into another where it is not. A trope, for Quintilian, is a form of verbal substitution and, in principle, the meaning or thought, remains unchanged. Thus, when I say, "Bob sure is handsome," and everybody knows Bob is the ugliest man alive, this would be an example of what Quintilian calls tropic irony or what Vlastos terms, "simple irony" (9.1.4, 9.2.44; Vlastos 1991: 31).

Figural irony, however, is more complex. First, a figure is a rhetorical practice that does not necessarily involve changes in words at all (9.1.7). One speaks in the later tradition of a "figure of thought." In some ways, this contrast between the figure of speech or "trope" and the figure of thought corresponds to Aristotle's distinction between irony as a form of "liberal jest" in the *Rhetoric* (1419b) and as form of self-fashioning in relation to truth in the *Nicomachean Ethics*. Both tropic and figural irony are "tropological" in the sense we used earlier, in that they each involve a "turning" from a putative ideal of completely nonfigural or literal speech – a speech of pure, transparent communication – to an ironic speech whose constitutive difference between what is "said" (*dictum*) and what is "understood" (*intellectum*) is foregrounded. But whereas Quintilian thinks of tropic irony as involving merely verbal substitution, the figure for him goes beyond the immediacies of word choice and strikes at the structure of thought itself.

Second, a figure for Quintilian can have two forms. The first is a *habitus* or form of thought: thus, any formalization of thought, its subjection to a set of canons, is a type of figure or *habitus*. This would include the subjecting of speech to disciplinary norms: legal speech, medical speech, scientific speech. The second is a "schema," a formalization of thought that has as its end the distinguishing of elegant speech or thought from the vulgar or simple (9.1.10–11). All formalizations are thus figures, and all figures are a shaping of thought that, insofar as they reveal themselves as a shaping of thought, say something other, something beyond that which the words themselves simply say.

> Sed si habitus quidam et quasi gestus sic appellandi sunt, id demum hoc loco accipi schema oportebit, quod sit a simplici atque in promptu posito dicendi modo poetice vel oratorie mutatum. Sic enim verum erit, aliam esse orationem ἀσχημάτιστον, id est carentem figuris, quod vitium non inter minima est, aliam ἐσχηματισμένην, id est figuratam. Verum id ipsum anguste Zoilus terminavit, qui id solum putaverit schema, quo aliud simulatur dici quam dicitur, quod sane vulgo quoque sic accipi scio; unde et figuratae controversiae quaedam, de quibus post paulo dicam, vocantur. Ergo figura sit arte aliqua novata forma dicendi. (9.1.13–14)

## PLACING THE SELF IN THE FIELD OF TRUTH

But if certain formalizations, gestures as it were, are to be referred to in this manner, in the end it will be proper that *schema* be accepted in this place, that is, as what is changed from a simple and spontaneous mode of speaking into a poetic or rhetorical form. It will then be true to say that there are two types of speaking, one the *aschematic*, which is lacking in figures and differing not the least from the barbarous, and the other, the *schematized*, which is figured. But Zoilus (the grammarian) has defined this idea very narrowly. He thought a schema to be this alone, that which gave the appearance of something else being said than what is being said. I know that in fact this is widely accepted. Hence certain topics of debate are known as "figured," which I shall discuss shortly. Therefore, let a figure be a certain form of speaking renewed by art.

Figures, then, are forms of speech and thought that have undergone a level of stylization and formalization. They, therefore, possess a level of performativity, a level on which the meaning and its expression have been worked in a way that is irreducible either to the nature and quality of the referent or to the spontaneous and unmediated utterance of the speaker. Rather that performativity is what makes the utterance receivable, *credibilis,* by the audience as something other than barbarous, other than a fault, *vitium,* and hence potentially as the truth, as locatable on a cognitive map of meaning (9.1.19). Yet the work, the performativity is, in itself a moment of nonmeaning or obscurity, a moment that exceeds the signified insofar as it is indexical of the ironic, a moment in which "what seems to be said is different from what is said." As such, all receivable statements for the Roman orator are inherently ironic in that the *dictum* ("the said") and the *intellectum* ("the understood") are, therefore, of necessity noncoincidental, or in Quintilian's earlier formulation *diversum* ("at variance").

Irony as a figure of thought is later qualified as a species of allegory dependent on a series of metaphors in which the fictive, the made quality of the performance appears, but is not confessed:

> At in figura totius voluntatis fictio est apparens magis quam confessa, ut illic verba sint verbis diversa, hic sensus †sermoni et voci† et tota interim causae conformatio; cum etiam vita universa ironiam habere videatur, qualis est visa Socratis (nam ideo dictus εἴρων, agens imperitum, et admiratorem aliorum tanquam sapientium) ut, quemadmodum ἀλληγορίαν facit continua μεταφορά, sic hoc schema faciat tropos ille contextus. (9.2.46–47)

> But this artifice concerning the whole intention in the figure is more apparent than confessed, so that in the former (the trope), words are at variance (*diversa*) with words, here the sense and sometimes the whole proof of our case is at variance with the utterance and the voice. Sometimes an entire life seems to possess irony, as is seen in the case of Socrates, for he is called an "ironist," acting as though he were an ignorant man, though he pretended to admire the wisdom of others. As a continuous series of metaphors becomes a species of allegory, so an unbroken series of tropes becomes a schema.

Such irony, which extends through the whole length of a narrative or even a life, as in the case of Socrates, can never be resolved into the simple tropic irony of saying one thing but meaning the simple opposite. It is never decodable as simply when you say A, you mean B, or when you say "handsome," you mean "ugly," or when you say "larch" in the field of truth, you mean "rhododendron," because in effect there

# THEORY DOES NOT EXIST

is no simple outside and hence no opposite. There is only the performance (de Man 1983: 210, 220–21).

## III

> When we perceive a green object we tend to have the thought that the object in front of us is green. ... the content of the thought, what it represents, is a propositional item. In this sense there is a *lekton* ["sayable"] corresponding to every human impression or thought; and it is in this sense that the *lekton* is what one has in mind when one is thinking something and when one is saying what one is thinking. (Frede 1994: 112)

> Ironists who are inclined to philosophize see the choice between vocabularies as made neither within a neutral and universal metavocabulary nor by an attempt to fight one's way past appearances to the real, but simply by playing the new off against the old. (Rorty 1989: 73)

What then is a speaker of truth? When I stand in the field and I perceive a birch, it is because the data provided by my senses have undergone a certain formalization, which has turned that set of givens into a proposition. That proposition may either be assented to ("yes, this is a birch") or not ("no, it is a larch"), but it can only become a proposition by entering language, by becoming sayable. Through this subjection to the *logos*, both I and the referent, to which my thought and speech gesture, begin to make the journey not only to the universal, the categories of birches, larches, and trees, but also through language itself into the lives, speeches, and desires of others. In the moment of constituting intelligible experience, we become alienated from ourselves – selves that are ultimately, nostalgic imaginary constructs – in irremediable ways.

Moreover, these constructed, fictive selves, selves which are always animated by the voice of the other, must at the same time undertake a further "ethical" labor of refashioning, even poeticizing, themselves in such a way that the propositions their experience generates will ultimately be receivable, and even attractive to listeners who themselves are similarly plural. Under such circumstances, any sort of simple model of speaking the truth, of fidelity to the referent, of transparent speech beyond the seductions of a meretricious rhetoric is not only naïve, but indefensible and even terroristic: a violent subjection of the multiplicity of the self to the jargon of authenticity. All maps are stylizations. All topographies are sets of *topoi, loci communes*. Every here and now, as Hegel demonstrated, is irreducibly plural.

How then does the speaker of truth, the orator who seeks to persuade and convince his auditors, navigate this difficult terrain? Ancient rhetorical theory and ancient philosophic rhetoric provide startlingly (post)modern responses. Our frankness (*libertas*) is only made possible through stylization. We come to be perceived as people who take up an intelligible relation to truth, not through our asserverations but as ironists. The ironist is not the speaker with the air of truth, the *alētheutikos*, but the speaker who performs the gap between himself and an impossible sincerity. He is not the speaker who calls a spade a spade, but the one who plays a speaker who calls a spade a spade, and in so doing calls our attention to both the play and the spade. He is the philosopher who tells you repeatedly that he, unlike those who have come before, is not *deinos legein*: unless of course by *deinos legein*, you mean someone who speaks the truth.

## Works Cited

Artaud, Antonin. 1964. *Le théâtre et son double suivi de Le théâtre de Séraphin*. Paris.

Bakhtin, M. M. 1981. *The Dialogic Imagination*. Ed. Michael Holquist. Trans. Caryl Emerson and Michael Holquist. Austin: University of Texas Press.

———. 1986. *Speech Genres and Other Late Essays*. Eds. Caryl. Emerson and Michael. Holquist. Trans. V. W. McGee. Austin: University of Texas Press.

Bakhtin, M. M., and P. M. Medvedev. 1985. *The Formal Method in Literary Scholarship: A Critical Introduction to Sociological Poetics*. Trans. Albert J. Wehrle. Cambridge, Mass.

Bauman, Richard. 1984. *Verbal Art as Performance*. Prospect Heights, Il.

Clark, Donald Lemen. 1957. *Rhetoric in Greco-Roman Education*. New York.

Davis, Gregson. 2010. "The Biographical and Social Foundations of Horace's Poetic Voice." *A Companion to Horace*. Ed Gregson Davis. Malden: Blackwell. 7–33.

de Man, Paul. 1983. "The Rhetoric of Temporality." *Blindness and Insight: Essays in the Rhetoric of Contemporary Criticism*. 2nd ed. Minneapolis: University of Minneapolis Press.

Derrida, Jacques. 1993. *Khôra*. Paris: Galilée.

Eco, Umberto. 1976. *A Theory of Semiotics*. Bloomington: Indiana University Press.

Fitzgerald, William. 1995. *Catullan Provocations: Lyric Poetry and the Drama of Position*. Berkeley: University of California Press.

Foucault, Michel. 2012. *Du gouvernement des vivants. Cours au Collège de France, 1979–1980*. Ed. Michel Senellart. Paris: EHESS, Gallimard, Seuil.

Frank, Jill. 2005. *A Democracy of Distinction: Aristotle and the Work of Politics*. Chicago: University of Chicago Press.

Frede, Michael. 1994. "The Stoic Notion of a Lekton." Ed. Stephen Everson. *Language: Companions to Ancient Thought* 3. Cambridge: Cambridge University Press. 109–28.

Freudenburg, Kirk. 1993. *The Walking Muse: Horace on the Theory of Satire*. Princeton: Princeton University Press.

———. 2001. *Satires of Rome: Threatening Poses from Lucilius to Juvenal*. Cambridge: Cambridge University Press.

Frow, John. 1986. *Marxism and Literary History*. Cambridge: Harvard University Press.

Goldschmidt, Victor. 2003. *Le paradigme dans la dialectique platonicienne*. Paris: Blackwell.

Habinek, Thomas. 2005. *Ancient Rhetoric and Oratory*. Malden: Blackwell.

Hadot, Pierre. 1995. *Qu'est-ce que la philosophie antique?* Paris: Folio.

Hampton, Cynthia. 1990. *Pleasure, Knowledge, and Being: An Analysis of Plato's Philebus*. Albany: SUNY.

Hankinson, R. J. 2003. "Stoic Epistemology." *The Cambridge Companion to the Stoics*. Ed. Brad Inwood. Cambridge: Cambridge University Press. 59–84.

Hegel, G. W. F. 1977. *Hegel's Phenomenology of the Spirit*. Trans. A. V. Miller. Oxford: Oxford University Press.

Holquist, Michael. 1990. *Dialogism: Bakhtin and his World*. London: Routledge.

Lacan, Jacques. 1975. *Le séminaire XX: Encore*. Ed. Jacques-Alain Miller. Paris: Seuil.

Leeman, Anton D., Harm Pinkster, and Edwin Rabie. 1989. *De Oratore Libri III*, Band 3. Heidelberg: Universitätsverlag Winter.

Mankin, David. 2011. *Cicero: de Oratore Book III*. Cambridge: Cambridge University Press.

May, James M., and Jakob Wisse. 2001. *Cicero: On the Ideal Orator*. Oxford: Oxford University Press.

Miller, Paul Allen. 1998. "Catullan Consciousness, the 'Care of the Self,' and the Force of the Negative in History," *Rethinking Sexuality: Foucault and Classical Antiquity*. Eds. David H. J. Larmour, Paul Allen Miller, and Charles Platter Princeton: Princeton University Press. 171–203.

———. 2004. *Subjecting Verses: Latin Love Elegy and the Emergence of the Real*. Princeton: Princeton University Press.

40 THEORY DOES NOT EXIST

———. 2005. *Latin Verse Satire: An Anthology and Reader.* London: Routledge.

———. 2010a. "Persius, Irony, and Truth." *American Journal of Philology* 131. 233–58.

———. 2010b. "The Platonic Remainder: Khora and the Corpus Platonicum." *Plato and Derrida.* Ed. Miriam Leonard. Oxford: Oxford University Press. 321–41.

———. 2017. "Rhetoric and Deconstruction." *The Oxford Handbook of Rhetorical Studies.* Ed. Michael McDonald. Oxford: Oxford University Press. 695–707.

Morson, Gary Saul, and Caryl Emerson. 1990. *Mikhail Bakhtin: Creation of a Prosaics.* Stanford: Stanford University Press.

Nehamas, Alexander. 1998. *The Art of Living: Socratic Reflections from Plato to Foucault.* Berkeley: University of California Press.

Noonan, Harold, and Ben Curtis. 2014. "Identity," in Edward N. Zalta, ed., *The Stanford Encyclopedia of Philosophy* (Summer 2014 Edition). http://plato.stanford.edu/archives/sum2014/entries/identity/.

Nussbaum, Martha C. 1994. *The Therapy of Desire: Theory and Practice in Hellenistic Ethics.* Princeton: Princeton University Press.

Parkhurst, Michael. 1995. "Adorno and the Practice of Theory," *Rethinking MARXISM* 8: 38–59.

Ragland-Sullivan, Ellie. 1986. *Jacques Lacan and the Philosophy of Psychoanalysis.* Urbana: University of Illinois Press.

Rorty, Richard. 1989. *Contingency, Irony, and Solidarity.* Cambridge: Cambridge University Press.

Saussure, Ferdinand de. 1959. *Course in General Linguistics.* Eds. Charles Bally and Albert Sechehaye in collaboration with Albert Riedlinger. Trans. Wade Baskin. New York: Columbia University Press.

Stampacchia, G. 1982. "Schiavitù e libertà nelle 'Satire' di Orazio." *Index* 11: 193–219.

Syme, Ronald. 1939. *The Roman Revolution.* Oxford: Oxford University Press.

Todorov, Tzvetan. 1984. *Mikhail Bakhtin: The Dialogical Principle.* Trans. Wlad Godzich. Minneapolis: University of Minnesota Press.

Too, Yun Lee. 1995. *The Rhetoric of Identity in Isocrates.* Cambridge: Cambridge University Press.

Tzounakas, Spyridon. 2005. "Persius on his Predecessors: A Re-Examination." *Classical Quarterly* 55.559–71.

Vlastos, Gregory. 1991. *Socrates: Ironist and Moral Philosopher.* Ithaca: Cornell University Press.

Voloshinov, V. N. 1986. *Marxism and the Philosophy of Language.* Trans. Ladislav Matejka and I. R. Titunik. Cambridge: Harvard University Press.

White, Nicholas P., trans. 2003. *Sophist. Plato: Complete Works.* Ed. John M. Cooper. Assoc. Ed. D. S. Hutchison. Indianapolis: Hackett.

Wilkinson, Augustus S. 2002. *Cicero: De Oratore I–III.* Bristol: Bristol Classical Press.

Wirzsubski, C. 1950. *Libertas as a Political Idea at Rome During the Late Republic and Early Principate.* Cambridge: Cambridge University Press.

Wittgenstein, Ludwig. 1973. *Philosophical Investigations.* 3rd ed. Trans. G. E. M. Anscombe. London: Pearson.

Žižek, Slavoj. 1989. *The Sublime Object of Ideology.* London Routledge.

———. 1991. *Looking Awry: An Introduction to Jacques Lacan through Popular Culture.* Cambridge: MIT Press.

———. 1993. *Tarrying with the Negative: Kant, Hegel, and the Critique of Ideology.* Durham: Duke University Press.

# Chapter 4

# RHETORIC AND DECONSTRUCTION: PLATO, THE SOPHISTS, AND PHILOSOPHY[1]

... if one bears in mind that in a certain sense Socrates and the Sophists held the same position and that Socrates actually struck at their very roots by carrying through their position, by destroying the halfness in which the Sophists set their minds at ease, so that Socrates by defeating the Sophists was thereby in a certain sense himself the greatest Sophist, one already perceives a possibility for Aristophanes to identify him with the Sophists. (Kierkegaard 1989: 138–39)

In "Plato's Pharmacy," Derrida demonstrates the way in which the ambivalent signifier *pharmakon*, meaning both poison and medicine, deconstructs the opposition between speech and writing that subtends the *Phaedrus*. That opposition, in turn, is based upon an even more fundamental one between internality and externality (Derrida 1981: 103). Speech is the reflection of truth because it emanates from the inside and is directly present to consciousness. Writing is secondary and derivative, existing as an externalization of a prior moment of interiority, i.e., thought as silent speech (Stoekl 1992: 201). The deconstruction of the priority of speech over writing, through the latter being characterized as a *pharmakon* and hence as both a salutary healing agent and a foreign noxious other, is itself a deconstruction of the priority of truth over its external and derivative manipulation through formalized practices of speech and writing: i.e., rhetoric. Rhetoric as a practice is associated throughout the Platonic corpus with the sophists and is generally opposed to philosophy defined as the pursuit of truth. Derrida in his deconstructive reading of the opposition between speech and writing in the *Phaedrus* demonstrates that, in effect, Plato himself deconstructs the opposition between rhetoric and philosophy through the deployment of philosophy's initial, constitutive trope, Socratic irony, as figured by the duplicitous *pharmakon*. The result is that rather than philosophy and sophistry being mutually exclusive alternatives, each becomes a moment within the other, which can never be fully sublimated. Philosophy on this view, I contend, is less a policing of the borders of discourse than a series of

---

1  This paper has benefited enormously from the ongoing dialog sustained by the University of South Carolina Ancient Philosophy reading group. My particular debt to the criticism and insight of Jill Frank a brief note cannot due justice to. I owe her most in those areas where we continue to disagree.

persuasive interventions in the ongoing dialogue that constitutes the movement of truth in time.

More precisely, in "Plato's Pharmacy," Derrida argues that writing as a *pharmakon*, both medicine and poison, becomes the deconstructive hinge around which truth and philosophy are articulated in their opposition to sophistry and rhetoric. The *Phaedrus*, thus, becomes the site in which rhetoric and philosophy are constituted as opposed practices that nonetheless assume and depend on each other. As such, the *Phaedrus* occupies a crucial position in the history of philosophy and rhetoric. It is no accident, therefore, that Cicero begins his *De Oratore* with Scaevola saying to Crassus, "why don't we imitate that Socrates who is in Plato's *Phaedrus*?" (1.7.27). The speakers then contend: first that humans excel animals insofar as they come together in speech (in Greek the *logos*) (1.8.32); second, that Plato only makes philosophy triumph over rhetoric in the *Gorgias*, because he is the superior orator (1.11.47); and finally that the superior orator must be more desirous of the truth than contention and should be lacking in no point of knowledge (1.11.48). In short, according to Cicero's reading of the *Phaedrus*, the ideal orator is the pinnacle of human achievement precisely owing to his participation in rational discourse. The philosopher can only assert his primacy over the rhetorician insofar as he is himself the ideal orator and, in that capacity, he must be the image of the *sapiens*, the wise man of the philosophical tradition. Thus, while Derrida's concentration on the *pharmakon* deconstructs the opposition between rhetoric and philosophy, the simultaneous assertion and dismantling of the opposition is as old as the practices themselves (Rorty 1989: 134). Their co-constitution in relation to the question of truth has, from the beginning, been the ground of both their difference and their ultimate interdependence (Derrida 1992: 266–67).

In this chapter, I first look at Derrida's definition of the sophist and sophistry in "Plato's Pharmacy." Second, I examine Derrida's treatment of Socratic irony in relation to the problem of truth. Third, I read a passage from the *Phaedrus* that puts into question the possibility of truth as a form of presence or internality rigorously separated from external repetition and hence from rhetorical manipulation. Over the course of these three movements, I outline a concept of ironic philosophy and rhetoric, which does not allow them either to be thought separately or considered identical. Rather it insistently asks, in the manner of Cicero, "cur non imitamur Socratem illum Platonis"?

# I

> Plato paints his "wise men" with a deliberately broad brush in this dialogue because the art of philosophy he advocates is not only a discipline but also a theoretical stance available to … the practitioners of a wide range of traditional arts, including rhetoricians, poets, and lawgivers. (Ferrari 1987: 234n12).

While Plato's discussion of the sophists and their association with the teaching of rhetoric is scattered throughout the *Phaedrus*, the first mention occurs near the beginning. Here to Phaedrus's question of whether he accepts the traditional myth

## RHETORIC AND DECONSTRUCTION

concerning the kidnapping of Oreithuia by Boreas, Socrates responds that to distrust it would mean to accept the kind of rationalizing account offered by the sophists (Robin 1966: 6n1):

> But if I were to disbelieve it, as do the wise (*hoi sophoi*), I would not be strange, but then acting like a sophist (*sophizomenos*) I would say that Boreas (the North Wind) took her over the nearby rock, while she was playing with Pharmaceia and thus she is said to have died with Boreas taking her. (229c6–d1)[2]

Socrates, however, says that he does not have time for such speculations, which are endless (230a1–2). Instead, he follows the Delphic injunction to know himself and is completely occupied with determining whether he is a more tangled and covetous beast than *Tuphon*, the son of a hundred headed giant and father of the winds (Hes. *Th.* 306), or he is a tamer and simpler animal, who is not puffed up (*atuphos*) with pride. There is, in fact, an elaborate play in this passage on Tuphon as the father of Boreas. Yet, this same name is also as a common noun meaning "delusion." Socrates has clearly not completely separated himself from sophistic practices of mythological exegesis and invention.[3] Instead, through an elaborate rhetorical figure that involves taking the word as both the proper name of a mythological character and as a common noun describing a mental state, he has trumped the sophists at their own game (in the same manner in which he trumps Lysias twice). He moves to a space, which is both parasitic upon sophistic practices of rationalization and transcends their claims to immediate power. He does not explain myth in terms of a more fundamental "reality," but rather uses myth to problematize the practices of "explanation" that were hegemonic in both traditional thought (Homer, the poets, the oral tradition) and the brave new world of the sophists. Rather than offering a univocal decoding of the myth of Boreas and Oreithuia, he has ironically[4] appropriated it. He does not simply reject sophistic rationalization but uses it both to play within the realm of myth (Tuphon as the father of Boreas) and

---

2  Unless otherwise specified, all translations are my own.

3  I refer here to "invention" in the classical sense, not the creation of something *ex nihilo*, but the coming upon something (*invenire*) that was in one sense already there but not found before. Plato's Socrates, even when "creates" myths, as he does in his great second speech in the *Phaedrus* almost never invents them from whole cloth. His practice is rather citational.

4  Irony refers to the creation of doubled, often conflicting, levels of meaning. It is a function in language of the emergence of moments of nonmeaning. In any given moment of multiplicities of meaning, there is a necessary moment of difference that cannot be recuperated within meaning itself. Irony is not just a literary device. As the example of Socrates demonstrates, the turn toward irony is the first necessary step in the construction of the concept. Irony, in this context, represents a tropic turning from the immediate that opens an alternative space of eidetic construction. Thus, the use of this rhetorical trope on the part of Socrates in his conversations with his fellow Athenians is not merely an exercise in sarcasm, wit, or false modesty, but also what makes possible the vision of another register of existence, another self, another form of meaning. It is the linguistic turn that makes possible the doubling of the empirical by the transcendental (i.e., the beyond of the immediate) and hence the critical.

44 THEORY DOES NOT EXIST

within its sophistic rationalization (*tuphon* as delusion), thereby creating a new more complex form that is both turned to the task of self-knowledge and self-conscious of its own delusionary character.

Nonetheless, that self and its truth do not exist separately from the realms of myth and rationalization. Self-knowledge, as Derrida notes, proceeds through a form of externalization:

> It is not perceived. Only interpreted, read, deciphered. A hermeneutics *assigns* intuition. An inscription, the *Delphikon gramma*, which is anything but an oracle, prescribes through its silent cipher; it signifies as one signifies an order—autoscopy and autognosis. The very activities that Socrates thinks can be contrasted to the hermeneutic adventure of myths,[5] which he leaves to the sophists (229d). (Derrida 1981: 69, emphasis his)

The sophists, then, are the purveyors of an externalized rationality: a commodity or product (*Sophist* 223b–224d). As such, for Derrida, their knowledge is of a piece with what it purports to explain: myth as an externalization and repetition of thought, passed from one hearer to the next. Like the speech of Lysias, which Phaedrus carries under his cloak, sophistic knowledge travels from hand to hand: an object of economic and cultural exchange that must be contrasted with an authentic knowledge of the self and its truth (Derrida 1981: 75; Brisson and Pradeau 2007: 143–45).

Myth from this point of view is related to true knowledge in much the same fashion as writing. Each represents a seeming externality, as the sophist does in relation to the philosopher:

> Books, the dead and rigid knowledge shut up in *biblia*, piles of histories, nomenclatures, recipes and formulas learned by heart, all this is as foreign to living knowledge and dialectics as the *pharmakon* is to medical science. And myth to true knowledge. (Derrida 1981: 73, see also 103)

These distinctions are all quite classical. But Socrates too is a teller of myths, not only on the level of commentator, as in the case of Tuphon, but also on the grand scale, in the great myth of his second speech and in the story of Thamus and Theuth, the Egyptian inventor of writing. It is in the latter that Thamus refers to writing as a *pharmakon* (275a6), though the word and the concept have been haunting the dialog from the moment Phaedrus introduces Pharmaceia into the myth of Boreas and Oreithuia. Indeed, it is worth noting that Pharmaceia is a character who appears nowhere in classical literature outside of Plato. The *pharmakon* of writing is presaged by Pharmaceia ("the poisoner"), who appears to have been invented for this occasion. Writing, Thamus tells us, is not an aid to memory (*mnêmê*), but a reminder (*hupomnêmata*),

---

5  This is an overly strict binary. The "hermeneutic adventure" of myth is not completely left to the sophists, as the rest of this essay makes clear. Derrida's later problematization of the relation between Plato and Socrates in *La carte postale* (1980) and of the contrast between *muthos* and *logos* in *Khôra* (1993) demonstrates that he too would move beyond such stark positions.

an external supplement that threatens to supplant the internality of thought with the dead letter. It threatens to reduce the spontaneous and the self-present to the alienated, material, and external (cf. Miller 2007: 136–38).

Theuth, then, is presented not as an inventor, not as the first finder or father of a discourse but as a divine bureaucrat (Nightingale 1995: 166). Writing is a technocratic operation, a secondary manipulation of a given set of tools (274e8–10; Derrida 1981: 86). None of this is out of character with his mythic identity. Traditionally, Theuth is son of Ra, the sun god. As the moon he takes Ra's place. He is often a participant in plots and conspiracies to usurp the throne. During the reign of Osiris, according to some sources, he conspires with Seth for the former's overthrow (though in other versions he is instrumental in the healing of Horus). But in every case, he is the god of repetition. He is never the thing itself but always signifies something else, always re-fers beyond himself, substituting for a lost original (Müller 1918: 33–34, 84–85, 90–91, 118, 126; Derrida 1981: 87–93). He is not unlike Phaedrus carrying the speech of another. But Lysias too is a Theuth figure—a sophist, an external manipulator of signs, whose cynical lucubrations on love threaten to displace the thing itself, Eros in all its manic intensity.

In many ways, this relation between copy and original, and hence the problem of reference, is central to Platonic philosophy. It is at the heart of the critique of *mimêsis* in Book 10 of the *Republic*. And while this indictment is problematized both in its immediate context (the myth of Er) and in the dialogue as a whole (a mimetic work in which Socrates plays all the parts [Slezák 1999: 79–80]), it is perhaps most saliently called into question by the image of the sun in Book 6. In this passage, Socrates uses the sun as a likeness or myth to discuss the good, since its direct presentation is not possible. As Luc Brisson observes, myth in Plato is a form of semblance or *mimêsis* and hence is susceptible to the same critique of usurping the authority of the original as writing, poetry, and rhetoric (Brisson 1998: 66, 69–70). At the same time, the good in and of itself, which by definition knows no single instantiation, can only be imitated through the reproduction or recounting of a likeness, the imitation of an imitation, since the original is by definition never immediately present to us (Brisson 1998: 103–104).

In *Republic 6*, Glaucon asks Socrates to "go through" or "explain" (*dieltheis*) the good so that he might also understand the other virtues. The latter replies that he would love to but is unable. "For those things, at least as they seem (*tou ge dokountos*) to me now, appear (*phainetai*) to go beyond the present undertaking. But now what appears (*phainetai*) to be the offspring of the good and most like it, I would like to say" (506d4–e5). We must be attentive to Plato's words here. The story of the sun will not tell us what the good is in itself, nor will it be a "going through" of the concept. Rather, it will be the recounting of an appearance of the way things seem to Socrates "now" via an offspring or a likeness. If we were to graph the steps, it would look something like the following (good⇒Socrates' opinion⇒the appearance of that opinion⇒the likeness/offspring). There may well be other ways to conceive of this relation, but at every point Plato is at great pains to emphasize that we are dealing with a representation of the way the good seems at a certain point in space and time. In short, we are dealing with a myth, an imitation of an imitation (Derrida 1981: 82–84). We are dealing with an offspring whose father, as Socrates says of writing (275e), is not there to vouchsafe his lineage, a bastard (cf. *Timaeus* 52b).

But to what extent is the father ever present in the son? To what extent can Socrates guarantee the lineage of the myths he recounts, of Plato, or of the writings in which he himself appears? At what point can priority be guaranteed, and, if it cannot, then where does repetition end and originality begin? This last question is precisely what is at stake in Derrida's argument on the reversibility of the relation between Socrates and Plato in *La Carte Postale* (1980: 27, 35, 54, 68, 141; cf. Derrida and Roudinesco 2001:21; Blondell 2002: 110–11). If Socrates continues to play within the realm of myth and repetition, how then do we differentiate Socrates from a sophist, or, as Kierkegaard contends and Cicero argues in *De Oratore*, is such a distinction fundamentally impossible? I would contend that it is the permeability, and yet necessity, of such distinctions that Derrida and Plato's Socrates seek insistently to remind us of.

As Derrida notes in *Khôra*, it is Socrates who at the beginning of the *Timaeus* ranges himself with the *genos mimetikōn*, the poets and sophists (1993: 54–58). Moreover, if the sophist is defined as he who appears (*phainētai*) to have the knowledge of many things (*Sophist* 232a1–2), but who is in fact merely the imitator (*mimētēs*) of the wise man (268c1), then for Socrates to be rigorously differentiated from the sophist, he would have to deploy a knowledge that exists outside appearance and imitation, outside inscription and myth, and hence outside "the outside" itself (Derrida 1981: 106–107). But what Socrates provides us time and again is a likeness or myth, from the sun, the cave, and Er in the *Republic*, to the final myth of the *Gorgias*, to the great speech and the story of Theuth in the *Phaedrus*.

Myth is not a mere accidental ornament or illustration but a necessary supplement to the *logos* and dialectic (Robin 1966: xcvi; Zuckert 1996: 218). The archive of received semblances—myths, speeches hidden under one's cloak, writing itself—in the final analysis can never be completely dissociated from knowledge. Thus, even the myths deployed by Socrates in his great speech are derived from the poetic tradition, the lore of Pythagoreanism, the mysteries, and Egyptian myth (Robin 1966: lxxix–lxxxvii, 44n1, 50n3; 158–60; Thomson 1973: xxvi–xxvii, 43–74; Morgan 1992: 231–39; Heitsch 1993: 95, 98–107). As Berger argues, the great speech pretends "to be a spontaneous ecstatic outburst when it is actually a citational pastiche" (1994: 102).

But if Plato's Socratic myths derive from the archive, at what point do they too cease to represent the live "movement of truth" and become instead sophistic markers to be manipulated, chits, counters on a game board (Derrida 1981: 109)? At what point does even memory itself, what Thamus cites as the opposite of writing's set of reminders, become just another form of externalization, a repetition and imitation?

A limitless memory would … be not memory but infinite self-presence. Memory … needs signs in order to recall the non-present, with which it is necessarily in relation. The movement of dialectics bears witness to this. Memory is thus contaminated by its first substitute: *hypomnēsis*. But what Plato *dreams* of is a memory with no sign. That is, with no supplement. A *mnēmē* with no *hypomnēsis*, no *pharmakon*. (Derrida 1981: 109, emphasis his)

# RHETORIC AND DECONSTRUCTION 47

Memory, thus, is predicated on forgetting, on that which must be *recalled*, on the movement of reference, and hence of the sign and writing (Stoekl 1992: 202). As Freud observes at the end of *The Interpretation of Dreams* consciousness itself would be impossible without repression (1965: 587–82). The unconscious, the voice of the other within the heart of identity, is the condition of possibility of self-awareness. Thus even the beautiful boy whose sight provokes the memory of the beautiful itself in the soul is always a sign standing for a memory recalling a perception, a reference leading to a recollection of an imitation (*Phaedrus* 254b4–c4). As such philosophy and rhetoric can never be rigorously distinguished, but each must always be the reflection that threatens to turn into the other, recto and verso (Derrida 1981: 111–12, cf. 108). Socrates, in the end, is Theuth (Derrida 1980: 59–60).

## II

[A]ll deconstruction is also a logic of the spectral and of haunting, of survival: neither present nor absent, neither living nor dead …. (Derrida 1996: 45)

And if there is a name for that which simultaneously brings together and separates the classical style [of philosophy] from the deconstructive, the least inappropriate would without doubt be irony. Irony should be understood here as the radical and assumed non-simplicity of meaning. (Kambouchner 2008: 60)

To simply stop at the impossibility of finally, in all due rigor, distinguishing rhetoric from philosophy, sophistry from love of wisdom, outside from inside, would be radically insufficient. Must there not, in the end, be a meaningful distinction between coercion, between being "tamed by argument" (*Republic* 554d2), or engaging in mere repetition, and genuine assent, persuasion, a thought of one's own. The question is always, how is that decision made?[6] If language itself only functions in virtue of repetition, and repetition signifies a form of externality and hence the presence of the other in the same, then in what sense can a meaningful authenticity obtain, a claim to assent that is not an index of coercion? "Persuasive eloquence (*peithô*) is the power to break in, to carry off, to seduce internally, to ravish invisibly" (Derrida 1981: 116). Is there a form of persuasion that is not an invasion of the self by the other, whether wielded by the practitioner of the Socratic elenchus or of the philosophically informed eloquence advocated by Cicero?

One answer, I would contend, is found precisely in Socratic irony as Derrida understands it. Irony is a moment of discursive turning. It seeks neither to establish a level of unbreachable internality nor to say there is no difference between inside and outside, truth and repetition. Rather it seeks to establish truth and authencity as the moment of tropic turning when one double-faced *pharmakon* encounters the next. As such, it depends on the very difference it calls into question:

Irony does not consist in the dissolution of a sophistic charm or in the dismantling of an occult substance or power through analysis and questioning. It does not consist in undoing

---

6  I am here dependent on the arguments of Frank (2016).

48 THEORY DOES NOT EXIST

the charlatanesque confidence of a *pharmakeus* [magician, poisoner] from the vantage point of some obstinate instance of transparent reason or innocent *logos*. Socratic irony precipitates out one *pharmakon* by bringing it in contact with another *pharmakon*. Or rather, it reverses the *pharmakon*'s powers and turns *its* surface over—thus taking effect, being recorded and dated, in the act of classing the *pharmakon*, through the fact that the *pharmakon* properly consists in a certain inconsistency, a certain impropriety, this nonidentity-with-itself always allowing it to be turned against itself. (Derrida 1981: 119, emphasis his).

Irony is precisely the trope by which the outside becomes the inside and vice versa. It is the turn by which Socrates becomes the wisest of men through the knowledge of his own ignorance. But that self-knowledge can never be a settled fact, lest it become precisely a moment of sophistic externality, another counter moved on a game board of discursive combat (cf. *Republic* 487a10–e8). The salutary awareness of one's own inner lack can only be proven time and again through the questioning of others, through leading them to the recognition of their ignorance as well, through the love of wisdom in the moment of tropic turning (Miller and Platter 2010: 160–61).

The self-knowledge of the Socratic philosopher, then, is always sought through engagement with the other (Derrida 1981: 121). For Plato and Derrida, philosophy begins at the moment of aporia, at the moment of undecidability in which the opposition between knowledge and ignorance, inside and outside, authenticity and imitation first becomes possible. And it ends when those distinctions become givens, become counters to be moved in an argumentative game, rather than self-questioning *pharmaka* that in the movement of truth exhibit an infinite openness to their own turning (Gasché 2002: 106, 115, 118; Blondell 2002: 42; Hunter 2004: 86–87; cf. Derrida 1994: 21). That turning, if it is to retain its fidelity to truth, must question the givenness of its own terms. It must mark the point in which the opposition on which it depends serves as a moment of constitutive opacity that points to the necessity of another terrain, a beyond of its own closure, and hence to the beginning of a knowledge that cannot be formulated only in terms of the exclusion (and therefore covert inclusion) of its opposite (Gadamer 1991: 4–5; Courtine 2008: 26).

Thus at the end of the *Greater Alcibiades*, the question arises of how one comes to know the self. If the self is the soul and the soul is not visible even to the mind's eye, then, how is the call to self-knowledge not a very bad joke? The answer, Socrates claims, is that one comes to know one's own soul as it is reflected in the eyes and soul of the other. The practice of dialectic, of question and answer, of the joint search for truth, in the context of desire, becomes the way in which the self becomes visible through and as the other, the inside through and as the outside (Hadot 1995: 56–57, 103; Blondell 2002: 100).

> Socrates: By the gods—that admirable Delphic inscription we just mentioned—did we understand it?
> Alcibiades: What's the point of bringing that up again, Socrates?
> Socrates: I'll tell you what I suspect that inscription means, and what advice it's giving us.
>    There may not be many examples of it, except the case of sight.

# RHETORIC AND DECONSTRUCTION

Alcibiades: What do you mean by that?

Socrates: You think about it, too. If the inscription took our eyes to be men and advised them, "See thyself," how would we understand such advice? Shouldn't the eye be looking at something in which it could see itself?

Alcibiades: Obviously.

Socrates: Then let's think of something that allows us to see both it and ourselves when we look at it.

Alcibiades: Obviously, Socrates, you mean mirrors and that sort of thing.

Socrates: Quite right. And isn't there something like that in the eye, which we see with?

Alcibiades: Certainly.

Socrates: I'm sure you've noticed that when a man looks into an eye his face appears in it, like in a mirror. We call this the 'pupil', for it's a sort of miniature of the man who's looking.

Alcibiades: You're right.

Socrates: Then an eye will see itself if it observes an eye and looks at the best part of it, the part with which it can see.

Alcibiades: So it seems.

Socrates: But it won't see itself if it looks at anything else in a man, or anything else at all, unless it's similar to the eye.

Alcibiades: You're right.

Socrates: So if an eye is to see itself, it must look at an eye, and at that region of it in which the good activity of an eye actually occurs, and this, I presume, is seeing.

Alcibiades: That's right.

Socrates: Thus, if the soul, Alcibiades, is to know itself, it must look at a soul, and especially at that region in which what makes a soul good, wisdom, occurs, and at anything else similar to it. (*Alcibiades* 132c–133b; Hutchinson 1997: 591–92)

In this erotically charged moment, Socrates and Alcibiades look into each other's eyes and into each others' souls, and each sees himself in and through the other. In the same way, in the *Phaedrus*, the beloved, who receives the desire of the lover and reflects back his own beauty begins himself to desire as well and in that desire sees himself in his lover as though in a mirror (255b7–d6). Self and other, then, are neither mutually exclusive nor meaningless terms. Rather each is only the object of knowledge insofar as it is the predicate of the other, and truth lies not only in their difference but also in the ironic tropic movement that defines their interrelation.

The structure of the ironic *pharmakon*, then, is never that of an either/or question, but always that of a neither/nor statement. A detour of time and difference, a moment of alienation, is precisely what makes authenticity possible.

If the *pharmakon* is "ambivalent," it is because it constitutes the medium in which opposites are opposed, the movement and the play that links them among themselves, reverses them or makes one side cross over into the other (soul/body, good/evil, inside/outside, memory/forgetfulness, speech/writing, etc.). It is on the basis of this play or movement that the opposites or differences are stopped by Plato. The *pharmakon* is the movement, the locus, and the play: (the production of) difference. (Derrida 1981: 127)

# THEORY DOES NOT EXIST

Derrida in this passage betrays his own residually traditional reading of Plato in the assumption that the text of the *Phaedrus*, which deploys the ambivalences and ironies that he charts, tries to "stop" the currents it unleashes (Shankman 1994b: 8). Plato here is conceived of as one with Platonism and the philosophy transmitted under that name (Ferrari 1987: 214; Berger 1994: 76, 114). In later texts, Derrida demonstrates that this is an oversimplification, that Platonism is but a moment in, or an abstraction from, the Platonic text whose ironic overdetermination deconstructs it (Derrida 1993: 81–83; cf. Ferrari 1987: 207, 220; Alliez 1992: 226; Halperin 1994: 62; Loraux 1996: 169).

In the end, the ironic production of truth functions in precisely the opposite fashion to the logic of the *pharmakos* or "scapegoat," the *pharmakon*'s etymological cousin. Where the *pharmakon* embodies the most fundamental ambiguities and thus serves as the ground of difference, the *pharmakos* represents the attempt to expel the other in the name of the same. Where the logic of the *pharmakon* is endlessly open, that of the *pharmakos* aspires to closure and the monologic (Derrida 1981: 128–34; Stoekl 1992: 204). The *pharmakon* cannot but be ironic; the *pharmakos* represents the aspiration to the univocal. In this context, Plato's final ironic hyperbole in the *Phaedrus*, his advocacy of writing on the soul (278a3), is a gesture toward openness, a gesture which makes possible a vision of the self that is not auto-entombed, a salutary internalization of the external.

## III

Phaedrus: Who are they and where have you a heard better speech than this?

Socrates: Now I really can't say. But it's clear I've heard them, whether they be lovely Sappho or wise Anacreon or some prose writers? What sort of proof do I offer in support? I have a strange fullness in my breast, divine Phaedrus, and I perceive that I am able to say different things, which would not be worse, on this same topic. I know well that I have not at all thought about these matters, being conscious of my own ignorance. Indeed, I think, the only possibility left is that I have been filled through my ears from the streams of others, like a pitcher. But on account of a certain stupidity, I have forgotten this very thing, how and from whom I heard them. (*Phaedrus*, 235c1–d3)

This passage, which has largely gone unnoticed in the scholarship, contains all the elements we have discussed concerning the relation between rhetoric and philosophy in the *Phaedrus* and "Plato's Pharmacy." I conclude by offering a reading of it. Phaedrus's initial question is aimed at defending Lysias's speech against Socrates' charge that it had not treated the matter in depth (234e4–235a3) but had simply repeated the same things time and again (235a3–b9), "Who are these speakers and where did you hear them?" This is both a challenge and a genuine inquiry. If there are better speakers, Phaedrus would love to hear them.

Socrates, however, frustrates Phaedrus's request. He cannot remember where he has heard them or who they were. We must ask ourselves "is this not a case of Socratic irony?" Socrates has just cited "Ancient and wise men and women" as his authorities (235b6). He must have some idea who they are. Moreover, as the next clause makes clear, Sappho and Anacreon, along with unnamed prose writers, loom large among them.

Socrates has been filled (*plēres, peplērēsthai*) with the words of others: poets and writers. These others, according to the ontology offered in *Republic* 10, are themselves the imitators of imitations, manipulators of externalities like the sophists, mythographers, and Theuth. If we take his statement at face value, Socrates as their secondary and self-proclaimed forgetful reporter would thus be of an even more fallen state. Yet face value is hard to come by. For one thing, in Socrates' second discourse the inspired poet participates in a form of divine madness second only to that of priests and prophets (245a1–8). For another, we can only accept the monologically negative reading of this passage if we disregard the irony of Socrates' claim that he does not know where or from whom he has heard such speeches.

The proof that Socrates has heard these speeches is that he feels his own breast now full. He is inspired: ready, if not to break out in song then at least in speech. But since he "knows" that he is "without learning" (*amathia*), then, it must be the case that he has been filled up like an urn from the streams of others. That is since he knows that he is empty, then his fullness must be purely external. Since he knows that he knows nothing, then his knowledge must not be genuine but artificial, factitious, an imitation of an imitation. Yet as the *Apology* teaches, it precisely because he knows he knows nothing that Socrates is the wisest of men (22e6–23c1). Moreover, in the *Symposium*, Socrates not only denies that wisdom can simply be poured from one individual to another (175d–e), but also that it can be exchanged, that Alcibiades can trade his favors for that which Socrates hides within himself (218e–219b; Miller 2008 121–32). Thus if Socrates is ironic when he claims not to remember where he heard these speeches are we also to assume that he is ironic in his claim of ignorance or *amathia*? And what would it mean for him to be ironic in this claim particularly given the repeated assurances in the passage that Socrates "knows this well" and is "conscious" of this ignorance, especially when the claim itself is almost identical with that offered in the *Apology* as an explanation of the Delphic oracle? Does he know or not know? Is he full or empty? And if he is full, has he been filled from the streams of others or, as in the case of the beloved who receives the stream of desire from the lover, does his own desire awaken and become a way of seeing himself through the other? The ironic tone makes a one-sided answer fundamentally impossible, even as it invites us to think beyond the antinomies in which it is couched (de Man 1983: 220–22; Rorty 1989: 73–74).

Perhaps, though there is a simpler solution. This is not a blanket claim Socrates offers here. It is local and specific and serves to preface his first speech, which he will renounce and then deliver his second speech as a palinode, in the manner of the poet Stesichorus (242d12–243b7). The first speech is precisely an example of what should not be done, of bad speech. This is what happens when one is filled up with the words of another, with words from the outside, when one becomes a sophist or rhetorician. Yet, as we already hinted in noting the precedent invoked for the second speech, it too derives from a poet. It too floods in from the outside. It too depends on that which is secondary and derivative. Indeed, in terms of Socrates' use of elements derived from the Mysteries, Pythagoreanism, and other sources, have we not already indicated that the second speech is a tissue of citations? But if that is the case, then the passage we have been explicating with its multiple layers of ironic displacement, claims and

# THEORY DOES NOT EXIST

counterclaims, applies every bit as much to the second speech as it does to the first. Indeed, on the most profound level, all language comes to us, poured through our ears from the streams of others. Even the *Republic*, which on one level banishes the poets from the ideal city, is itself filled with poetic citations. Nonetheless, not all outsides are created equal. In Socrates' first speech, and in Lysias's before that, reference is deployed to an ontologically prior reality, to an outside that justifies the power the speaker seeks to wield, in much the same way as the sophistic explication of the myth of Boreas and Oreithuia seeks to ground it in a more fundamental level of signification. In Socrates's second speech and in the larger Platonic practice of Socratic citationality, the practice of reference to the poets, to local myth, to exotic tales from Egypt, ultimately seeks not to reproduce the sophistic claim to discursive power, but to turn that practice against itself, to re-fer to the act of referring to per se.

If there is no original word, then, at what point do we distinguish internal from external, philosophy as the authentic pursuit of truth from rhetoric as the secondary manipulation of language? We don't. The moment such a distinction is made, the moment the play of difference is arrested, then language, words themselves become dead letters, tokens moved on a playing board. The second answer, though, is precisely to acknowledge the infinite irony of this temporal play. Primary and secondary, inside and outside are not fixed terms with fixed meanings, but neither are they meaningless. Rather only when Socrates ceases to ask questions, when he simply accepts being the wisest of men, does his proof become a sophistry and rhetoric the antithesis of philosophy. Likewise, only when deconstruction becomes a formalized procedure—rather than an event, an unveiling—does it too become just another style, another tropological routine (Courtine 2008: 20; Crépon 2008: 37).

## Bibliography

Alliez, Eric. 1992. "Ontologie et logographie. La pharmacie, Platon et le simulacre." *Nos Grecs et leurs modernes*. Ed. Barbara Cassin. Paris: Seuil. 211–31.

Berger, Harry, Jr. 1994. "*Phaedrus* and the Politics of Inscriptions." Shankman 1994a. 76–114.

Blondell, Ruby. 2002. *The Play of Character in Plato's Dialogues*. Cambridge: Cambridge University Press.

Brisson, Luc. 1998. *Plato the Mythmaker*. Trans and Ed. Gerard Nadaff. Chicago: University of Chicago Press.

Brisson, Luc et Jean-François Pardeau. 2007. *Dictionnaire Platon*. Paris: Ellipses.

Courtine, Jean-François. 2008. "L'ABC de la deconstruction." *Derrida, la tradition de la philosophie*. Eds. Marc Crépon and Frédéric Worms. Paris: Galilée. 11–26.

Crépon, Marc. 2008. "Déconstruction et traduction: Le passage à la philosophie." *Derrida, la tradition de la philosophie*. Eds. Marc Crépon and Frédéric Worms. Paris: Galilée. 27–44.

de Man, Paul. 1983. "The Rhetoric of Temporality." *Blindness and Insight: Essays in the Rhetoric of Contemporary Criticism*. 2nd ed. rev. Minneapolis: U of Minnesota P. 187–228.

Derrida, Jacques. 1980. *La Carte Postale: de Socrate à Freud et au-delà*. Paris: Aubier-Flammarion.

———. 1981. "Plato's Pharmacy." *Dissemination*. Trans. Barbara Johnson. Chicago: University of Chicago Press. 61–171.

———. 1992. "Nous autres Grecs." *Nos Grkecs et leurs modernes*. Ed. Barbara Cassin. Paris: Seuil. 251–73.

———. 1993. *Khôra*. Paris: Galilée.

———. 1994. *Politiques de l'amitié, suivi de L'oreille de Heidegger*. Paris: Galilée.

———. 1996. "Résistances." *Résistances de la psychanalyse*. Paris: Galilée. 11–53. Original = 1992.

# RHETORIC AND DECONSTRUCTION

Derrida, Jacques and Elisabeth Roudinesco. 2001. *De quoi demain ... : Dialogue*. Paris: Fayard/ Galilée.

Ferrari, G. R. F. 1987. *Listening to the Cicadas: A Study of Plato's Phaedrus*. Cambridge: Cambridge University Press.

Frank, Jill. 2016. "The Power of Persuasion in Plato." Lecture given at Duke.

Freud, Sigmund. 1965. *The Interpretation of Dreams*. Trans. James Strachey. New York: Avon Books.

Gadamer, Hans-Georg. 1991. *Plato's Dialectical Ethics: Phenomenological Interpretations Relating to the Philebus*. Trans. Robert M. Wallace. New Haven: Yale University Press.

Gasché, Rodolphe. 2002. "L'expérience aporétique aux origines de la pensée. Platon, Heidegger, Derrida." *Etudes françaises* 38: 103–21.

Hadot, Pierre. 1995. *Qu'est-ce que la philosophie antique?* Paris: Gallimard.

Halperin, David M. 1994. "Plato and the Erotics of Narrativity." Shankman 1994a. 43–75.

Heitsch, Ernst. 1993. *Phaidros*. Göttingen: Vandenhoeck & Ruprecht.

Hunter, Richard. 2004. *Plato's Symposium*. Oxford: Oxford University Press.

Hutchinson, D. S., trans. 1997. "Alcibiades." *Plato: Complete Works*. Ed. John M Cooper. Assoc. ed. D. S. Hutchinson. Indianapolis: Hackett. 557–95.

Kambouchner, Denis. 2008. "L'ironie et deconstruction: Le problème des classiques." *Derrida, la tradition de la philosophie*. Eds. Marc Crépon and Frédéric Worms. Paris: Galilée. 45–63.

Kierkegaard, Søren. 1989. *The Concept of Irony with Continual Reference to Socrates. Notes of Schelling's Berlin Lectures*. Ed. and trans. Howard V. Hong and Edna H. Hong. Princeton: Princeton University Press.

Loraux, Nicole. 1996. *Né de la terre: Mythe et politique à Athènes*. Paris: Seuil.

Miller, Paul Allen. 2007. *Postmodern Spiritual Practices: The Construction of the Subject and the Reception of Plato in Lacan, Derrida, and Foucault*. Columbus: Ohio State University Press.

Miller, Paul Allen and Charles Platter. 2010. *Plato's Apology of Socrates: A Commentary*. Norman: Oklahoma University Press.

Morgan, Michael L. 1992. "Plato and Greek Religion." *The Cambridge Companion to Plato*. Ed. Richard Kraut. Cambridge: Cambridge University Press. 227–47.

Müller, W. Max. 1918. "Egyptian." *The Mythology of All Races*, vol. 12. Ed. Louis Herbert Grey. 1–245.

Nightingale, Andrea Wilson. 1995. *Genres in Dialogue: Plato and the Construct of Philosophy*. Cambridge: Cambridge University Press.

Robin, Léon. 1966. "Notice." Platon: Phèdre. Paris: Société d'Edition <<Les Belles Lettres>>. vii–ccv. Original = 1933.

Rorty, Richard. 1989. *Contingency, Irony, and Solidarity*. Cambridge: Cambridge University Press.

Shankman, Steven, ed. 1994a. *Plato and Postmodernism*. Glenside, PA: Aldine Press.

———. 1994b. "Plato and Postmodernism." Shankman 1994a. 3–28.

Stoekl, Allan. 1992. *Agonies of the Intellectual: Commitment, Subjectivity and the Performative in the 20th Century French Tradition*. Lincoln: University of Nebraska Press.

Szlezák, Thomas A. 1999. *Reading Plato*. Trans. Graham Zanker. London: Routledge. Original 1993.

Zuckert, Catherine H. 1996. *Postmodern Platos: Nietzsche, Heidegger, Gadamer, Strauss, Derrida*. Chicago: University of Chicago Press.

# Chapter 5

# THE PLATONIC REMAINDER: DERRIDA'S *KHÔRA* AND THE *CORPUS PLATONICUM*

In *Khôra*, Derrida offers his reading of one of Plato's most fascinating and problematic texts. The *Timaeus* is central to the history of western thought and wildly eccentric. Translated into Latin by Cicero and later by Chalcidius, it was for many centuries the only Platonic text available in the west. Its metaphysical speculations as interpreted through the lens of Augustinian neo-Platonism came to pass for Platonism *tout court* and were refined and elaborated by the monks at Chartres (Rivaud 1963: 3–5). Yet in point of fact the text is anything but typical of the Platonic corpus, consisting as it does of an introductory dialogue (17a–27b) followed by a long speech in which Timaeus of Locris, a presumed Pythagorean, tells the tale of how the Demiurge or divine craftsman created the universe through imitating a set of pre-existing eternal essences or forms (27c–92c). Halfway through, however, the speech of Timaeus encounters a hiccup and our speaker must pause and begin again (47e). If the divine Demiurge creates perfect copies of the intelligible essences in the world of sense, then how would those imitations differ from the originals, and if they were indeed perfect copies—and why would a divine craftsman produce anything less?—then how are we to explain the manifest change and corruption of the world of our experience? Surely, these copies are not part of the world of intelligibles, which belong to the realm of being rather than that of becoming. A new beginning must be made, which accounts for this "wandering cause" (πλανωμένης … αἰτίας, 48a7) that limits and at the same times makes possible the Demiurge's labor of reproducing the intelligible order in the world of sense (Sallis 1999: 70; McCabe 1994: 175, 180–81). This "cause" is the famous *khōra*, the mother or receptacle of creation (50a–51b). A second story of how the world was fashioned then follows and the dialogue ends.

Any reader of the Platonic dialogues will note that one element we have come to associate with the Platonic text is missing from the summary given above: Socrates. Now this absence is neither unique nor total. As is well known, in the *Laws*, Plato's final dialogue, Socrates does not appear at all, nor does he have his accustomed prominence in the *Critias*, the sequel to the *Timaeus*, nor in the *Sophist* or *Statesman*. The last two dialogues, however, are characterized by direct and intense dialectical interchange, which recalls the more Socratic dialogues, while the *Timaeus* and the unfinished *Critias* alone feature neither a prominent role for Socrates nor any

56 THEORY DOES NOT EXIST

meaningful dialectical exchange.[1] They are atypical in their organization and presentation.

These issues of literary form and style of argument are never incidental to the interpretation of Platonic philosophy, as much recent Anglo-American scholarship, as well as an older French tradition, have shown, (Hunter 2004: 22–27; Blondell 2002: 4–5, 42; Szelizák 1999: 85; Diès 1966: xvi; Koyré 1962: 18). To account for the strangeness of the *Timaeus*, then, is at least in part to account for the nature of the text itself. It is, in fact, an atypical dialogue that has been misread as a straightforward metaphysical treatise (Rivaud 1963: 38). Yet in many ways there is little that could be further from the concerns of Platonic dialogic practice and its fundamentally ethical form of inquiry (Blondell 2002: 42; Gadamer 1991: 2, 10–11; Hadot 1995: 102–6; Koyré 1962: 20; Festugière 1950: 42–43, 191). As such, the accidental centrality of the *Timaeus* in the transmission of Plato and Platonism has perhaps accounted as much as anything for the perceived dogmatism often thought to characterize the Platonic project. In fact, the dialogues themselves present less a set of unqualified assertions than an open and relentless field of experimentation and inquiry (Hunter 2004: 86–87).

In many ways, the *Timaeus* is a dialogue that wears its problematic nature on its sleeve. Read outside the Latinate theological framework that dominated its early reception, it bears countless signs that Timaeus's speech is to be received with inverted commas. As Mary Margaret McCabe writes

> The reader must take the *Timaeus* with several large pinches of salt. For here is a dialogue whose central sections is a myth, presented to a Socrates, hilarious at completing the *Republic*, by Timaeus, the "expert" in cosmology. Just that short description should be enough to make us worry about how to read the dialogue. After all, Plato is the writer who warns us against the deceptions of storytelling; and Socrates was the gadfly who never accepted the expertise of others. So we should be wary of the myth and its setting and attentive to the explicit epistemological background to Timaeus's disquisition. (1994: 162)

Yet while McCabe's cautions are well-heeded by the unwary reader, they are, if anything, too timid. They assume that Socrates' references to the previous day's conversation on the constitution of the ideal city allude to the *Republic* and that the *Timaeus* is thus to be taken as the sequel to the story found there. The present dialogue would provide the metaphysical account for how the ideal city could be made flesh. Critias's unfinished sequel on the myth of Atlantis would then represent a quasi-historical testing of these theses in the crucible of experience, or at least myth. Such a reading goes back to Proclus and is reflected in the manuscript tradition, where the *Timaeus* frequently

---

1 The *locus classicus* is Vlastos's famous grouping of the dialogues into the categories of Socratic, Platonic, and late dialogues, in which the true Socratic dialectic or *elenchus* is only found in the early Socratic or aporetic dialogues (1991: 46–56, 115, 117). This view has never been widely accepted, at least in its dogmatic form, outside of the Anglo-American analytic tradition and today is questioned even there. See Miller (2007: chapters 4 and 5); Blondell (2002: 10–13); Annas (1993: 19); Wallace (1991: xv); Plato, *Sophist* (230a–d); *Theaetetus* (187b–c, 210a–d).

# THE PLATONIC REMAINDER

appears immediately following the *Republic* in the codices (Sallis 1999: 21–22). Yet, however venerable its provenance, this interpretation has been decisively refuted. First, it is impossible to reconcile the conflicting dramatic dates of the dialogues, so that the conversation referred to in the *Timaeus* cannot be that which took place in Polemarchus's home in the *Republic* (Sallis 1999: 22–23; Rivaud 1963: 19). Second, despite certain similarities, the content of the two visions of the ideal state cannot be reconciled. While there are numerous differences between the cities imagined in the *Timaeus* and the *Republic* (Sallis 1999: 20–23; Rivaud 1963: 19), the most basic is that the city discussed in the *Timaeus* does not include anything mentioned after Book 5 in the *Republic*. In short, the *Timaeus* presents the ideal city without the philosopher. This *polis* is a model of static harmony that remains within the cave and without the challenge and the science of dialectic to enlighten it (Sallis 1999: 23–24).

If, as everyone from McCabe to Rivaud recognizes, the *Timaeus* comes to us surrounded by hermeneutic cautions, then, Timaeus's speech is anything but a dogmatic set of metaphysical assertions that we are invited simply to accept. It is rather a story that self-consciously labels itself as concerned with the world of appearance. It does not present certainties, but only a likely account (εἰκὸς λόγος 29c, 30b, 44c, 48d, 54d, 68b) or tale (εἰκός μῦθος 29d, 68d) (Brisson 1998: 129–30; Rivaud 1963: 8, 11–13): for, as Socrates observes, poets and philosophers alike must take experience as the ground of their representations, and hence their descriptions of the ideal city of Socrates' imagining will always fall short, for all are dealing in the realm of imitations and likenesses, not certainties (19d).

Only the world of intelligible being in itself can produce certain knowledge. The realm of perception and likeness, of experience and becoming, whose genesis Timaeus ultimately describes, is also the world of seeming, appearance, or opinion (δόκειν, δόξα, 27d–28a). Thus, while formal proofs will be possible for those things which yield certainty, for creation the likely story will have to suffice:

> Timaeus: But if we should provide accounts no less likely than any other, it is necessary to welcome them, remembering that I, the speaker, and you, my judges, are merely human, so that it is proper that we accept the likely tale about these matters and seek nothing more definite than this. (29c7–d2)[2]

Thus, Timaeus's discourse far from constituting a set of unchanging truths, in fact, labels itself as at best a likeness, a tale, a poetic invention of the type Socrates compared his own imitative discourse to at the beginning of the dialogue. Moreover, it is a discourse that is prefaced by Critias's own bizarre tale of how he has inherited from his grandfather a story of Athens's ancient past, which his grandfather learned from Solon, who had in turn learned it from the Egyptian priests, who themselves had recorded it in their otherwise unintelligible hieroglyphs on the walls of a temple. Timaeus's myth of creation is in fact merely to serve as a prelude to Critias's retelling of this tale, which he had last heard in childhood, but has spent the previous night

---

2  All translations are my own unless otherwise noted.

58                      THEORY DOES NOT EXIST

attempting to recover the memory of (Sallis 1999: 38).[3] In such a situation, why should
we view Timaeus's discourse any less skeptically than Critias's own? At every moment,
Plato frames Timaeus's discourse with doubts and qualifications (Berger 2005: 471–72).[4]

None of this means, however, that we should not take that discourse with great
seriousness. Timaeus's tale is far too long, far too elaborate, and far too technically
based in the scientific and mathematical speculations of the day to be simply dismissed.
Rather this text, with its multiple layers of quotation marks, its multiple cautions, its
ironic self-comparison of Socrates to the poets and sophists themselves, requires us to
undertake a double reading (Sallis 1999: 30; Derrida 1993a: 59). Like the Demiurge
himself, we as readers and lovers of wisdom must be mimetic artists (ποιητής 28c3)
who move constantly between the intelligible essences and their likenesses in the world
of appearance, experience, and becoming, occupying a third register that is neither
and both (28a6–b2; Derrida 1993a: 54–58; Sallis 1999: 51). The cosmology of the
*Timaeus* must then be taken simultaneously literally and figuratively: as a parody of its
own dogmatic pretensions that also demands to be taken seriously (McCabe 1994: 176).
It requires the infinite labor of the reader who can never penetrate the last of the
quotation marks nor can refuse the content therein (Zuckert 1996: 235). It is into this
bottomless discourse, this *mise-en-abyme* of endless reflection, that Derrida's reading
steps. The *Timaeus* is, in fact, an unfinalizable dialogue in which each moment of
positing is also a moment of irony and interrogation, of simultaneous acceptance and
active separation (Loraux 1996: 169–70; compare Derrida 1994: 112). As such, it is not
unique, for this is the double labor that characterizes the Platonic dialectic from the *Ion*
and the *Apology* to the *Philebus* and the *Timaeus* (Blondell 2002: 100; Hadot 1995: 110;
Gadamer 1991: 4–5; Robin 1985: lxvii).


                                    I

Written as homage to Jean-Pierre Vernant, *Khôra*, like all of Derrida, seeks simultaneously
to accept and go beyond the terms of the text being read (Derrida and Roudinesco
2001: 16–19). In *Mythe et société en Grèce ancienne*, Vernant had posited a fundamental
opposition between *muthos* and *logos*, with the latter representing a discourse founded
on noncontradiciton, a quasi-Aristotelian logic of the excluded middle, and the former

---

3  In the *Critias*, we learn that he in fact possessed a written copy. The *Critias* is generally
   considered unfinished so it is difficult to judge whether this inconsistency is the product of
   incomplete revision or meant to reveal dishonesty on the part of Critias.
4  Berger's acceptance of Proclus's identification of Critias with the member of the Thirty
   is no longer generally admitted. The majority opinion favors Critias's grandfather, who
   was also Plato's ancestor (Nails 2002: 106–11; Sallis 1999: 32).
       In late antiquity, there clearly arose a desire to strip Timaeus's speech of the quotation
   marks and create a straightforward dogmatic discourse in its place. Thus, a spurious work
   ostensibly authored by Timaeus himself appeared, *On the Nature of the Cosmos and the Soul*.
   It poses as the original from which Plato supposedly cribbed his more baroque and ambiguous
   copy. For a good summary and analysis, see Sallis (1999: 146–50).

# THE PLATONIC REMAINDER

being a narrative discourse that thrives precisely on ambiguity and indeterminacy. The key passage Derrida cites runs as follows:

> Thus, myth puts into play a form of logic which could be called—in contrast to the logic of noncontradiction of the philosophers—a logic of the ambiguous, of the equivocal, of polarity. How can one formulate, or even formalize, these see-saw operations, which flip any term into its opposite whilst at the same time keeping them both apart, from another point of view? The mythologist was left with drawing up, in conclusion, this statement of deficit, and to turn to the linguists, logicians, mathematicians, that they might supply him with the tool he lacked: the structural model of a logic which could not be that of binarity, of the yes or no, a logic other than the logic of the *logos*. (Vernant 1974: 250)[5]

The doubleness discussed in this passage has recognizable structural affinities with the double movement of the Platonic dialectic in general, as described above, and with Timaeus's own "likely" discourse, which in various places is qualified now as *muthos*, now as *logos*. The attractiveness of such a position to a Derridean reading of the *Timaeus*, one which posits a double form of discourse in which binarity is both constituted and undermined, is too obvious to require extensive comment.

Nonetheless, the opposition between *muthos* and *logos* that Vernant posits is only the first step in what Derrida stages as Plato's deconstruction of Vernant, because it is precisely the *Timaeus*'s formulation of the *khōra* that will ultimately call this opposition into question. *Khōra*, as we shall see, stands as the prephilosophical, prenarrative moment that makes the construction of both *muthos* and *logos* possible, even as it reveals their essential complicity (Derrida 1993a: 30). It is that which neither participates in the intelligible essences per se nor constitutes the realm of their mimetic instantiation. As such, it is neither being nor becoming, neither essence nor appearance, neither proof nor tale (Derrida 1993a: 15–18, 68). This essay proceeds from the perspective of this "neither/nor," which as we shall see is also a "both/and," and which characterizes both Plato's *khōra* and Derrida's *Khôra*.[6] It will argue three things: first, that Derrida's reading of the *Timaeus* in *Khôra* is critical to our understanding of Derrida; second, that it is critical to our understanding of Plato; and third, that the ultimate subject matter of both Plato's and Derrida's *khōra* is not the validity of a particular metaphysical concept, but the constitution of philosophy per se as an ironic turning from the present and immediate to the deferred, and hence toward the possibility of difference and the event, in the fullest sense of the word (Derrida 1994: 85–87, 247).

Let us go over these points in more detail before taking each in turn as the object of further investigation. First, the reading of the *khōra* in the *Timaeus* is critical to our understanding of Derrida because it contains certain clear homologies with his earlier readings of Plato as evidenced in "La pharmacie de Platon" and *La carte postale*, among

---

5   I cite Vernant in the translation of Ian McLeod, where it prefaces the translation of Derrida's *Khôra* (1995: 88), as the original prefaces Derrida's French (1993a: 14).

6   "The oscillation that we have just spoken of is not one oscillation among others, an oscillation between two poles. It oscillates between two types of oscillation: the double exclusion (*neither/nor*) and the participation (*at the same time … both this and that*)" (Derrida 1993a: 19).

60 THEORY DOES NOT EXIST

other texts. There is thus a Derridean reading of Plato, which *Khôra* allows us to see with unusual clarity, by drawing our attention to what in the *Timaeus* escapes both metaphysics and myth, and hence to what constitutes their simultaneous beyond and necessary precondition (1993a: 15–16). *Khôra*, thus, names the "place" that is no place (*atopia*)[7] that allows place (defined logical space, *topos*) to take place (the possibility of its eventuality, and thus of the event) (1993a: 94–95). *Khôra*, therefore, functions as an incomplete totalization of the non-spaces, non-concepts that had earlier been delineated by Derrida's meditations on the problems of the *pharmakon, différance*, aporia, and the "unlimited." *Khôra* thus reveals not only the structure of Derrida's recurring engagement with Plato, but the centrality of the Platonic corpus to the Derridean project.

Second, to the same degree that *Khôra* reveals the centrality of the Platonic corpus to the Derridean project it also reveals the centrality of the *corpus/corps* in Plato. It discloses the presence of a constitutive otherness or remainder in the Platonic text that can neither be subsumed into the purely intelligible nor reduced to the unintelligible, which is in fact a category of intelligibility. Rather, *khōra* names precisely that which necessarily precedes the opposition of the intelligible and the unintelligible (Derrida 1993a: 21, 37, 95–96). It is therefore that element in Plato that always resists its assimilation into Platonism (Derrida 1993a: 81–83) and hence into a philosophical tradition that privileges the absolute self-presence of disembodied reason. Yet, as Diotima reminds us in the *Symposium*, the moment of pure self-presence is not only the end (in both senses of the term) of human life—only the gods possess the intelligible per se—but also the end of that desire (*erōs*) that is called philosophy.

Thus, third, *khōra* as such names that "place," the literal meaning of the word, that both exceeds philosophy and makes it possible. It is quite literally, an atopic place, one that is not defined by the logic of the *topos*, a delimited area within a grid, but a form of clearing that opens the possibility of the object world and the space it de-*fines* (Zuckert 1996: 235; Sallis 1999: 98, 121, 153–54). It is thus no accident, then that Timaeus introduces the section in which the *khōra* is named as a "strange," "out of the way," "out of place discourse" (*atopos*, 48d5). And it is for this reason, he says, that the god must be invoked to bring him and his listeners through safely to a discourse of likely appearance/opinion (πρὸς τὸ τῶν εἰκοντῶν δόγμα, 48d5-6). In this final section of the essay, then, it is argued that the place, which is no place ("lieu sans lieu," Derrida 1993a: 59)[8], which is the *khōra*, is in fact the "space" or nonspace—the atopic moment—of Socratic irony per se, understood as the perpetual hinge point between a given statement's denotative content and its figurative doubling. *Khōra* names, I contend, the clearing that makes the joining of these two levels of signification possible and hence creates the opening necessary for the construction and deployment of philosophical concepts. Thus, while the *khōra* is a mythico-metaphysical philosopheme (i.e., a narrative deduction from the intelligible that functions in philosophical discourse but does not rise to the level of the concept)[9]

---

7  Socrates is frequently referred to as being *atopos* (Vlastos 1991: 1n1; Hadot 1995: 57).

8  Compare Leonard (2005: 213).

9  On the *khōra* as the deduction of a necessary "vide fugace" inside a world of plenitude, see Rivaud (1963: 65–70).

# THE PLATONIC REMAINDER

introduced in the late Platonic *Timaeus*, in fact, its function, as read by Derrida, is ultimately the same as that of Socratic irony itself: it names the space of the constitution of philosophy, defined as a form of discourse that is not simply a set of statements about those things which are the case. This last argument, in turn, will be illustrated with a reading of the passage from the *Apology* where Socrates claims that he *should* in fact be brought into court and condemned to death if he abandons the post the god had assigned to him and ceases to philosophize.

## II

Derrida's engagement with the Platonic corpus is longstanding. From his early response to Foucault's *Histoire de la folie* (1967) to the now classic "Plato's Pharmacy" (1972) through *La Carte Postale* (1980) to *Khôra* (1993) and *Politiques de l'amitié* (1994), Derrida has always returned to the founding gestures of occidental philosophy and their simultaneous encoding and resistance in the Platonic corpus.[10] Central to each of these engagements is a dramatization of reason or the *logos's* engagement with its other (Derrida 1992: 260, 269). The question of the other, however, can never be posed in terms of that which reason defines as its opposite, because that would be the other as defined by and within reason. It must always be posed in terms of the absolute other. Only the absolute other that resists all gestures of dialectical recuperation can truly withstand the hegemony of calculating reason and thus simultaneously ground it and uncrown it. The question of the absolute other is also of central importance because it is only the presence (or better, the non-presence) of the absolute other that makes difference possible, that keeps the world as world from collapsing into the stasis of an idealist and totalitarian unity. Thus, the possibility of meaning, action, decision, and history depends on that which eludes all possible totalization, i.e., the other in its radical difference from the same (Derrida 1993b: 68).

In *Khôra*, Derrida's reading of the *Timaeus*, in many ways Plato's most speculative of dialogues, this moment is located in the conception of the *khōra* itself. On the most basic level, *khōra* is a Greek word that means "place." In the dialogue, however, *khōra* functions as a sort of ground that makes human reason, creation, and ultimately the ontic itself possible. Yet, it can never be included within them. The *khôra* at once exceeds and fails to rise to the threshold of being, of having a defined existence. Thus when the divine Demiurge crafts the cosmos in the *Timaeus*, it takes the ideal forms of intelligibility and deploys them as if they were a set of stamps or *typoi* (50c), which it impresses on the formless as justice, goodness, tableness, chairness, etc. to produce the individual instantiations of the things of the world: i.e., a just act, a good man, a table, a chair. *Khōra* is the place in which this activity occurs. It at once precedes and exceeds the creation of the intelligible universe, because it is both that which receives the stamp of the intelligible and that which in itself remains unchanged by that stamp,

---

10  See Derrida (1992: 262–67); Derrida and Roudinesco (2001: 38); Miller (2007: chapter 5); Leonard (2005: 189–215; 2000); Loraux (1996: 169); Alliez (1992: 226); Wolff (1992: 235).

62                                    THEORY DOES NOT EXIST

like the base from which a perfume is made or the gold worked by a goldsmith (50b–e; Derrida 1993a: 94–95; Zuckert 1996: 236). *Khōra* is the condition of the possibility of the world as world, as cosmos, but it is always radically other from, and hence incomprehensible by, either the intelligibles per se or their mimetic instantiations (Derrida 1993a: 16, 28).

*Khōra* is thus a third *genos* or type (48e–49a, 52a–b). It is at once self-identical and eternal—an attribute of being and the intelligible rather than of becoming and the sensible—yet in itself it remains impervious to reason per se (51a–b; Sallis 1999: 98; Zuckert 1996: 236; McCabe 1994: 187; Wolff 1992: 245).[11] At the same time, inasmuch as it is not the defined space of the Aristotelian *topos* nor of Cartesian extension, the space in which objects appear, but a kind of pre-ontic clearing that makes the topical possible, it cannot be apprehended directly through the senses (McCabe: 1996: 181; Derrida 1993a: 58; Rivaud 1963: 66). Plato has Timaeus state the paradox of its apprehension directly:

> The third *genos*, the always existing *khōra*, that does not receive destruction, but provides the seat for all things that come into being, this is not perceptible through sensation but by a certain bastard reasoning, which is scarcely credible, toward which we look in dreams. And we say that it is necessary that everything be somewhere in some place (*topos*) and occupy a certain *khōra*,[12] and that which is nowhere on earth nor under heaven is nothing. Moreover, concerning all these things and those that are their kin, and concerning their true and waking nature, under the conditions of this dream state we are not able, when roused, to speak the truth and make distinctions, but use a likeness, since the thing itself does not come to be in that which is of its same nature, but is always said to be the image of some other thing, and it is therefore proper that it come to be in something else—if that nature is to have being in any way—or that it be completely nothing. As for what really exists in reality, the *logos* of exact truth is a support: to wit, so long as anything is one thing and something else another, neither ever becomes one thing in the other, becoming simultaneously the same thing and two. (52a8–d1)

This passage is one of the most important and most tortured in the whole dialogue. The *khōra* is only apprehensible in a state that is like a dream: i.e., a state that is neither that of pure sensation nor of pure reason, but a kind of hybrid, which is nonetheless more than just mixture of the two (Sallis 1998: 407–8). The *khōra* is thus perceived through a form of apprehension in which the opposition between the categories of the noetic and the fantasmatic qualities of sensation has not yet come to be.[13] It is thus susceptible to neither *logos* nor *muthos* as modes of comprehension, but represents a third *genos* that makes their opposition possible, one which thus simultaneously precedes and exceeds them: "so long as anything is one thing and something else another."

---

11  On the third type and the *khōra* as the ground of Being and the good in the *Republic* (509–16), see Zuckert (1996: 240) and Sallis (1998: 404).

12  On this careful distinction, see Sallis (1999: 121).

13  Compare *Timaeus* 71e–72a on the relation of the dream state to prophecy and reason.

# THE PLATONIC REMAINDER

In this sense then, the deconstructive *khōra* functions in Derrida's reading of the *Timaeus* in much the same way as the *pharmakon* does in his reading of the *Phaedrus*.[14] It names that which eludes the logic of the same. Neither salutary medicine nor deadly poison, and yet both, the *pharmakon* names that moment of absolute externality on which the distinctions between speech and writing, love and lust, philosophy and rhetoric, *dialogos* and *logographos*, *muthos* and *logos* depend. It is the space that allows these binaries to arise. Yet, as the moment of the distinction that makes them possible, it cannot be absorbed into them. It can never occupy either position in a stable manner (Derrida 1972: 96–98, 112–17, 127; Allen 2000: 85; Ferrari 1987: 207; Oudemans and Lardinois 1987: 88).

By the same token, the *apeiron* or the "unlimited" in Derrida's reading of the *Philebus* in *La carte postale* is that which is both prior to the imposition of the limit, i.e., that which makes the unit or entity possible (as well as the collection of those units into larger intelligible wholes), and that which is the beyond the limit, the infinite, the transcendental (24a–26d).[15] The latter is the ideal telos of the logical process of collection, just as it is also the starting point for its opposite, the process of division (14a–20a). Division, according to Plato, moves from the intelligible one, which by definition can know no limit, to its smallest possible instantiation, and ultimately below the threshold of being to the realm of that which is before the limit itself.[16] The unlimited is therefore that which both precedes and exceeds reason, just as the *pharmakon* precedes and exceeds the possibility of the binary, and the *khōra* precedes and exceeds creation itself (Hampton 1990: 43; Gadamer 1988: 260).[17] The *apeiron* is thus, as Derrida notes, the anticipation of Freud's *Thanatos* in *Beyond the Pleasure Principle* (1961). It names that which is beyond the libidinal accounting of the pleasure and the reality principles and which can only be conceived of as a form of nonexistence or death (Derrida 1980: 180–81, 425–27; Zuckert 1996: 233). In the same way, the *khōra* both eludes the forms and their instantiations, both creator and created, to signify a form of nonexistence that makes existence possible. It is the womb and tomb of the ontic.[18]

## III

The *khōra* thus conceived is not just central to the Derridean enterprise or to the latter's reading of Plato, but to Platonic philosophy per se. This is a central point, for it has become common to conflate Plato with Platonism, i.e., with the doctrine of the forms as the telos of a Platonic system, and hence to read the *khōra* itself as merely an odd remainder,

---

14  Derrida makes the analogy explicitly (1972: 184–86).

15  Compare Frede (1992: 428–29, 43); Gadamer (1991: 131); Hampton (1990: 44); Gosling (1975: 200); Diès (1966: xxvii–xxviii).

16  See Gadamer (1991: 80–81, 120–21); Hampton (1990: 87–88); Gosling (1975: xiv); Diès (1966: xix, xxv); Boussoulas (1952: 171).

17  For a detailed list of textual parallels between the *Timaeus* and the *Philebus*, see Rivaud (1963: 21–22).

18  Compare Copjec (2002: 33) on the *Timaeus*'s anticipation of the death drive's relation to the primordial mother.

# THEORY DOES NOT EXIST

a bump in the road on the way to establishing the theory of abstract intelligibles. The *khōra* is thus the feminine (*Tim.* 50d–51a; Sallis 1998: 407), or a form of "bastard reasoning" (*Tim.* 52b), that which must be surpassed with a certain embarrassment on the way to the erection of a cosmos, properly understood. But what I want to argue here is that this attempt to see the *khōra* as secondary, degraded, or somehow inessential is a fundamental misreading of the Platonic corpus: for the metaphysics of closure, while a necessary moment in the theory of forms as a totalizing unity of the self-identical, is also one that is deliberately and self-consciously deferred throughout the Platonic corpus (Castel-Bouchouchi 2003: 186–87). Indeed, it precisely the *khōra*'s status as neither eidetic form nor ontic imitation, but as a third type that keeps the Platonic dialectic open (48a7).

The irresolvable tension between these three moments—the same, its imitation, and the other that makes them possible but also limits them through the force of a necessity that cannot submit to pure reason—is not a dialectical hiccup to be surpassed in an ultimate gesture of recuperation, sublimation, and ultimately exclusion, as Irigaray would argue in her reading of the myth of the cave (1974), but one whose pursuit and preservation lies at the heart of the Platonic enterprise. Thus, as Diotima, that supreme representative of the Platonic feminine, observes, the human participates in the divine and the self-identical, precisely to the degree that it is not identical with itself, that it is characterized by irreducible difference:

> What is called "careful attention" [*meletan*] presupposes the transitory nature of knowledge: for forgetting is the departure of knowledge, but careful attention is its return, by implanting a new memory in place of that which has departed, it preserves knowledge so that it seems to be the same. In this manner, every mortal is preserved, not as wholly self-identical like the divine, but with the departing being replaced by something new, yet similar, left in its place. By this means, the mortal, both the body and everything else [...] partakes of the immortal; but immortality is something else. (*Sym.* 208a4–b4)

The telos of a truly philosophical desire, one that seeks wisdom, then, is not absolute self-presence but the recognition of its simultaneous impossibility and desirability for mortals. In the same way, Socrates in the *Apology* is the "wisest of men" because he alone is both *sophos* and knows that he knows nothing. Likewise, coming to *aporia*, "helplessness" or "perplexity," as Socrates acknowledges in the *Theaetetus*, represents not the failure of philosophy, but the opportunity to recognize the limits of one's thought, its own constitutive otherness, and hence the chance to think anew (*Theae.* 187b–c, 210a–d; Blondell 2002: 124).

This recognition presents itself on the level of form, not just content. It is no accident that Plato never wrote a treatise and that the dialogue remains central to his philosophical method from the *Laches* to the *Timaeus* (Diès 1966: xvi). For the purpose and function of Socratic dialogue as presented in the Platonic corpus is not to transmit a bounded body of specific, reproducible, codifiable (and hence commodifiable) knowledge or *tekhnē* (Nightingale 1995: 49), but to induce Socrates' interlocutors, and ultimately Plato's readers, to scrutinize their own opinions in order to strive to rid themselves of false presumptions and self-contradictions (*Soph.* 230a–d), even as they recognize that these contradictions summon the soul to *philosophia*. The dialogue form thus both codifies the principle of otherness in the figure of the interlocutor and at the same time calls attention to its own fictive status through its dramatic form (Hunter 2004: 22–23). The purpose of Socratic dialogue and Platonic storytelling then is not to produce an impossible self-identity, which is both the province of the divine and, in its unchanging nature, indistinguishable from death, but to come know the irreducible other at the very heart of our identity and hence induce a radically new practice of the self, which strives for the divine in the recognition of its impossibility. To that extent, the dialogue is the formal correlate of the *aporia* induced by Socratic questioning (Blondell 2002: 42), and, as the moment of undecidability, it occupies the same logical nonspace (*atopia*) as the *khōra* in the creation myth of the *Timaeus*.

## IV

The *khōra* as such names that place that both exceeds the desire named philosophy and makes it possible. As was noted earlier, one reading, then, of the place, which is no place, that is the *khōra* is in fact the atopic space of irony, understood as a perpetual hinge point between a given statement's denotative content and its figurative doubling. *Khōra* names, I contend, the clearing that makes the joining of these two levels of signification possible and hence creates the opening necessary for the construction and deployment of philosophical concepts. Thus, while the *khōra* is a mythico-metaphysical philosopheme, in fact, its function, as read by Derrida, is ultimately the same as that of Socratic irony itself: it names that which makes possible the constitution of philosophy as a form of discourse that is not simply a set of truth claims, but one that seeks transcendence and hence transformation on what Deleuze and Guattari would call the plane of immanence (2005: 30–68). Clearly this is not irony as it is commonly understood, nor is it complex irony as defined by Gregory Vlastos—a statement that on one level is false but on another true.[19] It goes well beyond that (Nehamas 1998: 46–98). Rather Socratic irony ultimately creates an opening that makes possible the interrogation of true and false, ironic and literal, and hence also serves as their ground and precondition. In Derridian terms, Socratic irony consists in the reflexive self-conscious deployment of the *pharmakon*, or the unlimited, or the *khôra*'s double-sided nature against itself:

> Socratic irony precipitates out one *pharmakon* by bringing it into contact with another. Or rather it reverses the *pharmakon*'s powers and turns *its* surface—thus taking effect, being recorded and dated, in the act of classing the *pharmakon*, through the fact that the *pharmakon* properly consists in a certain inconsistency, a certain impropriety, this nonidentity-with-itself always allowing it to be turned against itself. (Derrida 1981: 119; 1972: 136, emphasis his)

---

19 "In 'simple' irony what is said just isn't what is meant: taken in its ordinary commonly understood sense the statement is false. In 'complex' irony what is said both is and isn't what is meant: its surface content is meant to be true in one sense, false in another" (Vlastos 1991: 31).

66  THEORY DOES NOT EXIST

Philosophy, then, I would contend, at least as Plato understood it and as it is still understood today in many quarters, i.e., "the critical work that thought brings against itself … the endeavor to know how and to what extent it might be possible to think differently, instead of legitimating what is already known" (Foucault 1986: 9), is precisely the discourse that happens in this ironic, atopic space.

To illustrate this point, let us examine a crucial passage in the *Apology* (29a2-4). Socrates, in response to the capital charge of atheism or impiety, responds that the real impiety would be to give up his philosophical vocation. Indeed, he should more properly be brought into court on such charges if he were to ignore the Delphic oracle's statement that he was the wisest of men or should he cease his quest to understand what that statement means through the interrogation of himself and others. "And it would be a terrible thing, and truly then someone should drag me into court on the grounds that I do not believe the gods exist since I would be disobeying the oracle, fearing death, and thinking myself to be something when I am not." Of course, it is precisely by adhering to his understanding of the oracle that Socrates has provoked these charges in the first place and been brought to trial for his life.

Nonetheless Socrates, in this passage, not only skillfully turns around the accusation of Meletus and the other prosecutors, he also troubles the distinction between the merely literal and the simply ironic in important ways. Indeed, there are several difficulties with taking Socrates' statement as literally true. First, if we are to accept the truth of Socrates' assertion in this passage, then we must also accept as literally true that the god appointed Socrates to the mission of testing himself and others. Yet as Socrates emphasizes in the sentence immediately preceding this one, that appointment is merely Socrates' interpretation of the Delphic oracle's pronouncement to Chaerephon that he was the wisest of men. The latter was a statement that even Socrates found incredible and set out to disprove.[20] Socrates, of course, ultimately does validate the claim of the god by demonstrating that he alone is aware of his own ignorance. Thus, his statement that the god had assigned to him the mission of testing himself and his fellow citizens, through questioning their pretensions to knowledge, rests solely on Socrates' construal of an oracular message that he himself finds incredible. Moreover, the core of that message, as Socrates understands it, is not a stable statement of fact, rather it is an ironic assertion that the wisest man is not he who has the most positive knowledge, but he who most profoundly recognizes his own lack of knowledge and can therefore begin, through a genuine care of the self, the unfinalizable pursuit of *arete*. Thus, even the most literal reading of the present passage is dependent in the last analysis on an ironic statement in which the normal meaning of the word *sophos* is converted into its seeming opposite. Second, a literal reading of the present passage presumes that Socrates believes that people should actually be dragged into court for the failure to follow their own idiosyncratic interpretations of the divine will. This is not only absurd on its face, but also finds no support elsewhere in the Platonic corpus.

---

20 Moreover, Chaerephon, it should be note, is often portrayed in Plato as "a little mad," so it is unclear how reliable a vehicle he is for relaying the will of the god (Nails 2002: 86).

# THE PLATONIC REMAINDER

Nevertheless, none of this is to say that we are not to understand that Socrates means every word he says. It is quite clear that he does not see his choice of the philosophic life as arbitrary. It *is* his duty, and he *is* willing to die in the defense of it. As such, this duty transcends the scope of normal human life and is to that extent divine. Hence, it *would* be impious to flee or ignore it, in which case Meletus *would* have grounds for charging Socrates with failing to honor the gods.

Consequently, Socrates' statement at *Apology* 29a2-4 can be taken neither in a strictly literal, referential sense—it is not a proposition about the world—nor can it be understood as ironic in the common Greek sense of "shamming, meaning one thing and saying another." It is both and therefore opens a space—a *khōra*—that can be fully assimilated to neither one of these positions, a space in which language does not merely reproduce the world of the given—be it facts or forms—but somehow radically precedes and exceeds both the given and its simple negation. It opens the world and our experience of it to a systematic interrogation and transformation. The recognition of this opening, one might argue, of this place without place, is the very origin of philosophy: the recognition of the plane of immanence in which the concept qua concept first comes to be.

## V

In sum, then, *Khôra* is no minor codicil to the Derridean testament, nor a mere remainder to that of Plato. It is both central to the legacy of deconstruction and to an ongoing genealogy of the present. In this work, Derrida not only shows himself to be a skilled interpreter of Plato but also demonstrates the continuing importance of the Platonic text to our own canons of self-understanding. *Khôra* reveals both the fundamental opening that is constitutive of Platonic philosophy and the very *atopia* or non-space that makes philosophy itself possible—not as the mere reproduction of the same, an endless series of imitations and legitimations, but as the attempt to turn thought back on itself and so come to think differently. This ironic doubling does not seek merely to reproduce an original but to encounter what we have labeled the absolute other, and what Plato denominates as a force of necessity, a wondering cause, that makes possible the mimetic labor of creation performed by the Demiurge, the ποίησις, in its necessary difference. In the *khōra*, in the third *genos* that is neither transcendental original nor empirical copy, the *Timaeus*, then, presents the unassimilable remainder that is at once constitutive of, and foreign to, the *corpus Platonicum*. The philosopher, in the end, seeks not to hold up a mirror to nature but to reflect on and through it so as to fashion it and ourselves anew.

## Works Cited

Annas, Julia. 1993. *The Morality of Happiness*. New York: Oxford University Press.

Allen, Danielle S. 2000. *The World of Prometheus: The Politics of Punishing in Democratic Athens*. Princeton: Princeton University Press.

Alliez, Eric. 1992. "Ontologie et logographie. La pharmacie, Platon et le simulacre." *Nos Grecs et leurs modernes*. Ed. Barbara Cassin. Paris: Seuil. 211–31.

Berger, Harry, Jr. 2005. "The Athenian Terrorist: Plato's Portrayal of Critias." *Situated Utterances: Texts and Cultural Representations*. New York: Fordham University Press. 455–89.

68 THEORY DOES NOT EXIST

Blondell, Ruby. 2002. *The Play of Character in Plato's Dialogues*. Cambridge: Cambridge University Press.

Boussoulas, Nicolas-Isidore. 1952. *L'être et la composition des mixtes dans le <<Philèbe>> de Platon*. Paris: Presses Universitaires de France.

Brisson, Luc. 1998. *Plato the Mythmaker*. Trans and Ed. Gerard Nadaff. Chicago: University of Chicago Press.

Castel-Bouchouchi, Anissa. 2003. "Foucault et le paradoxe du platonisme." *Foucault et la philosophie antique*. Eds. Frédéric Gros et Carlos Lévy. Paris: Kimé, 2003. 175–93.

Copjec, Joan. 2002. *Imagine There's No Woman: Ethics and Sublimation*. Cambridge, MA: MIT Press.

Deleuze, Gilles, and Félix Guattari. 2005. *Qu'est-ce que la philosophie?* Paris: Minuit.

Derrida, Jacques. 1967. "Cogito et *Histoire de la Folie*." *L'écriture et la différence*. Paris: Seuil. 51–97

———. 1972. "La pharmacie de Platon." *La dissémination*. Paris: Seuil. 74–196.

———. 1980. *La Carte Postale: de Socrate à Freud et au-delà*. Paris: Aubier-Flammarion.

———. 1981. "Plato's Pharmacy." *Dissemination*. Trans. Barbara Johnson. Chicago: University of Chicago Press. 61–171.

———. 1992. "Nous autres Grecs." *Nos Grecs et leurs modernes*. Ed. Barbara Cassin. Paris: Seuil. 251–73.

———. 1993a. *Khôra*. Paris: Galilée.

———. 1993b. *Spectres de Marx*. Paris: Galilée.

———. 1994. *Politiques de l'amitié, suivi de L'oreille de Heidegger*. Paris: Galilée.

———. 1995. "Khôra." Trans. Ian McLeod. *On the Name*. Ed. Thomas Dutoit. Stanford: Stanford University Press.

Derrida, Jacques and Elisabeth Roudinesco. 2001. *De quoi demain … : Dialogue*. Paris: Fayard/Galilée.

Diès, Auguste. 1966. "Notice." *Platon: Philèbe*. Paris: Société d'Edition <<Les Belles Lettres>>. vii–cxii. Original = 1941.

Ferrari, G. R. F. 1987. *Listening to the Cicadas: A Study of Plato's* Phaedrus. Cambridge: Cambridge University Press.

Festugière, A. J. 1950. *Contemplation et vie contemplative selon Platon*. 2nd ed. Paris: Vrin. Original, 1935.

Foucault, Michel, 1986. *The Use of Pleasures*. Volume 2 of *History of Sexuality*. Trans. Robert Hurley. New York Pantheon.

Frede, Dorothea. 1992. "Disintegration and Integration: Pleasure and Pain in Plato's *Philebus*." *The Cambridge Companion to Plato*. Ed. Richard Kraut. Cambridge: Cambridge University Press. 425–63.

Freud, Sigmund. 1961. *Beyond the Pleasure Principle*. Trans. James Strachey. The Standard Edition. New York: Norton.

Gadamer, Hans-Georg. 1988. "Reply to Nicholas P. White." Trans. Robert C. Norton and Dennis J. Schmidt. *Platonic Writings, Platonic Readings*. Ed. Charles L. Griswold, Jr. New York: Routledge. 258–66.

———. 1991. *Plato's Dialectical Ethics: Phenomenological Interpretations Relating to the Philebus*. Trans. Robert M. Wallace. New Haven: Yale University Press.

Gosling, J. C. B. 1975. *Plato: Philebus, Translated with Notes and Commentary*. Oxford: Clarendon Press.

Hadot, Pierre. 1995. *Qu'est-ce que la philosophie antique?* Paris: Gallimard.

Hampton, Cynthia. 1990. *Pleasure, Knowledge and Being: An Analysis of Plato's Philebus*. Albany: SUNY Press.

Hunter, Richard. 2004. *Plato's Symposium*. Oxford: Oxford University Press.

Irigaray, Luce. 1974. *Speculum, De l'autre femme*. Paris: Minuit.

Koyré, Alexandre. 1962. *Introduction à la lecture de Platon, suivi de Entretiens sur Descartes*. Paris: Gallimard.

## THE PLATONIC REMAINDER

Leonard, Miriam. 2000. "The 'Politiques de l'amitié': Derrida's Greeks and a national politics of classical scholarship." *Proceedings of The Cambridge Philological Society* 46: 45–78.

———. 2005. *Athens in Paris: Ancient Greece and the Political in Post-War French Thought.* Oxford: Oxford University Press.

Loraux, Nicole. 1996. *Né de la terre: Mythe et politique à Athènes.* Paris: Seuil.

McCabe, Mary Margaret. 1994. *Plato's Individuals.* Princeton: Princeton University Press.

Miller, Paul Allen. 2007. *Postmodern Spiritual Practices: The Construction of the Subject and the Reception of Plato in Lacan, Derrida, and Foucault.* Columbus: Ohio State University Press.

Nails, Deborah. 2002. *The People of Plato.* Indianapolis: Hackett.

Nehamas, Alexander. 1998. *The Art of Living: Socratic Reflections from Plato to Foucault.* Berkeley: University of California Press.

Nightingale, Andrea Wilson. 1995. *Genres in Dialogue: Plato and the Construct of Philosophy.* Cambridge: Cambridge University Press.

Oudemans, Th. C. W. and A. P. M. H. Lardinois. 1987. *Tragic Ambiguity: Anthropology, Philosophy, and Sophocles' Antigone.* Leiden: Brill.

Rivaud, Albert. 1963. "Notice." *Platon: Timée.* Paris: Société d'Edition <<Les Belles Lettres>>. 3–123. Original = 1925.

Robin, Léon. 1985. "Notice." *Platon: Phèdre.* Paris: Société d'Edition <<Les Belles Lettres>>. vii–ccv. Original = 1933.

Sallis, John. 1998. "Daydream." *Revue internationale de philosophie* 52: 397–410.

———. 1999. *Chorology: On Beginning in Plato's Timaeus.* Bloomington: Indiana University Press.

Szelizák, Thomas A. 1999. *Reading Plato.* Trans. Graham Zanker. London: Routledge. Original 1993.

Vernant, Jean-Pierre. 1974. *Mythe et société en Grèce ancienne.* Paris: Maspero.

Vlastos, Gregory. 1991. *Socrates, Ironist and Moral Philosopher.* Ithaca, NY: Cornell University Press.

Wallace, Robert W. 1991. "Introduction." Hans-Georg Gadamer. 1991. *Plato's Dialectical Ethics: Phenomenological Interpretations Relating to the Philebus.* Trans. Robert M. Wallace. New Haven: Yale University Press. ix–xxiii.

Wolff, Francis. 1992. "Trios. Deleuze, Derrida, Foucault, historiens du platonisme." *Nos Grecs et leurs modernes.* Ed. Barbara Cassin. Paris: Seuil. 232–48.

Zuckert, Catherine H. 1996. *Postmodern Platos: Nietzsche, Heidegger, Gadamer, Strauss, Derrida.* Chicago: University of Chicago Press.

# Chapter 6

# CICERO READS DERRIDA READING CICERO: A POLITICS AND A FRIENDSHIP TO COME[1]

The reciprocal possession and fusion toward which the tender tend, is nothing other than an (unnatural) principle of perversion at the heart of the natural law of attraction and repulsion. We could compare it to the death drive or to a demonic principle. It would come to haunt virtue. If it were really thus, friendship would both be the sign, the symptom, the representative of this possible perversion, and what guards us against it. (Derrida 1994: 287) [2]

Therefore, firm, stable, and constant men are to be chosen, of which type there is a great shortage. And it is difficult to judge truly except through experience. However, it is necessary to have the experience in friendship itself. So, friendship runs ahead of judgment and takes away the power of experiential testing. (Cicero, *Laelius, De Amicitia* 62)

In 1994, Derrida published the *Politics of Friendship*, a major work that followed on the heels of 1993's *Specters of Marx* and *Khora*. The latter two, while generally considered among Derrida's most important statements on Marx and Plato, were also, as he acknowledges, long deferred continuations of dialogues begun in his seminar twenty years prior. As I have shown (2016: chapter 2), *Specters of Marx* and *Khora* while possessed of undoubtedly complex genealogies, in many ways represent a settling of accounts with Julia Kristeva, Philippe Sollers, and the editorial collective that surrounded the avant-garde journal, *Tel Quel*. In the early 1970s, in the wake of the failed May 68 student uprising in Paris, political turmoil swept the lecture halls and seminar rooms of France. Many, searching for an authentically revolutionary alternative to the failed model of Soviet Marxism, turned to Mao's theory of cultural revolution. When Derrida refused to commit himself, there was a quiet but decisive break with *Tel Quel*.[3] As a result, the once fast friends, Derrida, Sollers, and Kristeva, never spoke again, even once Sollers and Kristeva renounced politics upon their return from China (de Nooy 1998: 79–80, 90–91; Peeters 2010: 221–22, 263–292, 419–20). In 1993, Derrida revisited the themes of his 1970 seminar, as he acknowledges in a note to *Khôra* (1993b: 101–02n7), giving his final pronouncement on his debate with Kristeva on the status of Plato's use of the term *khōra* in the *Timaeus* and publishing for the first time a full-fledged reading of

---

1   This paper is dedicated to the friends I think about each and every day.
2   All translations are my own, unless otherwise noted.
3   See for example the politically charged interview with Guy Scarpetta and Jean-Louis Houdebine reprinted in *Positions* (1972b: 51–133).

72                              THEORY DOES NOT EXIST

Marx in *Specters of Marx* (1993a). Old debates and the specter of lost friends were clearly on his mind.

The following year, in 1994, Derrida published the aptly titled *Politics of Friendship*, a book about the history of the concept of friendship in the west from Plato to Blanchot by way of Cicero, Montaigne, Nietzsche and Carl Schmitt.[4] It is also a book about the inseparability of politics from a concept of both the friend and its mirror image, the enemy (Derrida 1994: 91). And it is a book that returns again and again to a possibly apocryphal saying of Aristotle's recorded by Diogenes Laertius (5.21), "Oh my friends, there is no friend,"[5] an adage subsequently cited by Montaigne, Nietzsche, and Blanchot. The true friend, as the saying makes apparent, is the (all but) impossible exception (Derrida 1994: 19, citing Cicero, *Laelius de Amicitia* 22). That rare true friend is portrayed throughout much of the tradition as a veritable second self, as the other of myself who reflects my self to myself (cf. Pangle 2003: 66, 70). And yet my friend, as friend, remains other. And insofar as my friend remains other, he or she, as my second self, has the potential to call the integrity, the sufficiency, of my self into question. There is a potential violence in friendship: a violence that recalls the passion of love.

Thus, Derrida notes, Cicero observes both that *amicitia* receives its name from love (*amor*) and that each sets the soul aflame (*exardescit*) (*Laelius de Amicitia*, 26, 100, cited by Derrida 1994: 195).[6] Yet, the flames of passion only too easily become those of hatred. The context for Derrida's observation is a discussion of Montaigne's retelling of Cicero's anecdote about Gaius Blossius and the revolutionary tribune Tiberius

---

4   Pangle 2003 covers many of the same authors referring to them as "a single tradition" (5). Her evaluation of the *Politics of Friendship* as simply contending that "we should befriend everyone" (192) fails to come to grips with Derrida's text.

5   "ὤ φίλοι, οὐδεὶς φίλος." This is the reading of all the manuscripts. Diogenes is here citing a collection of Aristotle's sayings assembled by Phavorinos. Thus is also the reading of all the texts in the philosophical tradition that Derrida cites: "Montaigne, Florian, Kant, Nietzsche, Blanchot, Deguy" (1994: 219). And it is the preferred reading of the translations he cites: Genaille's 1965 edition in French, an 1806 edition in German cited without the author, and Ortiz y Sainz's 1985 Spanish translation (Derrida 1994: 219–220n1), although he is aware of others (1994: 236–37). Nonetheless, most modern philological editions follow Causabon's emendation to "ᾧ φίλοι, οὐδεὶς φίλος," meaning the man who has many friends has none. See Marcovich (1999), with his apparatus; Huebnerus (1981), with his commentary; Long (1964); and Hicks (1925). This emendation, as Derrida (1994: 237), notes is based on the next sentence in Diogenes, which says "but it is also in the seventh book of Aristotle's ethics." Unfortunately, nothing like the sentiment of the famous interjection can be found in either the *Nicomachean* or the *Eudemian Ethics*. Nonetheless, the notion that real friends are rare and that one who has many friends has no real friends is common in both works. In the end, Derrida (1994: 241–44) argues that the differences between the two versions are less than they first appear, since both emphasize the rarity of true friendship in a context that simultaneously acknowledges the (plural) existence of people we call "friends." Derrida primarily refers to the first, what he calls the "canonical," version throughout the *Politics of Friendship*, both because this is the dominant version that has gone into the philosophical tradition and presumably because he appreciates the aporia at the heart of its "performative contradiction" (1994: 240).

6   I follow Derrida and cite Robert Combès's 1971 Budé edition.

# CICERO READS DERRIDA READING CICERO

Gracchus. The question in the original dialogue is how far should love (*amor*) go in friendship (*amicitia*) (*Laelius de Amicitia*, 36), even to the point of treason? Blossius, in the aftermath of Gracchus's murder at the hands of a senatorial mob, is asked by Laelius, the main speaker of the dialogue, if his friendship with Gracchus would have extended all the way to burning down the Capitol, should the latter have demanded it. Blossius replies, "He never would have wanted that, but if he had, I would have obeyed." In this passage, the fire of love and the fire of treason momentarily become one. A single will unites these two friends, who nonetheless remain forever separate, torn apart by political murder. As Derrida comments, "The friendship between these two men who are like brothers, that too is the passion of love" (1994: 211). Laelius condemns Blossius's answer: true friendship, he contends, is to be founded on virtue.

> Nulla est igitur excusatio peccati si amici causa peccaveris; nam cum conciliatrix amicitiae virtutis opinio fuerit, difficile est amicitiam manere si a virtute defeceris. (37)

> Therefore, there is no excuse for evil if you did it for the sake of a friend, for since an impression of virtue was what brought the friendship together, it is difficult for friendship to continue if you should be lacking in virtue.

Nonetheless, who could say Blossius was not, in fact, a true friend of Gracchus, Blossius who, as Laelius admits, stayed when others abandoned him (*a ... amicis derelictum*)? Montaigne, by contrast, who recounts this same tale, praises Blossius's response, because the perfect friend both knows and ultimately controls the will of the other – who is after all a second self (1962: 188). He would never allow him to demand such a thing. And yet Blossius, as Laelius acknowledges, did in the end commit treason, fleeing to Asia and joining the rebellion of Aristonicus, after whose defeat he committed suicide. Derrida summarizes his reading of these passages in Montaigne and Cicero as follows:

> Friendship is only able to exist among good men, repeats Cicero.[7] Reason and virtue cannot be *private*. They are not able to enter into conflict with the public matter. These concepts of virtue or reason are from the beginning tailored to the space of the *res publica*. (Derrida 1994: 211, emphasis his)

But, insofar as friendship represents a passionate commitment of the self to the other as its reflection, as the other whose love enflames (*exardescit*), then it also represents the potential for burning down the temples of the state (*in Capitolium ferre faces*): for treason, subversion, and death, for virtue to become perversion.

The friend, we read, possesses the power of a love that threatens the boundaries of both the self and the community, even as it affirms them in their identity. This duality is implicit in Cicero and Montaigne, but, as Derrida observes, becomes explicit in Nietzsche and Schmitt. Friendship, from this perspective, increasingly represents the power of the other in the self, of a second self, and so, in the very instant of maximum identification between self and other, the friend (*Freund*) can become

---

7  Citing *Laelius de amicitia, nisi in bonis amicitiam esse non posse* (18).

the enemy (*Feind*). He can become the brother of absolute hostility, the other in whose death we live (Derrida 1994: 170–76, 188, 287). This is the central problem, with all its complications and overdeterminations, that Cicero's *De Amicitia* allows Derrida to explore: the friend as both a second self and a possible enemy of the state, and thus the friend as a model for a politics and friendship to come. It is along this porous boundary between friend and foe, self and other, life and death that Derrida situates the complex set of meditations that make up the *Politics of Friendship*. It is here that he founds his search for what he terms another politics and another friendship: a politics and a friendship not opposed to what has come before but beyond the opposition of self and other on which the possibility of both friendship and enmity, community and conflict have been predicated heretofore (Derrida 1993a: 68, 102; 1994: 42, 126–29, 246). "Oh my friends, there are no friends."

Derrida thus does not begin the *Politics of Friendship* with Aristotle or Plato, both of whom receive considerable attention, but with Cicero. His inquiry, while it is in a profound sense historical, tracing sets of oppositional structures that have shaped our ability to conceptualize both friendship and the political from antiquity to the present, is not chronological. Derrida begins the *Politics of Friendship* with an epigraph from Cicero that simultaneously frames the argument of the book as a whole and calls into question one of our most fundamental oppositions, that between life and death: "quocirca et absentes adsunt [...] et, quod difficilius dictu est, mortui vivunt." ["Wherefore even the absent are present [...] and, what is more difficult to say, the dead live."] (*Laelius de Amicitia* 23; Derrida 1994: 9). Nor is this epigraph an isolated quotation, a mere rhetorical flourish. The opening chapter begins with a careful reading of Cicero's text, with special emphasis on the concept of the friend as an *exemplar* of the self: a simultaneous original and copy. My friend is my likeness, and I am his reflection, we are both the same and necessarily different. For Derrida, Ciceronian friendships confound the ontological categories that normally govern our thought and hence our world, and Cicero is more than aware of the paradoxes thus created (Derrida 1994: 19–20). To quote the Cicero passage in full:

> Verum enim amicum qui intuetur, tamquam *exemplar* aliquod intuetur sui. Quocirca et absentes adsunt, et egentes abundant, et imbecilli valent, et quod difficilius dictu est, mortui vivunt: tantus eos honos, memoria, desiderium prosequitur amicorum. ex quo illorum beata mors videtur, horum vita laudabilis. (23, emphasis mine)

> For he who perceives a true friend, it is as though he perceives a *model* of himself. Wherefore the absent are present, the poor are rich, the weak are strong, and what is more difficult to say, the dead live: so great is the respect, the memory, and the desire that follows after our friends. Hence for the ones death seems happy and for the others life is worthy of praise.

Derrida's great merit in choosing this passage as his epigraph is to take Cicero at his word, not to fob off his claims as rhetorical exaggeration or derivative philosophizing, but actually to think the logic of the *exemplar* in relation to friendship, politics, and death the three great topics of Cicero's text and his own. "Those who grimace before discourses on the undecidable believe they are in a strong position, as we know, but they ought to begin by taking after a certain Cicero" (Derrida 1994: 21).

If we are to take Cicero at least as seriously as Derrida does, we would do well to remember the dramatic occasion of the dialogue. Laelius's great friend, Scipio Africanus Aemilianus, has just died under mysterious circumstances while at the height of his personal and political powers (129 BCE). Laelius's sons in-law have come to visit and inquire how he is handling his grief.

We would also do well to keep in mind that Cicero wrote the dialogue in 44 BCE, shortly after the assassination of Caesar. It was a time of political turmoil, when one's friends only too easily became one's enemies, when true friendship was especially precious and rare, and when death lurked on every side (Pangle 2003: 105).[8] *De Amicitia* is then a dialogue in which a primary speaker (long dead) speaks about his rare friendship with a great political leader and general Scipio Africanus, who has recently died. Written in the context of the recent death of another great political leader and general (Cicero's sometimes friend), it also recounts the death of other controversial political leaders (e.g., Gracchus) and their friends (e.g., Blossius). Finally, *De Amicitia* is dramatically situated as the sequel to Cicero's *De Republica*, which takes place just before the death of Scipio. Ending with Scipio's vision of the afterlife, the famous *Somnium Scipionis*, it recounts his image of the ideal constitution of the Roman republic at a time of acknowledged political strife (Nicgorski 2008). Thus politics, friendship, death, and remembrance are all deeply intertwined in *De Amicitia*, as friend and enemy, self and other, exemplar and exemplified establish complex and shifting positions in what has often been read as nothing more than a simple panegyric of friendship.

In *De Amicitia*, then, as Derrida underlines, the dead live (*mortui vivunt*). Scipio is an almost palpable presence. He lives on through Laelius, whose exemplar he is. But he is not alone. All the characters of the dialogue are long dead by 44, and yet we hear them still. Caesar is dead. Death itself lives, it threatens Cicero and the republic, but it also promises that they might live on, not quite immortal, like a god, but haunting our thoughts and our discourse, even our unconscious assumptions, as exemplars of themselves. Only their death makes this afterlife possible. Exemplarity depends on finitude. "A friendship, of the Ciceronian kind, would be the possibility of citing myself in an exemplary manner, by signing in advance my own funeral oration, the best, perhaps, but it is never certain that the friend will pronounce it standing on his own feet when I will no longer be" (Derrida 1994: 21). Such a friendship between immortals would be inconceivable. They do not live in our memory. Without death, friendship as we understand it, would not exist, nor would enmity.

Perhaps then we should take Derrida at his word too: there is a reason why Cicero leads off the *Politics of Friendship*. It too is a haunted text. Haunted by the friends who

---

8   For many years one of the commonest translations of *amicitia* was "political alliance." While more recent scholarship and Cicero's own work shows that this was an oversimplification, the Roman republican elite were highly politicized and friendships, though certainly not excluding genuine affection, were often as much or more the product of expediency as they were of the true and perfect friendship Laelius emphasizes in the dialogue (22). See Brunt (1988) for a good overview and Konstan (1997: 122–48). The politics of friendship for the Roman elite was less a paradox than a truism.

are no longer friends – "oh my friends, there are no friends!" – haunted by the friends who are no more: the text alludes to the death of Paul de Man and ends with Blanchot's powerful confession of his friendship for Foucault, a friendship that could only be declared after his death. Blanchot's silent friendship is, in some ways, Derrida's as well. He and Foucault had been close. Foucault had been his tutor at the École normale supérieure. They had fallen out at the end of the sixties, not spoken for years, only to be reconciled shortly before Foucault's death (Peeters 2010: 492; cf. Miller 2007: chap. 4). "Without trying to hide it, you will have understood it, I would like to speak here about the men and women with whom a rare friendship has bound me: that is to say I also want to speak to *them*" (Derrida 1994: 335, emphasis, his).

The specters that haunt Derrida's text are not just those of past political and intellectual struggles, friends who are no longer friends, Sollers and Kristeva, and friends who are no more, de Man and Foucault, but also the promise of a friendship to come, one that exceeds politics, that exceeds the constraints of communal life. Such a friendship is by definition not present, yet not wholly absent, if it is still to come, if there is a place for it to come. It is exemplified by those moments of the past that while no longer fully present possess the promise of a future: Scipio and Laelius, Cicero and Atticus, Montaigne and La Boétie, Blanchot and Foucault. It is a friendship that in the very moment of constituting the affective bonds that both produce and are formed by the communal, have the potential to posit a politics to come, one which would truly be a politics of friendship as the search for justice, for virtue, and ultimately for "a certain democracy, which would no longer be an insult to the friendship we have tried to think" (1994: 340). This is the struggle for a justice, a politics, and a friendship to come that is never quite present, but not unreal. "Oh my friends, there are no friends."

This friendship to come, like that evoked so movingly by Laelius when speaking of Scipio, adheres to a spectral logic that Derrida had described the year before in *Specters of Marx* as a form of transcendence that exceeds the oppositional categories of presence and absence, being and nonbeing:

> To be just: beyond the living present in general – and its simple negative inverse. Spectral moment, a moment that no longer pertains to time, if one understands by this noun the linkage of modalized presents (past present, actual present: "now," future present). [...] Furtive and tempestuous, the apparition of the specter does not pertain to this time, it does not give the time, *"Enter the Ghost, exit the Ghost, re-enter the Ghost" (Hamlet)*. (Derrida 1993a: 17, emphasis his)

The search for justice – to be just – is the search for this friendship to come. Nonetheless, the demarcation of friend from foe, what Carl Schmitt – as cited by Derrida – describes as the origin of the political, always threatens to overturn the moment that determines friendship into its opposite, into a moment of struggle, hostility, and even death (1994: 95, 103, 176). Friendship comes to be, comes to be most fully in the moment of death, when it is gone, and yet the dead live on, as our exemplar, as our promise of justice to come (*à venir*). This logic of a future possibility, which inheres in the past, and which is never quite present, is what Derrida punningly refers to in *Specters of Marx* as an "hauntologie," "neither living nor dead, neither present nor absent, but [...] a specter. It is not a matter

# CICERO READS DERRIDA READING CICERO

of ontology, of a discourse on the being of being, on the essence of life or death" (Derrida 1993a: 89). But this logic is exactly what Cicero articulates in the passage Derrida uses as his opening epigraph the following year to describe the phenomenon of true friendship as a moment irreducible to the demands of the present, the facts of the past, or a future already determined in its being (Derrida 1994: 46–47, 54–55, 86–88).

There is then nothing accidental in Derrida's choice of Cicero to begin the *Politics of Friendship*. In many ways, it is the perfect text for the complex meditation on friendship, politics, enmity, and death, which follows. Nonetheless, the text with which Derrida opens his discussion, and to which he refers throughout the course of the book, has been all but neglected in the literature on Derrida and on Cicero's reception.[9] This does both texts short shrift. Each of them is more complex and more personal than has been generally realized.

*De Amicitia*, like *The Politics of Friendship*, is from the beginning predicated on the possibility of at least a double reading (cf. Laurand 1928: 8n2). In his preface, Cicero tell us that he is responding to the request of his dearest friend, Atticus to write a work on friendship, with obvious reference to their own (4). *De Amicitia* is his response to that request. Notwithstanding the elaborate story of how Cicero came to know the contents of Laelius's discourse on friendship, which will be discussed below, it strains credibility to believe that even if such a conversation did in fact take place that Scaevola, Laelius's son-in-law, would have transmitted it to Cicero intact, or that Cicero would have remembered that transmission with anything approaching detailed accuracy forty-four years later. We are clearly dealing with a literary construction and one that in the first instance responds to the request of Cicero's friend for such a text (Combès 1971: ix–xxvii). Consequently, everything said by Laelius of his relationship with Scipio and the political conflicts that characterized the end of second century may also be read as a commentary on Cicero's friendship with Atticus and on the politics of his day.

As Cicero explains in a passage worthy of Derrida:

> Tu uelim a me animum parumper auertas, Laelium loqui ipsum putes. C. Fannius et Q. Mucius ad socerum ueniunt post mortem Africani; ab his sermo oritur, respondet Laelius, cuius tota disputatio est de amicitia, quam legens te ipse cognosces. (5)

---

9 Derrida's reception of antiquity has been a topic of increasing interest in recent years, see inter alia Zuckert 1996, Miller 1999, Leonard 2000, Leonard 2005, Miller 2007, and Leonard's edited volume, *Derrida and Antiquity* 2010. Most of these efforts focus on Derrida's reception of Greek philosophy in texts like "La pharmacie de Platon" (1972a), *La carte postale* (1980), "Nous autres Grecs" (1990), and *Khôra* (1993b). His engagement with the Latin tradition has been largely ignored. Leonard's 2010 volume does contain one essay on his use of the Latin Christian tradition, but only passing mentions of Cicero. Konstan (1997) acknowledges Derrida's text (10) and has a brief discussion of Cicero (130–37) but the two are not connected. Von Heyking and Avramenko's (2008) collection features a discussion of the relationship between *De Republica* and *De Amicitia* (Nicgorski 2008), and briefer mentions of *The Politics of Friendship* (Salkever 2008: 72; Avrameko 2008: 304–06; Gebhardt 2008: 341–42), but again the connection between the two works is never drawn. The sole work to discuss Derrida's reading of Cicero is Lau (2007: 419).

I would wish you to turn your attention a little away from me; you should think Laelius himself is speaking. C. Fannius and Q. Mucius come to their father-in-law after the death of Africanus; the conversation begins with them, Laelius responds. His whole discourse is about friendship. When reading it, you will recognize yourself.

Through the deliberate act of turning your attention, or more literally your soul (*animum*) from me, you should perform the act of thinking/imagining that Laelius (long dead) is speaking, and in performing this act while reading you will know/recognize yourself. Or as Derrida himself said, "Without trying to hide it, you will have understood it, I would like to speak here about the men and women with whom a rare friendship has bound me: that is to say I also want to speak to *them*." But in fact Cicero says more here than just you will know I am speaking to and about you when you read Laelius's discourse, as Derrida invites us to imagine he is speaking to and about his friends when we read his discussion of Blanchot on the death of Foucault. Cicero also says that in performing the imaginative act of believing Laelius rather than Cicero is speaking, Atticus will recognize himself, meaning at least three things, which are not mutually exclusive. 1.) Atticus will recognize that Laelius is talking about Atticus (rather than Scipio), in which case he will see that Laelius actually is Cicero, in spite of the imaginative act of thinking otherwise. 2.) Atticus will recognize Laelius as himself, in which case he will see that Laelius is actually talking about Cicero. These two options, however, are really the same. Insofar as the friend is the exemplar of the friend, an embodiment of the self in the other, and hence the one lives on in the other even after death, then each can recognize themselves in the other, and in so far as Laelius is the avatar of the one he is also the avatar of the other. Thus, Derrida defines "the exemplar, that Ciceronian model of friendship with which we decided to begin" as both the "original and the reproducible type, the face and its mirror, the one and the other" (1994: 189).

The third option is actually the most literal, but also the most complex. Atticus will, in reading the dialogue, quite literally come to know himself. It is only through the exteriorization of the self, through the exemplary value of the friend, but also through the imaginative act of turning one's spirit (*avertere animum*) that we come to see ourselves in the mirror of the other. Cicero's text in its ability to bring back the dead, to allow the specter of Laelius to evoke the specter of Scipio, and then to invite each of us to transpose ourselves into those spaces, even as we recognize our difference from those spaces, opens up a new dimension which is not of the order of being (ontology) but represents its transcendence and its promise (hauntology). And it is this dimension of future possibility – rooted in the attachments of the past – that is the promise of friendship both on the level of the individual and the community. The friend as a second self who crosses the categories of being opens up new possibilities of existence, creating new forms of self-recognition and hence self-transformation.

Self-knowledge and self-transformation, moreover, have been the fundamental mission of philosophy – i.e., the pursuit of wisdom (*sophia*) as its friend (*philos*) – since the time of Socrates. Thus, much of the *Apology* centers on Socrates' attempt to understand the Delphic oracle's response to Chaerophon that Socrates is the wisest of men. The latter is initially puzzled by the oracle since he knows that he "knows nothing either great or small" (21b4–5), and so Socrates sets out to refute it by going to those who do seem to know something and proving that they are wiser than he. In each case, however, those that seem to have divine wisdom are shown not to have it but to be deluded, since they think they know what they do not. After a number of these encounters, Socrates concludes that he truly *is* the wisest of men, because at least he knows that he knows nothing. Moreover, in coming to that knowledge, he in fact fulfills the Delphic oracle's primary injunction: *gnōthi seauton*, "know yourself."[10] The beginning of wisdom, the beginning of its pursuit, and hence its love (*philia*), Socrates teaches us, comes with the knowledge of one's own lack, a knowledge which comes not from solitary introspection but from the questioning of others and from the self-reflection that results from the encounter with the other (Hadot 1995: 56–57, 103; Blondell 2002: 100). This is the lesson of both the *Apology* and the *Symposium*. The friend is a special case of this moment of self-reflection through the other, as evoked in the famous passage from the *Alcibiades* where knowledge of one's own soul is said to be acquired through looking into the soul of another, in the same way that one sees one's own reflection by staring into the eyes of the other (132c–133b).[11] But this is a lesson perhaps most strongly made by Cicero's logic of the friend as an *exemplar* of the self.

It is no accident, then, that Socrates' proclamation as the wisest of men is cited twice right at the beginning of *De Amicitia*, immediately after the passage in which Atticus is told that if he imagines that he hears Laelius rather than Cicero speaking in the dialogue, he will not only recognize himself, and hence their friendship, but he will also come to know himself. The first citation comes at the very opening of the dialogue. Fannius directly compares Laelius, who was known as *sapiens* ("the wise, the philosopher"), to Socrates, saying that Socrates alone of the Greeks was truly wise and that he "had been judged the wisest by the oracle of Apollo" (7). Similarly, he claims that Laelius alone of the Romans is known as *sapiens* in this comprehensive sense.

> te ... non solum natura et moribus, verum etiam studio et doctrina esse sapientem, nec sicut volgus, sed ut eruditi solent appellare sapientem, qualem in reliqua Graecia neminem ... Athenis unum accepimus, et eum quidem etiam Apollinis oraculo sapientissimum iudicatum: hanc esse in te sapientiam existimant, ut omnia tua in te posita esse ducas, humanosque casus virtute inferiores putes. (6–7)

> They judge you wise not only in your nature and habits but also in your study and learning, not just as the crowd is accustomed to call someone wise, but as the learned do. We find no one like this in the rest of Greece. ... We recognize one in Athens, and this one indeed was judged the wisest by the oracle of Apollo. They believe that this Socratic wisdom is in you, with the result that you consider all your possessions to be lodged inside and you judge all human affairs of less value than virtue.

---

10  Cf. *Phaedrus* 230A.

11  Cf. *Phaedrus* 255b7–d6. "To submit to a mutual research, to search to know oneself through the detour and the language of the other, such is the operation that Socrates, recalling what the translator names the 'lesson of Delphi' (*tou Delphikou grammatos*), presents to Alcibiades as the antidote (*alexipharmakon*), the counter-potion (*Alcibiades* 132b)" (Derrida 1972a: 138).

80                              THEORY DOES NOT EXIST

Immediately afterward, Laelius repeats this same formula for naming Socrates, *istum quidem ipsum quem Apollo, ut ais, sapientissimum iudicavit* ["that very one indeed whom, as you say, Apollo judged the wisest man"] (10). Laelius, however, modestly refuses the title of *sapiens* in deference to the elder Cato, contending that Fannius should not place Socrates himself before Cato, since men praise the former's words but the latter's deeds.

This periphrastic formula for naming Socrates is used a third time but a few pages later when Laelius is discussing his views of the possibility of an afterlife, with reference to the death of Scipio. Laelius notes that he does not agree with the "recent Epicurean contention that the soul is destroyed with the body." Laelius trusts rather in the implicit wisdom of ancient Roman ancestor worship, in the practices of the Pythagoreans, and in the contention "eius qui Apollonis oraculo sapientissimus est iudicatus" ["of him who was judged the wisest by the oracle of Apollo"] that the soul is immortal (13). *De Amicitia* thus begins clearly under the sign of Socratic philosophy, and specifically under that canonized by the judgment of Apollo, naming Socrates as wisest of men because he knows what he does not know. He is possessed of the self-knowledge that comes from the ability to know the self through the encounter with the other, to become the friend of wisdom through the encounter with an exemplar of the self, and through that encounter to live on after death, as Scipio does himself.

Being the friend of wisdom (*philo-sophos*), then, in the first instance for Socrates involves self-knowledge. That self-knowledge takes place most directly through the encounter with the other, whether through dialectical questioning as exemplified in the *Apology*, through the beautiful boy or *erōmenos* in the *Phaedrus* and *Symposium*, or through the eyes of the mature friend and companion in the *Alcibiades*. In *De Amicitia*, this reflective or exemplary function is taken over most crucially by the friend in Laelius's speech and the double reading of it by Atticus, who sees himself and Cicero reflected in the dialogue and its characters. Those characters, in turn, exercise a reflective and exemplary function for the reader that like the friend bears a transverse relation to the most basic ontological categories of presence versus absence, living versus dead, that structure our existence. That is to say that, rather than falling squarely within those categories, the logic of the *exemplar* cuts across them, denying their mutual exclusivity and opening new possibilities of thought and existence.[12]

The practice of friendship is thus a profoundly philosophical act, but philosophy too is always haunted by the friend, by the absent presence of our founding affections. Indeed, as Derrida notes, friendship and philosophy have long been associated in the western tradition, from Plato's *Lysis* to Schmitt on war, politics, and the enemy:

> Friendship as philosophy, philosophy as friendship, philosophical friendship, friendship-philosophy will have always been in the West a concept indissociable in itself: no friendship without *philosophia*, no philosophy without *philia*. Friendship-philosophy: from the beginning we are inquiring about the politics *around* this hyphen. (Derrida 1994: 168, emphasis his)

One of Derrida's main interests, then, is in the politics that inhabit the joining of friendship with philosophy, whether in the case of his friendships with Kristeva, Sollers,

---

12  On the "syncategoreme" in Derrida, see Courtine (2008).

## CICERO READS DERRIDA READING CICERO

de Man, and Foucault or with those of Blossius and Gracchus, Scipio and Laelius, or Cicero and Atticus. And *De Amicitia* is precisely the text with which to open any such inquiry both in terms of its identification of friendship as a particular practice of philosophy and in terms of the politics that characterize the time of its writing, its dramatic context, and its direct thematic content.

Cicero's view of friendship is of particular interest to Derrida, as we have seen, precisely because of the way it cuts across traditional ontological categories, pointing to a position beyond the normative binary oppositions that structure them. Such a moment is of particular importance to Derrida's political thought because it points to the possibility of a radically new future. This is the argumentative level on which *The Politics of Friendship* represents a direct continuation of *Specters of Marx*. The spectral is a moment from the past that possesses a contradictory relation to the present and hence an openness to the future. Like Scipio in *De Amicitia* and the specter of communism at the beginning of the *Manifesto*, it is both present and absent. The spectral opens up the possibility for the emergence of that which is truly new, of what Derrida labels the "peut-être"[13]: the access to a dimension beyond simple facticity and its negation that can never be reduced to a pregiven teleology (1994: 54–55, 86).

At the joining point of these two contradictory impulses, which are nonetheless always-associated one with the other, philosophy and friendship, Derrida sees the possibility of such an opening. On the one hand, philosophy and virtue are always understood as embodying universal and hence public, as opposed to private, idiosyncratic values. And insofar as these values *are* public and thus serve to regulate exchanges and power relations between individuals (friends, colleagues, opponents) and/or groups of individuals (citizens, coworkers, enemies), they are inherently political (Derrida 1994: 211). On the other, the great friendships, which are cited again and again throughout history – Orestes and Pylades, Scipio and Laelius, Cicero and Atticus, Montaigne and La Boétie – are always dual and hence profoundly private. They are repeated exemplary pairs. "Citations of citations, therefore, on the subject of the possibility of citing the great friendships, the true ones. Even if they are more than two, the model (*exemplar*) will most often be furnished by a dual, by certain great couples of friends" (Derrida 1994: 96). Friendships are thus for both Cicero and Derrida unique private experiences grounded in an aspiration to the universal, and hence they are at once moments of great political peril (Blossius and Gracchus) and promise (Scipio and Laelius).

Democracy itself, Derrida argues, is situated at the crux of these same competing values of singularity and universalism.

> The question of democracy is opened in this fashion, the question of the citizen or the subject as a countable singularity. And that of a "universal fraternity." No democracy without the respect of singularity or of irreducible alterity, but no democracy without a "community of friends" (*koina ta philōn*), without the calculation of majorities, without identifiable, stabilizable, representable subjects who are equal among themselves. These two laws are irreducible one to the other. Tragically irreconcilable and forever wounding. (1994: 40)

---

13  The French for "perhaps," but more literally "is able to be."

82 THEORY DOES NOT EXIST

This same crux also characterizes the search through philosophy for self-knowledge. For such knowledge is, in the end, the search for the exemplary, reproducible self of virtue, the self reflected in the other: the friend. The care of the self is the care of the soul, of that within that does not fully die, of the specter, and hence of what is at once most authentically our own and what transcends our singularity. There is then a spectral hauntology, which lies at the base of friendship, philosophy, and democracy: the promise of a future that is at once radically particular (rooted in the affections of the past) and open to all and hence universalizable – a politics of friendship. "Oh my friends, there are no friends." And this possibility of a future is what Cicero's dialogue and its initial framing promise as well, even as it mourns the lost promises of the past, even as it is aware that every demarcation of friend from foe, of self from other, of citizen from alien is a violent wounding gesture, whose promise for tomorrow's survival is dependent on death today.

It is unsurprising, then, that Cicero's response to Atticus's request for him to praise (their) friendship is framed in terms of an ironic anecdote, one which is not about the ability of friendship to overcome all obstacles or transcend political differences, but about death and alienation. It tells how the friendship of Publius Sulpicius with the consul Quintus Pompeius Rufus suffered a fatal breach when the latter became tribune of the people during the Social Wars (91–87 BCE). Publius Sulpicius, Atticus's cousin by marriage, supported citizens' rights for the Italian allies and had allied himself with Gaius Marius and the cause of the people (*populares*). His former fast friend, Q. Pompeius Rufus, consul in 88 BCE, was a supporter of the aristocratic senatorial faction and allied himself with Sulla, his colleague in the consulship. With the aid of Marius, Sulpicius was able to pass a series of radical reform laws, but after Sulla marched on Rome, Sulpicius was captured and executed. Nonetheless, Pompeius was not saved. In the aftermath of Sulla's march on Rome and the slaughter of his political enemies, the consul, Pompeius Rufus, was killed by the soldiers of his cousin, Gnaeus Pompeius Strabo, when he tried to supersede the latter in their command. The whole of this story of friendship, politics, and death is invoked, in what seems an almost passing manner at the beginning of the dialogue to describe how Cicero came to know of the story of Laelius's discourse on his friendship with the recently deceased Scipio. But it also serves as a gloss on its subject matter. If Scipio and Laelius are the positive analogues to Cicero and Atticus, Sulpicius and Pompeius are their negative reflections in a time of civil war:

Memnisti enim profecto, Attice, et eo magis, quod P. Sulpicio utebare multum, cum is, tribunus plebis, capitali odio a Q. Pompeio, qui tum erat consul, dissideret, quocum coniunctissime et amantissime uixerat, quanta esset hominum uel admiratio uel querela. Itaque tum Scaevola, cum in eam ipsam mentionem incidisset, exposuit nobis sermonem Laeli de amicitia, habitum ab illo secum et cum altero genero, C. Fannio, Marci filio, paucis diebus post mortem Africani (2–3)

For you, Atticus, truly remember all the more, because you were often in Publius Sulpicius's company, how great was either the wonder or the complaint, when he as tribune of the people opposed with a deadly hatred Quintus Pompeius, who was then consul and with whom he had lived in the greatest possible familiarity and with the greatest possible love. And thus, Scaevola, when he had happened to mention this fact, revealed to us the discourse

CICERO READS DERRIDA READING CICERO            83

Laelius had held concerning friendship, when both he was present and Laelius's other son-in-law Gaius Fannius, the son of Marcus, a few days after the death of Africanus.

In the guise of motivating his knowledge of a dialogue that occurred before he was born (129 BCE), Cicero plunges us into a world of deadly politics, individual personalities, complex relations of friendship, enmity, family and other forms of filiation that were a mirror of his own troubled time.[14] The choice of this particular anecdote, moreover, is especially appropriate since it was the death of Sulpicius and the danger it exposed, that led Atticus to withdraw from politics and move to Athens for twenty years (85–65 BCE), whence came the cognomen by which he is popularly known.

*De Amicitia* begins, then, not with friendship per se but with death. Laelius is known as "the wise" (*sapiens*). He is said by Fannius to have both the practical wisdom of the Romans and the learned wisdom of the Greeks, and hence to be, as we have seen, a Roman Socrates. Given this reputation, people are asking Fannius and Scaevola, how Laelius is bearing up under the death of Scipio. Death and friendship are joined from the beginning of the dialogue. It seems Laelius has been absent from the most recent meeting of the College of the Augurs, Rome's official body of diviners, and the question asked is whether he was too stricken with grief to attend. Laelius assents to Scaevola's suggestion that his absence was because he was ill not because he was grief stricken. But he then disclaims the wisdom Fannius attributes to him, saying that he clearly is speaking as a friend (*amice*), but if wisdom should be attributed to anyone it should be to Cato, who bore the death of his grown son with such notable restraint (9–10). Laelius, however, continues by saying that if he were to deny being moved by the death of Scipio he would be lying. Indeed, he has been moved as he judges "no one ever will be." The wise man, the "philosopher" then, following a Stoic truism should be unmoved by events, and by this measure Laelius says he is not wise, but rather Cato is, and yet the wisdom of Cato is neither that of Laelius nor that exhibited by Cicero himself upon the death of his daughter a year and half earlier (Pangle 2003: 114; Falconer 1923: 116n.1). Laelius is grieved as no one ever has been and no one ever will be. His wisdom, then, if such it be called, is not to be unmoved by his friend's death, but to recognize that nothing bad has happened to Scipio. Indeed, if anything bad has happened to anyone it has happened to Laelius. But, he reminds us, to be grieved by one's own pains is the province of the lover not the friend (11).[15]

And yet the distinctions made here are troubled as soon as they are made. Laelius is in fact *sapiens*. Everyone calls him so, whether he grieves for his loss or not. The term comes to function as his cognomen (6). He is a philosopher, in the manner of Socrates, as Fannius tells us (7), and therefore, because of his wisdom, people seek to know how he bears the death of his friend. He is an exemplar of wisdom whose behavior they seek to replicate. Yet he has been absent from his official duties. Has the death of his friend

---

14  See Combès (1971: vii–xi) and Pangle (2003: 107).

15  Combès (1971: 8n1) observes the same theme is found in the *Tusculan Disputations* 1.111, which as Altman (2009) has shown serves as a *consolatio* for himself on his daughter's death, and in the *Brutus* 4.

caused this seeming lapse in virtue? Laelius at once assures us that "no" he has merely been ill, but that he is not wise, Cato was wise, wiser than Socrates himself. Why? Because of the manner in which he bore the death of his son. We are told no details nor do other ancient sources provide us much more (c.f., *De Senectute* 84). But the implication is clear that Cato would most certainly have not missed any of his official duties simply because of the death of a friend. Yet even though that is what certain philosophers (*sapientes*) qualify as wise, Laelius who is not wise, though others call him such (*sapiens*), will not deny that he has been moved. And indeed, as Scaevola makes clear, not to be moved by the death of such a friend would have been a failure of Laelius's humanity (*humanitatis*), if not his wisdom (8).

Are we therefore to assume that since Cato is wise and Cato is like the Stoics in his lack of public grief, that the Stoics therefore are the operative model of wisdom (*sapientia*) for Laelius, rather than Socrates, whose status as the wisest of men is evoked no less than three times at the beginning of the dialogue? Such an assumption would be hasty and an oversimplification. Indeed, Laelius later rejects the Stoic model as "hard" and more befitting a "stump" or "stone" than a "human being" (48). Such men may be termed *sapientes*, but ultimately, they may not be so wise (Pangle 2003: 114–14; Altman 2009). Indeed, the term *sapiens* seems increasingly ironic as the dialogue progresses. Thus, Laelius says in response to the Stoic contention that friendship is to be avoided as producing emotional entanglements:

> Quam ob rem, si cadit in sapientem animi dolor, qui profecto cadit, nisi ex eius animo exstirpatam humanitatem abritramur, quae causa est, cur amicitiam funditus tollamus e vita, ne aliquas propter eam suscipiamus molestias. (48)

> If therefore psychic pain befalls the wise man, which it certainly does, unless we judge that all humanity has been extirpated from his spirit, what cause is there for why we should remove friendship completely from our life, lest we suffer certain troubles because of it.

In this light, the statement that Cato is the wisest of men, because of the Stoic demeanor he exhibited at his son's death, is made to appear increasingly problematic. Such wisdom, if wisdom it be, is inhuman, the wisdom of a "stump" or "stone." Cato's "wisdom" ultimately leads us less to take him as our *exemplar* than to question who precisely is wise. By the same token, if we learn in *De Senectute* (84) that Cato's unflappable demeanor was founded more on his faith in the immortality of his son's soul than on what the *sapientes* consider wise, then we must ask whether there is not another wisdom, one that grounds our humanity in the experience of both friendship and loss, love and pain.

After disclaiming his own wisdom in favor of that of Cato and the *sapientes*, Laelius continues by saying that even though he has been "moved" as none will ever be moved, he takes comfort in the knowledge that nothing bad has happened to Scipio. For Scipio died at the height of his powers and reputation. A few more years of life would have added nothing. He either has ascended to the gods, as envisioned in the *Somnium Scipionis* at the end of *De republica* or, if death be the end, he experiences no harm (11–14). The conclusion is much the same as that found at the end of the *Apology* when Socrates contemplates his eminent death, and Laelius's reflection comes directly following the third mention of Socrates being judged wisest by the Delphic oracle.

# CICERO READS DERRIDA READING CICERO

Cato therefore may appear to be the wisest in accord with the teachings of the Stoics, but Laelius displays a deeper Socratic wisdom that valorizes both friendship and loss. Indeed, the distinction between the wise man and his opposite comes to be troubled in the course of the dialogue, not because either wisdom or philosophy are rejected per se, they are not. But it is troubled in the name of a friendship that is at once richer than any arid banishing of the emotions and more deeply implicated in the fabric of everyday life than any Epicurean retreat.

> Sed tamen recordatione nostrae amicitiae sic fruor, ut beate vixisse videar, quia cum Scipione vixerim, quocum mihi coniuncta cura de publica re et de privata fuit; quocum et domus fuit et militia communis et, id in quo est omnis vis amicitiae, voluntatum studiorum sententiarum summa consensio. Itaque non tam ista me sapientiae, quam modo Fannius commemoravit, fama delectat, falsa praesertim, quam quod amicitiae nostrae memoriam spero sempiternam fore. (15)

> But nonetheless I so enjoy the recollection of our friendship that I seem to have lived happily because I lived with Scipio, who was joined with me in the care of both public and private weal, and with whom I shared everything both at home and on campaign including that in which all the force of friendship is, complete agreement of wills, pursuits, and thoughts. And thus, that reputation for wisdom, which Fannius just recalled and is no doubt false, does not delight me so much as the fact that I hope the memory of our friendship will be eternal.

This friendship, however, happy though it may have been, included not only the pleasure of recollection, accompanied as it must be by grief and loss, but also the potential for conflict, enmity, even violence, for politics in short. Scipio and Laelius are shadowed throughout not only by Cicero and Atticus but also by Blossius and Gracchus as well as Sulpicius and Pompeius. In taking the risk of the Socratic encounter with the other, as opposed to Stoic detachment, Laelius exposes himself to the possibility of a friendship turned to enmity, of virtue turned to vice. This ever-present possibility is why great friendships are so rare. True friendships, we are told, are not mere relations of convenience or utility but they are rooted in nature and therefore eternal (32). Yet in the very next sentence we read that Scipio said, "nothing is more difficult than for friendship to endure to the end of life, because men's habits (*mores*) often change" (33).

Friendship rather is a risk that one enters into blind, as if in love. "Friendship runs ahead of judgment and takes away the power of experiential testing" (62). Laelius wants to differentiate his grief for Scipio from that of the lover who cares only for his own pain. But at the dialogue's end the flames (*exardescit*) of love (*amor*) and those of friendship (*amicitia*) are said to be the same, as each is named for the act of loving (*amando*) (100). This passage is clearly meant to recall two earlier moments in the dialogue. As Combès (1971) notes in his annotation of this passage, the same etymology of friendship being derived from love is cited by Laelius at 26, where friendship is said to arise more from the application of the soul in love than from the calculation of benefits. Likewise, the same verb, *exardescit,* appeared at 29, when we are told the movement of the soul in love causes "a certain wondrous magnitude of good will" to be kindled. Derrida, in turn, had clearly read his edition of Combès with some care since he chose to introduce the chapter in which he discusses Montaigne's and Cicero's varying judgments

86                                    THEORY DOES NOT EXIST

of Blossius's willingness to burn down the Capitol if Gracchus asked by quoting these
very passage from 26 and 100.

Thus Laelius, as we have seen, when he seems to draw a clear line between
wisdom and its opposite, ultimately undermines that opposition, not so as to destroy
the distinction, but so as to invite us to think about it in a more complex and nuanced
way. By the same token, when at the beginning of his speech he seeks to draw a clear
distinction between the friend and the lover, here too he undermines this strict dichotomy
over the course the dialogue, forcing us to think more carefully about the passions
ignited by the strength of our affections. Indeed, he signals this in the very terms
he uses to describe his loss, "Moveor enim, tali amico orbatus, qualis, ut abitror, nemo
umquam erit, ut confirmare possum, nemo certe fuit" ["For I am moved, having lost
such a friend, as I judge, no one ever will be and, as I am able to confirm, certainly no
one was"] (10). This passage calls to mind a formula that Catullus used for his beloved
Lesbia on several different occasions. In poem 8, she was "amata nobis quantum
amabitur nulla" ["loved by us as no one will be loved"] (5). This line is echoed almost
word for word in 37.12 and it is used again in expanded form at 87.1–2. There the focus
switches from the future to the past, "Nulla potest mulier tantum se dicere amatam/
vere quantum a me Lesbia amata mea est" ["No woman is able to say she is loved
so much as my Lesbia is loved by me."]. In each case, in Catullus as well as Cicero,
the essential point is that the emotional commitment of the speaker, who has suffered
a recent loss, is so great that it will never be equaled nor has it been equaled in the past.
If Cicero's Laelius uses an analogous formula immediately before his declaration
that he consoles himself with the knowledge that Scipio suffers no ill and that only
the lover, not the friend, is pained by his own discomfiture, then the separation of love
from friendship posited here can only be ironic for anyone who perceives the echo.

Still there is one final turn of screw. In Catullus's case, his loss is the loss of betrayal.
Love and hate in Catullus are two sides of the same coin (85). And though *amicitia* may be
proposed as the ideal towards which true love aspires (109.6), nonetheless the *benevolentia*
that springs into flame (*exardescit*) in Ciceronian friendship in Catullan *amor* is directly
contrasted with the desire by which one burns more intensely (72.5). The friendship
that moves Laelius, as none has even been moved, is the same passion that ignites
Blossius's devotion to Gracchus and that only too easily become Sulpicius's hatred for
Pompeius. Love is always on the cusp of turning into hate. Friendship is both the other
of love in its irrational self-centered passion and its mirror image. As Derrida writes
"The enemy, the enemy of morality in any case, is love. Not because it is the enemy,
but because, in the excess of attraction it unleashes, it gives way to rupture, to enmity,
to war. It carries hatred in it" (1994: 287). The ontological categories that define our
existence and that a certain Stoic rationality seeks to keep apart are forever crossed by
friendship as a moment of universal singularity, in which the dead live, the absent are
present, and in which too often the object of love, a friend, becomes our enemy.

In 1994, the year after publishing *Specters of Marx* and *Khôra*, Derrida brought out
*The Politics of Friendship*. In a text, in which he openly acknowledges he is talking to and
about his friends, some of whom have died, some of whom are no longer friends, some
of whom haunt the present, he turns in the first instance to Cicero. To many this may

## CICERO READS DERRIDA READING CICERO

seem an odd choice, and indeed though literally hundreds of items are published on each of these authors every year, this fact has gone all but unmentioned. It seems almost an accident. What possible relation could there be between this apotheosis of traditional western reason and a radical antiphilosopher of postmodernity?

Nonetheless, when the sloganeering is through, and the excuses for not reading or considering these texts, are pushed aside, we find a profound resonance between them. Cicero's text is far more nuanced, far more ironic, and, in places, far more undecideable than either its apologists or its denigrators have often been willing to accept. Derrida's text not only offers a far more informed and far more careful reading of Cicero than we might have expected, it is also a far more personal, far more moving meditation on love, friendship, politics, enmity, and death, than perhaps even his most ardent fans have been willing to admit. One cannot leave it and its reading of Cicero without being haunted by the promises of the past and the hope for a friendship, a politics, and a justice to come.

## Works Cited

Altman, William H. F. 2009. "Womanly Humanism in Cicero's Tusculan Disputations." *Transactions of the American Philological Association* 139: 411–445.

Avramenko, Richard. 2008. "Zarathustra and His Asinine Friends: Nietzsche and Taste as the Groundless Ground of Friendship." In von Heyking and Avramenko 2008. 287–314.

Blondell, Ruby. 2002. *The Play of Character in Plato's Dialogues*. Cambridge: Cambridge University Press.

Brunt, P. A. 1988. "*Amicitia* in the Late Roman Republic." *The Fall of the Roman Republic and Related Essays*. Oxford: Oxford University Press. 351–81.

Combès, Robert, ed. and trans. 1971. *Cicéron: Laelius de Amicitia*. Paris: Société d'Edition <<Les Belles Lettres>>.

Courtine, Jean-François. 2008. "L'ABC de la déconstruction." *Derrida, la tradition de la philosophie*. Eds. Marc Crépon and Frédéric Worms. Paris: Galilée.

de Nooy, Juliana. 1998. *Derrida, Kristeva, and the Dividing Line: An Articulation of Two Theories of Difference*. New York: Garland.

Derrida, Jacques. 1972a. "La pharmacie de Platon." *La dissémination*. Paris: Seuil. 74–196. Original 1968.

———. 1972b. *Positions*. Paris: Minuit.

———. 1980. *La carte postale: de Socrate à Freud et au-delà*. Paris: Aubier-Flammarion.

———. 1992. "Nous autres Grecs." *Nos Grecs et leurs modernes*. Ed. Barbara Cassin. Paris: Seuil. 251–73.

———. 1993a. *Spectres de Marx*. Paris: Galilée.

———. 1993b. *Khôra*. Paris: Galilée.

———. 1994. *Politiques de l'amitié, suivi de L'oreille de Heidegger*. Paris: Galilée.

Falconer, William Armistead. 1923. *Cicero: De Senectute, De Amicitia, De Divinatione*. Loeb Classical Library. Cambridge, MA: Harvard University Press.

Gebhardt, Jürgen. 2008. "Friendship, Trust, and the Political Order: A Critical Overview." In von Heyking and Avramenko 2008. 315–47.

Hadot, Pierre. 1995. *Qu'est-ce que la philosophie antique?* Paris: Gallimard.

Hicks, R. D, ed and trans. 1925. *Diogenes Laertius: Lives of Eminent Philosophers*. Cambridge: Harvard University Press.

Huebnerus, Henricus Gustavus. 1981. *Diogenes Laertius: De vitis, dogmatis et apthegmatis clarorum philosophorum libri decem*. Vols. 1 and 3. Hildesheim: Georg Olms Verlag. Original 1828.

Konstan, David. 1997. *Friendship in the Classical World*. Cambridge: Cambridge University Press.

Lau, Kwok-Ying. 2007. "Non-Familiarity and Otherness: Derrida's Hermeneutics of Friendship and its Political Implications." *Phenomenology 2005* 1.2: 417–40.

Laurand, L. 1928. *Cicéron: L'amitié*. Paris: Société d'Edition <<Les Belles Lettres>>.

Leonard, Miriam. 2000. "The 'Politiques de l'amitié': Derrida's Greeks and a national politics of classical scholarship." *Proceedings of The Cambridge Philological Society* 46: 45–78.

———. 2005. *Athens in Paris: Ancient Greece and the Political in Post-War French Thought*. Oxford: Oxford University Press.

———, ed. 2010. *Derrida and Antiquity*. Oxford: Oxford University Press.

Long, H. S. 1964. *Diogenes Laertii Vitae Philosophorum*. Oxford: Clarendon Press.

Marcovich, M. 1999. *Diogenes Laertius: Vitae Philosophorum*. Leipzig: Teubner.

Miller, Paul Allen. 1999. "The Classical Roots of Poststructuralism: Lacan, Derrida, and Foucault." *International Journal of the Classical Tradition* 5: 204–25.

———. 2007. *Postmodern Spiritual Practices: The Construction of the Subject and the Reception of Plato in Lacan, Derrida, and Foucault*. Columbus: Ohio State University Press.

———. 2016. *Diotima Among the Amazons: French Feminists Read Plato*. Oxford: Oxford University Press.

Montaigne, Michel de. 2017. *Oeuvres complètes*. Eds. Albert Thibaudet and Maurice Rat. Paris: Gallimard.

Nicgorski, Walter. 2008. "Cicero's Distinctive Voice in Friendship: *De Amicitia* and *De Re Publica*." In von Heyking and Avramenko 2008. 84–111.

Pangle, Lorraine Smith. 2003. *Aristotle and the Philosophy of Friendship*. Cambridge: Cambridge University Press.

Peeters, Benoît. 2010. *Derrida*. Paris: Flammarion.

Salkever, Stephen. 2008. "Taking Friendship Seriously: Aristotle on the Place(s) of *Philia* in Human Life." In von Heyking and Avramenko 2008. 53–83.

von Heyking, John and Richard Avramenko, eds. 2008. *Friendship and Politics: Essays in Political Thought*. Notre Dame: Notre Dame University Press.

Zuckert, Catherine H. 1996. *Postmodern Platos: Nietzsche, Heidegger, Gadamer, Strauss, Derrida*. Chicago: University of Chicago Press.

# Chapter 7

# ON BORDERS, RACE, AND INFINITE HOSPITALITY: FOUCAULT, DERRIDA, AND CAMUS

On the evening of June 17th, 2015, Dylann Roof joined a Bible study at Mother Emanuel Church in Charleston South Carolina. It is known as Mother Emanuel because it is the church from which all subsequent African Methodist Episcopal (AME) congregations sprang. The AME church was the first independent black denomination in the United States, and it was founded by slaves and freed slaves in Charleston, the port through which more than one third of all enslaved Africans entered the United States. Roof was welcomed into their Bible study. He participated for an hour before standing up, pulling a Glock 45, and shouting, "I have to do it. You rape our women and you're taking over our country. And you have to go" (Borden, Horwitz, Markon 2015). Nine people were killed. Three others survived their wounds. The next day, after his arrest, Dylann Roof, wearing a jacket with the flags of Rhodesia and apartheid South Africa, told police he had gone to Mother Emanuel in the hopes of starting a race war.

While it would be wrong to claim that Dylann Roof is typical, his act and his discourse are hardly a fluke. Racial violence has been a persistent part of the American imaginary from the founding of the country to the present: from slavery to the oft-repeated necessity to conquer, suppress, or annihilate the Native American population; to Donald Trump's campaign announcement that declared Mexican rapists were swarming across the border ("Leo Frank" 2018; Davis 2001: 280; Rushdy 2012: 123). Dylann Roof in Charleston, Robert Gregory Bowers at the Tree of Life Synagogue in Pittsburgh, the Charlottesville march, and David Duke are symptoms of a deep and persistent racism that has haunted American culture. In December 1890, a few days before the bloody massacre of 300 unarmed men, women, and children at Wounded Knee, South Dakota, and shortly after the murder of the Lakota holy man, Sitting Bull, L. Frank Baum, the beloved author of such children's classics as the *Wizard of Oz* opined in the Aberdeen, South Dakota newspaper he edited, the *Saturday Pioneer*:

> The proud spirit of the original owners of these vast prairies inherited through centuries of fierce and bloody wars for their possession, lingered last in the bosom of Sitting Bull. With his fall the nobility of the Redskin is extinguished, and what few are left are a pack of whining curs who lick the hand that smites them. The Whites, by law of conquest, by justice of civilization, are masters of the American continent, and the best safety of the frontier settlements will be secured by the total annihilation of the few remaining Indians. (Stallings 2007)

# THEORY DOES NOT EXIST

Baum was not despised or condemned for expressing sentiments barely distinguishable from the Nazis forty years later. Since the end of the Second World War and the dismantling of the Jim Crowe south, the direct articulation of such genocidal views and the open advocacy of racial violence have been largely unacceptable in civil discourse.[1] But it is important to realize how deeply violent racial fantasies have pervaded the discourse of the United States, modern Europe, and increasingly the world of nation states that fashioned themselves in their wake.

Historically speaking, the question of borders is not necessarily coterminous with that of race. There were borders to the ancient Roman Empire, lines beyond which the authority of the kings of Egypt, Persia, and ancient Israel did not cross, but in almost all these cases, no concept analogous to the notion of biological race existed or of the nation state as a topographical unity that coincided with a specific linguistic or genetic community (Anderson 1991: 172–73). The thought is nowhere found in the ancient Mediterranean that those on the other side of a border not only practiced different customs, spoke different languages, and even presented different skin tones, but were also fundamentally other, that they were a different species—not merely a different phenotype but a different genotype. Herodotus marvels at the strange customs of the Egyptians, Persians, and Scythians, but he does not question that they are *anthropoi* (humans). Saint Augustine was African, but he moved freely between Carthage, Hippo, and Rome. Biological racism simply did not exist as a pervasive discourse (Snowden 1970, 1983). But in the modern world, in the world of the nation state, the question of borders, the need for strong borders that divide one nation from another, almost always entails questions of "race." The need to draw strong lines between us and them, to have borders that are not simply an arbitrary convention or a contingent fact of history, that mark something in the real, it is felt, must point to something essential. Borders between nation states do not divide territories. They divide peoples, and when peoples are on the wrong side of the border, they need to go back to where they came from. The English belong in England, the French in France, the Dutch in the Netherlands. A state for every nation, and every nation should have a state. Israel for the Jews, Palestine for the Palestinians, and someday the Catalans and the Kurds (Anderson 1991: 3). Yet while the logic of this line of argument seems clear, it leads to violence and exclusion. This is the logic of fusing nationalism with racial conflict. It is the opposite of infinite hospitality. This is the logic of positing essential qualities based on phenotype, language, religion, or some combination thereof. Hutus versus Tutsis, Serbians versus Croats, Indians versus Pakistanis, Burmese versus Rohingyas, in each case the question of borders entails, determines, and creates questions of "race," that is, questions of who people are in their typological essence. Those who are other are posited as being different in their being, and therefore as being in some basic sense less human than we are (whoever we are), as people who threaten our identity, who threaten our being, and so who must be removed, or separated, or killed. "I have to do it. You rape our women and you're taking over our country. And you have to go."

---

1   See Sara Ahmed's discussion of "civil racism" (2008). See also Žižek's response (2010: 44). Many thanks to Zahi Zalloua for these references.

## ON BORDERS, RACE, AND INFINITE HOSPITALITY

Concepts of race are deeply implicated in concepts of national borders, and inherent in those concepts are fear, aggression, and violence. To oversimplify, in the modern world where there are questions of borders there are often questions of race, and where there are questions of race and borders, there is the necessity that these differences be both asserted and policed. In what follows, I explore an alternative relation to the other based on hospitality. First, I look at the history of "race war" as a trope within Western discourse. My purpose is to historicize and denaturalize our concepts of race, the nation, and national conflict, and thereby create a space for thinking differently. I will do this through a reading of Foucault's *Il faut défendre la société* and Benedict Anderson's *Imagined Communities*, though other texts could be included. Second, I engage with Derrida's notion of an unconditional or infinite hospitality, which derives from the work of Emanuel Levinas. In this latter incarnation, the term becomes a nexus between ethics and politics, particularly with regard to the history of Zionism, anti-Semitism, and the aporetical relationship between a terrestrial, political Jerusalem, and a transcendent Jerusalem to come. Third, my argument culminates with a reading of Albert Camus's story, "L'hôte," a title that can with equal justice be translated "The Host," "The Guest," and a word that is etymologically derived from the Latin *hostis*, meaning "stranger," "enemy," and "sacrificial victim," as in the eucharistic *host*. This story set in the Algerian conflict forces us to interrogate the meaning of each of these terms and then asks us to take responsibility for our freedom and to accept the freedom of the other. It ties together all the major themes of the essay: race, borders, the state, and hospitality. The role of the instructor in the isolated school in rural Algeria, who as French, is both a guest and the host of the prisoner left in his charge, and is in many ways analogous to the situation confronted by modern America; as we rule a land that we took from those who came before us and play host to guests on our southern border whose ancestors' historic claim to these lands exceed our own, and yet we cannot leave any more than we can return to a world before the nation state, before colonialism, to a mythical Eden before exploitation itself. "L'hôte" is good to think with.

## I

In 1976, Michel Foucault delivered his annual course at the Collège de France, entitled for that year, *Il faut défendre la société*. It is a wide-ranging set of lectures largely devoted to tracing the development in the early modern period of a discourse that sees the history of nations as a war between opposed races. These were not initially understood to be biological races, and these discourses certainly did not correspond to a racist worldview or to a scientific racism, such as became prominent in the 19th century and would later go on to underwrite Jim Crowe, manifest destiny, Nazi ideology, and European imperialism. Nonetheless, Foucault argues in many ways that these early and often obscure historical works provide the rhetorical and intellectual foundations that help make those later social and epistemic formations possible, and at minimum, demonstrate that these discourses have a specific and limited genealogy, which can be traced.

This type of history, he argues, was initially proposed as a counter-discourse to more traditional royalist narratives of continuity and lineal descendance. It was produced by writers seldom read today, such as Hotman, Boulainvilliers, and Thiers. These were often the writers of reaction, defending the rights of the nobility against an increasingly centralized monarchy. The beginning of the "modern" world is posited by these historians with the great invasions of the Vikings, the Normans, and the Franks, who mark an end to antiquity and the beginning of what will retrospectively be cast as the Middle Ages. They seek to differentiate themselves from that "Middle Age" precisely because they have "awoken" to the usurpation those invasions mark, "awoken" to the fact that there are Vandals in their midst who have stolen their property and power, and who must be resisted in the name of a return to a quasi-mythical past (Foucault 1997: 166). Their awareness and their counter-history are presented precisely as a rebirth, a renaissance of the nation.[2] But at the same time, these reactionary counter-historians are also forging, unbeknownst to them, a discourse of revolution (Foucault 1997: 119). Their work is founded on unearthing what they see as the secret history of the conquest of the nation, whether in the form of the Norman conquest of England or the invasion of the Franks and the Merovingian conquest of the indigenous Gallo-Romans. These writers present modernity as a break from antiquity, an illegitimate usurpation by hostile invaders.

Politics for them becomes war by other means, a struggle between implacable enemies that continues sometimes openly and sometimes covertly: history is a conflict not between ideas or interests but species, irreconcilable forms of being (Foucault 1997: 41). What began as a discourse that sought to explain the ways in which traditional rights and prerogatives were being usurped by the growth of a centralized state (see also Anderson 1974), whose functionaries are depicted as external invaders, gradually becomes appropriated by a variety of later actors to describe an internal struggle between opposed types, both racial (the Black, the Indian, the Jew) and sexual (the homosexual, the pervert) (Foucault 1997: 224). This racial discourse has its own mythology often derived from earlier Medieval and Germanic forms of storytelling. It produces elaborate fantasies of revenge, return, and the apocalyptic settling of accounts such as we see in Dylann Roof. "Race war" under this new paradigm ceases to be a form of historical explanation and becomes an aspiration, a dream, the final solution to an interminable problem:

> In this mythology, they tell how the great victories of the giants have little by little been forgotten and covered over; that there has been a twilight of the gods; that the heroes have been wounded or died and that the kings have fallen asleep in inaccessible caverns. It is also the theme of the rights and the goods of the first race, which have been trampled on by clever invaders; the theme of the secret war that continues; the theme of the plot that one must take up again to revive this war and chase away the invaders or enemies; the theme of tomorrow's famous battle that will bring back the forces of the long-vanquished and finally make them victors, victors who will neither know nor practice clemency. And it is thus

---

2  See Greene (1982) on the defining characteristic of the Renaissance as its self-differentiation from the Middle Ages and identification with a prior era of antiquity. See also Anderson on subsequent nationalism's self-construction as "awakening" from a long national slumber (1991: 195).

## ON BORDERS, RACE, AND INFINITE HOSPITALITY

that during the entire Middle Ages, and still later, there is continuously revived, linked to this theme of perpetual war, the great hope for the day of revenge, the wait for the emperor of the last days, for the *dux novus*, the new chief, the new guide, the new *Führer*; the idea of the fifth monarchy, of the third empire, or of the third *Reich*. (Foucault 1997: 48–49)

What Foucault attempts to demonstrate in this course at the Collège de France is that, beginning largely in the nineteenth century, this historical tradition, this counter-history of the repressed, conceived in terms of a battle between peoples, combined with these apocalyptic fantasies and their accompanying mythology, helps create a new discourse that subtends a growing biological and social racism, which sees the other race as now within our midst, as something that must be exposed, combatted, and eliminated. It is not simply that other peoples exist, but that they are essentially different, ontologically different, less than human, and can therefore never be accommodated or assimilated (Foucault 1997: 52–53). There is an increased focus on "racial purity" (Foucault 1997: 71).[3] Internal warfare becomes increasingly envisioned as a kind of autoimmune response to biological hazards as the body politic is medicalized (Foucault 1997: 194).

Often, in direct opposition to most ancient or traditional history, the social virtues to be emulated in this discourse are not those of Roman or Hellenistic civilization (Habinek 1998: 15–33) with its promiscuous cosmopolitanism, its race mixing, its necessary compromises and trade with the other; but those of the barbarian, who comes to represent purity, strength, and an unbridled white masculinity. We see hints of this in Rousseau's noble savage and romantic cults of authenticity and immediacy. But it comes into its full flower, Foucault notes, in the work of one of Boulainvillier's successors, Freret, who etymologized the word "franc" not to mean "free," but from the Latin, *ferox*, "proud, intrepid, arrogant, cruel." And it is from these and similar assumptions, in part, that we can trace the mythology of the "blonde beast" that makes its appearance at the end of the nineteenth century in Nietzsche and elsewhere, in which freedom is equated with "a taste for power and a determined avidity, an incapacity to serve but an ever-ready desire to subject" (Foucault 1997: 131).[4]

Benedict Anderson's now classic *Imagined Communities* comes to many similar conclusions working independently within the tradition of British Marxism.[5] Anderson

---

3  Foucault develops at some length the difference between a traditional, religious based anti-Judaism in Europe and a new racialized and biologized anti-Semitism that would lead to the holocaust (Foucault 1997: 76–77). See also Anderson (1991: 59, 149–50).

4  See Nietzsche, *Genealogy of Morals* 11, "At the centre of all these noble races we cannot fail to see the blond beast of prey, the magnificent blond beast avidly prowling round for spoil and victory; this hidden centre needs release from time to time, the beast must out again, must return to the wild: – Roman, Arabian, Germanic, Japanese nobility, Homeric heroes, Scandinavian Vikings – in this requirement they are all alike. It was the noble races which left the concept of 'barbarian' in their traces wherever they went; even their highest culture betrays the fact that they were conscious of this and indeed proud of it." (1994: 25).

5  While Anderson evidences a passing familiarity with Foucault, *Il faut défendre la société* was not published until 1997. The first edition of *Imagined Communities* was begun in 1978–79 (1991: xi).

94 THEORY DOES NOT EXIST

focuses less specifically on the discourse of race wars and more on that of nationalism and print capitalism (1991: 44, 134), and while Foucault is primarily concerned with developments in Europe; Anderson offers meticulous detail on developments in Latin America (1991: 47–65) and Southeast Asia (1991: 124–34, 155–62). For both, however, the concept of the nation, its association with a particular set of borders on a topographic grid, and the assumption that those who belong to the nation share certain essential characteristics is a modern phenomenon that has a specific genealogy and is in no way natural and therefore open to contest (1991: 6, 11–12, 19, 81, 113). Likewise, for both, however imaginary the ontological reality of nations, states, borders, and race may be, they all have, and in particular their nexus has, very real, often deadly, effects (1991: 45–46).

The recognition of the history of the discourse of nations, borders, and race, that is to say the genealogy of our modern racist discourse, even if only partial and incomplete has a number of consequences. First and foremost, it denaturalizes racial hatred. The notions that people have always hated, feared, and demonized those different from them, and that racism has always existed are simply factually wrong. If the contention is that difference has always existed and that *difference* has always been the basis of our *differences*, then fair enough, but this is utterly tautological. If the contention is that biologized racial hatred has always existed, that those who have a phenotype different from our own have always been seen as a potential danger to our own existence, a danger that requires managing, that requires borders to be enforced, that requires force; then that is demonstrably false, and indeed our racist discourse has a history, a shape, and a set of conventions, which once seen, becomes possible to modify. It becomes possible to think differently (Foucault 1984: 14–15). As Foucault says of Boulainvillier's own attempts to write the history of the usurpation of the rights of the traditional nobility, the production of history and of a genealogy is not simply an academic exercise but always, necessarily, a political exercise, an attempt to modify our understanding of the past, and hence to rewrite the possibilities of the present and the future:

> It is a question by the same token of modifying in their very dispositive and in their actual equilibrium, the relations of force. History is not simply an analysis and decoding of forces, it is a modifier. Consequently, control, the fact of having been correct in the order of historical knowledge, in brief, to speak the truth of history, is by that very fact to occupy a decisive strategic position. (Foucault 1997: 152)

Our academic discussions, to the extent that they modify other scholars' understanding of the field, and to the extent that they modify what we and others teach, have real if always highly mediated and indirect consequences. The effect of any one speech act is incalculable and perhaps infinitesimal, but the concatenation of those acts and their intercalation with the circumstances and relations of force that give rise to them inevitably, indeed ontologically must, leave their trace in the real. This is as true for literature and philosophy as it is for history and genealogy.

## ON BORDERS, RACE, AND INFINITE HOSPITALITY                95

## II

The essance[6] of what is, or rather of what *opens itself* to the beyond of being, is hospitality. (Derrida 1997: 90, emphasis his)

In many ways the 1990s represent the golden age of Derrida's thought. While the works of the late sixties and seventies rocketed Derrida to the status of an intellectual superstar, particularly in the United States, and those works remain astonishing for their pyrotechnic brilliance; nonetheless, the political and ethical engagement of works like *Spectres de Marx, La politique de l'amitié, Apories*, and *Les Adieux* may well constitute a more lasting contribution to our philosophical heritage. One of the most important concepts Derrida elaborates in this period is that of an unconditional or infinite hospitality: a hospitality without limits as a fundamental, ethical, and even epistemic principle that must always both square itself, and find itself in tension, with the responsibilities and decisions of its political engagement.

In this section, I will argue that his notion of an infinite hospitality—in its necessary and aporetical relationship with our inherited discourse of borders, boundaries, states, and therefore race—gives us one tool for rethinking the destructive and potentially genocidal logic of modern racial politics, of our inherited discourse of nations, race, and war. It does so in ways that do not simply seek to mollify the worst of those tendencies through a liberal appeal to individual rights or a neoliberal appeal to the economics of choice, which cannot think beyond the terms of a zero-sum game except through appealing to greater efficiency and productivity (the rising tide that lifts all boats), an appeal that offers no out to a politics of distribution and redistribution, a politics that inevitably sees what is yours as coming from what is mine. In short, it rests on a conceptual framework of boundaries and property that can always only see the other as a threat and that nourishes at its core a logic of *ressentiment*.

By contrast, the concept of an infinite hospitality rests not only on an unconditional openness to the other, but also on the recognition that there can be no one who is completely other, that we can do no other than to recognize, and thus in some sense welcome, the other, in short that "tout autre est tout autre" (Derrida 1996: 49).[7] That is to say, we are all guests constituted by the other who has welcomed us into our identity by their presence. Even in our *host*-ility we must recognize the *host (hôte)* who is always also a *guest (hôte)*, always a *host*-age, always the sacrificial *host* who makes us

---

6  A spelling that Levinas used to emphasize the participial derivation of the Latin *essentia*, drawing attention to the "process or event of being" (cited in Kosky 2001: 49; see Derrida 1997: 90n1).

7  This phrase, which first appears near the end of *Spectres de Marx* (1993a: 273), can be translated either "every other is completely other" or "every other is every other." The first emphasizes the incommensurability of otherness, its final inability to be assimilated to the same. The second recognizes that each other is, on a certain level, able to be substituted for every other, that all others are on some level the same, which in the final analysis would include both the self and the other. For a fuller explication, see Lawlor (2016: 107–109).

whole in the recognition of our primal wound, our original sin, the recognition of our finitude, which can itself only be constituted in relation to the unlimited, the boundless, the infinite. It is precisely eating from the tree of knowledge of good and evil that leads to our expulsion from the garden, the recognition of our own autonomy that renders us eternal exiles. We are guests in our own home, and while we can only open our homes to the other in the recognition of the boundaries of that home, by envisioning the door that lets the other in, by drawing those bounds within the real; nonetheless the constitution of that liminal space is always on some level an arbitrary moment of decision, and therefore we can always only be a guest in the house of the other that we welcome into our own (Derrida 1996: 28–29; Derrida 1997: 79–80).

While Derrida's thought derives from many sources, one of the most important for the concept of hospitality is Emmanuel Levinas. In his funeral oration for the great Jewish philosopher in 1995, he reminds us that Levinas's thought on hospitality begins with a primal affirmation. It begins with the gesture of saying yes and hence with unconditioned responsibility. It begins with a response to the other that founds and therefore precedes our freedom, because there is no freedom without the other and its welcome. There is no freedom in a space without determination, of indiscriminate uniformity. The *khōra* of Plato's *Timaeus* and of Derrida's essay of the same name from this period represents only the pure passivity of reception (*Timaeus* 50c–e, 51a–b2, 52a8–b4; Derrida 1993b; Miller 2016: chapter 2). It has no agency but is a pure and permanent suffering. Nor does freedom exist in a space where all is already determined, where there is no empty space of maneuver, and so where no response is needed or can be given to what the subject suffers:

> All the great themes to which the thought of Emmanuel Levinas has awakened us, first that of responsibility, but of an unlimited responsibility that goes beyond and precedes my freedom, that of an "unconditional yes" ... of a "*yes* more ancient than the spontaneous and the naïve," a *yes* that is in agreement with this rightness that is an "originary fidelity with regard to a permanent alliance." (Derrida 1997: 13, emphasis his)

Hospitality in this absolute sense is the welcome of the face of the other, the recognition of the other as unique and irreplaceable, through the offer to the other of my original face (Derrida 1997: 49). There is a tremendous vulnerability in this moment for both parties, an erasure of boundaries, or at least their transgression, which is always also a form of aggression. And it is here that the question of the third, of the law (of the father Lacan would say) must supervene, the moment in which *tout autre* becomes *tout autre* and hence the possibility of substitution arrives, of commutability and justice, but also of finitude and boundaries that put limits on that primal and unlimited "yes" that must always precede the freedom of our responsibility:

> As the third does not wait, the instance that opens ethics and justice is the instance of a quasi-transcendental or original, truly pre-original, betrayal. We could call it ontological from the moment it joins ethics to all that exceeds and betrays it (ontology, precisely, synchrony, totality, the State, politics, etc.). We could even see there an irrepressible evil or a radical perversion. Ill will is not able to be absent from it, as if its possibility, the haunting

# ON BORDERS, RACE, AND INFINITE HOSPITALITY 97

at least of its possibility, as if some pervertibility were not also the condition of the Good, of Justice, of Love, of Faith etc. And of perfectibility.

This spectral "possibility" is not, all the same, the abstraction of a liminal pervertibility. It would rather be the *impossibility* of controlling, of deciding, of determining a limit, the *impossibility* of situating oneself in order to maintain one's position, by certain criteria, certain norms, certain rules, the threshold that separates pervertibility from perversion. (1997: 68–69, emphasis his)

Thus, Derrida via Levinasian ethics teaches that we must always hold two opposed thoughts in our mind: the call to an original and originary affirmation of the other, the welcome and recognition of the face of the other with our own face, and the simultaneous necessity to have boundaries with that other, lest we consume the other and negate it in the moment of this affirmation.[8] This is in fact the ontological necessity of a bounding moment (what Plato in the *Philebus* calls *peras*), of an imposition of the law: a third position that would intervene in the primal and imaginary dyad to make ontic separation and hence the recognition of the other possible. Yet this moment of intervention is always in some sense a betrayal of the promise of immediacy, of unmediated love, and the imposition of a standard of substitution (John is x, Sally is x, every x is equivalent, and hence can be substituted one for the other in so far as it is x and not y). This moment comes through a variety of intermediaries: the law, justice, the State, that is, through the bounded entities of force that make possible the reality of our hospitality and that by limiting what should be, indeed must be, unlimited—if it is truly to be hospitality—conjure the specter of its own perversion.

And so, we confront the aporia of the decision between an ethics and a politics of hospitality, which in no way relieves us of our responsibility to make that decision or of the freedom to make it. Indeed, this aporia is the condition of our freedom, for if the decision were already made, if it were dictated by its own terms, then there would be no decision, and we would not be free to make it. Both ethics and politics as matters of human practice would be impossible. In the case of Levinas, this aporia is perhaps most poignantly presented in the case of Jerusalem, or more properly the two Jerusalems: the Jerusalem that is a call for justice for the fullest and highest realization of the Torah; and the Jerusalem that is a divided city, claimed by multiple peoples, multiple faiths, and yet indissociable from the very identity of what it means to be Jewish. As is sung at the end of the Passover Seder, "Next year in Jerusalem." It is both a geographical entity and a transcendental ideal. What precisely would an unconditional and infinite hospitality mean in this case (Derrida 1997: 91)? This is the moment of our decision as much today in Jerusalem as it is in the tent cities on the Mexican border, and as it was in Mother Emanuel the night she opened her arms to Dylann Roof. How do we welcome the other, how do we receive the threat of the other, what are the limits of our hospitality and how do those limits in themselves constitute the other as a threat?

---

8  See Zalloua's important reflections on Derrida's twin formulations, "Il faut bien manger" and "il faut bien vivre ensemble" for the Israeli-Palestinian conflict (2017: 120–23).

98 THEORY DOES NOT EXIST

It is in this context that Derrida first quotes Levinas from his work, *The Hour of the Nations*:

> One pertains to the messianic order when one has been able to admit the other among his own. That a people should accept those who come and install themselves in their home, foreigners that they are, with their customs and their costumes, with their speech and their smells, that it gives to him an *akhsania* as a place of shelter and place to breathe and to live— is a song to the glory of the God of Israel. (Derrida 1997: 133, citing Levinas)

He then continues in his own voice:

> That a people, in so far as they are a people, "accept those who come and install themselves in their home, foreigners that they are" that is the standard for popular and public engagement, a political *res publica* that does not reduce itself to "tolerance," unless that tolerance demands of itself the affirmation of a "love" without measure. (Derrida 1997: 133)

A political republic is not a heavenly one, but it may be one yet-to-come, one as yet unrealized, one haunted by the specter of its own perfectibility and hence pervertibility. The challenge Levinas and Derrida issue to us is to inscribe the promise of the Jerusalem of the Torah, of the heavenly Jerusalem "*in* the terrestrial Jerusalem," of the ethical within the political, of the possibility of infinite hospitality within the order of law, freedom, and the state (Derrida 1997: 193–97). Infinite hospitality can offer us a way to think differently about the nation and race, a way that acknowledged the possibility of violence, even as it seeks to welcome the other.

## III

In 1954 Albert Camus began writing *L'hôte*, which would appear in the middle of the Algerian war in the 1956 collection, *L'exil et le royaume*. Camus, a native of French Algeria and a veteran of the French Resistance in the Second World War, tells the story of a teacher who has requested an isolated post after the war. He lives and works in a small schoolhouse on the high plateau of Algeria. It is a winter's night, and his desert outpost is surrounded by snow, the first sign of relief from a devastating drought that has left the surrounding population near starvation and partially dependent on grain rations shipped from France and distributed by the teacher to his students and their families. As he looks from the school at the beginning of the story, he sees in the distance a gendarme, riding on a horse, leading an Arab prisoner bound by the hands and walking behind him. Slowly they make the climb up to the top of the plateau and they are offered shelter and mint tea by the teacher in an act of hospitality. At this moment, we believe we understand the title of the story. The teacher is the "host" and the gendarme, Balducci, and the nameless Arab are his "guests." He is a good "host" and loosens the bonds of the Arab prisoner and makes him as welcome as he can under the circumstances.

## ON BORDERS, RACE, AND INFINITE HOSPITALITY 99

Yet, this is no social call, nor a mere pause on a longer journey. The gendarme has brought the prisoner, *hostis*/enemy but also hostage, to the schoolteacher, so the latter can deliver him to the authorities in the next town. The teacher is taken aback and refuses. But the gendarme, a Corsican administering French justice in Algeria, makes clear that the police are stretched thin, that the local Arab population is on the edge of revolt, and that Daru, the schoolteacher, should consider himself mobilized "in a sense" for war. When asked what crime the Arab prisoner committed, it turns out to have little to do with an impending revolt and everything to do with the recent drought and ensuing famine. He had murdered his cousin in a dispute over a sack of grain, no doubt the same sacks Daru himself is charged with distributing to the local populace. The crime fills the instructor with disgust. But Balducci warns the teacher that he should be on his guard, that the village will try and take back the prisoner. He even leaves the teacher his pistol. In the end, Daru, the host, is the occupier of their land, the symbol of an authority they do not accept, an unwelcome guest. At the same time, when the teacher continues to refuse to accept the orders passed on by the gendarme, saying he will not deliver the prisoner to the authorities in the next town, the local version of the terrestrial Jerusalem, Balducci reminds him of his obligations and departs. He refuses Daru's gesture of walking him to the door, noting "It's not worth the trouble of being polite. You have offended me" (52).

The good host has become now the *hostis* of both the occupier and the occupied. He is without a clearly delineated position within the borders that are being drawn, being neither a member of the Arab community nor a loyal citizen of an occupying France. The hospitality that he has attempted to extend to all has nonetheless required him to make certain decisions, which have drawn a line beyond which he will not go. His isolated position in the schoolhouse on a high plateau is at once a metaphor and the real embodiment of what may in the end be an untenable but necessary position.

There follows an awkward evening with Daru and his unwanted prisoner forced to spend the night in the confines of the small schoolhouse surrounded by snow. The teacher offers the prisoner the universal sign of hospitality. He makes a simple meal of an omelet and a large pancake, which they share. The prisoner is puzzled by the gesture, which for the moment at least places them in the position of equality:

"Are you the judge?"
"No, I'm keeping you till tomorrow."
"Why do you eat with me?"
"I'm hungry." (53)

The simplicity of the response belies the humility of the gesture. In the world of the segregated lunch counters of the Jim Crow South, Apartheid South Africa, French Indochina, the occupier did not sup with the occupied, the oppressor with the oppressed. To do so is to admit of a vulnerability, a communion, that undermines hierarchy. The first gesture of *xenia*, the ancient Greek ritual of hospitality, which the *Odyssey* reenacts time and again, is to welcome the stranger, to offer him meat and drink, before you ask his name, before you know his business or social standing. The stranger is protected by the gods. The Arab prisoner, held by a man whom he thinks is the judge, the symbol of colonial authority, the Arab prisoner who murdered his cousin is puzzled by the gesture. "Why do you eat with me?" Because, like you, "I'm hungry."

They exchange a few more words and then Daru makes the prisoner's bed in the same simple room where he will sleep. The teacher passes a restless night. What will the prisoner do? At one point, he hears him stirring, and he regrets having put the gendarme's pistol away in the drawer. At another, he hears him get up and go outside. Will he escape and relieve Daru of the decision he must make? But then he hears him urinate and return to his bed. Have they formed a bond by spending this night together, like soldiers or other strangers who are thrown together in similar circumstances? Daru wants no part of any such forced fraternity.

The next morning, the teacher must make a decision. The entire affair disgusts him. On the one hand, the prisoner has committed a crime that he does not deny, a crime for which no justification is offered. On the other, to hand him over to the French judge in the next town feels dishonorable, and makes Daru complicit in the larger machinations of the law, the police, and necessarily the occupation for which he offers no justification:

> He found the man's stupid crime revolting, but to hand him over was a dishonor: just the thought of it drove him mad with humiliation. And he cursed his people who sent him this Arab and he cursed the man who dared to kill and had not known how to flee. (56)

He then sets out with the Arab prisoner. After walking for several hours, they reach an isolated spot in the road, and he hands the man a package:

> "Take this," he said. "There are dates, some bread, and sugar. It should hold you for a couple of days. Here's thirty bucks too" … "This way is the route to Tinguit. It's a two-hour walk. In Tinguit, there's the administration and the police. They are waiting on you … Over here is the path across the plateau. Two days walk from here you will find the pasture lands and they will welcome you and they will shelter you according to their law." (57)

The Bedouins too practiced a kind of Homeric *xenia* in which the stranger was always welcomed. In the land of the nomad, no man was not at home.

The prisoner again is perplexed. He tries to ask a question, but Daru cuts him off. "Be quiet. I am leaving you now" (57). He turns his back and heads off to the school. When he has gone some distance, he turns around and sees the Arab still glued to the spot. He stops and turns around several more times, but the Arab seems paralyzed. Eventually, at some distance, he turns around one more time and the prisoner, his guest, has chosen the route toward prison. He has been offered his freedom and he has chosen prison. We are not told why. Because that was what he had been taught he should do? Because freedom was the more frightening alternative? Because it somehow felt safer than the life of pure indeterminacy, a life truly without boundaries, a nomadic life where he would always be welcome and therefore never at home? The infinite hospitality of the nomad is more fearful than the all too familiar prison of our enemies, the occupiers we prefer because they give us definition, as hosts, as guests, as *hostes*, as hostages. The infinite hospitality of the heavenly Jerusalem can seem too much like slavery, too much like the indeterminacy of death, the unraveling of our identity in an infinite openness to the other, so much so that we actually prefer the known positions of the terrestrial Jerusalem, a land we can fight over, build a wall around, defend, a bag of grain for which we would slit the throat of our cousin—only if we must.

When Daru returns, he faces a final and potentially fatal irony. On the blackboard of the school, on the blackboard where at both the beginning and the end of the story it is mentioned that he has drawn the four major rivers of France—a symbolic evocation of the colonial subjection of the Algerian population to the history, the geography, and the culture of the occupying power, on that very blackboard is inscribed, "in a skillful hand," "You have handed over our brother. You will pay" (58). His gesture has been misread. He offered the man his freedom, and the man chose prison. The unbounded nature of the hospitality he offered—he took off his bonds, offered him food, drink, and shelter; he let the other choose his way—have become the bonds that may well lead to his own death. There is a history that makes his actions legible to others in ways he cannot himself control. He remains the occupier in the eyes of the other. The freedom of the heavenly Jerusalem is only visible, can only exist, as inscribed within the bounds of its imperfect counterpart: "as if its possibility, the haunting at least of its possibility, as if some pervertibility, were not also the condition of the Good, of Justice, of Love, of Faith etc. And of perfectibility."

## IV

I have, in fact, deliberately sanitized Camus's story. I have left out a certain mark of perversion, or perfectibility, it wears on its face. There is in the narration at several points a grotesque racialization of the other, a focus on certain physical features that mark the Arab as other, in contrast to the presumed unmarked whiteness of Daru and Balducci. This racialization focuses on a fleshly excess that seems to mark the Arab as forever unassimilable. When the Corsican Balducci first brings the prisoner in, we are told "Daru only saw his enormous lips, full, smooth, almost negroid; the nose however was straight, the eyes somber, full of fever" (48). Later when they share their supper, we read, "the fat lips opened a little" (53).

It is hard to know what to make of these racializing details. What is the point of view from which they are focalized? Is this Camus's own racism? Is this supposed to represent the racializing gaze of the colonial regime? Is it an example of the ways in which the discourse of a long held biological racism, itself rooted in an even older discursive regime that views historical conflict through the lens of "race wars," now determinedly fastens upon the fleshly details of groups of people to find boundaries and lines of demarcation, to ensure their otherness, an otherness that constitutes our identity as a people through their exclusion? To recall the English name of Foucault's course, *Society Must Be Defended*. Our very physicality becomes a kind of unintelligible excess that we invest with a surplus of social meaning, creating a moment of what Žižek following Lacan, would label "obscene enjoyment."[9] To quote one of my favorite and most wonderfully ironized lines from Malcom X, in which this very mechanism can be seen at work in its reversal, "some old, blue-eyed, brown-haired, bad smelling white man" (1960).

Black face itself, in its bizarre artificiality, becomes an unconscious recognition of these phenomena in which our very materiality is invested with an unacknowledged and obscene enjoyment that undergirds, reinforces, and sexualizes the borders that create our fantasies of identity, threat, and apocalypse. We see only too much evidence of these motifs in American political discourse. The Klan was created to defend the honor of "white womanhood." Latin America is sending caravans of racialized others headed to our borders. "They have women wrapped in duct tape in their back seats" (Mettler 2019). "I have to do it. You rape our women and you're taking over our country. And you have to go." This repulsive litany could be echoed by a thousand other quotations from the Protocols of the Elders of Zion, from Hutu radio broadcasts that incited the slaughter of Tutsis, from Serbian propaganda leading to the rape and murder of Bosnians. The very possibility of our perfection must by definition begin in our perversion, Derrida reminds us, in the embattled, terrestrial Jerusalem, in which we all dwell, in which our hospitality must be offered.

And this is why it is so incredibly important to recognize the historically limited nature of these racialized discourses. It has not always been thus. The nation state, as we understand it, is of relatively recent vintage. The notion that all Germans, all French, all Americans, should be gathered under a single legal authority on a single territory, is an idea that was not theorized or put into practice until the 18th and 19th centuries. As Foucault asks us to observe, it is no accident that this is the same period in which we see the emergence of biological racism and the more general notion of the biopolitical state.[10] Thus while the discursive and intellectual roots of the concept of race wars and of discriminating against in-groups and out-groups go much deeper, and phenomena such as anti-Semitism have an even longer and more complex genealogy, the idea that the boundaries of political states should coincide with the boundaries of particular "nations," and that these nations are expressions of an underlying ontological reality—nationality, blood, genetics—has a distinct and limited history; and it is no accident that that history coincides with the emergence of genocide as a defined historical phenomenon. *Blood and soil*. There is, in short, nothing natural about any of this. None of which is to say that people did not commit other horrible crimes in the distant past, that mass murder, slavery, and sexual oppression did not exist. But the recognition and discussion of the historical trajectories and limitations of these seemingly natural

---

9  See Lacan (1986: 356–57); Žižek (1992: 22, 134, 158–61; 2006: 310–11, 367–75); Janan (2009: 41–45).

10  See Brooke Holmes (2019) "bios also turns up at the heart of the bio- of biopower and biopolitics as it is first read by Foucault in terms of State racism and thanatopolitics—that is, as the determination of who must die to ensure the flourishing of a population conceived of as a racially pure community—in ways that are not always acknowledged but cannot be quarantined from our concept."

ON BORDERS, RACE, AND INFINITE HOSPITALITY 103

phenomena—race, nationality, borders, the state—means that they are not fated or decreed, that like Daru and his Arab prisoner, and like Mother Emanuel and Dylann Roof, we do have a choice. That choice is never outside of a context. And that context may pervert our intentions in the moment they seek perfection. But we do not have to choose the prison of the given; we can envision a world of infinite, nomadic hospitality, and of openness to the other, even as we must acknowledge that such openness will by necessity change us, that we, as we understand ourselves, may no longer exist, and that the heavenly Jerusalem of a democracy, of a governmentality to come, will require the ongoing and continuing transformation of the earthly Jerusalem, of its peoples, of its boundaries, and of its walls—so we may all breathe.

## Works Cited

Ahmed, Sara. 2008. "Liberal Multiculturalism is the Hegemony—It's an Empirical Fact—A Response to Slavoj Žižek," *Darkmatter: In the Ruins of Imperial Culture* (19 February 2008). https://libcom.org/article/liberal-multiculturalism-hegemony-its-empirical-fact-response-slavoj-zizek-sara-ahmed.

Anderson, Benedict. 1991. *Imagined Communities: Reflections on the Origin and Spread of Nationalism.* Rev. Edition. London: Verso.

Anderson, Perry. 1974. *Lineages of Absolutist State.* London: Verso.

Borden, Jeremy, Horwitz, Sari, Markon. 2015. "Officials: Suspect in Church Slayings Unrepentant Amid Outcry Over Racial Hatred." *The Washington Post.* June 19, 2015. www.washingtonpost.com/politics/south-carolina-governor-urges-death-penalty-charges-in-church-slayings/2015/06/19/3c039722-1678-11e5-9ddc-e3353542100c_story.html?utm_term=.6db4b9a77702.

Camus, Albert. 2008. *Oeuvres complètes.* Tome 4. Ed. Raymond Gay-Croisier. Paris: Gallimard.

Davis, Jack. E. 2001. *Race Against Time: Culture and Separation in Natchez since 1930.* Baton Rouge: Louisiana State University Press.

Derrida, Jacques. 1993a. *Spectres de Marx.* Paris: Galilée.

———. 1993b. *Khôra.* Paris: Galilée.

———. 1996. *Apories.* Paris: Galilée.

———. 1997. *Les Adieux.* Paris: Galilée.

Foucault, Michel. 1984. *L'usage des plaisirs. Histoire de la sexualité*, vol. 2. Paris: Gallimard.

———. 1997. *"Il faut défendre la société": Cours au Collège de France. 1976.* Eds. Mauro Bertani and Alessandro Fontana. Paris: Gallimard and Seuil.

Greene, Thomas. 1982. *The Light in Troy: Imitation and Discovery in Renaissance Poetics.* New Haven: Yale University Press.

Habinek, Thomas. 1998. *The Politics of Latin Literature: Writing, Identity, and Empire in Ancient Rome.* Princeton: Princeton University Press.

Holmes, Brooke. 2019. *"Bios." Political Concepts: A Critical Lexicon.* http://www.politicalconcepts.org/bios-brooke-holmes/.

Janan, Micaela. 2009. *Reflections in a Serpent's Eye: Thebes in Ovid's Metamorphoses.* Oxford: Oxford University Press.

Kosky, Jeffrey. 2001. *Levinas and the Philosophy of Religion.* Bloomington: Indiana University Press.

Lacan, Jacques. 1986. *Le séminaire VII: L'éthique de la psychanalyse.* Ed. Jacques-Alain Miller. Paris: Seuil.

Lawlor, Leonard. 2016. *From Violence to Speaking Out: Apocalypse and Expression in Foucault, Derrida, and Deleuze.* Edinburgh: University of Edinburgh Press.

"Leo Frank." Jewish Virtual Library. 2018. www.jewishvirtuallibrary.org/leo-frank.

Mettler, Karen. 2019. "Trump Again Mentions Taped-Up Women at the Border. Experts Don't Know What He Is Talking About." *The Washington Post*. January 25, 2019. www.washingtonpost.com/politics/2019/01/17/trumps-stories-taped-up-women-smuggled-into-us-are-divorced-reality-experts-say/.

Miller, Paul Allen. 2016. *Diotima at the Barricades: French Feminists Read Plato*. Oxford: Oxford University Press.

Rushdy, Ashraf H. A. 2012. *American Lynching*. New Haven: Yale University Press.

Nietzsche, Friedrich. 1994. *On the Genealogy of Morals*. Ed. Keith Ansell-Pearson. Trans. Carole Diethe. Cambridge: Cambridge University Press.

Snowden, Frank M. Jr. 1970. *Blacks in Antiquity: Ethiopians in the Greco-Roman Experience*. Cambridge: Harvard University Press.

———. 1983. *Before Color Prejudice: The Ancient View of Blacks*. Cambridge: Harvard University Press.

Stallings, A Walter. 2007. "L. Frank Baum's Editorials on the Sioux Nation." web.archive.org/web/20071209193251/http://www.northern.edu/hastingw/baumedts.htm.

X, Malcolm. *Speeches of Malcolm X*. 1960. www.wpafilmlibrary.com/videos/149365

Zalloua, Zahi. 2017. *Continental Philosophy and the Palestinian Question: Beyond the Jew and Greek*. London: Bloomsbury.

Žižek, Slavoj. 1992. *Enjoy Your Symptom: Jacques Lacan in Hollywood and Out*. London: Routledge.

———. 2006. *The Parallax View*. Cambridge: MIT University Press.

———. 2010. *Living in the End Times*. London: Verso.

# Chapter 8

# SARTRE, POLITICS, AND PSYCHOANALYSIS: IT DON'T MEAN A THING IF IT AINT GOT *DAS DING*[1]

In *Qu'est-ce que la littérature*, Sartre argues that literature is neither an exercise in pure aesthetics nor a mere reflection of pre-existing conditions but always an intentional act directed toward a specific audience. He challenges the writer to take responsibility for both the act and the audience to which it is addressed. In this way, he proposes that we produce a *littérature* that is both *engagée* and existentially authentic. His position is more nuanced than has often been recognized. He does not call for a mere "Literature of Ideas," in Nabokov's dismissive phrase,[2] nor does he demand the production of endless *romans à thèse* as is often alleged (Contat and Idt 1981: x). Rather, for Sartre, the author simultaneously creates and unveils an object (1948: 55) that in turn constitutes an invitation to the reader to participate in, and make possible, this unique moment of unveiling. "Écrire, c'est faire appel au lecteur pour qu'il fasse passer à l'existence objective le dévoilement que j'ai entrepris par le moyen du langage" ["To write is to make an appeal to the reader that he make enter into objective existence the act of unveiling that I have undertaken by the means of language"] (1948: 59).[3] The literary moment is not that of simple communication in which a pre-existing message is passed from one speaker to another, nor that of free play in which a fundamentally non-ideological, floating world is created. It is rather a moment of creation between author, reader, and text in which a fundamentally new object is called into existence through an act of profoundly situated and yet transcendent unveiling: transcendent precisely in so far as the act of unveiling does not exhaust itself in the moment (1948: 74–75).[4]

Engagement, then, is not something willed or refused, it is a fact of the authentic creative act. In calling into being an object that is fundamentally new, the literary work has changed the world from what it was prior to the conjoined acts of creation and reception that constitute it. This is true as much for mimetic forms as for more formalist ventures, since there is no attempt to present an image of the world through language

---

1 Many thanks to Greg Forter, David Wray, Meili Steele, and Pierre Zoberman who provided invaluable help and advice when this paper was written. It has been further updated and edited for the present collection.

2 Nabokov (1977: 286; see also 1973: 3, 121, 228–30; and 1989: 242, 336).

3 All translations are my own unless otherwise noted.

4 On the continuing value of Sartre's notion of the "situation" for literary and cultural study, see Tally (2023: 1).

that is not also the creation of a parallel world (1948: 29), or a world of difference. In choosing therefore to call into being one object rather than another, the author is responsible for the invitation to a specific act of unveiling that constitutes their creation. This is not a claim of authorial responsibility in the naïve sense that every act someone commits upon reading your text can be laid to your moral or ethical account, or that you are somehow fully self-present in the moment of creation, but in the precise philosophical sense that responsibility has been understood from Socrates to Bakhtin, i.e., you owe a response to the questions your act elicits. For whom are you writing, for what purpose, and why did you call into being this act of unveiling rather than another (1948: 29–30)? The answers you give open the possibility of a deeper dialogue leading to further symbolic, creative, and responsive acts, and reveal either a willingness to pursue the implications of your actions to their end (authenticity) or a refusal to acknowledge them in their finality (*mauvaise foi*, 1943: 84–85). "Écrire, c'est donc à la fois dévoiler le monde et le proposer comme une tâche à la générosité du lecteur" ["To write, is thus both to unveil the world and to propose it as a task to the reader's generosity"] (1948: 76). The act of unveiling itself must be, in the very complexity and principle of its construction, response-able: able to provoke and pursue the dialogue it engenders.

Although talk of authenticity, transcendence, engagement, and bad faith, as well as the concept of language as a means manipulated by the subject rather than as the ground of its constitution may sound *dépassé* (1948: 18), the challenge of Sartre's question remains fundamental. As writers, students, and consumers of literature, how do we justify this pursuit? More fundamentally, what is this pursuit? How can we give an account of it which neither degenerates into "the dead-end of formalist criticism" (de Man 1983) nor produces yet another, more sophisticated positivism? In short, what is literature? It would be naïve to assume that Sartre's postwar text is the last word on the subject. But it might be a good beginning.

Terry Eagleton's responds to Sartre's question, in *Literary Theory: An Introduction*, by saying that literature does not exist, only cultural semiotic systems. This is both typical and yet oddly idealist. To say that there is no such thing as literature because there is no single external object that corresponds to a consistent descriptive definition of it, is to assume that phenomenal objects exist outside the systems that describe them and render them visible qua objects of knowledge. This is classic idealism and, as a reader of Althusser and Lacan, Eagleton knows better. By this same logic, neither history nor society exist, since there exists no single consistent instantiation of them as an object separate from the set of assumptions and theoretical protocols that define and call them into existence as objects of study. Every science, on some level, must define and construct its own object.

Eagleton in the first and second editions of his seminal study proposes to replace literary theory with rhetorical and cultural studies (1996: 169–89). But cultural studies per se, as Eagleton later acknowledges (2003: chap. 1), cannot explain why we should teach and read poetry, novels, romances, or plays as opposed to Facebook posts, greeting cards, historical documents, or contracts. It is a position that calls the continued existence of literary study into question at a time when the humanities are under maximal threat, and it rests on the dubious assumption that culture is less imaginary than literature.

It is thus an ideological gambit that seeks to exert the hegemony of its own protocols and, in Sartrean fashion, to create and unveil its own object of study. To that extent I accept and applaud it. Cultural studies as a movement has in many ways been salutary. It successfully dethroned a narrow, stifling formalism that dominated Anglo-American literary criticism and theory from the time of Leavis and the New Criticism to the last gasps of American deconstruction. But it hardly answered, let alone disposed of Sartre's nagging question. The fact of the matter is that most of us who work in English or Comparative Literature departments still consider ourselves teachers of literature, even if we no longer know what that is[5].

In this essay, then, I take up Sartre's challenge, but I propose to move beyond the Marxian and existential terms in which he framed the question toward a post-Freudian definition founded on the works of Slavoj Žižek, Julia Kristeva, and Jacques Lacan. This is not as strange as it may sound: for, the Sartrean notion of authenticity and good faith is ultimately based on a concept of desire as *manque à l'être*. It is this lack at the heart of being that propels us forward in the project of our existence (1943: 625–25). Such a vocabulary is central to post-Freudian analysis as well, as exemplified in Lacan's echoing of Sartre (Lacan 1986: 229; Lacan 1973: 341; Ragland-Sullivan 1986: 43), and their common Hegelian and Heideggerian heritage (Butler 1987). But where for Sartre this lack is ontological, for post-Freudian analysis it is a fact of language: our lack is an effect of the castration we suffer upon entrance into the world of the Symbolic, that is of the a priori renunciation of plenitude that all human beings undergo when they enter into the world of difference, which makes articulated thought, and thus subjectivity, possible (Kristeva 1979: 11; Moi 1985: 99–100; Žižek 1992: 270).[6] It is for this reason, I would argue, that post-Freudian psychoanalysis escapes Sartre's strictures on the logical impossibility of repression. So long as the unconscious is seen as a substance in which ideas arise and are censored before they can come to consciousness, then the only way they can be censored is if they are already fully formed and known to exist by the subject. The subject thus becomes split against itself and can only engage in repression through a deliberate, knowing act of bad faith (1943: 85–90, 616–23). Such objections, however, hold no purchase on a conception of the unconscious as an effect of language. In the post-Freudian view, the unconscious is not a seething pit within but precisely that portion of enjoyment that haunts the institution of the subject itself. It is the voice of the Other, i.e., the meanings and significations that constitute our unique subject positions in relation to the pre-existing world and thus escape our conscious control even as they are the fabric out of which consciousness itself is made (Lacan 1973: 142, 167; Lacan 1986: 42; Ragland-Sullivan 1986: 221; Žižek in Hanlon 2001: 842).

---

5  Jeffrey Nealon's offers a grim assessment of literary study as traditionally pursued in English departments as having become "essentially a hobby— and a retrograde, frankly neo- racist one at that" (2022: 27).

6  The nostalgia may very well be for a plenitude that never existed. The moment described is logical rather than experiential. Indeed, by definition, the articulation of the experience of plenitude could not happen except once it has been lost. The feeling of "loss," therefore, is a back-formation.

108                    THEORY DOES NOT EXIST

Yet, my purpose in writing this text is not to call for a reconciliation of the Sartrean and Lacanian projects, both of which are well over a half-century old. It is to advance a concept of the literary object that can meet the demands of Sartre's question, which often still goes unanswered, and which in the contemporary crisis of the humanities only becomes more urgent. In this context, I argue that what we refer to when we say that we study the literary is a set of texts that problematize the dominant Symbolic system through a self-conscious manipulation of its founding contradictions. Literature is thus a practice of the letter that, through a concentration of signifying effects, points to a beyond of the Symbolic, to the irrational kernel of our enjoyment. In Kristevan terms, the literary is that form of writing that "by means of the polyvalence of sign and symbol, which unsettles naming and, by building up a plurality of connotations around the sign, affords the subject a chance to imagine the nonmeaning, or the true meaning of the Thing" (1989: 97). The Thing, here, refers to a concept first outlined by Lacan in his *Ethics of Psychoanalysis, das Ding*. By *das Ding*, Lacan means, "le hors-signifié. C'est en fonction de cet hors-signifié, et d'un rapport pathétique à lui, que le sujet conserve sa distance, et se constitue dans un mode de rapport, d'affect primaire, antérieure à tout refoulement" ["the beyond-of-the-signified. It is as a function of this beyond-of-the-signified and of an emotional relationship to it that the subject keeps its distance and is constituted in a kind of relationship characterized by primary affect, prior to any repression" (1986: 67/1992: 54)]. *Das Ding* is, then, the pre-object. It is that piece of the Real that is both in us and beyond us, hence the ground of desire (Silverman 2000: 16; Žižek 1989: 208–09; Žižek 1991: 169). The literary, on this view, is thus the unveiling through language of a fundamentally new object that, in the moment of its unveiling, points to a beyond of the very situated nature that its fundamentally linguistic and hence Symbolic character necessitates (Žižek 1992: 169–70).

This definition does not, I contend, produce a static essentialism: for every formation of the Symbolic is unique, as is every point of insertion in it, and thus every relationship to its beyond (Ragland-Sullivan 1986: 230–31, 299–305; Clément 1975: 16). The Imaginary, the Symbolic, and the Real are not reified things, but a set of logical relations presumed by the existence of the speaking subject (Julien 1990: 213–14; Mitchell and Rose 1982: 171n.6). The speaking subject only exists to the extent that it exists in language—defined as the total set of codes and syntagmatic relations that make articulated meaning possible—that is to say to the extent that it exists in the Symbolic (Althusser 1996: 72; Julien 1990: 176; Moxey 1991: 990). It is only a subject to the extent that it can project an image of itself, by means of which it can come to identify with the meanings into which it is born: this realm of projection and identification is the Imaginary (Julien 48–49 1990; Roudinesco 1997: 216). And finally, that subject is only finite (i.e., not God) to the extent that neither its self-projection nor the codes against which it projects itself constitute the sum total of existence, that is to say to the extent that the Real exists as the beyond of the Imaginary and the Symbolic (Ragland-Sullivan 1986: 188; Lacan 1975: 85). No one of these logical relations, however, has any necessary or prescribed content in and of itself. Moreover, this definition of the literary as "a practice of the letter that, through a concentration

## SARTRE, POLITICS, AND PSYCHOANALYSIS

of signifying effects, points to a beyond of the Symbolic" is fully historicizeable (Žižek 1989: 135), equally applicable across all genres of composition, and politically engaged in so far as the Symbolic system of any given social formation represents the dominant codes, syntaxes, and rules of substitution operative therein (Lacan 1986: 114–19, 128–29).

It may be objected that virtually any text may be read in this way, as in Eagleton's famous of example of the drunk pondering the metaphysical implications of the sign "dogs must be carried on the escalator" (1996: 6). This is quite true on one level. As Sartre was among the first to point out, literature is at least as much an act of reading as an act of writing. One *can* read the phonebook or subway signs as literature. But simply because such materials can be read as literature does not mean that all materials equally repay a literary reading. Eagleton exhausts the possibilities of his subway sign more quickly than he would either a Shakespearean sonnet or a speech by Macaulay. In the same fashion, virtually anything may become the object of a sociological analysis, but it is not clear that all objects equally repay the effort expended or yield as rich an experience. They do not all represent practices of the letter that produce in a sustained fashion the "sublime object."

The sublime object, to which, according to the Seminar on the *Ethics of Psychoanalysis*, the phenomenon of beauty[7] is intrinsically related, is that which is raised to the level of the Thing (Lacan 1986: 133). The Beautiful and the Sublime, then, become two aspects of the same Thing: the first representing the beyond of representation and the second representing the impossibility of that representation:

> although the suprasensible Idea/Thing cannot be represented in a direct, immediate way, one can represent the Idea "symbolically," in the guise of beauty (in other words, the beautiful is a way to represent to ourselves "analogically" the good in the phenomenal world); what the chaotic shapelessness of the of sublime phenomena renders visible, on the contrary, is the very impossibility of representing the suprasensible Idea/Thing. (Žižek 1992: 164)

The sublime object is not caught up in the endless substitutions of Symbolic exchange but occupies a place beyond the quotidian satisfactions of the pleasure and reality principles, and as such is cognate with perversion as Lacan defines it (Lacan 1986: 131).[8]

The Thing is, in Lacan's memorable phrase, that aspect of the Real that "suffers from the signifier." It appears within discourse as the place of "flocculation," the point of attraction to which shards of meaning, elements of signification, are attracted, where they are gathered into strands and chains (Lacan 1986: 142; 1992: 118). It does not appear directly but only through the representation of representations,

---

7  Lacan thus collapses Kant's categories of the beautiful and the sublime, but as Sussman (1993: 36) points out beauty in Kant is a "way-station between pure reason and the sublime." It presents the antinomies of pure reason: demanding the particular be apprehended within the universal, while maintaining its particularity. See also Sussman (1993: 28–29)

8  Compare Bataille (1957: 158–59).

the *Vorstellungsrepräsentanzen*. It is then the no-thing, the unrepresentable that nonetheless attracts the representation and its means, for our purposes, the literary.

The sublime object, therefore, is thus not what is searched for within the existing protocols of knowledge, but what is "found" or "created," while nonetheless inhering in the Symbolic as a necessary moment of its own self-betrayal. It is worth quoting from the *Séminaire* at some length on this difficult point:

> We come one again upon a fundamental structure, which allows us to articulate the fact that the Thing in question is, by virtue of its structure, open to being represented by what I called earlier … the Other thing.
>
> And that is the second characteristic of the Thing as veiled; it is by nature in the finding of the object, represented by something else.
>
> You cannot fail to see that in the celebrated expression of Picasso, "I do not seek, I find," that it is the finding (*trouver*), the *trobar* of the Provençal troubadours and the *trouvères*, and of all the schools of rhetoric, that takes precedence over the seeking.
>
> Obviously, what is found is sought, but sought in the paths of the signifier. Now the search is in a way an antipsychic search that by its place and function is beyond the pleasure principle. For according to the laws of the pleasure principle, the signifier projects into this beyond equalization, homeostasis, and the tendency to the uniform investment of the system of the self as such; it provokes its failure. The function of the pleasure principle is, in effect, to lead the subject from signifier to signifier, by generating as many signifiers as are required to maintain at as low a level as possible the tension that regulates the whole functioning of the psychic apparatus. (Lacan 1986: 143; Lacan 1992: 118–19)

The repetitive structures of most TV series offer a great example of what Lacan means by "searching" within the pleasure principle. They do not present a found object that breaks the frame of representation but seek to lead the viewer through an endless chain of substitutions, while assuring us that nothing has really changed. Mark Green will be the same sensitive, but slightly troubled character from one episode to the next of *ER*, so that even if he gets written out of the show, the structure is in place and continues on without him. There will be tensions and misadventures, but the basic representational reality, the foundation of our normative subjectivity, is never called into question. There is no answer of the Real: no ominously swing traffic light; no mysterious corpse wrapped in plastic, as in David Lynch's *Twin Peaks*. The question therefore is not one of high versus popular culture or literature versus television and cinema, but of the structures of signification.

To make my point more concrete, I will examine four sample texts, one each from Juvenal, Mallarmé, Leyner, and Sartre himself. I have deliberately chosen examples from different languages, genres, and periods. Thus, Juvenal represents satire from the Roman imperial period, Mallarmé highly wrought French symbolist poetry from the late nineteenth century, Leyner contemporary American experimental prose, and Sartre the realist novel. What I am offering is not a theory of poetry or prose, a theory of modernity or classicism, a theory of literary aesthetics or political engagement, but an examination of the ways in which certain practices of the letter "break apart the usual, univocal terms of language and reveal an irrepressible heterogeneity of multiple sounds and meanings" (Butler 1990: 81). It is an investigation into the literary as a signifying practice that points beyond language and thus always stands as a critique of a given formation of the Symbolic. And it is that meditation on the process of unveiling a radical new object that takes place between writer and reader in the literary moment that we call criticism.

My first example comes from Juvenal *Satire* 1, lines 147–49. In this poem written at the beginning of the second century CE, Juvenal asks who today can avoid writing satire when poets drone on incessantly about mythological minutiae and when senators' wives fight gladiators in the arena. It is the image of a world turned upside down. Such a view in itself, while well-anchored in the historical setting, would hardly represent a beyond of the Symbolic. It is rather its instantiation. Literary decadence, the inversion of gender roles, and the progressive degradation of traditional Roman morality are all standard tropes of Roman discourse from the time of Cato the Elder (2nd century BCE) to the coming into dominance of Christianity's messianic narrative. These are the classic bogey men of Roman aristocratic and patriarchal ideology (Miller 2004: 22–25). Juvenal deploys them ably. The mere citation of them confirms their power rather than relativizes or points beyond it.

Juvenal, however, does far more than simply reproduce the founding assumptions of Roman ideology. He exposes the rhetorical mechanisms by which this ideology is produced. He reveals the sleights of hand and the rules of substitution and syntactical enchainment that permit it to function. In the process, he produces a rift in the fabric of the Symbolic exposing the possibility of a world beyond—not so much a utopia as a world of unrelieved parapraxes from which all illusions of order have been swept away:

> Nil erit ulterius quod nostris moribus addat
> posteritas, eadem facient cupientque minores,
> omne in praecipiti vitium stetit.

> Posterity can add nothing more to our customs
> Our descendants will do and desire the same,
> All vice stands at the edge of a precipice.

Our vice has reached, in Peter Green's translation, "its ruinous zenith" (1974). What does it mean to say that time can add nothing more to our *mores*, our habits of life? History appears to have stopped. Moreover, why is addition or increase bad? We seem to have reached a saturation point at which no additional form of behavior can be absorbed into the Roman system of morality without pushing it over the precipice (Ferguson 1979: 122). We have reached rock bottom by going over the top. Thus, each new generation has brought an increasing variation in life (*addat*), and yet that increase can only be pictured as a decrease, a falling-off, or a deterioration within the existing Symbolic. "Our descendants will be *less* than ourselves." *Minores* is a common Latin term that both means descendants and yet carries with it an implicitly negative moral charge, "because they will do and desire the exact same things," *eadem*. Our elders, the *maiores*, are by definition our betters in Latin. The moral touchstone of

# 112 THEORY DOES NOT EXIST

traditional Latin discourse is the *mores maiorum*, "the customs of our elders." In Juvenal our descendants (*minores*) will be less (*minores*) than we are, however, because they will in fact be the same (*eadem*). Thus increase, decrease, and stasis, movement in time and paralysis, all become aligned with one another in a fashion that is both completely consonant with the dominant ideology and reveals its logical absurdity. We can only go down from here, which will be indistinguishable from up. The ruling fantasy that gives consistency to our sense of social order has been pulled back to reveal the inexpressible *Ding*.

Our second example is drawn from Mallarmé's "Sonnet en –yx," a poem whose complex intricacies of diction and etymological play go far beyond the scope of this paper.[9] I want to focus on one word, *ptyx*, a Greek term signifying a curve or fold (Cohn 1965: 141–42). It does not exist in normal French usage but appears in Homer in the first extant mention of writing in occidental poetry (Kromer 1971: 563–71). Before Mallarmé it appears only in Hugo's "Le satyre," where it is used as the name of a hill. The word signifies for Mallarmé the border between nonsense and meaning: the point at which existence folds back against itself in an act of reflection that conjures consciousness out of the nothingness enshrouding human existence. In the octave's rhyme scheme, *ptyx* is inserted between *Phénix* and *Styx*, corresponding to rebirth and nullity respectively. It thus constitutes the fold of language, the "aboli bibelot d'inanité sonore."

> Ses purs ongles très haut dédiant leur onyx,
> L'Angoisse, ce minuit, soutient, lampadophore,
> Maint rêve vespéral brûlé par le Phénix
> Que ne recueille pas de cinéraire amphore
> Sur les crédences, au salon vide: nul ptyx,
> Aboli bibelot d'inanité sonore,
> (Car le Maître est allé puiser des pleurs au Styx
> Avec ce seul objet dont le Néant s'honore).

> Her pure nails very high dedicating their onyx,
> Anguish, this midnight, sustains, lampadephore,
> Many a vesperal dream burned by the Phoenix
> That is not collected by any funerary amphora
> On the credenzas, in the empty salon: no ptyx,
> Abolished knickknack of empty sonority,
> (For the master has gone to search for tears in the Styx
> with this, the sole object with which Nothing is honored).

The poem is a complex meditation on nineteenth-century linguistic and historical theories, combined with a Hegelian reflection on the origin of consciousness in contradiction and conflict. Yet the whole is so tightly articulated and so overdetermined that the very act

---

9  For an extended reading in these terms, see Miller (1994).

of synthesis it attempts reveals the impossibility of that gesture and thus points beyond the totalizing theories on which it rests.

The *ptyx* is both a metonym for those linguistic and historical theories and a metaphor for the impossible fold or curve that would arrest the dissemination of meaning to which they attest. At the beginning of his mythology textbook, *Les dieux antiques*, Mallarmé describes how the primeval linguistic unity of the Indo-European peoples became fragmented, rendering a universal or perfect language impossible (1945: 1163–70). He argues that as a result of their migrations various dialects and, then, languages arose, and thus sound and meaning became separated from one another, making the direct expression of intentional meaning no longer possible. His proposed solution to this perceived crisis of language was to imagine a work of self-conscious poetic, linguistic, and cultural recuperation that would "donner un sens plus pur aux mots de la tribu" ("Give a purer meaning to the words of the tribe," "Tombeau d' Edgar Poe").[10]

The implications of this fall from an original state of linguistic grace and the subsequent need for a work of recuperation are central both to Mallarmé's conception of the "oeuvre pure" and the "Sonnet en yx" (1945: 366). According to the myth, as he tells it, in the beginning there was linguistic and cultural unity. It is the modern poet's task to recover this state of grace through a symbolic order that subsumes both the original unity and its subsequent fragmentation into a new, higher synthesis: "l'explication orphique de la terre" (Mallarmé 1945: 663; Langan 1986: 26–28). One means of pursuing this new symbolic order is through a thorough knowledge of the history of the language, its patterns of evolution, and their philosophical implications.

This interest in the poetic possibilities of historical philology is typical of the period (Balakian 1977: 85). In the latter half of the nineteenth century, comparative mythology and Indo-European linguistics offered revolutionary explanations for the origins of western culture. Their impact on Mallarmé can be seen most clearly in *Les dieux antiques* and *Les mots anglais*. *Les dieux antiques*, a free translation of George Cox's *Manual of Mythology* supplemented with passages from *The Mythology of the Aryan Nation*, shows both a general knowledge of the field and of the work of Cox's mentor, Max Müller (Mallarmé 1945: 1159–63). *Les mots anglais* displays a keen interest in the general theory of historical linguistics as well as the etymological roots of modern English and French (Mallarmé 1945: 901–02, 1050–51). Yet where Cox and Müller supply comforting narratives of historical and racial continuity, providing the raw materials for what will be developed by other hands into a scientific racism that reaches its apogee in Nazism, Mallarmé's poem presses these same concepts to the breaking point revealing the radically incommensurate nature of the individual

---

10 See Gilbert (1976: 110), "Mallarmé desired to return man and his world to their unique sources…. At these origins can be found the beginnings of all languages. During the course of history, adversity was established; expansion led to deterioration. Poetic language would return to this ideal source and be reborn as supreme."

114 THEORY DOES NOT EXIST

speaking subject to the historically constituted forms of signification out of which meaning is formed:

> On the credenzas, in the empty salon: no ptyx,
> Abolished knickknack of empty sonority,
> (For the master has gone to search for tears in the Styx
> with this, the sole object with which Nothing is honored).

Mallarmé in the "Sonnet en –yx" uses the etymologies of individual words,[11] as well as their mythological associations, to fashion a poem that enacts the roles of language and consciousness in the production and erosion of meaning. In each case, the etymological roots and their mythic connotations refer either to the cosmic cycles of the stars and sun—which Mallarmé believed embodied for early man the primal struggle between being and nothingness—or to the corresponding cycles of life and consciousness found in individual human beings. Indeed, it was Mallarmé's conviction, as well as Cox's, that all mythology and all religious and philosophical concepts stem from primitive humanity's attempt to name and understand the eternal cycling of the sun, its death and resurrection, or what Mallarmé termed "la tragédie de la Nature." Mythology itself was a product of the linguistic drift occasioned by the splitting of the original Indo-European, linguistic plenum, which caused terms that were formerly concrete and descriptive to become detached from their original context (Mallarmé 1945: 1050–51, 1163–70, 1274; Cox 1870: 31–38; Cohn 1965: 55, 140, 198).[12] The poet's impossible challenge, then, is not so much to deny history as to embody it within the compass of a single text. Hence, each of the etymologies examined in this sonnet refers to at least one of the following elements: light, dark, the curve as synecdoche for the cycle, or the convergence of opposites, as a synthetic movement embodying the previous three.

The first line is paradigmatic of the etymological patterning which runs throughout the poem. The relation of *ongles* and *onyx* is of particular interest. Set at opposite ends of the line, each is derived from the common root of both Greek *onux* and Latin *unguis*. *Onux* possesses a variety of meanings, but its primary sense is essentially that of *ongles*, the claws of an animal or the nails of a human. It is only by an extension of the initial set of qualities denoted by the word that it later came to mean a "veined gem," or more particularly "onyx" (Littré 1876; Liddell and Scott 1940). Thus, if we accept R. G. Cohn's interpretation of the *ongles* as "the distant cold stars which seem to be an organic part, a projection of the universal anguish [i.e. the *Angoisse* at the beginning of the second line]" (139–40), then we will observe a sort of overture being played on the harmonic relations that characterize the poem's imagery, the semantic content of its nouns, and

---

11 See Chassé (1954: 39), "Pour arriver à la compréhension du poète, l'essentiel est d'abord de bien se persuader que le vers: 'Donner un sens plus pur aux mots de la tribu' était une formule de signification très précise. A son point de vue, cette phrase, en langage clair, se traduisait ainsi: employer les mots dans un sens strictement étymologique."

12 Chassé claims Mallarmé was trying to invent an ideal language as close to Sanskrit as possible (1954: 36).

## SARTRE, POLITICS, AND PSYCHOANALYSIS

their etymology. For, Mallarmé, by increasing the gap between sound and meaning that separates *ongle* from *onux*, through a metaphorical transformation of nails into stars, has allowed the *ongles* to regain their original sound value [oniks], while permitting *onyx* to regain its original meaning ("nails").[13] Just as these two estranged moments of linguistic history converge at their point of derivation, *onux*, when they are projected to the apex of the night sky, so the line itself rolls up its ends to converge at the caesura between *haut* and *dédiant*. We thus find in this one line all the elements previously mentioned: light and dark; the cycle of the heavens; a convergence of opposites; and all achieved through an examination of the etymological root of the words at opposite ends of that same line. In the very first line, then, identity and difference are subsumed into a Hegelian unity of opposites.[14]

This sublimation of difference into unity, however, is but momentary. Its ideal self-identity is balanced by the powerful centrifugal forces inherent in the very history that produced it. The difference cannot be erased; *ongle* remains *ongle* and *onyx* onyx. They have not shifted positions on the page, nor been removed to a mythical vanishing point in Greek history, where the separate trajectories of their evolution would be annulled. The fold or *ptyx* that would allow them to be brought together exists neither within the poem, *nul ptyx*, nor in the French language. Even the imagery maintains this assertion of difference. For, while the white *ongles*, as the stars, are projected upon the dark night sky, the striped onyx remains a gem of the earth. The dualities effected by history are maintained, even in the moment of their denial. The white stars shine against the black background of night, while onyx consists in alternating bands of black and white. Unity and difference, light and dark, exist simultaneously, and are distributed equally throughout the line. Even the time of night *ce minuit*, reflects this dialectic, for midnight is by tradition the hour of greatest darkness, but also that in which the day begins its ascent. Yet, perhaps the most important indication of the mythic significance of this etymological and imagistic interaction resides in the observation that its effect is predicated on the initial projection by "Anguish" of the finite *ongles* onto the infinite heavens, thus ratifying their participation in the cyclic drama of the cosmos, even as it evokes the lost object that is the Symbolic representation of a plenitude that is beyond signification: *das Ding*.

The "Sonnet en –yx" is a very different poem from Juvenal's. The moral and political eschatology of traditional Roman discourse has been replaced with the metaphysical melancholy of *fin de siècle* France. But in both cases, what distinguishes these passages as literary is a certain practice of the letter, a certain manipulation of the signifying

---

13  It should be noted that the process that permits this metaphorical transformation is the same as what originally allowed the Greek *onux* to refer to "onyx" as well as "nails," an extension of meaning through abstraction of the image.

14  See Hegel (§73), "Everything is grounded in the unity of identity and non-identity, of one and other, of sameness and distinction, of affirmation and negation. The Absolute is essentially dialectical. Dialectic is the essence of Being or Being as *essence*. Essence is the *sufficient ground* of all that seems to be non-absolute or finite. A is non-A: The Absolute maintains itself in that which seems to escape it."

116 THEORY DOES NOT EXIST

substance that reveals the logical limits of the Symbolic structures that make signification possible. In neither case, however, are those manipulations extra-historical or extra-ideological. The literary is not only inconceivable outside of ideology, it, like any other speech-act, is constructed from the raw materials of social life. The question is not one of whether literature is contaminated by ideology, but of what literature does with the ideological materials out of which it is rightly and necessarily made. Both Juvenal and Mallarmé reveal a beyond of the Symbolic, but in each case a beyond that could only be constructed within a precisely located set of historically determined structures. In both cases, they reveal the ultimate impossibility of the Symbolic systems out of which they are constituted ever producing the stable, homogeneous sets of meanings and corresponding social unities of which their respective dominant ideologies dream. They do so less by adopting a position of conscious opposition to that ideology, which could only be articulated in the terms of the reigning Symbolic and thus subject to its immediate cooption, than through the invitation to the reader to collaborate in the unveiling of fundamentally new object (or non-object, more precisely) that reveals the limits of the Symbolic from within.

My penultimate example, from Mark Leyner's collection *I Smell Esther Williams*, is perhaps the best illustration of my thesis of the simultaneously local and transcendent nature of the literary. Leyner combines popular American culture with a camp writing style and absurdist sense of humor to produce a postmodern prose that pushes contemporary idiom to the breaking point.[15] His work is saturated with the most mundane elements of our immediate ideological universe and yet he manages to reveal the depthless spaces that lie just below their signifying surface. The following is from his story "The Young American Poets":

> In lieu of kidnapping, more and more young people are having children of their own. Mayonnaise gone bad can be lethal and I wonder if being a stewardess is the vaunted career it once was. Ms. Eggnog left me a note: "Dear Mark, Go fuck yourself. I can't stand it anymore. They're lulling us into a false sense of security about radioactivity." I began to suspect some sleight of hand involving the bonds my grandparents held in escrow. I sent the little money I had left to Charo. (78)

In this passage, a series of deft maneuvers simultaneously reveals the vapidity of normal life, lacerates our reigning paranoia, and celebrates the weightless joy of pure semiosis. We move from the reversal of the expected tabloid headline on childless couples kidnapping babies from hospitals to the mock seriousness of "Hints from Heloise" warning us of the dangers of spoiled mayonnaise. The eggs in the mayonnaise, in turn—picture the jar of Helmans in your refrigerator—give rise to Ms. Eggnog whose affair with the author has turned as sour as a carton of old milk ("Dear Mark, Go fuck yourself"). This association of mass-produced consumer products and sexuality turned bad ("fucking eggnog!") in turn picks up on the earlier phrase lamenting the lost glories of the airline stewardess, that 60's and 70's icon of corporate produced sexuality.

---

15 I owe my discovery of Leyner to Moraru's insightful article (2001).

# SARTRE, POLITICS, AND PSYCHOANALYSIS

"Coffee, tea, or me?" Yet it is not "Mark" or his "fucking" that Ms. Eggnog cannot stand, but the radioactivity produced by the same dark corporate forces that have churned out the mayonnaise, holiday dairy products, and dimly remembered visions of sexy stewardae. That same constellation of late capitalist forces leads the narrator to fear the worst for his grandparents' bonds. Yet, these are the same forces he celebrates in that ultimate icon of the culture industry's vapidity, Charo—forever singing "goochie, goochie" as she dances for the doddering Xavier Cougat, who is old enough to be her grandfather. At least, she doesn't have to worry about her bonds.

The transitions in this passage are dizzying and the implications far from exhausted by this quick analysis. The amazing thing is not how disjointed it all seems, but just the opposite, how each disparate object seems deeply implicated in the next. The chain of association linking these found objects from the detritus of contemporary American life in Leyner's prose reveals the profound coherence and simultaneous inanity of our Symbolic ground. The postmodern American culture of the late twentieth century is revealed as an absurd, paranoid, and yet oddly joyous romp, a complex web of nothing. To follow the associative syntax and diction closely is ultimately to feel the foundations of that existence shimmer lightly in the air.

The evacuation of the illusion of substance in an era whose clearest cultural icons were *Survivor* and Donald Trump may hardly seem counterhegemonic. Contemporary consumer capitalism is itself a constant exchange of images with no real demand for foundational experiences and use values (Eagleton 2003: chapter 2). Yet, there is something sinister in Leyner's weightless world: the paranoia, the floating affect reveal a Symbolic system that has no legitimate claim upon us in any strong sense of the word and yet produces tangible effects and manipulations. The very sense of freedom this weightlessness on one level celebrates, on another level is the sign of the sheer arbitrary nature and abjectness of our subjection. The revelation of that subjection, the unveiling of the *Ding* that lies behind and constitutes our freedom, remains a fundamentally demystifying gesture. Moreover, it is not at all clear that consumer capitalism, especially in the United States, views itself as the postmodern romp it many respects became. Reaganism, Thatcherism, and their ideological offspring, Bushism and Trumpism, remain dependent on the belief that the bourgeois values of God, Country, Family, and Freedom underpin Western capital's continuing world hegemony. Such foundational beliefs may well be a cynical illusion in the world of global consumer capitalism and populist culture wars, but they have real consequences, nonetheless. It would have been very difficult to persuade thousands of American soldiers to kill and be killed in the sands of Iraq for Charo and *The Apprentice*. The illusion of solidity is persistent

My final example comes from Sartre himself. Although Sartre and Lacan differed on many things, most particularly their conceptions of language and the unconscious, their basic aesthetic positions, as outlined here, are not without certain complementarities. This can no doubt be laid at the door in part of their respective debts to Heidegger and Hegel, and their common Parisian intellectual milieu (Ragland-Sullivan 1986: 91; Roudinesco 1997: 98).

118 THEORY DOES NOT EXIST

Nonetheless, this coincidence of interests would be nothing more than a mere cultural and intellectual curiosity if it did not have potentially powerful theoretical and political ramifications. Thus, for both Sartre and Lacan the subject remains central. This is what separates Lacan from many of his postmodern confreres (Žižek 1989: 174–75). The Lacanian subject may be at its core a moment of sheer absence or the negation of all positive substance, but it is also central in that role. The talking cure depends on the existence of the tortured subject on the couch, perpetually discovering the facticity of its own constructions and defenses, its own constitutive relation to the Other (Lacan 1986: 347, 351; Freiberger 2000: 225–26, 237–38). Nor should it be forgotten that for Sartre himself in *L'être et le néant*, the authentic subject is on the side of *le néant*, not *l'être*: it is not a substance, but a perpetual Hegelian negation. All the same, as noted above, Lacan does not accept either Sartre's position of the subject being a posited ontological given, nor that of its ability through lucidity to come to an ideal self-presence of good faith. For Lacan, the subject is always constituted through language, and always therefore irremediably severed from itself (Dowling 1984: 91).

Nonetheless, once these allowances are made, the Lacan of the *Ethics* and the Sartre of *Qu'est-ce que la littérature* each have something to offer the other in terms of a theory of literature. Sartre brings three things to the table. The first is the urgency of the question: what is literature? What is this thing we think we read, produce, and study? The second is the formulation of literature not as a reified pre-existing object, a Platonic form, but as an invitation to a collaborative unveiling of a fundamentally new object that at once reflects and re-forms the world. The third is the consciousness of the necessarily political nature of any such collaborative unveiling of the literary object. What Lacan has on offer is three very different things. The first is his conception of the Imaginary, the Symbolic, and the Real as the three primary orders of existence. This triangular structure has the advantage of allowing us to theorize the relation of language to the subject in a very precise way without ever collapsing one term into the other. The second is his concept of *das Ding* as the preSymbolic kernel of our enjoyment. Last is his concept of the sublime object as that which is raised to the dignity of *das Ding*, i.e., as that which is created within the Symbolic in such a way as to always point beyond it and its pre-existing constructions.

Literature, then, is a practice of the letter that comes as an invitation to the reader to constitute or unveil a sublime object. That invitation comes in the form of a concentration of signifying effects that folds back a given Symbolic formation against itself and so points to its own beyond. Neither that beyond nor the Symbolic itself are static unchanging objects, but situated moments whose precise contours are constituted in the instant of the issuing of the invitation: that is to say, when reader and text enter into the relation of co-constitution and unveiling.

Our final passage, then, is from the second volume of Sartre's *Les chemins de la liberté*, *Le Sursis*, and will show more precisely how this particular reading of Lacan and his heirs is able to offer a convincing answer to Sartre's question. *Le Sursis* is a vast multi-perspectival novel set on the eve of the Second World War, in the days leading up to the French mobilization in September 1938. It is at once realistic and written in a kind of cinematic technique that involves rapid cuts between fictional characters and historical

# SARTRE, POLITICS, AND PSYCHOANALYSIS

actors, leading to the possibility of a final synthesis in which all the individual points of view are taken up into a single larger historical and narrative vision. The passage in question is at once programmatic for the novel as a whole and an avowal of the fundamental impossibility, and simultaneous necessity, of its narrative project. This passage both acknowledges the necessity of the omniscient "God's eye" point of view that such a narrative style creates and denies the possibility of the existence of such a perspective *tout court*. As such, the single most programmatic statement in the novel, the one in which the author offer his most explicit metanarratalogical reflections, is also a deconstruction of the novel's own narrative technique. That technique, however, as is made clear, is a product not of just formal exigencies, but also carries with it certain essential political, ethical, and epistemological demands:

> Un corps énorme, une planète, dans un espace à cent millions de dimensions; les êtres à trois dimensions ne pouvaient même pas l'imaginer. Et pourtant chaque dimension était une conscience autonome. Si on essayait de regarder la planète en face, elle s'effondrait en miettes, il ne restait plus que des consciences. Cent millions de consciences libres dont chacune voyait des murs, un bout de cigare rougeoyant, des visages familiers, et construisait sa destiné sous sa propre responsabilité. Et pourtant, si l'on était une de ces consciences on s'apercevait à d'imperceptibles effleurements, à d'insensibles changements, qu'on etait solidaire d'un gigantesque et invisible polypier. La guerre: chacun est libre et pourtant les jeux sont faits. Elle est là, elle est partout, c'est la totalité de toutes mes pensées, de toutes les paroles d'Hitler, de tous les actes de Gomez, mais personne n'est là pour faire le total. Elle n'existe que pour dieu. Mais Dieu n'existe pas. Et pourtant la guerre existe. (Sartre 1981: 1024–25)

> A vast body, a planet, in a space of one hundred million dimensions; three-dimensional beings could not even imagine it. And yet each dimension was an autonomous consciousness. If one tried to look directly at the planet, it would fall to pieces, there would be only consciousnesses. One hundred million free consciousnesses, each one of which saw walls, the glowing end of a cigar, familiar faces, and constructed its destiny under its own responsibility. And yet, if you were one of these consciousnesses, you would become aware through the lightest of touches, through insensible changes, that you were part of a giant and invisible coral reef. The war: everyone is free and yet the bets are made. It's there; it's everywhere, it's the totality of all my thoughts, all Hitler's words, all Gomez's acts: but no one is there to add it up. It exists only for God. But God does not exist. And yet the war exists.

As Jameson says of this passage, it is an "agonized and self-canceling passage" in which the simultaneous impossibility and necessity of totality is vividly evoked (1981: 57). The world must make sense because history has a direction. It is not random. In September of 1938, the world of Western Europe was moving inexorably toward war. And yet, the illusion of the inexorable march toward war masks the countless independent actions of millions of responsible actors, no one of whose individual actions could be predicted with any certainty. In addition, such a vision of radical individual freedom was the very condition of the political solidarity that was necessary if war was to be stopped: for only an appeal to these individual's ethical freedom could justify a call to action that might stop the slide toward catastrophe. In a world where people are not responsible for their actions, the call for them to act differently is a non sequitur. And yet, the appeal to the individual actors' ethical freedom just as clearly masks the fact that they are indeed part of a vast process, an organism, whose contours they cannot see or even posit, and yet it determines not only the context of their actions, but their import as well.

These positions are contradictory. They cannot exist in the same logical universe, and yet they must if any sense is to be made either of the events of September 1938 or those leading to our current climate catastrophe. What Sartre's novel in general, and this passage in particular, achieves is the concretization and representation of this logical impossibility. This is literature's job. "Totality is affirmed in the very moment whereby it is denied, and represented in the same language that denies it all possible representation" (Jameson 57). In doing so, Sartre marshals the categories and conventions of modernism's ethical pathos, the twentieth century's elegy for the bourgeois individual, to unveil an object that simultaneously transcends those categories and yet never falls into a facile deterministic materialism. It turns the very Symbolic resources of twentieth century phenomenological philosophy and of Sartrean existentialism against themselves to create a sublime object that evokes the lost image of the reassuring totality—*das Ding* as the lost object—and mourns its loss as the condition of our acting as subjects in history.

If space allowed, similar demonstrations could be made of the practice of the letter in an even wider variety of texts. In fact, the range of examples is only limited by the knowledge of the reader. Literary analysis, as here described, in no way precludes examining these same texts as communicative acts. But literature is a practice of the letter that in its dialogic relation with the reading public simultaneously unveils and creates an object that not only reproduces the founding assumptions of the reigning Symbolic, but also pushes those assumptions to the point at which they reveal their own historical, structural, and ultimately ontological limitations, and hence their beyond. Through the literary an excess of meaning is produced that threatens the very ground of our experience, revealing a sublime object: *das Ding*, the point of flocculation, the navel of our dream of representation.

## Works Cited

Althusser, Louis. 1996. "Letters to D." *Writings on Psychoanalysis: Freud and Lacan*. Eds. Olivier Corpet and François Matheron, Trans. Jeffrey Mehlman. New York: Columbia Univesity Press. 33–77.

Balakian, Anna. 1977. *The Symbolist Movement: A Critical Appraisal*. New York: New York University Press.

Bataille, Georges. 1957. *L'érotisme*. Paris: Minuit.

Butler, Judith. 1990. *Gender Trouble: Feminism and the Subversion of Identity*. New York: Routledge.

———. 1987 *Subjects of Desire: Hegelian Reflections in Twentieth Century France*. New York: Columbia University Press.

Chassé, Charles. 1954. *Les clés de Mallarmé*. Paris: Aubier.

Clément, Cathérine. 1975. "La Coupable." *La jeune née*. Paris: Union Générale d'Edition,. 8–113.

Cohn, R. G. 1965. *Towards the Poems of Mallarmé*. Berkeley: University of California Press.

Contat, Michel and Geneviève Idt. 1981. "Préface" to Jean-Paul Sartre, *Oeuvres romanesques*. Ed. Michel Contat and Michel Rybalka, with the collaboration of Geneviève Idt and George H. Bauer. Paris: Gallimard. ix–xxxiii.

## SARTRE, POLITICS, AND PSYCHOANALYSIS

Cox, George W. 1870. *The Mythology of the Aryan Nations*, vol. 1. London: Longmans, Green, and Co.

de Man, Paul. 1983. "The Dead-End of Formalist Criticism." *Blindness and Insight: Essays in the Rhetoric of Contemporary Criticism*. 2nd ed. Minneapolis: University of Minnesota Press. 229–45.

Dowling, William C 1984. *Jameson, Althusser, Marx: An Introduction to the Political Unconscious*. Ithaca: Cornell University Press.

Eagleton, Terry. 1996. *Literary Theory: An Introduction*. 2nd ed. Minneapolis: University of Minnesota Press.

———. 2003. *After Theory*. New York: Basic Books.

Ferguson, John. 1979. *Juvenal: The Satires*. New York: St. Martin's Press.

Freiberger, Erich D. 2000 "'Heads I Win, Tails You Lose': Wittgenstein, Plato, and the Role of Construction and Deconstruction in Psychoanalysis and Ethics." *Lacan in America*. Ed. Jean Michel Rabaté. New York: The Other Press. 223–46.

Gilbert, Paula. 1976. *The Aesthetics of Stéphane Mallarmé in Relation to his Public*. Madison: Farleigh Dickinson University Press.

Green, Peter. 1974. *Juvenal: The Sixteen Satires*. London: Penguin.

Hanlon, Christopher. 2001. "Psychoanalysis and the Post-Political: An Interview with Slavoj Žižek." *New Literary History* 32: 1–22.

Hegel, G. W. F. 1959. *Encyclopedia of Philosophy*. Trans. Gustav Emil Mueller. New York: Philosophical Library.

Jameson, Fredric. 1981. *The Political Unconscious: Narrative as a Socially Symbolic Act*. Ithaca: Cornell University Press.

Julien, Philippe. 1990. *Pour lire Jacques Lacan*. 2nd ed. Paris: E.P.E.L.

Kristeva, Julia. 1989. *Black Sun: Depression and Melancholia*. Trans. Leon S. Roudiez. New York: Columbia University Press.

———. 1979. "Le temps des femmes." *Cahiers de recherché de S. T. D. Paris VII* 5: 5–18.

Kromer, Gretchen. 1971 "The Redoubtable PTYX." *Modern Language Notes* 86: 563–72.

Lacan, Jacques. 1973. *Le Séminaire. Livre XI: Les quatre concepts fondementaux de la psychanalyse*. Ed. Jacques-Alain Miller. Paris: Seuil.

———. 1975. *Le Séminaire. Livre XX: Encore*. Ed. Jacques-Alain Miller. Paris: Seuil.

———. 1986. *Le Séminaire. Livre VII: L'éthique de la psychanalyse*. Ed. Jacques-Alain Miller. Paris: Seuil.

———. 1992. *The Seminar of Jacques Lacan. Book VII: The Ethics of Psychoanalysis, 1959–60*. Ed. Jacques-Alain Miller. Trans. Dennis Porter. New York: W. W. Norton.

Langan, Janine D. 1986. *Hegel and Mallarmé*. Lanham: University Press of America.

Liddell, Henry George and Robert Scott. 1940. *A Greek English Lexicon*, 9th ed. Revised by Sir Henry Stuart Jones with the assistance of Roderick McKenzie. Oxford: Oxford University Press.

Littré, E. 1876. *Dictionnaire de la langue française*. Paris: Hachette.

Mallarmé, Stéphane. 1945 *Oeuvres complètes de Mallarmé*. Eds. Henri Mondor and G. Jean-Aubry. Paris: Editions Gallimard.

Miller, Paul Allen. 1994. "Black and White Mythology: Etymology and Dialectics in Mallarmé's 'Sonnet en –yx.'" *Texas Studies in Literature and Language* 36: 184–211.

———. 2004. *Subjecting Verses: Latin Love Elegy and the Emergence of the Real*. Princeton: Princeton University Press.

Mitchell, Juliet and Jacqueline Rose, eds. 1982. Jacques Lacan, "Seminar of 21 January 1975." *Feminine Sexuality: Jacques Lacan and the Ecole Freudienne*. Trans Jacqueline Rose. New York: Pantheon. 62–71.

Moi, Toril. 1985. *Sexual/Textual Politics: Feminist Literary Theory*. New York: Routledge.

Moraru, Christian. 2001. "Intertextual Bodies: Three Steps on the Ladder of Posthumanity." *Intertexts* 5: 46–60.

Moxey, Keith P. F. 1991. "Semiotics and the Social History of Art." *New Literary History* 22: 985–99.

Nabokov, Vladimir. 1973. *Strong Opinions*. New York: McGraw Hill.

———. 1977. *Lolita*. New York: Berkley Publishing.

———. 1989. *Selected Letters 1940–1977*. Eds. Dmitri Nabokov and Matthew J. Bruccoli. San Diego: Harcourt, Brace, Jovanovich.

Nealon, Jeffrey. 2022. *Elegy for Literature*. London: Anthem.

Ragland-Sullivan, Ellie. 1986. *Jacques Lacan and the Philosophy of Psychoanalysis*. Urbana: University of Illinois Press.

Roudinesco, Elizabeth. 1997. *Jacques Lacan*. Trans. Barbara Bray. New York: Coumbia University Press.

Sartre, Jean-Paul. 1943. *L'être et le néant: essai d'ontologie phénoménologique*. Paris: Gallimard.

———. 1948. *Qu'est-ce que la littérature*. Paris: Gallimard.

———. 1981. Oeuvres romanesques. Eds. Michel Contat and Michel Rybalka, with the collaboration of Geneviève Idt and George H. Bauer. Paris: Gallimard.

Silverman, Kaja. 2000. *World Spectators*. Stanford: Stanford University Press.

Sussman, Henry. 1993. *Psyche and Text: The Sublime and Grandiose in Literature, Psychopathology, and Culture*. Albany: SUNY Press.

Tally, Robert Jr. 2023. *The Critical Situation: Vexed Perspectives in Postmodern Literary Studies*. London: Anthem.

Žižek, Slavoj. 1989. *The Sublime Object of Ideology*. London: Verso.

———. 1991. *Looking Awry: An Introduction to Jacques Lacan through Popular Culture*. Cambridge: MIT Press.

———. 1992. *Enjoy Your Symptom: Jacques Lacan in Hollywood and Out*. New York: Routledge.

# Chapter 9

# ENJOYMENT BEYOND THE PLEASURE PRINCIPLE: *ANTIGONE*, JULIAN OF NORWICH, AND THE *USE OF PLEASURES*

In 1984 Michel Foucault published the long awaited sequel to his *Histoire de la sexualité*. *The Use of Pleasures*, as volume two was titled, ends with a final chapter called "True Love," which offers a reading of Plato's *Symposium* and *Phaedrus*. In many ways, this chapter is crucial to understanding Foucault's whole project in the *History of Sexuality*. For one thing, it takes up and responds to Lacan's reading of the *Symposium* in his well-known 1961 seminar on transference and thus is central to understanding the relation between the *Histoire* and psychoanalysis. For Lacan, the essence of the *Symposium* is its exploration of the transferential relationship and the logic of substitution that relation implies between Socrates, Alcibiades, and Agathon.[1] In his reading, Alcibiades and Agathon, while not identical, are substitutable as objects of desire, insofar as each of them is beautiful. At the same time, Socrates is the object of Alcibiades' desire precisely because Alcibiades desires to be his object. Subject and object, desire and its tokens, all become part of an economy of substitution in which Agathon (literally "Mr. Good") and Alcibiades (the beautiful boy par excellence) become place holders in a dance that leads from the empirical to the sublime through a logic of transference and counter-transference as all three characters play musical couches at the conclusion of Plato's great dialogue.

Foucault's reading, in the end, does not so much contest Lacan's interpretation as historicize it, asking how it is that Love or Desire (*Eros*) came to be seen as a problem of truth rather than a simple question of regime or of the "use" of pleasures. As we shall see later, in so doing, he offers a powerful recontextualization of psychoanalysis's framing of desire in relation to the "truth" of the subject. But Lacan's seminar on transference was the second in a sequence devoted to texts from antiquity. The first was 1960's *The Ethics of Psychoanalysis*, which featured an extended reading of the *Antigone* (1986). And while Foucault offers an important response to the problem of desire and its relation to truth, as first posited by Plato and reinterpreted by Freud and Lacan, he does not do the same for *Antigone*. This, as we shall see, constitutes an important lacuna: for the *Antigone* does not so much pose the *Symposium's* question of desire's relation to truth and to an economy of substitutions, according to Lacan, as posit the possibility of an enjoyment, of a drive, that goes beyond any such economy, beyond all calculation, and

---

1 For a fuller reading of Lacan's interpretation of the *Symposium*, see my *Postmodern Spiritual Practices* (2007: chapter 4), and for Kristeva's response and her polemic with Foucault, Miller (2016: chapter 3).

124 THEORY DOES NOT EXIST

hence beyond the pleasure principle. This is a possibility the *History of Sexuality* does not directly consider. When at the end of Volume One Foucault asks us to imagine a world not founded on sexuality, but on bodies and pleasures (1976), he is positing a utopia that Alcibiades might well have understood but one that has no room for Antigone and her choice of death. Moreover *Antigone* is not a unique case in this regard, as we shall demonstrate later, when we read what is many ways a sister text: the visionary writings of the medieval anchorite, Julian of Norwich.

To fully understands the stakes of Foucault's final chapter of Volume Two of the *History of Sexuality*, however, we must also come to see how his reading offers a counterdiscourse to another famous psychoanalytic interpretation of the *Symposium*, one that is contemporary with his own and one that takes direct aim at what it terms his "sado-masochistic" "homosexual" discourse, Julia Kristeva's *Tales of Love*. Kristeva's text not only opens with a reading of the same Platonic dialogues as Foucault but it also makes pointed allusions to Foucault's person using phrases such as "our archeologists of love" and defining all homosexuality as characterized by sado-masochistic domination. Nor is this a single reference. The association of homosexuality, sado-masochism, and Foucault is repeated in more menacing and less flattering terms in Kristeva's thinly veiled portrait of the philosopher in her *roman à clef, Les samouraïs*. At the same time, her title in French *Histoires d'amour* (plural) constitutes a clear rejoinder to the *Histoire de la sexualité* (singular).

Indeed, as I have shown elsewhere, there can be little doubt at whom Kristeva's barbs are aimed.[2] On a theoretical level the differences are substantial as well. In *Histoires d'amour*, Kristeva begins by seeking to trace the way in which a desire that first received theoretical articulation in the *Phaedrus* and the *Symposium*—a desire that she views as pederastic and phallic, if not directly "penile"—was able to become not the discourse of "sex" or "sexuality," terms whose genealogy Foucault is tracing, but the phenomenon of "love." This latter term, in so far as it necessarily includes an articulation of the maternal for Kristeva, is actively heteroerotic (Kristeva 1983: 65–66).[3] *Histoires d'amour* is a direct response to the entire project of the *Histoire de la Sexualité* as articulated in Volume One and in Foucault's various interviews, lectures, and courses at the Collège de France, which led up to the publication of Volumes Two and Three in 1984.[4]

---

2  This complex set of responsions is worked out at length in chapter 3 of Miller (2016).

3  *Histoires d'amour* reprints Kristeva's important earlier text (1976) on maternal love, "Stabat mater" (1983: 225–47).

4  The Parisian intellectual community was a very small world. The first public indications of Foucault's interest in antiquity are signaled in 1981, most prominently by his lectures at the Collège de France on the topic "Subjéctivité et vérité," where he is discussing Plato's *Alcibiades*, Artemidorus, Plutarch, Galen, and Musonius Rufus with regard to the concepts of the "use of pleasures" and the "care of the self" (1994c). But see also the 1981 lecture "Sexualité et solitude," that announces many of the concerns articulated in the preface to Volume 2 of the *Histoire* (1994d). A 1982 interview in *Salmagundi* indicates that the change in Foucault's focus was by then well known (1994e: 321). The same interview also presents sado-masochism not as the essence of the male homosexual relation, as Kristeva presents it, but as an "innovation" developed to fight the "boredom" ensuing from the too easy access of the mere "sexual act" (1994e: 330–32). The lectures making up *L'herméneutique du sujet* were given in the spring of 1982 (2001).

ENJOYMENT BEYOND THE PLEASURE PRINCIPLE 125

Certainly, the responsions between the two texts are very clear. Where Foucault in volume 2 of *Histoire de la sexualité* concentrates on the masculine "use of pleasure," outlining an ancient discursive regime covering "The Moral Problematization of the Pleasures," "Dietetics," "Economics," and "Erotics," only coming to "True Love," in the very last chapter, Kristeva begins her *Histoires d'amour* with the same Platonic texts under the heading, "Maniacal Eros, Sublime Eros, On Masculine *Sexuality*" (emphasis mine). Where Foucault asks how we moved from ancient pleasure and desire to the modern sexual regime, Kristeva asks how did we move from a masculine sexuality focused on desire to the possibility of love, highlighting the almost total exclusion of the feminine and the maternal from the texts that constitute the archive of Foucault's genealogy of the desiring and largely pederastic subject.[5] The opposition between the discourse of "love" and the genealogy of "sexuality" could not be more explicit in Kristeva's framing.[6] Indeed, as Kristeva says in her unflattering portrait of Foucault's alter ego, Scherner, in *Les Samouraïs*, "cet homme n'aime pas, c'est évident" ["this man does not love, it's obvious"] (Kristeva 1990: 182).[7]

Of course, according to the received wisdom concerning the antagonism between Foucauldian and psychoanalytic approaches to the history of sexuality and hence, as the story goes, between phallic queer theory and a more maternal feminist discourse, this antagonism should come as no surprise (cf. Eribon 1994: 259; Richlin 1998; Dean 2003: 241; Leonard 2005: 88). We see this same conflict played out in the early polemics surrounding David Halperin's work (1995: 121) and in Joan Copjec's 1994 critique of Foucault and the "historicists."[8] More recently, Guilia Sissa has attacked Foucault for a simple and straightforward opposition to psychoanalysis in all forms (2008). This paper argues that the received wisdom, however, is an oversimplification: (a) that Foucault's work is not opposed to psychoanalysis per se but rather offers a historicization of it (Dean 2003: 241–42; Armstrong 2005: 131, 269);[9] (b) that insofar as it offers a historicization, it represents a critique of the kind of normalizing tendencies found in Kristeva's discourse, tendencies that are not universally accepted in psychoanalytic thought (Lacan certainly never argues that all homosexuals are sado-masochists); and (c) that the psychoanalytic response to a Foucauldian model of bodies and pleasures cannot be found in the refusal of its own discursive history, or in the assertion of ahistorical sexual norms, but precisely in terms of that which lies beyond Foucault's model of reciprocity, of an exchange of pleasures, of an economy of substitutions. This beyond of the pleasure principle, which Freud names the death drive, I would argue is decisively represented in two examples of a discourse that cannot be reduced to the normative: Antigone's "no" and Julian of Norwich's hallucinatory identification with a suffering,

---

5  On Foucault's exclusion of the feminine, see Dean-Jones (1993: 72); Macey (1993: 358); Richlin (1998); and Nikolchina (2004: 106–10).

6  On the other hand, Kristeva seems completely uninterested in Foucault's problematic of masculine friendship (1994a).

7  The unabashed heteronormativity of Kristeva's discourse is startlingly.

8  See its continuation in Copjec (2002: 29–30) and compare Žižek (1992: 123–24).

9  I have discussed this extensively in Miller (2007), see especially 208–11.

feminized body of Christ. Lastly (d), the present paper observes that this beyond of the pleasure principle, which Foucault's *History* finds difficult to articulate, is in both the figures of Antigone and of Julian associated with the feminine, maternal body. The latter, as has been widely observed, constitutes a blind spot in the discourse of both Foucault and Lacan, a lacuna which receives decisive articulation in Kristeva's question at the end of her own reading of the *Symposium*, "Et les femmes, dans tout cela? " ["And women in all this?"] (1983: 68) : for even in the *Symposium*, which features the speech of Diotima, the desire for the good (*to agathon/Agathon*) is ultimately predicated on the body of the beautiful boy (Alcibiades). Likewise, in Plato's other great dialogue on Eros, the *Phaedrus*, the female is all but completely absent. The exclusion of the specificity of the feminine and the maternal from these discourses is precisely the exclusion of that which cannot be mapped onto a totalizing discourse of pleasure and utility.[10]

## 1. For the Love of Foucault

The fundamental question Foucault poses in volumes 2 and 3 of the *History of Sexuality* is whence came the subject to be figured as one who desires (Foucault 1984a 12; Kremer-Marietti 1985: 247, 251–52)? At what point and how did the self's relation to itself become an erotic mystery in need of its own hermeneutic? How, in turn, did that self-relation come to define its relation to a truth that was at once internal to the subject and yet opaque, in need of ever more refined methods of self-observation and interpretation? And how did that hidden truth come to be defined as the essence of our desire? In many ways, these questions both assume the problematic of desire as defined by Lacanian psychoanalysis and they posit a time when the subject could be defined differently, when the way it problematized its relation to both itself and the object of desire were fundamentally different, and when the pleasures of *Erōs* were to be used, managed, and cultivated (hence the *use* of pleasures) rather than deciphered, interpreted, and plumbed in relation to truth.

The Platonic texts occupy a crucial position in this genealogy of the sexual subject. In many ways, Foucault's reading of the *Symposium* is not that dissimilar to Lacan's (Leonard 2005: 171–72). His emphasis is less on the fixed roles of *erastēs* and *erōmenos*, subject and object, dominator and dominated, than on the permeability and substitutability of those roles in Plato's understanding of "true love." Foucault is interested in those roles' capacity to develop into networks of reciprocity centered on the figure of Socrates and their potential thereby to undermine the inherent dissymmetry of the classical pederastic relation in favor of a more fluid shifting of roles in which Socrates becomes both the pursuer and the pursued (as with Alcibiades).

---

10   Without going too far into the details of his argument or of its limitations, it should be noted that Lacan's later identification of the feminine with the "not-all" names woman as what gives the lie to the masculine's pretensions to totalization. For the importance Lacan's formulation and its limitations, see inter alia Lacan (1975: 13, 68–75, 94); Roudinesco (1997: 369); Janan (1994: 28); and the next essay in this book.

# ENJOYMENT BEYOND THE PLEASURE PRINCIPLE

Prior to the Platonic theorization of love's relation to truth in the *Symposium* and the *Phaedrus*, according to Foucault, erotic relations were primarily reflected on in terms of when, how, and to whom an adolescent boy should submit. As Foucault, however, documents in some detail this was a relationship fraught with peril for the young man. On the one hand, pederasty was an established practice with a set of rules that functioned to introduce the young man into male society, teach him acceptable norms of behavior, and establish affective ties with older males of the same class. On the other hand, if that same young man was to go on to assume a dominant role in society as the head of a household and a political subject, his role as the penetrated submissive would threaten to undermine him. Hence, there was a constant question of whether and to whom a youth should submit and a high value placed on spiritual ties and eventual friendship, all in a highly charged erotic atmosphere (Foucault 1984a: 74–96, 232–37, 253; cf. Calame 1977: 423–26; Halperin 1990b: 267).

Foucault argues that we first observe the familiar dissymmetries of the traditional pederastic relation being called into question in Aristophanes' myth of the androgyne in the *Symposium*. Socrates in his later speech goes a step further. He posits a reciprocity that undermines a strict partition of roles. In Socrates' great speech in the *Phaedrus* and Diotima's in the *Symposium*, the ontological question –what is love?—becomes primary (Foucault 1984a: 258–59). The concern becomes less what are the traits to be desired in a lover or a beloved, and how might the pleasures deriving from those traits be used in a praiseworthy fashion, than what does it mean to love. The lover's inherent lack becomes the condition of his desire, and *Erōs* becomes the intermediary between that lack and the object that incarnates the possibility of its fulfillment—the beautiful boy, the beauty of the soul, the beautiful per se, wisdom, the good (Foucault 1984a: 260).

In the Platonic texts, on Foucault's reading, what had been a series of practices centered on the proper use of pleasure are being replaced by a reciprocal practice of self-reflection through the other, which is undertaken in the common pursuit of love's ontological truth (Foucault 1984a: 267). Thus, from a genealogical perspective, the *Symposium* and the *Phaedrus* mark a decisive turning point in the history of the desiring subject and lay the groundwork for its eventual transformation into the subject of sexuality. Foucault thus returns at the end of volume 2 to the fundamental question he poses at its beginning: how is it that "western man has been led to recognize himself as the subject of desire"?

> One thus sees marked one of the points where the interrogation of the man of desire will be formed. This does not mean that Platonic erotics dismissed at one blow and definitively an ethic of pleasures and their usage. One will on the contrary see how this ethic continued to develop and transform itself. But the tradition of thought that derives from Plato will play an important role, much later, when the problematization of sexual behavior will be re-elaborated beginning with the soul of concupiscence and the deciphering of its secrets. (Foucault 1984a: 268)

The truths of the desiring soul, as Lacan's reading of the *Symposium* testified, were the province of psychoanalysis. Foucault's response to Lacan, and by implication to Kristeva, is not to offer a direct refutation of the psychoanalytic reading of Plato's text,

128 THEORY DOES NOT EXIST

but it is precisely to show how the *Symposium* itself makes that reading possible and thereby situates that reading within a certain historical frame. The psychoanalytic explanation of the text and the authorization of a certain therapeutic practice based on that reading are shown to be effects rather than accounts of that text. The psychoanalytic reading, thus, from the Foucauldian point of view is the product of a contingent and limited discursive structure, rather than the discursive event that brings that structure to visibility. No wonder Kristeva's reaction is so phobic, if we accept Foucault's thesis—and it has a certain undeniable cogency—then the very vantage point from which *Histoires d'amour* is written is already discursively compromised, is already an effect of the very narratives it seeks to categorize, document, and explain.

There is a kind of breathtaking intellectual jujitsu on display in this final chapter of the *Use of Pleasures* in which Foucault shows that he can explain the master discourse that purports to explain his desire. He can demonstrate the genealogy and hence contingency of that discourse, positing in its stead an alternative universe of bodies and pleasures, a discourse not focused on deciphering the inner truth of our desire through a variety of confessional and speculative practices, but on the use, management, and enjoyment of reciprocal pleasures. Why should this be so threatening to psychoanalysis? It is certainly not the case that Foucault ever pronounces a generic anathema on psychoanalytic thought and on many occasions speaks positively about it, particularly about Lacan (see for example his remarks after the latter's death, 1994).[11] He does oppose a binarizing, normalizing discourse, and he does want to argue that the discursive practices of psychoanalysis have a history, and that history means that psychoanalytic discourse is always as much an effect of the practices it seeks to explain as it is a neutral barometer of their truth. But must psychoanalysis really have a transhistorical warrant for its discursive practices in order for its claims to have explanatory and even therapeutic power? Is it not the case that every science constructs and reconstructs its object as its own discourse evolves internally and is inflected by interactions with other discourses? The object of Aristotle's *Physics* is not ours but ours is inconceivable without Aristotle's.

The crucial question, then, is not whether Foucault is "opposed" to psychoanalysis, or whether the historicization of psychoanalytic discourse necessarily invalidates its claims, but whether there are phenomena described by analytic discourse that the *Use of Pleasures* cannot explain. I would argue there are, and they are precisely those that are beyond the economy of exchange that constitutes the pleasure principle. Cognitive science, behaviorism, Foucault's project of a positive description of a regime of bodies and pleasures, all assume on some level a realm of rational choice, assume that people make choices based on what gives them the most pleasure or reward, without making judgments about what constitutes that pleasure. But what if that is not always the case?

---

11  See also Foucault's statements in *L'herméneutique du sujet* (2001: 31–32, 180–82). For more on this complex and often oversimplified "antagonism, which is not one," see Eribon (1994: 234–38, 248–57), Lane (2000: 312–19, 324, 344), Rabaté (2003: 7–8), Shepherdson (2003: 150n. 15), and Castel-Bouchouchi (2003: 188–89).

## ENJOYMENT BEYOND THE PLEASURE PRINCIPLE

## 2. How do you solve a problem like Antigone?

This same utilitarian paradigm of maximizing pleasure is Freud's essential model as well until *Beyond the Pleasure* and the positing of the death drive. *Beyond the Pleasure Principle* asks precisely: what if there were a drive that could not be reduced to the search for pleasure, that could not enter into an exchange process wherein pleasure was sought and unpleasure avoided? What would that drive look like and would it not exceed all calculative modes, all resolution into a normalizing discourse of utility, all cognitive mapping? In a sense, by positing a radical perversity at the heart of human existence, a move that is exorbitant to all modes of reciprocity or exchange, the later Freud, as Lacan and Žižek contend, also posits the possibility of a radical ethics and a radical freedom. The emblem of this ethics in Lacan and Žižek is Antigone, and she and her choice, I would claim, have no position within Foucault's compelling genealogy. Her choice to die, to bury her brother even though she knows it means certain death and even though she knows he possessed no personal qualities that warrant this sacrifice, is unintelligible from any kind of positivist, cognitive, or utilitarian perspective (Lacan 1986; Miller 2007: chapter 3). The archetypical free act, according to this Lacanian and Žižekian view is precisely the self-relating consciousness's ability to say "no" to that to which, from the perspective of pleasure or utility, it should assent (Žižek 2006: 168, 177).

It is this "no," moreover, that is the ground of the ethical, not as a series of pre-existing codes that regulate and determine our behavior, but as the ground on which choice can be posited as transcendent to a calculation of potential costs and benefits. Antigone's freedom is not a function of the ability to pursue pleasure or to maximize utility, but it is rather a function of the very ability to refuse pleasure or utility in return for no obvious good. It is the ability to choose unaccountable *gratuité*: not because of its superior moral value or a specious nobility, but precisely as the possibility of doing otherwise, of thinking differently, as the moment of constitutive excess that every ethics must assume.[12]

Antigone by choosing the impossible, by choosing her death, also chooses the singular and unrepeatable, the moment that when generalized to the level of a rule becomes madness, and a moment that from an economic point of view can only be pictured as an unaccountable perversity. Yet that choice of negation and of an absolute Ought only has meaning in relation to the Is, in relation to a world of normative, calculative reason represented by Creon and the written laws of this world. It has no value in and of itself. The ethical act as an index of freedom can only exist at the impossible point of the joining of these two worlds of Is and Ought, at the moment of parallax that brings them both into view at once and that, as Sophocles saw so well, constitutes the moment of their tragic excess and enjoyment.

The ethical imperative is to insist on desire even beyond the realm of goods, beyond the realm of things that can be inscribed within the pleasure principle (Zupančič 2003: 179). The realm of goods is the domain of social exchange. Freedom within it is defined as the ability to dispose of your goods as you wish, so long as you

---

12  The preceding paragraphs owe much to Žižek (2006).

do so within the established social rules governing their exchange. This is the realm of bourgeois calculation: one good is exchanged for another based on a calculus of their relative pleasure and utility in relation to the potential unpleasure and pain they might produce. Within this realm, it makes no sense to choose pain, for pain to be a form of enjoyment. The ethics of psychoanalysis, as modeled by Antigone, however, is beyond "the good" and hence also beyond "evil." It is beyond any reckoning of relative pain, even one as refined and sublime as that found in Dante's hell. It posits a form of enjoyment that is beyond the pleasure principle, and hence beyond any set of normative oppositions (see Lacan 1986: 269–70; Žižek 1992: 77–78; and Zupančič 2003: 175–76).

True ethical action, then, insofar as it takes Antigone for its model, does not simply reproduce society's founding assumptions and our imaginary identification with those assumptions (Žižek 1992: 12). True ethical and moral action is creative. It introduces something fundamentally new into the world. It creates a space for our existence. The role of analysis is to make this act possible, not to make us comfortable with what already exists (Lacan 1986: 30). On this level, it is Oedipus himself in his self-inflicted blindness that can serve as our model:

> He does not know that in attaining happiness, conjugal happiness and that of his profession as king, as the guide of a happy city, he is sleeping with his mother. The question can be asked: what does this treatment that he inflicts upon himself [i.e., blinding] signify? What treatment? He renounces that which held him captive. In truth, he was conned, duped, by his very access to happiness. Beyond the providing of goods and services [*service des biens*], beyond even his complete success in providing these, he enters the zone in which he searches for his desire. (Lacan 1986: 352)

The ethical act creates a fundamentally new object for our desire, one which has not existed before, and it is our ethical obligation to bring this object into existence, "not to cede on our desire" (Lacan 1986: 370–71), not to accept the compromises and substitutions that our daily truck with reality principle proposes, but to go beyond the pleasure and its binary twin.

Freud, in fact, defines the pleasure principle as one of the self-preservative or ego instincts. The reality principle is its reflex and represents, not the Real, but our socially constructed picture of the world that places limits on our pursuit of pleasure so as to avoid unpleasure. The reality principle is, then, not beyond the pleasure principle but a direct outgrowth of it. It is a set of norms, codes, representations, and rules of conduct that are an immediate product of the Symbolic, Lacan's term for the world of regulated signifying practices (Lacan 1986: 42–43). Yet, the pleasure and reality principles are not all. Their attempt to constitute a closed totality always produces an inassimilable remainder. Freud's argument is founded on concrete observations of the repetition compulsions of traumatized veterans of World War I and other examples taken from his case histories. Here he detected the existence of a drive for a kind of satisfaction that cannot be accounted for by our daily seeking of immediate pleasures or by the fact of our settling for the kind of substitute satisfactions the reality principle offers in their stead. This drive represents the search for an absolute, pure satisfaction

ENJOYMENT BEYOND THE PLEASURE PRINCIPLE131

that transcends the very bounds of our identity and threatens it with destruction (Žižek 1992: 48). Freud would label it the death drive or Thanatos, as opposed to the pleasure principle or Eros.

Antigone's decision to defy Creon's decree and bury Polynices is such an act, one that consciously seeks death. Antigone knows full well what the results of her action will be. She makes no effort to defend Polynices's attack upon Thebes, nor does she deny Creon's argument that Eteocles and Polynices should not be accorded the same honors based on their actions (Lacan 1986: 290, 323–25; Guyomard 1992: 106; Benardete 1999: 6).[13] Burying Polynices is simply something she must do. Her choice is beyond the realm of rational calculation and the collective norms of satisfaction it implies, beyond any notion of pros and cons, beyond the pleasure and reality principles (Lacan 1986: 78, 281; Žižek 1991: 25). Hers is a stance that transcends the very oppositions that structure our daily social and moral lives. It is a form of radical enjoyment:

> Antigone: for me, it is a beautiful thing to die doing this.
> Dear to him I will lie with this dear one,
> Having committed holy crimes. (lines 72–75)

Nor can her choice be naturalized by a political logic. She is not giving her life for her country or for any other articulated principle. She is not a martyr for a recognized cause. Because her choice of death cannot be understood according to strictly rational calculations, and she makes no attempt to justify it within those norms, she cannot be read as representing a simple antithesis of freedom to tyranny, or of the individual to the state (Lacan 1986: 281; Žižek 1992: 77–78).

In fact, as she acknowledges, she had chosen death before Creon's decree against the burial of Polynices had been promulgated, and she defines herself to Ismene as one already belonging to the realm of the dead: "You live on! My soul has long since died so that it might serve the dead" (ll. 559–60; see Lacan 1986: 315, 326; Guyomard 1992: 106). Again, in lines 460–62, Antigone says that she knew she would die, even if Creon had not issued his edict, and that if she died before her time, so much the better:

> For I knew very well that I would die—why not—
> Even if you had not made your pronouncements; but if before my time
> I will die, I will count it as a gain.[14]

Antigone seeks death not because of Creon's decree, but almost in spite of it. Thus Jebb glosses line 461, "Even if thou hadst not proclaimed death as the penalty of infringing the edict" (1900: ad loc). Antigone has, in fact, "long since" been dead. That is her

---

13  See Johnson (1997: 374) on "the excessive, or at least self-destructive, nature of her attachment to Polynices in *Antigone*, observed by every reader of the play."
14  "In contrast to Creon's crass mercantilism (221–22, 1035–39nn.), Ant. uses the term to mean 'a true benefit'" (Griffith 1999: ad loc).

132 THEORY DOES NOT EXIST

nature, as indicated by her very name: "she who is *against*, or *in place of, generation*," i.e., the reproductive force of life (Benardete 1999: 18, 199). She is the bride of Hades (cf. lines 654, 806–16, 1236–41; Griffith 1999: 52). Creon's edict provides but the moment in which her desire is realized (Benardete 1999: 72–73).

## 3. Julian of Norwich: Suffering as Enjoyment

Antigone is important for her emblematic value and for the role she has played in western ethical reflection from Hegel to Lacan and Butler, but she is hardly alone. Our second example, Julian of Norwich, is less well known but equally salient. Julian was a fourteenth-century anchorite who lived in a cell attached to Saint Julian's church in the busy port town of Norwich. She is also the first woman writer in English. In her two texts, she tells vividly of her desire to experience Christ's wounds, of her prayer to identify with his passion, to feel the joy of his suffering. Like Antigone, Julian's enjoyment, her drive, cannot be framed in terms of an economic or utilitarian calculus. To reduce her experience to a masochistic inversion of the pleasure principle is to propose a tautological absurdity: "all human beings are motivated by pleasure, thus when people act in a manner that appears to court pain it must really be a source of pleasure, therefore all human beings are motivated by pleasure." Now *this* is a normalizing discourse in spades. And it is precisely what Freud's positing of the death drive sought to escape.

Julian, then, is an important test case if we are not to assume that Antigone represents a singular exception, and a fictional one at that. Julian's discourse is striking to say the least. She does not praise Jesus for his suffering. She does not thank him for the sacrifice he made for her, nor does she seek to exchange his pain for her eternal pleasure in what has become an all too common contemporary Christian calculus.[15] Julian was *not* an advocate of the "prosperity gospel." No, Julian wants "to suffer with" Christ (ST 3).[16] In a vision she has, which comes in a moment of illness, Christ appears, "And suddenly I saw the red blood trickling down from under the crown of thorns, all hot, freshly, plentifully, vividly" (ST 3). There is an immediacy to the vision. You can all but smell the blood, the sweat, the odor of the unwashed, corruptible bodies the vision implies.

Julian in her vision has an ecstatic relation to the suffering of Jesus, one that is explicitly sexualized. At one point, she observes that Jesus stands above the Virgin only in the "blessed Manhood of Christ" (ST4). But while his suffering is sexualized and eroticized, it does not fall within the economy of the "pleasure principle." It cannot be analyzed in terms of a drive towards pleasure that is tempered by the demands of the "reality principle" (Freud 1961: 4; Lacan 1986: 29; Derrida 1980: 249, 304–305,

---

15 One of my students complained when I made her class read this text that Julian could not have been a Christian because "Jesus suffered so we wouldn't have to."

16 Two texts come down to us from Julian. They are known respectively as the "Short Text" (henceforth ST) and the "Long Text" (henceforth LT). The numbers in the parenthetical citations refer to the chapters in the original.

# ENJOYMENT BEYOND THE PLEASURE PRINCIPLE

425–27). It is beyond that. It is beyond sublimation. His suffering is an end in itself. It *is* love. It has no exchange value. It answers no need. It meets no desire. It accepts no substitutions. It is a drive (Žižek 1992: 48; Žižek 2006: 62; Copjec 2000: 278–79; Copjec 2002: 38–39). It is not masochistic pleasure in self-degradation but suffering as the pure expression of love:

> We are his joy, we are his reward, we are his glory, we are his crown. What I am describing causes Jesus such great pleasure that he thinks nothing of all his hardship and his bitter suffering and his cruel and shameful death. And in these words, "if I could suffer more, I would suffer more," I saw truly that if he might die once for each man who shall be saved as he died once for all, love would never let him rest until he had done it. And when he had done it, he would still think nothing of it out of love; for everything seems a trifle to him in comparison with his love. And he showed me this very seriously, saying these words, "If I could suffer more." *He did not say, "if it were necessary to suffer more," but "if I could suffer more"; for if he could suffer more, he would, even if it were not necessary.* (ST 12, emphasis mine)

The limit on his suffering is not predicated on the demands of his pleasure, nor is it any necessity that mandates that he suffer, a need for a certain quantity of atonement. The limit on his suffering is simply an absolute limit to his capacity for suffering/pleasure/love. It is beyond any rational accounting of the pursuit of pleasure and the avoidance of pain. It is beyond the pleasure principle.

In answer to Julian's fevered prayer, Jesus appears. He opens his wound to her and "the blood and water that was within flowed out" (ST 13). This stream serves not as a blood sacrifice, but as an example of the blissful suffering that "purges us and makes us know ourselves" (ST 13). It serves, as Foucault would say, as a kind of spiritual practice" aimed at transforming the self, but it is irreducible to a simple exchange (Foucault 2001: 16–17). His pain is the moment of our redemption, not because it means we will *not* suffer, but precisely in order that we become one with that pain and are nourished by it. In her vision, Julian writes:

> Here I saw a great union between Christ and us, as I understand it; for when he was in pain, we were in pain. And all creatures who were capable of suffering, suffered with him, that is to say, all the creatures that god has made to serve us. At the time of Christ's dying, the firmament and the earth failed for sorrow, each according to their own nature. For it is their natural property to recognize as their God him in whom all their power is grounded; when he failed then by their very natures they had as far as possible to fail with him from sorrow at his pain. (LT 18)

Jesus like Antigone seeks not to avoid suffering but to embrace it. That suffering, in turn, becomes our suffering and as such becomes the means of access to a world beyond the calculations of exchange.

This suffering, this pain becomes a source of enjoyment (*jouissance*) beyond the pleasure principle, an investment of self in what threatens the self's destruction. Jesus says to Julian, "It is a joy, a delight, and an endless happiness to me that I ever endured suffering for you, and if I could suffer more, I would suffer more" (LT 22). His suffering in turn becomes the mother's breast that suckles us, the anguish that tenderly fosters our bliss and annihilation. Jesus, by virtue of his "Manhood," is our mother:

> We know that our mothers only bring us into the world to suffer and die, but our true mother, Jesus, who is all love, bears us into joy and eternal life; blessed may he be! So he sustains us within himself in love and was in labour for the full time until he suffered the sharpest pangs and the most grievous sufferings that ever were or shall be, and at last he died. ...
>
> The mother can give her child milk to suck, but our dear mother Jesus can feed us with himself, and he does so most generously and most tenderly with the holy sacrament which is the previous food of life itself. ...
>
> The mother can lay the child tenderly to her breast, but our tender mother Jesus, he can familiarly lead us into his blessed breast through his sweet open side, and show within part of the Godhead and the joys of heaven, with spiritual certainty of endless bliss. ... he says "look how I love you," looking into his side and rejoicing (LT 60).

Christ's suffering becomes the means of our birth. His wound becomes both our wound and the breast at which we suckle: the canal through which we are born. His manhood is his motherhood, his suffering our birth. We endlessly devour him and through that ingestion we come to share in his suffering and thereby come to experience a form of radical enjoyment: the ecstasy of the eucharist.

I am not of course saying that Julian's visions cannot be allegorized as a form of pleasure. This *is* a discourse of enjoyment. But it cannot be reduced *simply* to pleasure, and it certainly cannot be reduced to the pleasure principle, with its series of economic exchanges to maximize pleasure and avoid unpleasure: making all the compromises and trade-offs necessary to insure that, in the vast accountancy of the soul, our debits and credits balance, our books are in order. *It* is *beyond* that. As Socrates demonstrates in the *Philebus*, it is not the life of knowledge that is better than the life of pleasure, but it is the life of knowledge with pleasure, the life in which the enjoyment of knowledge can never be reduced to simple pleasure, which is the best life.

Neither Foucault's *Use of Pleasure* nor Kristeva's normalizing binarism can fully account for this beyond envisioned by Freud and embodied by Antigone and Julian, and it is this beyond that presents a possibility of freedom and that in its refusal of the economics of exchange makes ethics, beauty, and—dare I say it?—even the good possible. At the same time, Foucault's reading of the *Symposium* presents a decisive challenge to any form of psychoanalysis that would set itself up as the arbiter of truth, that would claim to be beyond history, beyond the conditions of its own birth.

In the end, it is the suffering body, the maternal body, the body of birth, death, and ecstasy, which stands as the limit and the condition of both these discourses—psychoanalysis and genealogy. And as the limit condition of these discourses, this feminine, maternal body in all its intensity and fragility must always gesture to a beyond of all (phallic) discursive economies, to a beyond of all possible exchanges and substitutions, and to a beyond metonymically embodied in Antigone's "no" and Julian's endlessly suffering Christ of enjoyment.

# ENJOYMENT BEYOND THE PLEASURE PRINCIPLE

## Works Cited

Armstrong, Richard. 2005. *A Compulsion for Antiquity: Freud and the Ancient World.* Ithaca: Cornell University Press.

Benardete, Seth. 1999. *Sacred Transgressions: A Reading of Sophocles' Antigone.* South Bend, IN: St. Augustine's Press.

Calame, Claude. 1977. *Les choeurs de jeunes filles en Grèce archaïque*, vol.1. Roma: Edizioni dell' Ateneo e Bizzarri.

Castel-Bouchouchi, Anissa. 2003. "Foucault et le paradoxe du platonisme." *Foucault et la philosophie antique.* Eds. Frédéric Gros et Carlos Lévy. Paris: Kimé. 175–93.

Copjec, Joan. 1994. *Read My Desire: Lacan Against the Historicists.* Cambridge, MA: MIT Press.

———. 2000. "The Body as Viewing Instrument: The Strut of Vision." *Lacan in America.* Ed. Jean-Michel Rabaté. New York: The Other Press. 277–308.

———. 2002. *Imagine There's No Woman: Ethics and Sublimation.* Cambridge, MA: MIT Press.

Dean, Tim. 2003. "Lacan and Queer Theory." *The Cambridge Companion to Lacan.* Ed. Jean-Michel Rabaté. Cambridge: Cambridge University Press. 238–52.

Dean-Jones, Lesley. 1993. "The Politics of Pleasure: Female Sexual Appetite in the Hippocratic Corpus." *Helios* 19: 72–91.

Derrida, Jacques. 1980. *La carte postale: de Socrate à Freud et au-delà.* Paris: Aubier-Flammarion.

Eribon, Didier. 1994. *Michel Foucault et ses contemporains.* Paris: Fayard.

Foucault, Michel. 1976. *La volonté de savoir. Histoire de la sexualité*, vol. 1. Paris: Gallimard.

———. 1984a. *L'usage des plaisirs. Histoire de la sexualité*, vol. 2. Paris: Gallimard.

———. 1994a. "De l'amitié comme mode de vie." In *Dits et écrits: 1954–1988*, vol. 4. Eds. Daniel Defert and François Ewalt. Paris: Gallimard. 163–67.

———. 1994b. "Lacan, le <<libérateur>> de la psychanalyse." Trans. A. Ghizzardi. In *Dits et écrits: 1954–1988*, vol. 4. Eds. Daniel Defert and François Ewalt. Paris: Gallimard. 204–205.

———. 1994c. "Subjectivité et vérité." In *Dits et écrits: 1954–1988*, vol. 4. Eds. Daniel Defert and François Ewalt. Paris: Gallimard. 213–18.

———. 1994d. "Sexualité et solitude." In *Dits et écrits: 1954–1988*, vol. 4. Eds. Daniel Defert and François Ewalt. Paris: Gallimard. 168–81.

———. 1994e. "Choix sexuel, acte sexuel." In *Dits et écrits: 1954–1988*, vol. 4. Eds. Daniel Defert and François Ewalt. Paris: Gallimard. 320–35.

———. 2001. *L'Herméneutique du sujet: Cours au Collège de France. 1981–1982.* Ed. Frédéric Gros. Paris: Gallimard/Seuil.

Freud, Sigmund. 1961. *Beyond the Pleasure Principle.* Trans. James Strachey. The Standard Edition. New York: Norton.

Griffith, Mark. 1999. *Sophocles: Antigone.* Cambridge: Cambridge University Press.

Guyomard, Patrick. 1992. *La jouissance du tragique: Antigone, Lacan et le désir de l'analyste.* Paris: Aubier.

Halperin, David M. 1990. "Why is Diotima a Woman? Platonic Erōs and the Figuration of Gender." *Before Sexuality: The Construction of Erotic Experience in the Ancient Greek World.* Eds. David M. Halperin, John J. Winkler, and Froma Zeitlin. Princeton: Princeton University Press. 257–308.

———. 1995. *Saint Foucault: Towards a Gay Hagiography.* New York: Oxford University Press.

Janan, Micaela. 1994. "When the Lamp is Shattered": Desire and Narrative in Catullus. Carbondale: Southern Illinois University Press.

Jebb, Richard. 1900. *Sophocles The Plays and Fragments with Critical Notes, Commentary, and Translation in English Prose. Part III. The Antigone.* 3rd ed. Cambridge: Cambridge University Press.

Johnson, Patricia. 1997. "Woman's Third Face: A Psycho/Social Reconsideration of Sophocles' *Antigone.*" *Arethusa* 30: 369–98.

Kremer-Marietti, Angèle. 1985. *Michel Foucault: Archéologie et généalogie.* 2nd ed. Paris: Livre de Poche.

Kristeva, Julia. 1983. *Histoires d'amour*. Paris: Denoël.
———. 1990. *Les Samouraïs*. Paris: Gallimard.
Lacan, Jacques. 1975. *Le séminaire livre XX: Encore*. Ed. Jacques-Alain Miller. Paris: Seuil.
———. 1986. *Le séminaire livre VII: L'éthique de la psychanalyse*. Ed. Jacques-Alain Miller. Paris: Seuil.
———. 1991. *Le séminaire livre VIII: Le transfert*. Ed. Jacques-Alain Miller. Paris: Seuil.
Lane, Christopher. 2000. "The Experience of the Outside: Foucault and Psychoanalysis." *Lacan in America*. Ed. Jean-Michel Rabaté. New York: The Other Press. 309–47.
Leonard, Miriam. 2005. *Athens in Paris: Ancient Greece and the Political in Post-War French Thought*. Oxford: Oxford University Press.
Macey, David. 1993. *The Lives of Michel Foucault*. New York: Pantheon.
Miller, Paul Allen. 2007. *Postmodern Spiritual Practices: The Construction of the Subject and the Reception of Plato in Lacan, Derrida, and Foucault*. Columbus: Ohio State University Press.
———. 2016. *Diotima at the Barricades: French Feminists Read Plato*. Oxford: Oxford University Press.
Nikolchina, Miglena. 2004. *Matricide in Language: Writing Theory in Kristeva and Woolf*. New York: Other Press.
Norwich, Julian of. 1998. *Revelations of Divine Love*. Trans. Elizabeth Spearing. Introduction and notes by A. C. Spearing. London: Penguin.
Rabaté, Jean-Michel. 2003. "Lacan's Turn to Freud." *Cambridge Companion to Lacan*. Ed. Jean-Michel Rabaté. Cambridge: Cambridge University Press. 1–24.
Richlin, Amy. 1998. "Foucault's History of Sexuality: A Useful Theory for Women?" *Rethinking Sexuality: Foucault and Classical Antiquity*. Eds. David H. J. Larmour, Paul Allen Miller, and Charles Platter. Princeton: Princeton University Press. 138–70.
Roudinesco, Elisabeth. 1997. *Jacques Lacan*. Trans. Barbara Bray. Columbia University Press.
Shepherdson, Charles. 2003. "Lacan and Philosophy." *The Cambridge Companion to Lacan*. Ed. Jean-Michel Rabaté. Cambridge: Cambridge University Press. 116–52.
Sissa, Giulia. 2008. *Sex and Sensuality in the Ancient World*. Trans. George Staunton. New Haven: Yale University Press.
Žižek, Slavoj. 1991. *Looking Awry: An Introduction to Jacques Lacan through Popular Culture*. Cambridge, MA: MIT Press.
———. 1992. *Enjoy Your Symptom: Jacques Lacan in Hollywood and Out*. New York and London: Routledge.
———. 2006. *The Parallax View*. Cambridge: MIT Press.
Zupančič, Alenka. 2003. "Ethics and Tragedy in Lacan." *Cambridge Companion to Lacan*. Ed. Jean-Michel Rabaté. Cambridge: Cambridge University Press. 173–90.

# Chapter 10

# LACAN LE CON: LUCE TELLS JACQUES OFF

This paper begins with the paradox that French feminism from the 1970s to the present constitutes itself both in reaction to and in the tradition of the psychoanalytic theory of Jacques Lacan.[1] Exemplary in this regard is the case of Luce Irigaray. A member of Lacan's *École freudienne* at Paris until her expulsion in 1974, after the publication of *Speculum de l'autre femme* (a move that cannot help but recall Lacan's own exclusion from the Hôpitale Ste. Anne ten years before), Irigaray's work is both grounded in the Lacanian theory of the subject's sexualization in language and deeply critical of it. Of the many places in which this ambivalent and all but oedipal relation between teacher and student is played out, it is perhaps best seen in her essay "Cosi fan tutti." In this tour de force, Irigaray revisits Lacan's *Séminaire XX, Encore* on female sexuality, and through a strategy of extensive quotation, commentary, and parody presents the discourse of the master in the guise of a Mozartian comedy of seduction, only with the genders reversed (Mozart's title was "Cosi fan tutte"). In "Cosi fan tutti," we see the subject presumed to know travestied by the Other.

Parody, of course, as Bakhtin tells us, is always double-voiced.[2] In parodic texts, by definition the voice being parodied cannot be absolutely distinguished from the voice of the parodist, if the effect is not to be lost and the discourse degenerate into a monologic attack that seeks to annihilate rather than subvert the other. Two systems of accentuation are present in parodic texts, each in its most extreme manifestations clearly distinguishable from the other, but also each overlapping with and mutually determining the other at precisely those moments of contact that make parody possible. Parodic discourse is, thus, always already internally dialogized. Consequently, it must presume the authoritative status of the speech it seeks to inhabit (Bakhtin 1981: 68–69, 75–76; Morson 1989: 63, 65, 73). Parody, therefore, always begins with a concession to the ground of the other but continues with a simultaneous refusal to grant that territory absolute status and with an imperative that the monologic dreams of the other be relativized and opened to the speech of the interlocutor. Such is the case in "Cosi fan tutti." As Elizabeth Weed has argued, "Virtually every element of the essay ... comes

---

1 See inter alia, Moi (1985: 99), "Cixous, Irigaray, and Kristeva are all heavily indebted to Lacan's (post-) structuralist reading of Freud ... " ; and Weed 8 (1994: 7).

2 See Bakhtin (1984: 127), "... parody was inseparably linked to a carnival sense of the world. Parodying is the creation of a decrowning double; it is that same 'world turned inside out.' For this reason parody is ambivalent." On the distinction between negative, monological satire and the ambivalence of carnival, see Miller (1998).

138     THEORY DOES NOT EXIST

from the twentieth *Séminaire*" (1994: 90). Consequently, the point where Lacan's discourse leaves off and Irigaray's begins is impossible to determine with absolute precision, yet the result is not the annulling of either Lacan's or Irigaray's discursive claims, but rather the opening of the former to the interrogation of the latter. "Cosi fan tutti," then, is one of the purest manifestations of the dialogical possibilities inherent in Irigaray's concept of a feminist mimetic discourse.[3]

This inherently complex situation is further complicated by several factors. In a real sense, Lacan's discourse is self-parodic. When Lacan says, "elles ne savent pas ce qu'elles disent, c'est toute la différence entre elles et moi," ["they don't know what they are saying, that's the whole difference between them and me"] (1975: 68), it must be remembered that for Lacan knowledge, *le savoir*, is itself constituted within the phallic order of the Symbolic, that realm of ordered rationality and noncontradiction that psychoanalysis, both in spite of and because of its scientific pretensions, must always see as a mystified realm of rationalization and one whose protocols Lacan's own discursive practice violates at every turn.[4]

> Lacan … sees the knowledge (*savoir*) involved in Symbolic processes as indissociable from the knowledge (*connaissance*) produced in the early Imaginary demarcations of 'psyche' and 'body,' a *connaissance* that is, in turn, activated differently in the Symbolic depending on whether the subject is sexed through language as male or female. If anything, Lacan sees women as knowing they don't know what they're saying—by virtue of their position in the Symbolic order—while men are dupes of Truth. (Weed 1994: 89)

Women don't "know" what they are saying because the feminine position within the phallic economy is located outside the Symbolic, but it is only within the Symbolic that "knowledge" defined as information processed in accord with the formal dictates of reason (i.e., the laws of Symbolic substitution recognized by a given community) can occur. Lacan, Irigaray, and indeed Kristeva and Cixous all agree that woman is not representable within the phallic order of the Symbolic.[5] It is for

---

3  Irigaray (1977a: 183), "elles sont <<objets>> pour et entre hommes et ne peuvent, par ailleurs, que mimer un <<langage>> qu'elles n'ont pas produit" ["they are 'objects' for and between men and besides they are only able to mime a 'language' that they have not produced"]. See also Irigaray (1977b: 76–77); Herndl (1991: 11); Schwab (1991: 57–59); and Weed (1994: 82).

4  On the Symbolic as a realm of ordered rationality, see Janan (1994: 35, 79); Butler (1990: 82–83); and Kristeva (1980: 22).

5  See Janan (1994: 28), "for Lacan, Woman is a position outside clear meaning and grammatical language—she is *hors-sens*, 'outside meaning/sense.' As such, Woman signifies the antithesis of masculine certitude, based on identification with rules, order, Law. Thus, the feminine is for Lacan an attitude toward knowledge and procedure, rather than a category defined strictly by gender"; and Goux (1990: 223). On woman as unrepresentable within the Symbolic, see Lacan (1975: 74); Irigaray (1977a: 184), "Les femmes … vont assurer la possibilité de l'usage et de circulation du symbolique sans y être pour autant partie prenante. C'est le non-accès, pour elles qui établit l'ordre social" ["Women are going to assure the possibility of the usage and the circulation of the Symbolic without however taking part in it. It is their non-access that establishes the social order"]; Irigaray (1977c: 25); Moi (1985: 117, 133–34, 163, 166); Butler (1990: 9–10, 27–28, 154 n. 27); Goux (1990: 147); Herndl (1991: 16); Weed (1994: 81, 88–90).

# LACAN LE CON

this reason that Lacan argues that "La femme" does not exist, since the article "la" implies a universal and the concept of universality is the logical category that constitutes the very heart of the Symbolic order.[6] Woman thus represents a hole in the Symbolic, not because she is lacking (although that is the only way the patriarchal Symbolic can represent her) but because she is exorbitant in relation to its totalizing claims. The shudder of her *jouissance* takes place beyond words and thus beyond the Symbolic's power to categorize, anatomize, and atomize. It partakes of that Real from which the primary repression of our entry into the Symbolic has forever severed us.[7] She gives the lie to the Symbolic's claim to representing universality, *le tout*. She says no to that. She is thus the *pas-toute*, "Ce n'est pas parce qu'elle est pas toute dans la fonction phallique qu'elle y est pas du tout. Elle y est pas pas du tout. Elle y est à plein, Mais il y a quelque chose en plus" ["It is not because she is not whole in the phallic function that she is the not-at-all there. She is not not-at-all there. She is fully there, But, there is something else."] (Lacan 175: 69 see also 13 and 75). She is the ground on which the phallic figure of totality is erected, the space that makes its calculation possible. As Irigaray observes,

> Donc le <<tout>>–de x, mais aussi du système—aura déjà prescrit le <<pas-toute>> de chaque mise en relation particulière, et ce <<tout>> ne l'est que par une définition de l'extension qui ne peut se passer de projection sur un espace-plan <<donné>>, dont l'entre, les entre(s), seront évalués grâce à des repères de type ponctuel. (Irigaray 1977c: 106–107)

> Therefore the "all"—of x but also of the system—will have already prescribed the "not-all" of each particular relationship, and this "all" is only all by means of a definition of extension that must be projected onto a given spatial grid, from which the in-between, the in-betweens between/enters them, will be evaluated in relation to defined points on the grid.

Thus, her excess, which the Symbolic figures as lack, is his necessity.

Lacan then like Irigaray does not seek "to consolidate but to interrogate" the realm of phallic knowledge (Weed 1994: 87). Indeed, it is the phallic order's *jouissance de l'organe* that he later defines as both masturbation—the Other being present only as an imaginary phantasm—and the "jouissance of the idiot" (Lacan 1975: 75; Julien 1990: 210). Thus, when Lacan claims for himself the realm of phallic mastery in the form of a knowledge denied to women, what he claims is a realm of scientistic idiocy that his own discursive practice consistently reveals as mystified in its claims to totality. The logical conclusion of such a line of reasoning, therefore, is that Lacan speaks ironically from the position of the woman, of the "not-all," and hence the untotalizeable.[8] It is for this reason

---

6  Lacan (1975: 53, 54, 57, 64, and 68) "Il n'y a pas *La* femme, article défini pour désigner l'universel" ["There is no *The* woman, the definite article designating the universal"]. See Kristeva (1979: 15) for her reading of this passage.

7  Lacan (1975: 13, 57, 69, 76–77); Irigaray (1977d: 87–88, 95, 109); Julien (1990: 173, 176, 208); Butler (1990: 56); Janan (1994: 30); Eagleton (1996: 68).

8  Weed (1994: 89), "since Lacan knows enough to play the prick, he knows that it is little more than *woman* that he plays after all," emphasis hers.

140 THEORY DOES NOT EXIST

that he includes his own *Écrits* under the category of mystical writings, a mode of discourse which he, Irigaray, and other French feminists see as intimately connected to the discursive position of the feminine.[9]

The destabilizing force of this parodical paradox—Lacan the phallic master presumed to know and hence idiot ("pauvre petit con") speaking from the position of the excluded, of what is unintelligible to knowledge, and thus from the position of woman ("le con"), being parodied by a woman whom he has himself excluded ("quel con!")—is dizzying. It is further underlined, however, by Irigaray's own "mimetic style" which deliberately assumes the discourse of the Other, to reveal what it excludes, its founding repressions. Such a parodic, catachretic style is mandated for women, she argues, precisely because they are excluded from the phallic realm of discourse. As such their speech is always the speech of the Other which can only be made their own through the subversion of the norms of phallic discourse by means of its own devices. This, of course, is a position all but indistinguishable from Lacan's own. It implies that women, i.e. real empirical women, can speak the phallic tongue, and that *woman*, and consequently sex and gender generally, is an epistemological and discursive construct, not a biological reality. Hence women can be men, though they lose in the process that which makes them women, becoming pricks instead.[10] This too is completely Lacanian. On the one hand, Lacan argues that men and women "have not the least prediscursive reality," that "men, women, and children are only signifiers" (1975: 34, 39). On the other, he notes that women are "free" to take up (that is to say, not constitutionally prohibited from) the masculine side of the equation (1975: 67), while anyone can inscribe his or herself in the feminine position, i.e., outside the realm of the logical and universal and within the world of the mystical (Lacan 1975: 74–75, see also 68 and 70). Such a position leaves Lacan open to the charge of repeating the traditional identification of women with emotion rather reason (Murphy 1991: 48). The fact that Lacan, however, includes his own *Écrits* under the sign of the feminine and the mystical looks more like an interrogation than a simple acceptance of this dichotomy. Woman thus names a moment that escapes phallic discourse, a moment outside the pain of castration, the self-mutilation that access to the Symbolic demands, a deformation that real empirical women must suffer every bit as much as men if they are to enter the realm of the discursive.[11]

But what does it mean to say that real, empirical women can become men, can be castrated, can become phallic masters presumed to know and hence idiots ("pauvres petits cons")? What effect does this have on them? What does it mean to

---

9 Lacan (1975: 70–71); Janan (1994: 30); Moi (1985: 136–37); Kristeva (1983: 223–47) links mysticism with the maternal.

10 Weed (1994: 81); Irigaray (1977a: 183); Irigaray (1977e: 189); Irigaray (1974: 165), "Toute théorie du <<sujet>> aura toujours été appropriée au <<masculin>>. À s'y assujetir, la femme renonce à son insu à la spécificité de son rapport à l'imaginaire" ["Any theory of the 'subject' will have always been appropriated by the 'masculine.' To subject herself to it, woman, without knowing it, renounces the specificity of her relation to the Imaginary"].

11 Janan (1994: 29–30); Lacan (1982: 168), "The woman has to undergo no more or less castration than the man."

say you can be a woman but to be a human (i.e., speaking) being you must become a man? There is a kind of double logic at work here in the case of women (all sorts) that does not necessarily have the same force for men (at least those that aren't women). The possibility of formulating these questions is owed to Lacan, but in the act of formulating them one crosses over the imperceptible line to Irigaray. For the root of these questions interrogates the very sexual imagery that subtends psychoanalytic discourse. The phallus may not be the penis, and patriarchy may be based on the idiotic confusion of these terms, but that sexism has real effects on real women (even, maybe especially, those who are men), and the continuing use of the term phallus, as inherited from Freud and ultimately from the ancient traditions of phallic worship, makes that confusion all but inevitable. To say that woman is a discursive construct may be true, as both Lacan and Irigaray would concede, but it does little to change the fact those who are inscribed with the anatomy we call female are disproportionately beaten, raped, and economically as well as socially repressed in western society from its inception to the present. This is a woman that Lacan can never be.

There are, of course, many kinds of women, especially when we define woman as a cultural category rather than a simple anatomical given. This, we should note, is another level on which Lacan's declaration that "woman does not exist" rings true, for as Clément has noted, "woman" rather than naming a definable ontological or even semiotic substance, "bizarrely incarnates that group of anomalies that reveals the failures of an overall system" (1975: 18). Women, on this view, might be defined as those who are denied access to the Symbolic except at the price of becoming that which they are not. Thus, Žižek may define the Symbolic as the place where we are what we pretend to be, but if what we pretend to be is abjected or rejected by the terms available in the Symbolic, then we must not only suffer castration but forever bear the second scar of inauthenticity (1991: 74).

Many of these women are also women Lacan can never be. He cannot share the gay man's intolerable experience of the closet, the double bind in which every word he uses, once he comes out, is marked with his sexuality and hence considered deceitful in its allegorization of language into eros, but in which, if he stays in the closet, no word is not a lie (Sedgwick 1990: 67–90; Halperin 1995: chapter 1). Lacan cannot bear the double scar of the lesbian as both woman and homosexual. His speech is not marked by the accents of racial, class, or colonial oppression. These are women he will never be. Of course, it could be argued that it obscures the specificity of women's oppression within a patriarchal culture to broaden the definition to such an extent as to include virtually all marginalized groups. And even Clément recognizes that "ultimately societies do not offer to everyone the same insertion into the Symbolic order," and part of our labor as responsible intellectuals must surely be to define the specificity of different marginalized groups in relation to both the Symbolic and its underlying support in the Real (1975: 17; cf., Žižek 1991: 29–32, 120; Lacan 1973: 60). Yet, as Lacan and Irigaray both agree, woman is a symptom of the limitations of the phallic economy. Irigaray, however, takes her critique further. For her "Women are the symptom of the exploitation of individuals by a society which remunerates them only partially, or not at all, for their 'labor'" (Irigaray 1977a: 184; Lacan 1982: 168).

# 142                    THEORY DOES NOT EXIST

This is a level of social and empirical specificity that Lacan's critique of the phallic never reached.

These observations, then, brings us to the heart of Irigaray's criticism of Lacan. She essentially makes two charges. First, Lacan's discourse never opens itself to a dialogue with real women who know this double pain of castration and Symbolic exclusion.

> La question de savoir si, dans sa logique, elles peuvent articuler quoi que ce soit, ou être entendues, n'est même pas posée. Ce serait accepter qu'il puisse y en avoir une autre, et qui dérange la sienne. C'est-à-dire, qui questionne la maîtrise. (Irigaray 1977d: 89)

> The question of knowing if, in his logic, they are able to articulate anything at all, or be understood, is not even posed. That would be to accept that there is another logic and that would disturb his. That is to say, it would question his mastery.

There is a lack in Lacan's discourse of what Bakhtin in his early ethical and later metalinguistic writings terms "addressivity" (Bakhtin 1986: 95–100; Morson and Emerson 1990: 75–76, 80, 131, 145; Felson-Rubin 2001: 23–30). Lacanian speech's own intense self-subversions, its own opening to the speech of the Other, is so complete as to allow no space for others to respond, and so leaves everything ultimately as it was (Weed 1994: 101). The position from which an empirical woman might articulate the particularities of her own desire, might address the pain of her own peculiar castration and the necessity of being a permanent eunuch within the phallic realm is never addressed.[12] Lacan may indeed know more than the members of the *Mouvement de libération des femmes* (*MLF*) who protest their exclusion from a phallic realm of discourse that Lacan knows to be empty and so in Socratic fashion he is the wiser since he knows that he does not know. These feminists may be self-defeating in their implicit acceptance of the fantasmatic reality projected by the phallic Symbolic as coincidental with the real, in their refusal to recognize a beyond of the Symbolic, the very register that guarantees their own continuing exclusion (Lacan 1975: 68–70; Lacan 1973: 50; Julien 1990: 143). For these women, Lacan notes, there is no *jouissance* beyond the phallic *jouissance* of the organ, a mechanical reduction that he punningly labels a connerie ["stupidity, silliness, something related to a cunt"].[13] Lacan in his rejection of their position may be seconded by Cixous'

---

12  Irigaray (1974: 88), "La géographie du plaisir féminin ne vaut pas qu'on l'écoute. Elles ne valent pas qu'on les écoute, surtout quand elles essaient de parler de leur plaisir..." ["The geography of feminine pleasure is not worth listening to. They are not worth listening to, especially when they try to talk about their pleasure"] and "les zones érogènes de la femme n'a, pour le psychanalyste, pas le moindre intérêt" ["the erogenous zones of the woman have, for the psychoanalyst, not the least interest"]. On Lacan being the eminence grise almost always lurking behind the figure of "the psychoanalyst" or even Freud in Irigaray, see Schwab (1991: 62).

13  On phallic *jouissance* as "jouissance de l'organe," see Lacan, (1975: 13); on the attempt to locate the "organs" of *jouissance féminine*, see Lacan (1975: 69–70); on phallic jouissance being equally the affair of women, see Lacan (1982: 168); on the misguided attempt to reduce mysticism and *jouissance* to fucking and hence to the *jouissance* of the organ, Lacan (1975: 70–71).

refusal to accept the *MLF* label of "feminist" and Irigaray's declaration that she does not seek a reversal of current power relations but rather their complete revision (Moi 1985: 103; Irigaray 1974: 32), but he does little to explain these feminists' desire to be included in this circle of phallic unknowing, and he does little to find or to create a dialogic space in which the sources of that peculiar pain can be articulated. Rather than any specific theoretical disagreement, it is this ethical project to create a new dialogic space for the articulation of women's desire, a space that has until now been defined by men and for men, that marks the point at which Irigaray's psychoanalytic project most definitively transcends its Lacanian roots.[14] Lacan, we might say, names the hole in the Symbolic that phallic discourse seeks to hide under the signifier woman, while Irigaray seeks to make that hole, that interstitial space metonymically signified by the figure of lips, a recognized site for the generation of alternative significations not already defined by men or already colonized by the psychoanalyst.[15]

> Beyond classical oppositions of love and hate, liquid and ice—a threshold that is always *half-open*. The threshold of the *lips*, which are strangers to dichotomy and oppositions. Gathered one against the other but without any possible suture, at least of a real kind. They do not absorb the world into or through themselves, provided they are not misused and reduced to a means of consumption or consummation. They offer a shape of welcome, but do not assimilate, reduce, or swallow up. (Irigaray 1993: 18, see also 1974: 178.)

Lacan points to the inadequacy of phallic discourse, while Irigaray seeks to make those inadequacies the basis of a new form of discourse that speaks from the void: *parler femme*.[16]

Second, and this point is a logical corollary of the first, Irigaray charges Lacan with being, in essence, a positivist. His description of the way things are may in fact be true, and the importance of that description must never be underestimated, yet he gives no hint as to how things might be different. "Psychoanalytic theory," she concedes, "articulates thus the truth about the status of feminine sexuality, and the sexual relation. But it stops there. Refusing to interpret the historical determinants of its own discourse.... it remains the captive of phallocentrism, which it strives to make a universal and eternal value" (Irigaray 1977d: 99). In short, according to Irigaray, psychoanalysis as practiced by Lacan is not only insufficiently dialogical in its lack of addressivity to those whose bodies are socially inscribed with the marks of the feminine, it is also insufficiently dialectical in its failure to historicize its own position (Weed 1994: 87, 99).

---

14  Weed (1994: 89–91 and 99), "it is her insistence on positive sexual difference, what she calls the ethic of sexual difference, that marks the difference between her and Lacan."

15  Irigaray (1993: 10), "everywhere and in everything men define the function and social role of women, right down to the sexual identity women are to have." See also 14.

16  On the similarity between Cixous' *écriture féminine* and Irigaray's *parler femme*, see Moi (1985: 143), "Irigaray's vision of femininity and feminine language remains almost indistinguishable from Cixous's."

# THEORY DOES NOT EXIST

Women *are* banished from subjectivity within the Symbolic. This *is* the point of ideological closure within the phallic economy of signification (Weed 1994: 100). Lacan is correct in this, and Irigaray does not contest it as an observation on the status quo. But whose interests are served by this state of affairs? What are its historical determinants? Whose hole, for example, is plugged by the production of new subjects within the paternal law? Is it her lack or his that the child fills? Why must that hole always be conceived of as hers, in the manner of Freud, thus allowing her to enter the sexual relation only through motherhood, though for Lacan it too is conceived of as a function rather than an ontological substance? Who benefits from this state of affairs?

> "With this jouissance that she is not-all, that is to say, which renders her in part absent insofar as being a subject, she will find the cork of this 'a' that will be her child."
>
> Ah yes ... Once again [Encore] ... Without a child, no father? ... For what? For whom? are these "a" corks good, then?
>
> For all things, in all cases, just so long as she is not a "subject," so long as she cannot disrupt through her speech, her desire, *her jouissance*, the operation of language that makes the law, or of the prevailing organization of power. (Irigaray 1977d: 92, citing Lacan 1975: 36)

So long as woman's speech is silent, as Lacan says and Irigaray agrees it is in phallic discourse, then the prevailing order goes unchallenged. "If we continue to speak the same language, we will reproduce the same history" (Irigaray 1977f: 205). There is no disagreement on this level. Yet, description especially when it is as powerful and convincing as it is in the case of Lacan, all too easily, unwittingly, slides over into prescription so that the system of phallic dominance, in all its idiocy, is made to appear eternal when no alternative is posited (Butler 1990: 55; Weed 1994: 100–102; compare Jameson 1991: 5–6). To paraphrase Marx in the *Theses on Feuerbach*, the psychoanalysts "have only interpreted the world, in various ways; the point, however, is to change it" (1978: 145).

One way in which psychoanalytic theory in general and Lacan in particular can be opened up to the voice of the other is by deconstructing their master terms to reveal the submerged other. To do so is, in effect, to ask Lacan's own question, what is the desire of the analyst, and more particularly what is the desire of Freud (Lacan 1973: 18–20). This indeed is the hallmark of Lacan's own self-proclaimed "return to Freud," taking Freud seriously enough to read his texts in a psychoanalytic fashion (Julien 1990: 63–66). What I'm advocating here, then, may in a strict sense be called a "return to Lacan," in which once more the central question is what is the desire of the analyst? Such a strategy is in close solidarity with Irigaray herself who, as Toril Moi and others have observed, is in many ways a deconstructive reader (Moi 1985: 138; Schwab 1991: 61; Weed 1994: 100).

A good place to begin is with the transcendental signifier or the phallus itself. Why do we call it the phallus? Why not the mother? What kind of history and what sort of imaginary identifications does this terminology imply, if not the continuity of a system of genders founded on patriarchy in which penis and phallus are made to

# LACAN LE CON

145

appear interchangeable (Butler 1990: 106)? What is lost in castration from a Lacanian perspective if not that Imaginary plenitude in which subject and object, mother and child are one? This mythical oneness, which would prevent the functioning of the Symbolic since it would preclude signification's founding lack or absence (i.e., the necessary ontological incompletion that opens the space of re-presentation), this primal unity, which the loss of the phallus through the intervention of the *nom du père* signifies, could just as easily, just as logically, be viewed as the severance from the maternal body rather than as the loss of the phallic enjoyment in the oedipal moment (Lacan, 1975: 74; Kristeva 1979: 11; Eagleton 1996: 16;). Irigaray herself writes, "Lacan specifies that what is lacking in castration is not so much the penis— the real organ—as the phallus or signifier of desire. And it is in the mother before all else that castration ought to be located..." (1977g: 57–58).[17] Why then is the phallus not the mother? Is there not here an implicit erasure of the maternal body whose loss is signified as the deprivation of Imaginary plenitude? These terms inherited from Freud are loaded with levels of patriarchal signification that, while descriptive of the system of genders and the mode of subjectivation operative in western culture, also seem to foreclose the possibility of change. Is there not an uninvestigated libidinal and ideological investment in the continuing use of this system of imagery? What *is* the desire of the analyst?

On another level, the phallus is the transcendental signifier governing the Symbolic system, the magic wand that everybody desires, the absent presence whose permanent lack of a signified provides the opening or *coupure* that makes possible the system of phallic knowledge—defined as a body of protocols abstracted from the incomprehensible particularity of the Real (Lacan 1975: 74; Julien 1990: 124, 146; Janan 1994: 20). It is in fact this abstraction and hence separation from the Real that enables the Symbolic to produce the concept of universality, the category on which any notion of scientific law must ultimately rest, and from which *La femme* is excluded. It is this founding slippage of castration that makes the Symbolic a system of differences rather than identities, so that exchange becomes possible, knowledge is able to grow and change, words and concepts can evolve, since the moment of identity or presence, and hence stasis, is always deferred (Lacan 1975: 40; Janan 1994: 47).

But the transcendental signifier is itself a contradictory concept. As a signifier, it necessarily inhabits the realm of the material, the concrete that cannot be reduced to the universal without leaving a remainder, trace, or scar. As such, it would historically be located on the feminine side of patriarchal ideology's governing matrix of binary oppositions, which since the time of Plato and Aristotle has identified woman with the material as opposed to the spiritual, the sensible rather than the intelligible, matter rather than form, the signifier rather than the signified (Cixous 1975: 114–15; Goux 1990: 231; Butler 1990: 12). Within this ideology, the masculine should be

---

17  See Moi (1985: 99–100), especially, "The loss or lack suffered is the loss of the maternal body, and from now on the desire for the mother or the imaginary unity with her must be repressed."

# THEORY DOES NOT EXIST

the realm of the signified but cannot, for as Lacan himself knows, there is in point of fact no signified per se, only an endless chain of signifiers whose shifting system of differences is founded on the absent phallus, the token of the masculine (1966). Consequently, the primary opposition on which the term transcendental signifier rests can only collapse since the difference that defines signifiers, as opposed to signifieds, is elided and with it the opposition between the phallus and the feminine as well. The masculinist aspiration to pure meaning can never be fulfilled. Its result will only be the production of more signifiers signifying lack, which is traditionally the realm of woman but is also what the absent phallus represents. Indeed, this same double bind in which woman is simultaneously viewed as both lack (without the phallus) and plenitude, the unintelligible material before the schism of the Law, and in which man is represented as both wielder of the phallus and as the spiritual negation of the merely material, marks western culture from archaic Greece to the beginning of the modern era. In each case, both halves of the binary opposition Phallus/mother, signifier/signified, man/woman contain the same essential elements, representing simultaneously materiality and lack. Only the relative accents placed on the terms are different. Thus, woman in the theory of hysteria from Hippocrates through the *Encyclopédie* is considered to be more material than man is, since her mental stability, and thus her capacity for spirituality, are conceived of as a direct expression of the activity of her *hyster* or reproductive organs. Yet those same organs are granted no positive existence within representation but are instead viewed as constructed in the form of an absence or lack. Man, on the other hand, is conceived of both as representing the spiritual in relation to woman's material and as the bearer of a phallus capable of filling woman's lack. He is both the negation of the merely material and the plenitude that fills her absence. Each gender's identity is thus compounded from the same set of contradictory terms.[18] The real opposition between them is not an expression of different ontological, or even logical, substances but of power. The deconstruction of this oppositions' ideological basis shows not only the factitious nature of the West's dominant sexual ideology, but also how these oppositions have been mobilized to erase female experience.

In sum, the phallus marks a lack whose presence would mean the end of subjectivity and a return to the maternal, Imaginary womb. Its absence is the presence of the law of the father, and as such its inherited imagery represents an ideological inversion designed to conceal that law's roots in the maternal. Lacanian psychoanalysis lays the foundation that allows us to formulate this problem, but does it not take the next step. For that we need Irigaray, dialogue, and change.

---

18 On hysteria and women's bodies, ancient and modern see: the following articles in the *Encyclopédie* "Femme (jurisp.)," "Femme (morale)," "Fureur utérine," "Génération (Physiologie)," "Homme," "Hystérique (passion ou affection)," "Matrice, en anatomie," "Matrice, maladies de la (Médecine)," "Satyriasis (Médecine)," "Vagin (Maladies particulières du vagin)," "Vapeurs,"; and Lefkowitz (1981: 13–16), 23–24; Foucault (1984a: 21–23, 56, 99, 135–36, 145); Foucault (1984b: 137, 168); Laqueur (1990: 59, 61, 107–110); Dean-Jones 1992: 73–79).

## LACAN LE CON

147

# Works Cited

Bakhtin, Mikhail. 1981. "From the Prehistory of Novelistic Discourse." *The Dialogic Imagination.* Ed. Michael Holquist. Trans. Caryl Emerson and Michael Holquist. Austin: University of Texas Press. 41–83.

———. 1984. *Problems of Dostoevsky's Poetics.* Ed. and trans. Caryl Emerson. Minneapolis: University of Minnesota Press.

———. 1986. "The Problem of Speech Genres." *Speech Genres and Other Late Essays.* Eds. Caryl Emerson and Michael Holquist. Trans. Vern McGee. Austin: University of Texas Press. 60–102.

Bauer, Dale M. and S. Jaret McKinstry, eds. 1991. *Feminism, Bakhtin and the Dialogic.* Albany: SUNY Press.

Butler, Judith. 1990. *Gender Trouble: Feminism and the Subversion of Identity.* New York: Routledge.

Cixous, Hélène. 1975. "Sorties." *La jeune née.* Paris: Union Génerale d'Edition. 114–245.

Clément, Cathérine B. 1975. "La coupable." *La jeune née.* Paris: Union Génerale d'Edition. 8–113.

Dean-Jones, Leslie. 1992 "The Politics of Pleasure: Female Sexual Appetite in the Hippocratic Corpus," *Helios* 19: 72–91.

Eagleton, Terry. 1996. *Literary Theory: An Introduction.* 2nd ed. Minneapolis: University of Minnesota Press.

Felson-Rubin, Nancy. 2001. "Recollecting Discordant Courtship." *Carnivalizing Discourse: Bakhtin and the Other.* Eds. Peter I. Barta, Paul Allen Miller, Charles Platter, and David Shepherd. London: Routledge. 23–50.

Foucault, Michel. 1984a *L'usage des plaisirs. Histoire de la sexualité*, vol. 2. Paris: Gallimard.

———. 1984b. *Le souci de soi. Histoire de la sexualité*, vol. 3. Paris: Gallimard.

Goux, Jean Joseph. 1990. *Symbolic Economies After Marx and Freud.* Trans. Jennifer Curtiss Gage. Ithaca: Cornell University Press.

Halperin, David M. 1995. *Saint Foucault: Towards a Gay Hagiography.* New York: Oxford University Press.

Herndl, Diane Price. 1991. "The Dilemmas of a Feminine Dialogic." In Bauer and McKinstry, 7–24.

Irigaray, Luce. 1974. *Speculum de l'autre femme.* Paris: Minuit.

———. 1977a. "Le marché des femmes." *Ce sexe qui n'en est pas un.* Paris: Minuit. 167–85.

———. 1977b. "Pouvoir du discours, subordination du féminin." *Ce sexe qui n'en est pas un.* Paris: Minuit. 65–82.

———. 1977c. "Ce sexe qui n'en est pas un." *Ce sexe qui n'en est pas un.* Paris: Minuit. 23–32.

———. 1977d. "Cosi fan tutti." *Ce sexe qui n'en est pas un.* Paris: Minuit. 83–101.

———. 1977e. "Des marchandises entre elles." *Ce sexe qui n'en est pas un.* Paris: Minuit. 189–93.

———. 1977f. "Quand nos lèvres se parlent." *Ce sexe qui n'en est pas un.* Paris: Minuit. 205–17.

———. 1977g. "Retour sur la théorie psychanalytique." *Ce sexe qui n'en est pas un.* Paris: Minuit. 35–64.

———. 1993. "Body Against Body in Relation to the Mother." *Sexes and Genealogies.* Trans. Gillian C. Gill. New York: Columbia University Press. 7–22.

Jameson, Fredric. 1991. *Postmodernism or the Cultural Logic of Late Capitalism.* London: Verso.

Janan, Micaela. 1994. *"When the Lamp is Shattered": Desire and Narrative in Catullus.* Carbondale: Southern Illinois University Press.

Julien, Phillipe. 1990. *Pour lire Jacques Lacan.* 2nd ed. Paris: E. P. E. L.

Kristeva, Julia. 1979. "Le temps des femmes." *Cahiers de rechereche de S. T. D. Paris VII* 5: 5–18.

———. 1980. *Pouvoirs de l'horreur: Essai de l'abjection.* Paris: Seuil.

———. 1983. *Histoires d'amour.* Paris: Edition Denoël. 223–47.

Lacan, Jacques. 1966. "L'instance de la lettre dans l'inconscient ou la raison depuis Freud." *Ecrits 1.* Paris: Seuil. 249–89.

———. 1973. *Le séminaire livre XI: Les quatre concepts fondamentaux psychanalytiques.* Ed. Jacques Alain Miller. Paris: Seuil.

148 THEORY DOES NOT EXIST

————. 1975. *Le séminaire livre XX: Encore*. Ed. Jacques-Alain Miller. Paris: Seuil.

————. 1982. "Seminar of 21 January 1975." *Feminine Sexuality: Jacques Lacan and the Ecole Freudienne*. Eds. Juliet Mitchell and Jacqueline Rose. Trans. Jacqueline Rose. New York: Pantheon. 162–71.

Laqueur, Thomas. 1990. *Making Sex: Body and Gender from the Greeks to Freud*. Cambridge: Harvard University Press.

Lefkowitz, Mary. 1981. *Heroines and Hysterics*. New York: St. Martin's.

Marx, Karl. 1978. "Theses on Feuerbach." *The Marx-Engels Reader*. Ed. Robert Tucker. New York: Norton. 143–45.

Miller, Paul Allen. 1998. "Images of Sterility: The Bodily Grotesque in Roman Satire." *Arethusa* 31: 257–83.

Moi, Toril. 1985. *Sexual/Textual Politics: Feminist Literary Theory*. London: Routledge.

Morson, Gary Saul. 1989. "Parody, History, and Metaparody." *Rethinking Bakhtin: Extensions and Challenges*. Eds. Gary Saul Morson and Caryl Emerson. Evanston, IL: Northwestern University Press. 63–86.

Morson, Gary Saul and Caryl Emerson. 1990. *Mikhail Bakhtin: Creation of a Prosaics*. Evanston, IL: Northwestern University Press.

Murphy, Patrick D. 1991. "Prolegomenon for an Ecofeminist Dialogics." In Bauer and McKinstry. 39–56.

Schwab, Gail M. 1991. "Irigarayan Dialogism: Play and Powerplay." In Bauer and McKinstry. 57–72.

Sedgwick, Eve Kosofsky. 1990. *Epistemology of the Closet*. Berkeley: University of California Press.

Weed, Elizabeth. 1994. "The Question of Style." *Engaging with Irigaray*. Eds. Carolyne Burke, Naomi Schor, and Margaret Whitford. New York: Columbia University Press. 79–109.

Žižek, Slavoj. 1991. *Looking Awry: An Introduction to Jacques Lacan through Popular Culture*. Cambridge, MA: MIT Press.

# Chapter 11

# THE REPEATABLE AND THE UNREPEATABLE: ŽIŽEK AND THE FUTURE OF THE HUMANITIES, OR ASSESSING SOCRATES[1]

I am not in any sense a wise man; I cannot claim as the child of my soul any discovery worthy of the name of wisdom. But with those who associate with me it is different. At first some of them may give the impression of being ignorant or stupid; but as time goes on and our association continues, all whom god permits are seen to make progress—a progress which is both amazing to other people and to themselves. And yet it is clear that this is not due to anything they have learned from me; it is that they discover within themselves a multitude of beautiful things, which they bring forth into the light. (*Theaetetus*, 150d, Cooper 1997: 167)

In Plato's *Theaetetus*, Euclides and Terpison listen to a version of a dialogue between Socrates and the young Theaetetus that took place many years ago and is read by a slave. At the very moment the dialogue is being read, the now grown Theaetetus lies dying in Athens from a case of dysentery contracted while on campaign in Corinth. The copy of the dialogue read by the slave is not a transcript, it is rather a reconstruction, a kind of historical fiction. Euclides tells Terpison that he took some notes at the time he witnessed the discussion, but readily admits he was unable to recall the whole thing from memory. Rather he went home and wrote down his initial recollections. Later, when on occasion he would journey from his home in Megara to Athens, he would consult with Socrates and then make corrections when he went back home. In this way, over an unspecified but clearly not short period of time, the dialogue came to have the form that the two men are portrayed as hearing and that we supposedly read today, even as we know that this too is a fiction, since our author is Plato, not his imagined Euclides, let alone Socrates himself. Determinate authority is hard to locate in the *Theaetetus*, to say the least.

---

1 I would not have written this essay if not for the invitation of my friend and colleague, Zahi Zalloua, to come and speak to his wonderfully bright students at Whitman College. I owe much to the inspiration and conversations derived from this extraordinary encounter. This article also owes much to the feedback and intellectual stimulation I have received from my colleagues Erik Doxtader, Jill Frank, Jeanne Garane, John Muckelbauer, and Nicholas Vazsonyi. Lastly, I owe a debt of gratitude to Jeffrey Di Leo and to the anonymous readers who have helped shape its final form.

150 THEORY DOES NOT EXIST

The subject of the dialogue is the nature of knowledge. Socrates approaches the young Theaetetus in the company of the geometer Theodorus and tries unsuccessfully to get each of them to offer a defensible definition of knowledge. A number of different formulations are essayed—knowledge is perception, knowledge is true judgment, knowledge is true judgment with an account (*logos*)—but all are ultimately found wanting (210b–d). This conclusion is an expression of the classic Socratic aporia, the moment of perplexity that many of the shorter and so-called early dialogues issue into, but which remains characteristic of the "Socratic method" even in what is generally considered a late Platonic dialogue concerned with more abstruse and technical philosophical matters.[2] Indeed, the founder of western philosophy as often as not produces no unambiguous results at the end of his inquiries, even the *Republic* itself is ultimately termed a fiction, a pattern laid up in heaven, certainly not an invariable prescription for political action, let alone a testable hypothesis (458a–b, 592a–b, 500c–501b). The *Symposium* too, for all its beautiful talk of love's power to lead the lover to the ideal, ends not with the priestess Diotima, but the drunken Alcibiades, Socrates's own former student and beloved (Hunter 2004: 10–11, 129–30; Wohl 2002: 163; Nehamas 1998: 61–68).

On a certain level then, Socrates as portrayed in the *Theaetetus* and elsewhere is a failure. Expressed in terms of the learning outcomes according to which higher education is increasingly forced to assess itself—i.e., formalizable, repeatable data points representing operational knowledge, skill sets, and material mastery—Socrates is indeed an abject failure. As we learn in the *Apology*, all he knows is that he knows nothing. Given that he started in ignorance and ended there as well, his objectively measurable progress would be negligible at best. But this objection is more than a mere joke at the expense of our colleagues in Institutional Assessment, for the question of what is the value of humanistic inquiry—that is what is the value of a form of education that cannot be expressed primarily in terms of the repeatable[3]—is central to the continuing existence of a type of learning that sees students not as the consumers of educational products, but as individuals engaged in the ethical and political process of creating meaningful lives for themselves and their communities. For the ideal of repeatability as expressed within a certain social scientific model that is currently hegemonic within higher education and underlies the concept of "testability" operative in many Psychology and Sociology departments is that of functional identity, i.e., of the ability of each data point in a given set to substitute for another of the same value. Yet that is exactly what is at stake in a Socratic dialogue. The arc of Socratic inquiry, from ignorance to its self-conscious recognition, leads back to its point of inception, but with a difference. And it is precisely

---

2  As opposed to the ethical concerns that dominate the *Crito*, the *Ion* the *Laches*, and the *Euthyphro*. See, however, chapter four of Miller 2007 and Blondell 2002: 12–13.

3  For a very different notion of the repeatable, one that necessarily always includes difference in repetition and thus distinguishes it from identity, see Deleuze's *Difference and Repetition* (1994). While the larger model I follow in this essay is inspired by Žižek's Lacanian psychoanalytic philosophy, which has certain points of difference with Deleuze, nonetheless, in terms of the critical opposition being established with a hegemonic instrumentalism and identitarianism the basic thrust of the argument is similar.

THE REPEATABLE AND THE UNREPEATABLE          151

that irreducible difference of self-conscious critical reflection in its necessary and unresolved dialectic with the repeatable, I want to argue, that is the foundational moment of humanities education as traditionally understood. Moreover, it is equally precisely the dialectic between critical difference and repetition that is in danger of being driven out of higher education by the intellectual assumptions, economic priorities, and political calculations that lie behind, but are also openly articulated within, today's "assessment movement."[4] The call to "accountability," as enunciated by the Spellings commission, envisioned higher education as "an industry" that produces a commodity (2006),[5] a product that is exchangeable in a market of goods and services and so measurable by a quantifiable universal equivalent that permits of exchange and fungibility (my iron is worth x amount of your cotton, my increased skill in manipulating mathematical, verbal, or computer languages is worth x amount of purchasing power).[6] It is of course precisely this concept of knowledge as an exchangeable commodity, one powerfully advocated by certain fifth century sophistic teachers of rhetoric, that Socrates ranges himself against when he declares in the *Apology* that he has never been the teacher of anyone and when in the *Symposium* he rejects Alcibiades' offer to trade his sexual favors for the secrets of wisdom that the latter supposes Socrates to be hiding deep within (Nightingale 1995: 59, 123–27).

Yet it is not enough to respond to the assessment movement that prefabricated learning outcomes are neither able to measure the worth of a Socrates nor offer the tools necessary for our students to "discover within themselves a multitude of beautiful things"—whether we are discussing the joy of genuine scientific discovery or of first encountering that perfect poem. And this is true whether we are addressing a progressive audience or conservatives who see themselves as defenders of western civilization.[7] What is needed are very precise arguments that demonstrate that it is in the unrepeatable, the different, that humanistic knowledge and education gains its most profound purchase; that the arc of Socratic knowledge is not simply a closed circle but represents the moment of awareness in finitude that grounds consciousness as self-reflection; and that it is this moment that the intellectual criteria on which assessment is based will extirpate if carried to

---

4  For a good general account of the "movement" and its importance in higher education, as well as its basic intellectual assumptions, see two articles in *InsideHigherEd*: Jaschik 2009; and Lederman 2008. For a sense of the kind of quantifiable research that the field is based on, and its roots in a certain narrow, social-scientific model, look at recent issues of *Assessment and Evaluation in Higher Education* published by Taylor and Francis.). One cannot help but wonder how Socrates would have been rated by his interlocutors in the *Apology*. It is also sobering (and at times humorous) to examine many of the "assessment tools" currently available. See for example, Student Assessment of Learning Gains 2008 (http://www.wcer.wisc.edu/salgains/instructor/default.asp) or the *Teaching Goals Inventory* (Angelo and Cross 1993). In the latter, one can rate on a scale of 1 to 5 the importance of developing "aesthetic appreciation" in your course. It is hard not to feel that Kant and Coleridge would have been perplexed. For an important critique, see Fendrich 2007.
5  See the report at http://www.ed.gov/about/bdscomm/list/hiedfuture/reports/final-report.pdf. Note also Labi 2007.
6  See the classic exposition in Marx, *Capital*, vol. 1, chapter 1.
7  See for example Knippenberg 2007.

152  THEORY DOES NOT EXIST

their logical extreme. These arguments are needed not primarily to persuade those who are the leaders of this movement, or even the college and university administrators who are currently being forced to respond to them, but to persuade ourselves of the necessity of resistance. They are needed if we are to elaborate a principled refusal to accept the definitions of knowledge and education presented by the advocates of assessment in the context of an education that would value the critical over the rote, the creative over the merely repetitive.

To make these arguments, I will turn to what may seem an unlikely source, a book by Slavoj Žižek, *The Parallax View*. This work offers a series of arguments for grounding our reflection in those areas that would traditionally fall under the categories of theology and metaphysics, cognitive science and philosophy of mind, and ethics and politics. It seeks the ground for those categories not in their own content, but in the constitutive moment of excess or difference that makes them possible, and which by definition can never be fully subsumed within them, and hence accounted for by them. In this work with all its manifest eccentricities, all its Socratic *atopia* or "strangeness," I contend we can find decisive arguments for rejecting a model of knowledge, and hence education, as the repeatable, the reproducible commodity of an industry, and in favor of embracing the Socratic moment of the unrepeatable as epitomized in the *Theaetetus*.

Indeed, if we reflect on the structure of this dialogue, we shall find all the major elements of Žižek's argument. First, knowledge of the true is not that which can be encompassed within a narrow definition that could then be applied in an unproblematic fashion to either validate or invalidate the truth of a given set of data. Nonetheless, in our critical reflection on what constitutes knowledge, we in fact move to a position that is beyond that from which we began, even if we still do not possess a comprehensive definition of what knowledge is. Moreover, this movement of self-consciousness positing and overcoming itself is precisely what constitutes the philosophic life (*Theaetetus* 172c–174a, 210 b–d), though in terms of learning outcomes it must be considered a failure.

Second, the true is not that which is opposed to the fictive or the poetic, but rather it is only through a process of making (*fictio, poiesis*) that the examination of truth and the opening of the arc of knowledge can begin. Hence, the dialogue itself is not only fashioned by Socrates through his craft as what he terms a midwife of the soul, bringing to birth the thoughts of others, but more basically the dialogue that we read in a real sense does not exist at all. It is the product of the memory, craft, and the revisionary process of Euclides that is in turn performed by a third party, the slave, all in the imagination of Plato. The object of the inquiry, thus, does not exist outside the framing that brings it to our view and gives birth both to it and to the ultimate aporia into which it issues. But that fictive process nonetheless leaves its trace in the Real, in the world beyond the frame of the text, bringing us to a different place from where we began, as signified by the fact that the dialogue itself does not return to the moment of its opening frame but rather ends with Socrates saying, "but let us meet here again in the morning," signifying both repetition and the unending nature of the philosophic life as we look forward to the next dialogue, *The Sophist*.

Third, what lurks around the edges of the *Theaetetus*, what frames the frame, is death. It is the dying Theaetetus himself that inspires Euclides and Terpison to

THE REPEATABLE AND THE UNREPEATABLE          153

listen to the dialogue, and at the dialogue's end Socrates takes his leave of Theaetetus and Theodorus to go to the *Stoa Basileia* to answer the indictment lodged against him that will ultimately lead to his death. This frame is no accident, nor would I contend is it separable from the dialogue's main content: for knowledge itself, at least in any humanly intelligible form, is only made possible by finitude. Without the separation from the object that our mortality implies, knowledge and ignorance are meaningless concepts. This is why in the *Symposium* philosophy itself is a function of our mortality and why the whole concept of divine knowledge is a nonsequitur, since knowledge implies reference—an act of re-fering one thing to another—and hence must logically include otherness and separation, and thus gaps, errors, lack, and ultimately death.

## II

We can recall one of the archetypal scenes from cartoons: while dancing a cat jumps up into the air and turns around its own axis: instead of falling back down toward the earth's surface in accordance with the normal laws of gravity, however, it remains for some time suspended in the air turning around in the levitated position as if caught in a loop of time, repeating the same circular movement again and again …. At such moments, the "normal" run of things, the "normal" process of being caught in the imbecilic inertia of material reality, is for a brief moment suspended; we enter the magical domain of a suspended animation, a kind of ethereal rotation which, as it were, sustains itself …. This rotary movement, in which the linear process of time is suspended in a repetitive loop, is drive at its most elementary. This, again, is "humanization" at its most zero-level: this self-propelling loop which suspends/disrupts linear temporal enchainment. (Žižek 2006: 63)

In this one seemingly flippant comparison, but in fact in this one exceedingly dense poetic image, is contained *in nuce* the entirety of Žižek's argument. While I do not have the luxury of covering the whole of Žižek's four hundred pages of pyrotechnic prose in the scope of a brief article, I do want to derive three conceptual axes from the image of the dancing feline, axes that are both central to his larger project and crucial to the more general thesis I am proposing. They are in schematic form: first, the loop of the fictive frame of truth; second, the loop of freedom and the problem of consciousness; and third, the loop of drive and the role of death in the constitution of humanistic knowledge. In the remainder of this essay, I examine each of these in turn, recognizing that their analytic separability is provisional at best, before returning to Socrates and the issue of assessment.

### A. The Fictive Frame of Truth

When Adorno declares poetry impossible after Auschwitz, this impossibility is an enabling impossibility: poetry is always, by definition, "about" something that cannot be addressed directly, only alluded to. (Žižek 2006: 350)

When I speak of the loop of the fictive frame of truth, I refer to a specific circular and repeated activity of framing that both defines the object and allows the truth of

154                    THEORY DOES NOT EXIST

the object thus defined to be produced. The Heracleitean flux of experience admits of no objects of knowledge beyond the sheer welter of sensation until such point as that vast many has been divided into various categories and reconstituted as a series of unities or ones. But the truth of the object qua object, then, is nothing more than the frame that produces it, and yet without a pre-existing object of experience the framing concept does not exist. We are here at the moment of the conflict between a pure reason of categories of understanding and an empirical knowledge of unmediated experience, a conflict which received its classic modern expression in Kant's *Critique of Pure Reason* (1958: 41, "Transcendental Aesthetic"),[8] but whose basic antinomian formulation can be traced back at least to Plato's *Philebus* and its complex meditations on the relations between the unlimited, the limited, the mixed, and the One.

Kant occupies an important position in the opening pages of Žižek's argument, and it is his first critique that provides the ground for the initial articulation of Žižek's concept of the parallax. "Parallax" is a term derived from astronomy referring to a phenomenon wherein the same celestial body, when viewed from two different perspectives, appears to be in two different positions relative to other figures in the heavens. As used by Žižek, moreover, it would apply equally well to concepts such as Heisenberg's uncertainty principle, according to which we may either know the velocity or the position of a photon or electron, but not both. In each case, it is pointless to ask which is the correct perspective, or to try to split the difference between the two: for the correct perspective is always both and is thus always inconsistent with itself. The truth of the object thus consists in the oscillation, or better rotation, between the two perspectives, in the gap that articulates and creates the shifting frames of reference and in the circle thus inscribed that constitutes the moment of observational self-awareness (Žižek 2006: 165, 172).[9] The truth of the object, then, can only be posited in terms of the subject's own clearly definable, self-conscious, aporia. It is precisely this moment of Socratic self-awareness, however—"at least I know that I know nothing"—which necessarily remains inexpressible as a discrete data point or a quantifiable learning outcome, and yet which founds the possibility of truth itself.

By the same token, as Žižek notes, the Kantian antinomies of reason, as outlined in the first critique, are also not susceptible of synthesis: nor is it the case that a given thesis (e.g., "the world has a beginning in time, and is also limited in time and space") is correct but its antithesis (e.g., "the world has no beginning, and no limits in space; it is infinite as regards both time and space") incorrect (Žižek 2006: 20; compare Kant *CPR* 1958: 211–25, "Transcendental Dialectic," 2.2.2). The antinomies are, in short, in and of themselves perfectly parallactic, signifying only at the point of their impossible joining, that is on the level of what Kant terms "transcendental ideality" (*CPR* 1958: 244–46, "Critical Solution of the Cosmological Conflict of Reason with Itself"). In the Kantian universe, neither the merely empirical nor the purely categorical rise to the level of knowledge except from the perspective of their joining

---

8   Hereafter *CPR*.

9   Žižek's position was anticipated from a completely different disciplinary perspective by Friedrich's *The Language Parallax* (1986).

# THE REPEATABLE AND THE UNREPEATABLE
## 155

in the transcendental dimension, which does not abolish their difference, but rather articulates the (im)possibility of their parallactic encounter.[10] The transcendental thus names not a moment of closure but the moment of excess in which neither the manifold of the senses nor the concepts by which we frame the manifold so as to make it yield intelligible intuitions constitute the totality of experience (Kant *CPR* 1958: 42, "Transcendental Aesthetic"). It names not a substance or a thing but the space or moment of a difference that cannot be recuperated into our pre-existing categories of meaning.[11] It is this difference, this moment of noncoincidence that constitutes the axis around which the dancing cat of knowledge spins, the point of excess that allows it momentarily and gaily to defy gravity. It is also that of the Socratic aporia at the end of the *Theaetetus*, which affirms that though we have advanced no measurable distance along the road of defining what knowledge is, and thus cannot recuperate the steps we have taken into a pre-existing teleology, which would affirm the absolute identity between those steps and the final cause for which the journey was undertaken, nonetheless, we are not in the same position as before we left. Even if from one perspective we have gone around in a perfect circle, from another we have come back to somewhere else: and it is the difference defined by the joining of these two perspectives that constitutes the knowledge thus produced. That journey, the arc of its movement, the loop of its circulation has produced a certain excess, a certain irreducible difference. But this difference, this gap is not nothing. Indeed, it is this difference that as Kant so forcefully articulated in his concept of the transcendental makes knowledge possible. The scientific discovery, the work of artistic genius, the philosophical insight that may be taught, transmitted, and tested are predicated on, producible within, and, ultimately, only authentically possessed in the movement of the articulation of that difference.

The gap of the transcendental, which is what is gestured to in the moment of aporetic realization, and which constitutes the axis around which the dancing cat spins, names, then, precisely the distance created by what can only be called fiction (*fictum*: "the made" < *fingo -ere*), i.e., the excess whose distance from the Real makes the latter visible by articulating the space between the pre-existing categories of thought (and their own necessary, internal logic) and the simply given. It is, at the same time, the constitutive power of this moment of irreducible difference that gives the lie to the fantasy of total knowledge, of complete accountability, for such a fantasy must by definition be able completely to account for itself, including the difference that makes it possible. It must render itself either epiphenomenal, a moment of surplus or excess in a vast machinic structure, or it must posit the totality of

---

10  See Žižek, "What Kant does is to change the very terms of the debate; his solution—the transcendental turn—is unique in that it, first, rejects the ontological closure: it recognizes a certain fundamental and irreducible limitation ('finitude') of the human condition, which is why the two poles, rational and sensual, active and passive, can never be fully mediated-reconciled …. Far from designating a 'synthesis' of the two dimensions, the Kantian 'transcendental' stands, rather, for their irreducible gap 'as such': the 'transcendental' points to something in this gap, a new dimension which cannot be reduced to either of the two positive terms between which the gap is gaping" (2006: 21).

11  It is on this level that Žižek's acknowledgement of the convergence between his concept of the "minimal difference" and Derrida's of "différance" makes itself felt (Žižek 2006: 11).

156                              THEORY DOES NOT EXIST

knowledge as itself radically incomplete (Žižek 2006: 168). Knowledge, then, is the effect of the joining of the frames of the fictive or the made to the flux of the empirical. As such, the difference between the framing and the framed only becomes visible in the shift from one frame to the next, only in the parallactic view of the object from two irreconcilable perspectives that necessarily posit their own excess, i.e., the aporetic axis of rotation that makes their articulation possible.

Finally, it is at the moment of this shift, of the rotation of the arc of knowledge, that we must also posit the subject, as the moment of efficient drive and desire that shifts the gears from one set of frames to the next. This, as Žižek observes, is also the moment in which we must move from an essentially Kantian model to that of Hegel:

> The basic Hegelian correction of Kant is thus that the three domains of reason (theoretical, practical, aesthetic) emerged through the shift in the subject's attitude, that is through "bracketing": the object of science emerges through bracketing moral and aesthetic judgments; the moral emerges through bracketing cognitive-theoretical and aesthetic concerns; and the aesthetic domain emerges through bracketing theoretical and moral concerns. For example, when we bracket moral and aesthetic concerns, a human being appears as non-free, totally conditioned by the causal nexus; if on the contrary, we bracket theoretical concerns, he or she appears as a free autonomous being. Thus antinomies should not be reified—the antinomic positions emerge through shifts in the subject's attitude. (Žižek 2006: 50)

Frames then are not eternal static forms, but evolving categories of intelligibility that in response to the desires and drives of the subject carve different objects out of the manifold of sensation. The gap between those frames themselves and the objects they define is the space of the parallactic, the constitutive excess that is ultimately the truth of both the object and of the subject whose act of making constitutes it.[12]

The truth, then, is not in fact that which is yielded by the pre-existing categories of meaning, whose content was established before the moment of investigation, but

---

12  This moment beyond the categories of understanding and desire is what Lacan, Žižek's ultimate intellectual reference, termed the Real. The Real as Žižek argues is parallactic and not substantial. It is perceptible only in the shift from one perspective to the other or, better yet, as the moment of their aporetic emergence and joining (Žižek 2006: 27). In this respect, when we think of the Real, we are to recall the Kantian "thing in itself," which also in fact exists only as the excess that makes possible the articulation of the pure categories of thought (the positively noumenal) and the realm of appearance, the phenomenal, and as such names their impossible unity. The thing in itself is, in fact, on the side of the object, what the transcendental is on the side of the subject: each is only visible as the parallactic moment of the shift between frames, as an undecideable and hence aporetical excess or difference (Kant *CPR* 1958: 152–55, "The Ground of the Distinction of All Objects in General into Phenomena and Noumena," and 240, "Transcendental Idealism as the Key to the Solution of the Cosmological Dialectic"; Žižek 1989: 172, 177, 204–5).

   On the crucial distinction between the object of pure thought (the positively noumenal), the object of appearance (phenomenal), and the thing in itself as the ground of critical thought, see Colletti 1979: 86–110. Compare also Kolakowski 1978: 45 and Cassirer 1981: 285.

# THE REPEATABLE AND THE UNREPEATABLE            157

that which is beyond meaning and hence on the side of the Real (Žižek 2006: 181).
It is not a learning outcome or a skill to be mastered. The truth is what becomes visible
in the movement of those categories and the objects they frame. It is consequently
predicated on those categories' constitutive lack of identity with both the object of
their apperception and with themselves (see Žižek 2006: 106–107). It becomes visible
in their very poetic or made quality as they constitute the arc or loop of the fictive
frame of truth. Indeed, it is in the very plasticity of the work of art, of the work of
poetic indirection, that this parallactic movement is perhaps most foregrounded and
consequently becomes most visible (Žižek 2006: 147). Thus, paradoxically, we approach
most closely the Truth that is beyond the established categories of meaning, the Truth
to which the Socratic aporia of the *Theaetetus* both gestures and gives rise, through
the fictive, the metaphorical, and the poetic, through that which is precisely (im)possible
after Auschwitz (Žižek 2006: 169; Gasché 2002).

## B. The Loop of Freedom

> What strikes us is how evolutionist or cognitivist accounts always seem to stumble over
> the same deadlock: after we have constructed an artificial intelligence machine which
> can solve even very complex problems, the question crops up: "But if it can do it precisely
> as a machine, as a blind operating entity, why does it need (self-) awareness to do it?"
> So the more consciousness is demonstrated to be marginal, unnecessary, nonfunctional,
> the more it becomes enigmatic—here it is consciousness itself which is the Real …. (Žižek
> 2006: 177)

One of the many wagers of the *Parallax View* is on freedom in almost a Sartrean fashion.[13]
Although Žižek is careful never to put the matter that baldly, and indeed in one crucial
sense the two positions are ultimately irreconcilable: for where the Sartrean subject's
freedom is predicated on the possibility of an unrelenting lucidity, and a fundamental
denial of the reality of the unconscious (Sartre 1943: 616–35), for Žižek it is our own inner,
inescapable opacity that is constitutive of our freedom (2006: 244). Yet in both cases,
as perhaps most memorably bodied forth in Sartre's *Nausée*, it is indeed the superfluous
quality of consciousness, its own constitutive excess, its *gratuité*, that is its most profound
index of escaping the realm of total, linear determination.

The loop of freedom is thus not the denial of either necessity or of the reality
of determination. It is rather the traumatic irruption of a moment of excess, of
the strictly unnecessary (Žižek 2006: 92). But that excess, in turn, must be assumed,
must be taken up (Žižek 2006: 204, 243). It becomes part of the subject's fictive arc,
a moment that can be schematized strictly neither as the seeking of immediate pleasure
nor the avoidance of pain, and yet is purposeful, made (Žižek 2006: 203). At the same
time, it is neither strictly epiphenomenal, having no effective relation to the causal
chain, nor is it the necessary result of that chain, but exists precisely at the parallactic
moment between these two antinomian instances: a curve, a swerve, a perversion.

---

13  See, for example, Žižek 2006: 322.

It points to a fundamental openness, a moment of surplus within being itself—its own uncertainty principle (Žižek 2006: 172). If the Real were completely whole, closed, and self-consistent—completely beyond the symbolic forms and categories we deploy to create, stabilize, define, and consequently intervene in it—then the play of appearances, the possibility of parallax, and the self-reflective loop of consciousness itself, with its ethical and political commitments, would strictly be impossible (Žižek 2006: 106–107). Nonetheless, appearance implies difference, not just between itself and the Real, but within the Real that gave rise to it. A unidimensional world of pure positivity knows neither meaning nor change. It is inert: a piece of meat, a marble slab, the meaningless whir of the machine. It is the gap, the excess, the unaccountable that introduces the play of meaning and the possibility of self-awareness.

It is, then, the fictive loop of consciousness as a moment of simultaneous surplus and opacity in relation to a fundamentally parallactic Real that also makes possible the ethical, and that makes possible the ontology of the ethical dimension proper, which must posit the possibility of an Ought separate from the Is. As Žižek observes:

> When Lacan asserts that ethics belongs to the realm of the Real, is it not that—to put it in Kantian terms—he is claiming that, in our fleeting temporal reality with no ultimate ontological grounding, the ethical, the unconditional demand of our duty, is our only contact with the Eternal (noumenal)? The question is thus not simply that of how Ought emerges out of IS, the positive order of Being, or how to assert the ethical as external—irreducible—to the order of Being ... but that of the place of Ought within the very order of Being: within what ontology is the ethical dimension proper possible without being reduced to an epiphenomenon (in the style of Spinoza, for whom Ought simply indicates the limitation of our knowledge)? (Žižek 2006: 49).

The loop of freedom is therefore the very condition that is necessary for the ethical dimension to exist, and consequently for the whole question of what education should be to be meaningfully posed. Any form of assessment that does not directly engage precisely the gap on which that loop must be founded, the moment of ineradicable difference, is not only self-negating but unable to pose in coherent terms the following questions: what does it mean to know something, what is the truth, and what does it mean to be an ethical subject.

Yet, such a philosophical and psychoanalytic approach to consciousness runs squarely into the objections of cognitive science and evolutionary psychology. What these approaches have in common is a claim that our mental lives—our beliefs, our desires, our commitments—are a function of our hard wiring, and that hard wiring can be best read as a series of evolutionary adaptations to environmental demands. These approaches exhibit a variety of sophisticated responses to the problem of consciousness and the attendant question of the subject's freedom, and I cannot possibly do justice to them within the span of a brief article but will instead focus on Žižek's response (Žižek 2006: 177–78). That response, as might be expected, is not simple. On the one hand, cognitive approaches are perfectly at home with the decentered subject of psychoanalysis. For them, selfhood is a form of illusion, a collection of operations that has no single central organizing point, no Cartesian *res cogitans* coordinating all

THE REPEATABLE AND THE UNREPEATABLE 159

our various biological and information processing functions and subordinating them to a unified intent (Žižek 2006: 162–63). On the other hand, as a direct result of their viewing mental life as a series of interactive but dispersed adaptive functions, they are at a loss to explain the functionality of consciousness as what Žižek terms a "closed loop" of "negative self-relating." By this latter term, Žižek refers specifically to consciousness's ability to relate to the self in a fashion that changes the self in ways that cannot be captured under a concept of maximizing either individual pleasure or species adaptation (Žižek 2006: 168, 177). The classic example from the Lacanian perspective is Antigone. Her choice to die, to bury her brother even though she knows it means certain death, and even though she knows he possessed no inherent personal qualities that warrant this sacrifice is unintelligible from the cognitivist perspective (Lacan 1986; Miller 2007: chapter 3). The archetypical free act is thus the self-relating consciousness's ability to say "no" to that to which, from the perspective of pleasure or utility, it should assent.

It is this "no," moreover, this self-relating negation, that is the ground of the ethical per se, not as a series of pre-existing codes that regulate and determine our behavior, but as the ontological ground on which the Ought first separates itself from the Is. The loop of freedom is not a function of our ability to choose the life we wish, to pursue pleasure, or to be rational decision-makers maximizing utility, but it is rather a function, very precisely, of the ability to reflect back upon oneself and to refuse that life, that pleasure, that utility, in return for no obvious immediate good. It is to choose unaccountable *gratuité*: not because of its superior moral value or a specious nobility, but as the possibility of doing otherwise, as the moment of constitutive excess that every ethics must assume.

None of this is to deny the value of the vast mental mapping achieved by cognitive science and its ability to construct causal explanations for a wide range of human experiences, its ability to produce repeatable predictable results, which can be replicated through the sciences of artificial intelligence, cybernetics, and neurobiology, rather it is to note the moment of constitutive excess, the moment of difference that can never be accounted for per se within these paradigms. Antigone thus by choosing the impossible, by choosing her death, also chooses the singular and unrepeatable, the moment that when generalized to the level of a rule becomes madness, and a moment that can only be pictured as an unaccountable perversity from the perspective of the singular realm of the Is with its strict causal determinations. Yet that choice of the Ought and of negation only has meaning in relation to the Is, in relation to the world of normative, calculative reason represented by Creon and the written laws of this world. It has no value in and of itself. The ethical act as an index of the loop of freedom can only exist at the impossible point of the joining of these two worlds of Is and Ought, of the repeatable and the unrepeatable, at the moment of parallax that brings them both into view at once and that, as Sophocles saw so well, constitutes the moment of their tragic excess and enjoyment.

From the Žižekian and Lacanian, but also the Socratic and Sophoclean perspective, the subject is only a subject strictly to the extent that it remains opaque to the other, that it exists in the realm of the unrepeatable and that its acts can continue to trace their way within the Real, within the realm of Truth rather than pre-existing meaning (*doxa*).

160 THEORY DOES NOT EXIST

At the same time, the subject is only a subject on the condition that it appears to itself, that it reflects upon itself, and that its self-reflexivity remains ultimately incomplete, that a moment of inner opacity persists, a moment that refuses to let the circle be completely closed and the moment of aporia be reduced to the realm of reigning positivity. It is only in this moment that the chance of true action, a real event, and hence of ethics as a moment of self-determination can exist (Žižek 2006: 206, 244). It is that moment of opacity, the hard kernel of being that constitutes the axis around which the dancing cat of consciousness spins that represents the constitutive excess whose very surplus creates the ground on which the loop of fictive truth and the loop of freedom rejoin, but never quite merge with, one another in the parallactic.

## C. The Loop of Drive

Instinct is satiated by the object, but also extinguished by this very satiety. The instinct and the object finish each other off, as it were, as the former quickly has enough of the latter. The drive, on the other hand, does not finish so easily with its object, but keeps turning around it …. If the drive is not only satisfied, but continues to seek and derive satisfaction in the object, this has no doubt something to do with the splitting in the order of appearances of which Lacan speaks. The point is that drive does not aim beyond the ordinary object at the satisfaction to be attained on the other or thither side of it. This is what happens in the case of the oral instinct, where the goal is used to secure satisfaction of one's hunger. The food is merely the means by which the stomach gets filled. If the drive, on the contrary, is said to have no goal, but only an aim, this is because its object is no longer a means of attaining satisfaction, it is an end in itself; it is directly satisfying. (Copjec 2002: 38)

The loop of freedom, then, is not just another doctrine of philosophical humanism, not just a self-congratulatory way of asserting man's dignity or the ultimate self-transparency of man to man or man to god. It is rather founded on a fundamental opacity, on a moment of necessary aporia that refuses ever to collapse back into a logic of means and ends. It is this moment of aporia, of irreducible difference that makes meaning possible, that provides the necessary difference that allows for the fictive frame of truth and that consequently must also assume that the frame is never the object itself, even when that object is the self. Rather the loop of freedom, like the loop of the fictive frame of truth, is predicated on the fact that that loop can never be closed. To speak in Freudian terms, the loop itself is beyond the pleasure principle. It is beyond the chain of substitutions and exchanges that seek to restore a balance and equanimity between the subject and the constraints of its environment (Freud 1961; Žižek 1992: 48). The loop then, while having a directionality, an aim, can have no goal, can have no *telos* from which one can deduce a final cause and thus resolve the whole of its arc into a journey toward a predetermined end. The loop of freedom, then, far from representing either an adaptation of the organism to its environment or a triumph of rational self-presence over the darkness of self-division is precisely the moment of what Freud termed the death drive (Copjec 2000: 278–79). That is the obsessive turning round the unreachable object that cannot be resolved back into the terms of the play between the pleasure and the reality principles: Antigone's uncompromising, untreatable "no."

# THE REPEATABLE AND THE UNREPEATABLE 161

Ironically, then it is our inhuman excess that is constitutive of our humanity. As Žižek writes, the *"differentia specifica* which defines a human being is not the difference between man and animal ... but the difference between the human and the inhuman excess that is inherent to being-human" (Žižek 2006: 123). Or as Plato puts it in the *Symposium*, it is the very fact that we do not have wisdom that both makes us love it (*philosophein*) and never attain it: for to have it would be to be a god, and perfect beings in so far as they know no lack, and hence no difference between themselves and their objects, cannot be philosophers. Rather it is insofar as we all are in some sense like Alcibiades, drunken and besotted, and yet in love with that indefinable, unknowable something that Socrates carries within him, the *agalma* or icon that defines the difference between his coarse exterior and the possibility of unspeakable inner divinity, that we come to pursue the knowledge of the good, the just, and the beautiful, but also by definition never acquire it. The reduction of the pursuit of these goals to the acquisition of a set of predetermined outcomes, that is to a set of reproducible and hence exchangeable commodities under the twin aegises of the pleasure and the reality principles, is not only an oversimplification, but it is also by definition to make the pursuit of the traditional goals of humanistic education impossible. In the name of what passes for a strictly procedural notion of accountability, the assessment movement seeks to banish knowledge as the approach of truth, rather than reproduction of the already given.

The death drive, then, far from being a nihilistic desire for destruction, from a psychoanalytic perspective represents that within us, which is more than us and which is always therefore in the last analysis radically external to us: the gods, the Real. It is the other within that cannot be reduced to the dialectic of pleasure and adaptation. From a Lacanian point of view, human freedom exists only as the gap or *nonsequitur* represented by the human's fundamental maladaptation to its environment, its perverse excess (Žižek 2006: 231, 259–60). The death drive points strictly to that parallactic moment in which what from one perspective appears as the deeply internal becomes, from another perspective, the radically external. It constitutes the moment of excess that cognitive science and models of determinate causality can represent only as a gap. Its relation to the world of the repeatable is that of an unaccountable antinomy, and it consequently constitutes the aporetic center around which Socratic inquiry turns, the hole at the heart of being:

> The only way to account for the status of (self-)consciousness is to assert the ontological incompleteness of "reality" itself: there is "reality" [as the object of experience, investigation, signification] only insofar as there is an ontological gap, crack, in its very heart, that is to say, a traumatic excess, a foreign body which cannot be integrated into it.... in this momentary suspension of the positive order of reality, we confront the ontological gap on account of which "reality" is never a complete, self-enclosed positive order of being. It is only this experience of psychotic withdrawal from reality, of absolute self-contraction, which accounts for the mysterious "fact" of transcendental freedom: for a (self-)consciousness which is in effect "spontaneous," whose spontaneity is not an effect of misrecognition of some "objective" process. (Žižek 2006: 242)

The truly creative act, then, will not be that which affirms a given set of predetermined outcomes, but that which creates a silence, which clears a space, a moment of radical

162 THEORY DOES NOT EXIST

difference (Žižek 2006: 154–55). It is this moment of spacing that allows the true to appear within the loop of the fictive frame of truth, that makes possible freedom as the intersection of self-reflexivity with linear causality, and that constitutes the inhuman core of our humanity.

### III

Theaeteus: Oh yes, Socrates, I often wonder like mad what these things can mean; sometimes when I'm looking at them I begin to feel quite giddy.

Socrates: I dare say you do, my dear boy. It seems that Theodorus was not far from the truth when he guessed what kind of person you are. For this is an experience which is characteristic of a philosopher, this wondering: this is where philosophy begins and nowhere else. (*Theaetetus* 155c–d, Cooper 1997: 173)

The young Theaetetus, giddy with the prospect of philosophy in the shadow of his own death, converses with the sly Socrates, himself on the way to meet his appointment with mortality. The two are engaged in the pursuit of a defensible definition of knowledge, which itself is posed within the frame of a double fiction: that of Euclides and that of Plato. Their end is predetermined both by death and the structure of the fictive frame itself. Yet within that frame a marvelous space is opened up that can be reduced neither to the utility of the definition of truth thus arrived at—all the proposed formulas are ultimately found to be still born—nor to a set of discrete lessons learned. The openness of that space is signified by the fact that the represented fictive frame, that of Euclides, never closes, but we the readers theoretically continue to wonder infinitely within the space of inquiry, even as the limits of our own finitude are explicitly acknowledged.

The ontological status of that space is clearly problematic. It is neither that of the order of positive being nor does it simply not exist. Yet nonetheless it has real effects. It is the space of the aporia or parallax and exists only in the wavering moment that joins the loop of freedom to the realm of the repeatable, the exchangeable, and hence the commodifiable: the moment before our spinning cartoon cat looks down and sees the floor far beneath rising up to meet him. It is exactly this space, which Žižek in the wake of Socrates has defined, and which it has long been the task of the humanities to open. It is a space that cannot, in fact, exist outside the realm of positive repeatable knowledge—names, dates, doctrines, rules of logic and grammar—but which can never be exhausted by that knowledge, and which, more fundamentally, gives that knowledge itself meaning, allowing the bearer not only authentically to possess it but also to move beyond it. No one believes that the educator has no positive obligation to the student, but what she owes the young Alcibiades, Theaetetus, or Diotima is precisely *no* thing: not a list of boxes to be checked, but a space to be cleared into which "a multitude of beautiful things" can be "brought into the light"; not an object of exchange or a commodity, as Alicbiades supposes when he lies down with Socrates, but the recognition of the lack that figures our *philo-sophic* desire.

In the end, when Socrates in the *Apology* says that he is the wisest of men because he knows he knows nothing, what he says is neither simply true nor false. This infinitely

# THE REPEATABLE AND THE UNREPEATABLE 163

ironic statement can never be reduced to the ontological equivalent of a data point, a good, or a moment of species adaptation or of skill mastery. When Socrates says he knows nothing, this is one of the classic examples of Socratic irony. In terms of operational knowledge, it may very well be true. But this statement is also the claim to another kind of knowledge altogether. Moreover, the irony of the statement is only functional to the extent that the second meaning does not simply supersede the first. Both meanings must exist if the statement is to do its philosophic work: for it is indeed the parallactic joining of these two seemingly opposite claims in the same statement that is the provocation to inquiry. This is the moment at which the norms of what constitutes knowledge and wisdom, in dialogues like the *Theaetetus*, reveal their limits, and hence the moment in which thought, as opposed to repetition, begins. Socratic irony, thus, creates an opening that makes possible the radical interrogation of true and false and hence also serves as their necessary ground and precondition. If the forces behind the current assessment movement are successful and their epistemological model of repeatable, testable, and therefore quantifiable learning outcomes becomes hegemonic within our colleges and universities, then, the project of teaching students how to think in this most sustained and rigorous sense, and not just to be "knowledge workers," will be extinguished, and then Socrates will be assessed in much the same way as he was in an Athenian court 2500 years ago.

## Works Cited

Angelo, Thomas A. and Cross K. Patricia. 1993. *Teaching Goals Inventory.* https://tgi.its.uiowa.edu.

Blondell, Ruby. 2002. *The Play of Character in Plato's Dialogues.* Cambridge: Cambridge University Press.

Cassirer, Ernst. 1981. *Kant's Life and Thought.* Trans. James Haden. New Haven: Yale University Press.

Coletti, Lucio. 1979. *Marxism and Hegel.* Trans. Lawrence Garner. London: Verso.

Cooper, John M., ed. 1997. *Plato: Complete Works.* Assoc. ed. D. S. Hutchinson. Indianapolis: Hackett.

Copjec, Joan. 2000. "The Body as Viewing Instrument, or the Strut of Vision." *Lacan in America.* Ed. Jean-Michel Rabaté. New York: The Other Press. 237–308.

———. 2002. *Imagine There's No Woman: Ethics and Sublimation.* Cambridge: MIT Press.

Deleuze, Gilles. 1994. *Difference and Repetition.* Trans. Paul Patton. New York: Columbia University Press.

Fendrich, Laurie. 2007. "A Pedagogical Straitjacket." *Chronicle of Higher Education,* June 8. 53.40: B6.

Freud, Sigmund. 1961. *Beyond the Pleasure Principle.* Trans. James Strachey. New York: Norton.

Friedrich, Paul. 1986. *The Language Parallax: Linguistic Relativism and Poetic Indeterminacy.* Austin: University of Texas Press.

Gasché, Rodolphe. 2002. "L'expérience aporétique aux origins de la pensée. Platon, Heidegger, Derrida." *Études françaises* 38: 103–21.

Hunter, Richard. 2004. *Plato's Symposium.* Oxford: Oxford University Press.

Jaschik, Scott. 2009. "Assessing Assessment." *Inside Higher Ed.* https://www.insidehighered.com/news/2009/01/23/assessing-assessment.

Kant, Immanuel. 1958. *Critique of Pure Reason.* Trans. Norman Kemp Smith. New York: Modern Library.

Knippenberg, Joseph M. 2007. "Why Conservatives Should Be Leery of Government Mandated Assessment of Higher Education." https://www.academia.edu/503628/Why_Conservatives_Should_Be_Leery_of_Government_Mandated_Assessment_of_Higher_Education.

Kolakowski, Leszek. 1978. *Main Currents of Marxism. 1. The Founders.* Trans. P. S. Falla. Oxford: Oxford University Press.

Labi, Aisha. 2007. "International Assessment Effort Raises Concerns Among Education Groups." *Chronicle of Higher Education*, September 28. 54.5: A31.

Lacan, Jacques. 1986. *Le séminaire livre VII: L'éthique de la psychanalyse.* Ed. Jacques-Alain Miller. Paris: Seuil.

Lederman, Doug. 2008. "You can't measure what we teach." *Inside Higher Ed.* https://www.insidehighered.com/news/2008/12/04/you-cant-measure-what-we-teach.

Miller, Paul Allen. 2007. *Postmodern Spiritual Practices: The Construction of the Subject and the Reception of Plato in Lacan, Derrida, and Foucault.* Columbus: Ohio State University Press.

Nehamas, Alexander. 1998. *The Art of Living: Socratic Reflections from Plato to Foucault.* Berkeley: University of California Press.

Nightingale, Andrea Wilson. 1995. *Genres in Dialogue: Plato and the Construct of Philosophy.* Cambridge: Cambridge University Press.

Sartre, Jean-Paul. 1943. *L'être et le néant.* Paris: Gallimard.

Student Assessment of Learning Gains. 2008. http://www.wcer.wisc.edu/salgains/instructor/default.asp.

*A Test Of Leadership: Charting the Future of U.S. Higher Education, A Report of the Commission Appointed by Secretary of Education Margaret Spellings.* 2006. http://www.ed.gov/about/bdscomm/list/hiedfuture/reports/final-report.pdf.

Wohl, Victoria. 2002. *Love Among the Ruins: The Erotics of Democracy in Classical Athens.* Princeton: Princeton University Press.

Žižek, Slavoj. 1989. *The Sublime Object of Ideology.* London: Verso.

———. 2002. *Enjoy Your Symptom: Jacques Lacan in Hollywood and Out.* London: Routledge.

———. 2006. *The Parallax View.* Cambridge, MA: MIT Press.

# Chapter 12

# THEORY DOES NOT EXIST

Theory, as such, does not exist. I realize the perversity of this claim being made by a scholar who has written more than his fair share of books and articles in which the names of Derrida, Foucault, and Lacan, Kristeva, Irigaray, and Kofman loom large. Moreover, I fully appreciate the grave historical irony of any discussion of the vicissitudes of a non-existent theory in a cultural and political context in which the very project of enlightenment modernity seems increasingly imperiled, in which racism, sexism, and homophobia are on the rise, and in which the value of scientific reason (or reason *tout court*) is increasingly questioned. The fact that the science deniers themselves thrive in a media culture that is almost totally dependent on technology never seems to give them pause.

I speak, moreover, as someone who has sat in the Provost's office of a major research university and witnessed the flight of our students from subjects of real inquiry in both basic science and the humanities, who has heard the demands of their parents for immediate returns on their investments, and of governing boards that insist that the university be run "as a business," that outcomes be measurable and preferably spendable. I think we must pause in this time of crisis and ask very seriously "what are we doing?" Are we fiddling while Rome burns? The climate is rapidly degrading, racial nationalism is on the rise throughout the west, neo-fascists and their close kin are holding rallies and gaining electoral traction, children of immigrants have been put in cages, and the opposition is too often bogged down in infighting and finger pointing. It feels all too close to Europe in the 1930s. And here we are doing what academic students of theory do: dissecting the finer points of Derrida, consigning Latour to the ash heap of history, celebrating geocriticism, or investigating the depths of poetry and the Lacanian Real. Have we really nothing better to do? Perhaps not. *Indeed*, perhaps not: for I would argue that sometimes when we most seem to be doing nothing, we are in fact doing something crucial, something that must be done, precisely because it is no thing, because it is not an object with clearly defined borders that can produced, consumed, commodified, and assessed, because it offers the opportunity to rethink the ontic world as it has been given.

Increasingly I think the correct metaphor is not to picture ourselves as an elite collection of mandarins—which we must admit is how we appear to an all too large a public—occupants of the ivory tower who grow our fingernails long and argue about irrelevancies, while feeding at the trough of public education or on the largesse of the wealthy families who pay steep private school tuitions. Rather than thinking of Nero playing his lyre amidst the decadence of empire, when I consider my colleagues in the humanities who work long hours for mediocre pay and increasingly little job security to teach often apathetic undergraduates, to prepare graduate students for an all but nonexistent job market, and to produce scholarship on topics they love deeply but do not expect even their nearest and dearest to understand, I reflect back instead on the Irish Monks of the 5th and 6th centuries, who out on their windswept island copied ancient manuscripts by hand, manuscripts that the surrounding population and the barbarian hordes overrunning Europe could not read or understand and that they would have more readily burned for warmth than spent hours carefully, meticulously annotating and copying. It was those monks who in many ways preserved the conversation we name western civilization, and who through founding schools and monasteries across northern England produced figures such as Alcuin of York, who would go on to establish the cathedral school system under Charlemagne. That system in turn produced the Carolingian renaissance and later grew into the beginnings of the great universities of Europe, North America, and now much of the world.

Civilization is a delicate web that depends on long conversations extending over great expanses of time, and we should not fool ourselves about how easily its threads are snapped.[1] Rome actually fell. The Third Reich happened, as did Pol Pot, and ISIS. Bad shit happens. Basic questions about meaning, truth, justice, and ethics, about the importance of reading, thinking, writing, and reflecting, about the nature of the beautiful, the abject, and the sublime can only be posed in terms of the history of their previous usages, predications, and definitions. The capacity to interrogate our present condition, to imagine alternatives to it, and to persuade others to join us in trying to realize those alternatives—as well as the conceptual quality and texture of those alternatives— is dependent on the continuity and context of this conversation. The inability for the next generations to continue it or to understand the complex nature of its genealogy and the subtle determinations that differentiate it from calculations of pure utility or economic rationality is a real possibility. War, ecological disaster, educational mediocrity, the unwillingness to recognize or support that which cannot be subjected to a brutal immediate use all threaten to snap the threads that weave the text of this conversation.

If Irish monks seem too distant a metaphor for the role humanist scholarship plays in the preservation of civilization, think instead of a Jewish French philosopher of Algerian origin buying a postcard in the gift shop of the Bodleian library in Oxford. Derrida's famous postcard is itself taken from the frontispiece to a 13th century work of fortune telling by Matthew of Paris. The carefully hand-drawn image depicts two figures: one is seated at a desk producing a manuscript, in much the same manner as those very Irish monks would have done and as the actual monk who produced this work did; the other is standing behind the first and giving directions, perhaps even dictating what is being written. They are labeled respectively Socrates and Plato.

---

1 As my friend Carlos M. Amador reminds me (*per litteras*), "Threads snap with the everyday bleakness of human violence, but they reform, hide, and tie small, nearly imperceptible knots. We are utterly threaded." Indeed, some of those imperceptible knots can become not only bonds that link us but forms of bondage. Nazis read Goethe. Proud Boys fight to preserve "Western Civilization." We have to be able to hold in our heads simultaneously the possibilities of civilizational collapse, resurgence, and malevolence.

# THEORY DOES NOT EXIST

There are many ironies here, most of which Derrida himself unpacks in the course of *La carte postale* (1980), which begins as an epistolary novel, continues with Derrida's reading of Lacan's seminar on Poe's "Purloined Letter," and ends with an interview on the relation between Derrida's work and psychoanalysis. The frontispiece to Matthew of Paris's work eventually becomes the cover of Derrida's own. Among those ironies is the reversal of roles that seems to take place in the post card's depiction of Plato and Socrates. By tradition, and indeed in accordance with what can be presumed to be historical fact, Socrates did not write. He is the first philosopher in the west, the one from whom all subsequent ancient schools claimed their descent—the Platonic, Stoic, Cynic, Cyrenaic, Peripatetic, and Epicurean—yet he left no writings, and we know him only from the writings of his followers. Most famously, we know Socrates from the writings of Plato. The Socrates of Plato's *Apology, Symposium, Phaedrus*, and the *Republic* is etched in most of our minds and melds with Socrates himself for the vast majority of us. Yet he was hardly the only one. A very different Socrates emerges if you read Xenophon's *Apology, Symposium, Memorabilia*, or *Oikonomika*. Theodectes, whose work is now lost, produced yet another (Danzig 2003), and we would be very negligent if we were not to include the Socrates of Aristophanes' *Clouds*, whom Kierkegaard considered closest to the historical Socrates (Kierkegaard 1989: 128–56). The point here is not to determine which of these is the real Socrates, but rather to see that what a conventional intellectual history would view as a straight line from Socrates to Plato to Plato's readers, ultimately including Derrida and us is anything but straight. The Socrates that we know both really existed and no doubt had a profound influence on Plato as well as many others. He also so aggravated his uncomprehending fellow citizens that they had him executed, precisely for asking them uncomfortable questions. What is justice? What is the good? What is the beautiful? How should we organize the state so as to bring those forms into being? Yet, this same Socrates is also very much Plato's creation. Indeed, Socrates in a real sense took Plato's dictation. It was he who received Plato's inscription to precisely the extent that Plato was the young disciple able to receive his. The linear depiction of intellectual history, of philosophical debate, of the conversation that constitutes the thin but binding web of civilization, is an illusion. That history is a dialogue whose recursive temporality flows in both directions and whose content is never simply there to be received but must be actively constructed and responded to at each point of transmission or transference, at each postal relay.

And this is very much Derrida's point. His stance is ironic and mischievously humorous, but nonetheless deadly serious when he argues in *La carte postale* that we should not underestimate the influence of Freud's *Beyond the Pleasure Principle* on Plato's *Philebus* (Derrida 1980: 120; Miller 2007 139–41). The claim is at least a paradox. Traditional intellectual history assumes a univocal, irreversible system of transmission. Socrates teaches Plato. Plato teaches Aristotle. Jesus teaches the disciples. The disciples and the church fathers found the church. And the western *logos* is established and handed down to us: a divine mixture of Hellenic wisdom and Hebraic faith, in which Freud, Matthew Arnold and Charles Maurras all play their parts. Platonism's function has been to anchor that system of knowledge. Derrida's interrogation of Plato in relation to Freud, however, serves to show not simply the debt of Freud to Plato, but the way

168 THEORY DOES NOT EXIST

in which debt per se is the condition of possibility for any investment, the way in which each step forward must recreate its own past in a movement of double conditioning that is, yes, "always already" decentered. Thus, any given relay in the system of transmission of meaning must be radically historicized not only in terms of its debt to the past, but also in terms of the way that past itself becomes an object of transmission and hence potentially of appropriation and misappropriation as a condition of entering that system, of becoming a project, of becoming the future. The *Philebus*, as we know it, as we read it today, would not exist without Freud, Derrida argues, to precisely the same degree that Socrates would not exist without Plato, and there is no *Philebus* and no Socrates for us other than the ones we know (Derrida 1980: 36, 60–70, 180–207; Miller 2007: 151–66).

Nonetheless, it is all too easy to forget the contingencies upon which that post card from the past depends if it is to reach its destination, and indeed as Derrida argues within the same work against Lacan (Derrida 1980: 439–524), the letter does not in fact always arrive at its destination, or at least we must always keep open the possibility of its destruction or its loss. The entire structure of Derrida's meditation depends not only on the recursive temporality of his dialogue with Freud, Plato, and Socrates, and the vicissitudes that allowed the works of Plato to survive when so much from antiquity did not, including all the dialogues of Aristotle. It also depends on the production and preservation Matthew of Paris's book of prognostications, on the monks who drew Plato and Socrates in their own image, on the commitment to build and preserve the Bodlcian library in 1602, on the invention, continuation, and disruption of the epistolary novel, beginning with Ovid's *Heroides*, and on the commodification and reproduction of culture represented by the post card itself. At any point, the links in this chain, some salutary, others less so, could have been easily broken and what we take now for civilization could have been lost. There is nothing necessary about any of this surviving or continuing to survive, even though as we gather in our seminar rooms, give our lectures, and write our papers we all too often take for granted that it will.

What then does any of this have to do with theory or with antitheory for that matter? Everything and nothing. I am asking us to think seriously about what do we mean when we say we teach *theory*, we use *theory*, we apply *theory*, or we have moved beyond/after *theory*? Is theory a thing? Does it have an ontology? Is it something that was invented in Paris on or around 1968 or in American English and Comparative Literature Departments in the 1970s and 1980s? Or, like the poor, has it always been with us? Is it not in many ways the very conversation I have just described as the fabric of civilization itself? Is it not what makes possible thought not as simply a series of operations or reproducible skills, not as *tekhnē*, but as a fundamental questioning of the constitution of our object world that also, in a real sense, brings that world into being as an object of thought, experience, and radical change? And do we not in just as many ways do it a disservice by turning that conversation into a thing that one can either use or reject, adopt or dismiss?

Moreover, if it is a thing, if one can be either for or against theory, does it have different varieties or flavors? Can we move through our intellectual cafeteria line and take a helping of psychoanalysis, a bit of deconstruction, a side of Marxism, and a lovely little dollop of the new materialism for dessert? Is this not what our primers

# THEORY DOES NOT EXIST

and introduction to theory courses too often lead our students and those who would condemn us to believe, that these "methodologies" are separate entities that both somehow all fall under the magical term theory and yet are separable, and you can choose between them as your desire, your hunger, or your nutritional need sees fit? But is this not exactly what Derrida, in many ways the prime exemplar of theory and the "theoretical turn," in a work like *La carte postale* demonstrates not to be true, showing instead that Plato, Socrates, Freud, medieval monastic culture, theory, philosophy and postmodern capitalism are so interimplicated that the very notion that they could be separated from one another and dealt with as semiautonomous entities is precisely as absurd as trying to read Plato today without thinking of Freud.

In 1976, Michel Foucault delivered his annual course at the Collège de France, entitled that year, *Il faut défendre la société*. In it, he argues that history as a discourse has had two primary functions in western society after antiquity. The first, from the Middle Ages through the 18th century, was to legitimate the powers of the sovereign by tracing their origin to Rome. This strategy can be seen in sources as disparate as Geoffrey of Monmouth's 12th century *History of the Kings of Britain* and Ronsard's *Françiade*, as well as in Petrarch's famous statement, "what is there in history that is not the praise of Rome" (Foucault 1997: 65). The second function, however, is to conceptualize the history of nations as the chronicle of a war between opposed races. These were not initially understood to be biological races, and these discourses certainly did not correspond to a racist world-view or to a scientific racism, such as became prominent first in the 19th century and would later go on to underwrite Nazi ideology, Jim Crowe, manifest destiny, and European imperialism. Nonetheless, in many ways, these early, often obscure, historical works, Foucault argues, provide the rhetorical and intellectual foundations that make those later social and epistemic formations possible. They also provide a set of analytical and story-telling tools that underlie a variety of later models of historical development that see the primary motor of history as being an irreconcilable conflict between mutually exclusive, opposed populations, ranging from social Darwinism to the Stalinist purges.

This second type of history, which knows no analogue in either the ancient or the Medieval world, was initially proposed as a counter history. It opposed to the royal narrative of continuity and linear descendance from antiquity to the present a counter story of conquest, oppression, resistance, and wars of liberation. It was initially produced by writers seldom read today, such as Hotman, Boulainvilliers, and Thiers, as well as others long forgotten. These were often the writers of reaction, defending the rights of the nobility against an increasingly centralized monarchy, which had founded its legitimacy on arguments of continuity and lineal transmission. But at the same time, these reactionary counter historians were also forging the discourse of revolution. They present modernity as a break from antiquity, an illegitimate usurpation. Their discourse is founded on unearthing the secret history of the conquest of the nation, whether in the form of the Norman conquest in England or of the invasion of the Franks and the Merovingian conquest of the indigenous Gallo-Romans. These writers comb the archives to build their narratives, stories that would be decisive, as Foucault shows, both for Walter Scott and Marx himself (1997: 69, 87).

170                 THEORY DOES NOT EXIST

For many, Foucault's name is virtually as synonymous with theory as Derrida's. Together with Lacan, these three made up the ruling troika of what used to be known as "French theory." They were antihumanist Nietzscheans bent on upending the centrality of the subject, the self-evidence of liberalism, and the quiet verities of postwar American literary formalism. If the barbarians were at the gates, they spoke French, and if this was theory, then we should definitely be against it, as the likes of William Bennett (1992), Allan Bloom (1987), E. D. Hirsch (1987), or even René Wellek (1983) assured us (Derrida 1986: 12, 41–43n5; Derrida 1988: 34–35n.2; Miller 2016a). Theory, as thus portrayed, was indeed a thing, and it was bad: a vile abstraction that threatened to swamp all we valued beneath a welter of incomprehensible jargon and half-digested philosophy.

Yet what kind of "thing" was Foucault actually up to here and what would it mean to be for it, or for that matter, against it. If we ask him, the metaphor he offers is oddly enough not so dissimilar from that of the Irish monks I offered at beginning of this paper. He presents himself less as the Nietzschean superman and much more as the Nietzschean philologist. If he is a theorist, his theory is not one that can be either abstracted or generally applied, nor is it contemplative in the Aristotelian sense of *theoria*, but rather it is very much the product of the archive and the barely audible, often arcane, conversations contained therein:

> After all, the fact that the work I have presented you had this simultaneously fragmentary, repetitive, and discontinuous manner of presenting itself, would correspond closely to something that one could call a "feverish laziness," which characteristically affects the lovers of libraries, of documents, of references, of dusty writings, of texts that have never been read, of books which, as soon as they are printed, are closed up and sleep then on the shelves from which they are taken only several centuries later. All of this would go well with the busy idleness of those who profess a knowledge to no end, a sort of extravagant knowledge, the wealth of the parvenu whose exterior signs, as you well know, are found spread across the bottoms of their pages. That would be suitable for all those who identify with one of those most ancient but also most characteristic secret societies of the West, one of those strangely indestructible secret societies … which were formed early in Christianity, during the time no doubt of the first convents, on the border of the invasions, the fires, and the forests. I mean the great, tender and passionate free masonry of useless erudition. (1997: 6).

Of course, Foucault here does not so much mean that this knowledge is completely useless, any more than the manuscripts copied, annotated, and illuminated by those Irish monks were useless, even though no single one of those monks ever imagined the uses to which those manuscripts and their collective efforts would be put. Rather these are knowledges that are not completely subjected to or exhausted by immediate use, knowledges that have been swept aside or subjected by new, hegemonic configurations of power, knowledges that once unearthed reveal both the capillaries of knowledge and power that have nourished the dominant synthesis of the present and thereby offer new possibilities of thought, new forms of knowledge and truth.

They do not so much offer a "global theory" as the possibility of a local critique. Foucault's next remarks here are prescient. They recall very much the impasse faced by

# THEORY DOES NOT EXIST

the humanities in the modern American university, where we are constantly asked to justify our existence in terms of outcomes assessment, value added, and the income levels of our graduates. What contribution does a commentary on Origen's homily on the *Song of Songs*, a new reading of Montaigne's "Des cannibales," or a study of postcolonial film make to the reduction of student debt, to post graduate income levels, and to powering the infernal machine of endlessly increasing commodity production and consumption? Foucault's response is neither to fall back on claims of timeless values, which are only too obviously time bound, nor to submit to a narrowly conceived utilitarianism, but to call for and foster an insurrection of "subjected knowledges":

> [A] local critique is accomplished, it seems to me, through what we might call the "returns of knowledge." By "returns of knowledge," I mean the following: if it is true that in recent years we have often encountered at least on a superficial level a recurring motif: "not more books but life!" "not more knowledge, but reality," "not books, but cash," etc., it seems to me that under, across, and within this recurring motif, what we have seen produced is what might be called the insurrection of "subjected knowledges." (Foucault 1997: 8)

Now Foucault in these passages was as much addressing the anti-intellectualism of the Cultural Revolution as of the neoliberal state (Macey 1993: 217–19; Peeters 2010: 269–96; Miller 2016b: chapter 2). There is a sense in which the demand for immediate political utility is the obverse of the insistence on the assessment and commodification of all knowledge. But the subjected knowledges to which he is referring, the dusty tomes to which his attention was turned, revealed a world of hidden conversations and debates, which not only had been subjected to later hegemonic narratives but which also can be shown to have created the intellectual substructure of many of the best known discursive formations of the next two centuries. In the coming years, his attention would turn to the language of the confessional, of Stoic philosophy, and of ancient justifications for the courage to stand before your prince, your people, or your soul and tell the truth. These discourses, of course, spoke to a variety of contemporary concerns from the genealogy of psychoanalysis to the creation of a counter history of philosophy as a set of practices and forms of self-relation, rather than a body of doctrine, but in no case do they offer a global theory. They inform what Foucault termed the ontology of the present, i.e., the being of our present moment, the way in which reality is defined and exists for us, not in the form of a transcendental deduction, but as a thousand barely audible voices and institutions that inform, contradict, and determine one another and exist in a recursive relationship between present and past that in turn constitutes the future as a determined set of possibilities (Foucault 2008: 4–5, 22, 273, 285–86).

What then do we mean by theory? For my good friend and colleague, Zahi Zalloua, theory is defined by its opposition to philosophy. If philosophy seeks a world of pure thought, then theory is messy, impure, interdisciplinary. If philosophy seeks certainty, theory strives to be skeptical, to put itself forever in question, to be forever critical. If philosophy aims for the truth, the incontrovertible, the certain, theory is fictive, constructed, contingent. Hegel's *Logic*, Russell and Whitehead's *Principia Mathematica*, and Wittgenstein's *Tractatus* are philosophy by this definition, or at least that is what they very much aim to be. Kierkegaard, Nietzsche, and Derrida are theory, messy, literary, and skeptical. Zalloua in his closely argued and powerful book, *Theory's Autoimmunity* (2018), offers a ringing defense of theory as the critical self-analysis of reason from the standpoint of its own inscription.

Autoimmunity refers to the way in which the protective system of the body turns against itself as in such autoimmune disorders as lupus, rheumatoid arthritis, or ulcerative colitis. It is what happens when the body identifies the same as other, when the self starts to defend itself from itself, from the other that always exists within the self. Theory then names a move whereby reason, and more precisely reason's inscription into the material, its practice by a self, its critical recognition of its own historical contingency, turns on itself and undermines philosophy's claims to pure reason, to unadulterated certainty, to the absolute truth, at least in so far as those claims are actually made. Theory on this view is what turns reason from a protective coating into a gaping wound that allows the external to penetrate within us, to become recognized as the already internalized. It is what makes us vulnerable to the event, "Without autoimmunity nothing would happen; there would be no presence, no event of any kind. The event punctures the psychic shield afforded by our habits, which constitute our lifeless or quasi-mechanistic horizon" (Zalloua 2018: Introduction). Without the piercing of the envelope of self-protective identity, there is no encounter with the event or the other, but instead, as in *Beyond the Pleasure Principle*, or the *Philebus* for that matter, a return to a homeostatic sameness that is impossible to differentiate from either death or immortality.

And this, in turn, is precisely the argument in Plato's *Symposium*. Human beings can never possess wisdom but only the love of wisdom, *philosophia*, because to possess wisdom fully would mean to reach perfection, and the perfect is that from which nothing is missing. Those from whom nothing is missing do not experience love or desire because you cannot desire that which you fully possess. Therefore, only the gods possess wisdom and insofar as they must be completely bereft of desire, they must also be completely unmoved and unmoving, and therefore in the perfection of their immortality, they are indistinguishable from the dead (200a–203a). They are literally beyond the pleasure principle. But we humans, in our wounding imperfection,[2] in our openness to the other we do not possess, in our desire, in our traumatic autoimmunity and its shuddering *jouissance*, we must settle for mere philosophy, which names not certainty, not the possession of knowledge, but its simultaneous pursuit and lack. And so at the very origins of philosophy, when Plato dictates to Socrates, to Socrates who is the source of Plato's wisdom, we find theory, as defined by Zalloua, not opposed to philosophy, but as the very conditions of its existence qua philosophy.

The search for wisdom, however, comes to us in a variety of practices, none of which can be separated from their various forms of embodiment and inscription. It may be instructive at this point to turn our attention briefly to monks in a very different tradition from those in Ireland. Specifically, I would ask you to consider the Buddhist monks and hermits of China and Japan, the searchers for truth and enlightenment, who would

---

2  C.f. Aristophanes' myth of the androgyne.

## THEORY DOES NOT EXIST

173

leave their lives behind, sometimes lives of great privilege, go out and sit facing a wall for years at a time, practicing what in the vocabulary of the later Foucault would be termed "technologies of the self" or "the arts of existence."[3] As he would contend in his final lectures at the Collège de France, which focused on the ancient philosophy of the west rather than the east, these "technologies" and "arts" were best understood as "spiritual practices," practices of self-formation and reflection that prepared the subject to receive the truth and to perform acts of truth, or *alèthurgies* to use the term he coined in 1980 when beginning his examination of early Christian practices of confession and profession (Hadot 1995: 21–22; Foucault 2001: 16–17; compare Festugière 1950: 21–22; Foucault 2012: 8, 48, 79–81, 111–12, 151–57). As Plato emphasizes in his 7th letter, such practices, while deeply learned, did not simply involve the receiving and repeating of predigested information (or misinformation), but *tribē*: a labor, a continuous friction, that leads to the "spark" or "flame" of enlightenment (340–44; Foucault 2008: 51–56, 192–234). This is true philosophy according to Plato, and in this philosophical tradition, to which Foucault clearly affiliates himself, but in which he would also include Nietzsche, the Kant of *What is Enlightenment*, the Stoics, and the Cynics, the truth is never fully separable from the act that produces it, even as that act, to be an act of truth, an *alèthurgie*, must point beyond itself (Foucault 2001; 2008: 8–9, 29–36, 64, 322; 2009). The monks of Iona who produced the *Book of Kells* and other masterpieces of early Celtic art did not simply transmit the information that makes up our civilization, as if the conversation could be reduced to its separable referents, but they maintained, elaborated, and transmitted its practice, a form of writing and inscription that can never be reduced merely to the immediate utility of its products.

Bodhi Dharma came from the west. He sat for nine years facing a wall on Mount Song, bringing Buddhism and the practice of the Chan to China. To make sure he did not fall asleep but continued his meditation with full awareness, he slit his eyelids, seeking the moment of enlightenment. In an early Chan text, the *Song of the Jewel Mirror Awareness*, we read:

> Filling a silver bowl with snow
> Hiding a heron in the moonlight
> When you array them they are not the same;
> When you mix them, you know where they are.
> The meaning is not in the words,
> Yet it responds to the inquiring impulse. (Cleary 1980: 39)

These other monks, these *Rishis*, are the Buddhist seekers of enlightenment who know they have reached it precisely at the moment when the search itself becomes what is sought. The event, the moment when Being beyond the opposites (Radcliff and Radcliff 1993: 13–33), beyond the binary nature of opposed truths reveals

---

3  Foucault 1984: 35; 1994a: 415; 1994b: 617; 2001: 241–42; Kremer Marietti 1985: 251, 277; Nehamas 1998: 168–69; Gros 2001: 524–525.

174 THEORY DOES NOT EXIST

itself, is also the moment of its simultaneous disappearance (Mumonkan Case 19).[4] The fetishization of truth, the fantasy that you can possess it and be the god of Plato's *Symposium*, is also the moment when truth disappears, when enlightenment becomes both death and immortality, but also delusion (Suzuki 1970: 21–22). The search for the truth, for the *event* in the moment of its disclosure is no less authentic for the fact that in the grasping of the event it vanishes in a moment of self-occultation. The event itself is no thing and the attempt to reduce it to a thing, a reproducible entity, is to deny its status precisely as the event, a something beyond the endless reproduction of the given. An early Chan text tells the following anecdote.

> Once as Yaoshan [a Chan monk of the Tang dynasty] was sitting, Shitou [his master] saw him and asked "what are you doing here?" Yaoshan said, "I'm not doing anything." Shitou said, "Then you are just sitting idly." Yaoshan said, "if I were sitting idly, that would be doing something." Shitou said, "You said you are not doing; what aren't you doing?" Yaoshan said "Even the saints don't know." (Cleary 1980: 35)

The moment of aporia in these practices, as in the early Socratic dialogues, becomes the search for truth itself. Such koans, as in Socratic practice, force the practitioner, to think beyond the categories of the given. That search is not opposed to study. It is indeed founded on study, a study that always moves toward the truth, toward that which breaks through the fetishization of different formations of power, discourse, and knowledge, but not in the name of a cynical claim that there are no facts, that knowledge does not exist, but in the endless pursuit of a truth whose fundamental realization, as the event, as the triumph of the autoimmune response, is both the destruction of the sovereign self, as Zalloua recognizes so well, *and* its absolute realization. As the thirteenth century Zen Master, Dogen writes:

> To study the Buddha way is to study the self. To study the self is to forget the self. To forget the self is to be actualized by myriad things. When actualized by myriad things, your body and mind as well as the bodies and minds of others drop away. No trace of realization remains, and this no trace continues endlessly. (Tanahashi 1985: 70)

Let us take just a moment to examine what is happening in this extremely dense passage. Dogen tells us that the study of Buddhism is on a fundamental level a form of self-realization or spiritual practice in the Foucauldian sense. But rather than producing a shallow new age focus on the self, as a bounded, centered entity, as a thing, the search for enlightenment instead leads to a deconstruction of the narcisstic self, to the recognition that the self has no existence apart from the myriad things out of which and in relation to which it is constituted. This recognition in turn both undermines the mind body distinction and the radical separation of self from other on which that distinction depends. That undermining, in turn, means that the realization of

---

4 "Nanquan said, "The Way is not in the province of knowledge, yet not in the province of unknowing. Knowledge is false consciousness, unknowing is indifference. If you really arrive at the inimitable Way, it is like space, empty and open; how can you insist on affirmation and denial?' At these words, Zhaozhou was suddenly enlightened" (Cleary 1992: 94). Thanks to Charles Platter for the reference.

THEORY DOES NOT EXIST 175

the self is its disappearance, its reduction to a trace that both continues endlessly and has no definable ontic existence.

What the Chan and Zen traditions bring to this discussion, even if only briefly, is to reframe the problematization of what is theory and what is philosophy in a larger, less ethnocentric context. What Foucault would argue has become lost in the teaching of much academic philosophy, but is central to the philosophical tradition—and I think it is important to realize that neither he nor Derrida ever self-identified as theorists but always as philosophers—is the valorization of practices of truth, *askeses*, that undo the opposition of theory and philosophy, that foreground not truth as endlessly reproducible information, not as what any ass can google and then present as *his* truth, but as an intersubjective practice that always includes its own processes of reflection, verification, and materialization as integral to the act of veridiction (Foucault 2008: 318).

And this in turn really is the point. Philosophy *is* this practice, this conversation, across the centuries, across genres, ultimately across entire civilizations, that reflects, produces, and criticizes acts of truth. It exists as processes of reflection, verification, and materialization, whether that is in the rarefied forms of philosophies of science and formal logic or in Socrates on the streets of Athens challenging his fellow Athenians to say what it is they know, to define justice, and to care for themselves. Philosophy is constituted in all its manifold forms by this dialogue with its own archive and by the debates on what constitutes that archive. Theory, in so far as it seeks to challenge the hegemony of a certain vision of philosophical purity, is always dependent on its reinsertion in the dialogue with philosophy. In Socrates's great speech in the *Phaedrus*, we are not presented with a series of deductions, we are not offered a method of adjudicating the truth or falsity of a given set of propositions, nor are we offered a set of truths that can be formalized separately from their textual formulation. In the vision of the parade of souls approaching the gods and catching ever so slight a glimpse of the forms of beauty and the good, of the souls who guide their chariots pulled by the horse of spirit and the horse of sexual desire (246e–248c), we have a complex myth of love that is self-consciously poetic and derivative, even as it seeks to oppose itself to the rhetorical manipulations of Lysias's cynical speech and Socrates' first speech. Myth in Plato, as we argued in chapter 4, is not a mere accidental ornament or illustration but a necessary supplement to the *logos* and dialectic (Robin 1966: xcvi; Zuckert 1996: 218). The archive of received semblances in Plato—myths, speeches hidden under one's cloak, writing itself—in the final analysis can never be completely dissociated from the truth philosophy claims to speak and to adjudicate. Thus, even the myths deployed by Socrates in his great speech are derived from the poetic tradition, the lore of Pythagoreanism, the mysteries, and Egyptian myth (Robin 1966: lxxix–lxxxvii, 44n1, 50n3; 158–60; Thompson 1973: xxvi–xxvii, 43–74; Morgan 1992: 231–39; Heitsch 1993: 95, 98–107). As Berger argues, the great speech pretends "to be a spontaneous ecstatic outburst when it is actually a citational pastiche" (1994: 102). It undermines philosophy's attempt to immunize itself against the other. It is in short theory: present at the birth of philosophy even in its vision of the ideal. Theory is the precondition, supplement, and transcendence of philosophy. Theory is antitheory, and as theory qua theory, as a *thing*, it does not exist.

In the ancient world, the other of philosophy is not named theory but rhetoric, and this opposition is precisely what is put into play in the *Phaedrus*, which begins as an examination of the power of Lysias's cynical demonstration speech, advocating that a young man should only yield to one who is not in love with him, since all lovers are mad. The dialogue famously ends with a philosophical examination of how speeches should be made and an argument for the philosophical *logographer* or speechwriter. The *Phaedrus* in fact is the first example of a philosophical examination of rhetoric and, as such, is the great predecessor to Aristotle's *Rhetoric* and such important later works as Cicero's *De Oratore*. In the middle of the *Phaedrus*, we find Socrates' great speech. It turns Lysias's argument on its head, contending that the beloved should *only* yield to the suitor who is in love, precisely because he is mad, like the poet and ultimately the philosopher. Thus the central exemplar of philosophy's superiority to rhetoric, both as philosophy and as rhetoric, is a poetic speech in which the philosopher argues for his own constitutive madness.

Philosophy can never be pure. It is always derivative from rhetoric and poetry, from various practices of embodiment. In the end, this conclusion is not the product of a deconstructive reading or an elaborate theoretical argument but is directly stated within the dialogue. Philosophy is a response to a pre-existing set of conversations, acts of imagination, acts of truth, and acts of persuasion. When Socrates begins his critique of Lysias's speech, Phaedrus is incredulous. He asks, "where have you a heard better speech than this?" Socrates replies:

> Now I really can't say. But it's clear I've heard them, whether they be lovely Sappho or wise Anacreon or some prose writers? What sort of proof do I offer in support? I have a strange fullness in my breast, divine Phaedrus, and I perceive that I am able to say different things, which would not be worse, on this same topic. I know well that I have not at all thought about these matters, being conscious of my own ignorance. Indeed, I think, the only possibility left is that I have been filled through my ears from the streams of others, like a pitcher. But on account of a certain stupidity, I have forgotten this very thing, how and from whom I heard them. (*Phaedrus*, 235c1–d3)

This passage claims that Socrates is both ignorant and filled with information. He is, of course, being ironic, but not simply sarcastic. Every phrase in this passage overflows with meaning rather than simply points to its opposite. If there is no original word, then, at what point do we distinguish internal from external, philosophy as the authentic pursuit of truth from rhetoric or theory as the secondary manipulation of language? We don't. The moment such a distinction is made, the moment the play of difference is arrested, then language, words themselves become dead letters. The play of transmission is arrested; the letter ceases to arrive at its destination. The second answer, though, is to acknowledge the infinite irony of this temporal play. Primary and secondary, inside and outside are not fixed terms with fixed meanings, but neither are they meaningless. Rather only when Socrates ceases to ask questions, when he simply accepts being the wisest of men, does he cease to be in a complex, recursive, and mutually constitutive relationship with Plato, Freud and us, to be our inspiration and creation. Filled with the knowledge of others, like a pitcher, and completely ignorant, inspired and utterly derivative of the poets and writers of prose: philosophy is constituted both as itself and its other, as both theory and antitheory.

# THEORY DOES NOT EXIST

We make then a fundamental mistake in arguing for or against theory, as if theory were a thing that can be simply refused or accepted, anymore than can philosophy or rhetoric, at least within a world in which people still seek to discuss, persuade, or imagine. Rather, what I would contend we must do in our seminar rooms, our lecture halls, our journal articles and books is relentlessly to expose the myriad ways in which the very possibility of the existence of our civilization is dependent on this work, on the continuity of this work, even when it might appear to those outside that we are doing nothing. The very possibility of a self that cares for itself in relation to others, that distinguishes in a coherent and sustained fashion between truth and falsity, that is able to conceptualize and defend a moral universe beyond immediate utility, beyond the crushing brutality of pure exchange value, and that is not consumed by fear and hatred, by the death drive, is dependent up on the practices of truth, imagination, and persuasion that we preserve, refine, and continue in this conversation. The ontology of the present, as a present, is made up of the discourses that contribute to that conversation and of the practices that constitute them. By making those practices visible, we both transmit them and open them up to interrogation, criticism, and change. We make articulate resistance possible. By unearthing the dusty subjected knowledges and the barely audible voices that created them, we both enliven them and make new discursive options available. We make it possible to think, and thus to act, differently (Foucault 1984: 14–15). In doing so, we reveal the constitutive debt that the future not only owes the past, but the past the future, that Socrates always in a sense took dictation from a Plato that only Freud made possible. In doing so, we reveal the postal system, the material substructure that allows the letter to arrive at its destination: a gossamer like structure that is all too fragile in the strands that bind it together.

Yaoshan while meditating said in response to his master's query,

"I'm not doing anything." Shitou said, "Then you are just sitting idly." Yaoshan said, "if I were sitting idly, that would be doing something." Shitou said, "You said you are not doing; what aren't you doing?" Yaoshan said "Even the saints don't know." (Cleary 1980: 35)

The fact that even the saints don't know is precisely what makes this practice, our practice, at least *in potentia*, a radically transformative act: for when we sit in our studies, discuss in our seminar rooms, and lecture in our auditoriums, we may appear to be doing nothing, and indeed what we are doing is *no thing*. Yet I would contend that the conversation in which we are participating, the conversation that we name variously theory, philosophy, rhetoric, and literature, the search for truth, is itself both fundamental to the constitution of the world of things as things, as a set of defined ontic categories, and to the possibility of revolution in ways yet to be imagined.[5]

---

5   Many thanks to Anna Kornbluh and Irving Goh, whose articulate questions both at the initial presentation at the Society for Critical Exchange, and in subsequent conversation helped to sharpen my focus and make this a better paper. Thanks also to Steven Shankman for his constructive feedback and encouragement, and to my audience at the English Department at Ewha Woman's University in Seoul who heard a later version of this paper and whose lively response I greatly appreciated.

# Works Cited

Bennett, William J. 1992. *The De-Valuing of America: The Fight for Our Culture and Our Children.* New York: Touchstone.

Berger, Harry, Jr. 1994. "*Phaedrus* and the Politics of Inscriptions." *Plato and Postmodernism.* Ed. Steven Shankman. Glenside, PA: Aldine Press. 76–114.

Bloom, Allan. 1987. *The Closing of the American Mind.* New York: Simon and Schuster.

Cleary, Thomas, ed and trans. 1980. *Timeless Spring: A Soto Zen Anthology.* Tokyo and New York: Weatherhill.

———, ed. And trans. 1992. *No Barrier: Unlocking the Zen Koan.* New York: Bantam.

Danzig, Gabriel. 2003. "Apologizing for Socrates: Plato and Xenophon on Socrates' Behavior in Court." *Transactions of the America Philological Association* 133: 281–321.

Derrida, Jacques. 1980. *La carte postale: De Socrate à Freud et au-delà.* Paris: Flammarion.

———. 1986. *Memoires for Paul de Man.* The Wellek Library Lectures at the University of California Irvine. Trans. Eduardo Cadava, Jonathan Culler, Cecile Lindsay, and Avital Ronnell. New York: Columbia University Press.

———. 1988. *Mémoires pour Paul de Man.* Paris: Galilée.

Festugière, A. J. 1950. *Contemplation et vie contemplative selon Platon.* 2$^{nd}$ ed. Paris: Vrin. Original, 1935.

Foucault, Michel. 1984. *L'Usage des plaisirs. Histoire de la Sexualité.* Vol 2. Paris: Gallimard.

———. 1994a. "L'écriture de soi." *Dits et écrits: 1954–1988.* Vol. 4. Eds. Daniel Defert et François Ewalt. Paris: Gallimard. 415–30.

———. 1994b. "A propos de la généalogie de l'éthique: un aperçu du travail en cours." *Dits et écrits: 1954–1988.* Vol. 4. Eds. Daniel Defert et François Ewalt. Paris: Gallimard. 609–31.

———. 1997. "*Il faut défendre la société*": *Cours au Collège de France. 1976.* Eds. Mauro Bertani and Alessandro Fontana. Paris: Gallimard and Seuil.

———. 2001. *L'herméneutique du sujet: Cours au Collège de France. 1981–1982.* Ed. Frédéric Gros. Paris: Gallimard, Seuil.

———. 2008. *Le gouvernement de soi et des autres: Cours au Collège de France. 1982–1983.* Ed. Frédéric Gros. Paris: Gallimard and Seuil.

———. 2009. *Le courage de la vérité: Cours au Collège de France. 1984.* Ed. Frédéric Gros. Paris: Gallimard, EHESS, and Seuil.

———. 2012. *Du gouvernement des vivants: Cours au Collège de France. 1979–1980.* Ed. Michel Senellart. Paris: EHESS, Gallimard.

Gros, Frédéric. 2001. "Situation du cours" in Michel Foucault, *L'herméneutique du sujet: Cours au Collège de France. 1981–1982.* Ed. Frédéric Gros. Paris: Gallimard, Seuil. 487–526.

Hadot, Pierre. 1995. *Qu'est-ce que la philosophie antique.* Paris: Gallimard.

Heitsch, Ernst. 1993. *Phaidros.* Göttingen: Vandenhoeck & Ruprecht.

Hirsch, E.D. 1987. *Cultural Literacy: What Every American Needs to Know.* New York: Houghton Mifflin.

Kierkegaard, Søren. 1989. *The Concept of Irony with Continual Reference to Socrates.* Eds. and trans. Howard V. Hong and Edna H. Hong. Princeton: Princeton University Press.

Kremer-Marietti, Angèle. 1985. *Michel Foucault: Archéologie et Généalogie.* 2$^{nd}$ ed. Rev. Paris: Livre de poche.

Macey, David. 1993. *The Lives of Michel Foucault.* New York: Pantheon.

Miller, Paul Allen. 2007. *Postmodern Spiritual Practices: The Construction of the Subject and the Reception of Plato in Lacan, Derrida, and Foucault.* Columbus: Ohio State University Press.

———. 2016a. "Ghosts in the Politics of Friendship." *Dead Theory: Derrida, Death, and the Afterlife of Theory.* Ed. Jeffrey Di Leo. Bloomsbury. 111–32.

———. 2016b. *Diotima at Barricades: French Feminists Read Plato.* Oxford University Press.

Morgan, Michael L. 1992. "Plato and Greek Religion." *The Cambridge Companion to Plato.* Ed. Richard Kraut. Cambridge: Cambridge University Press. 227–47.

Nehamas, Alexander. 1998. *The Art of Living: Socratic Reflections from Plato to Foucault*. Berkeley: University of California Press.

Peeters, Benoît. 2010. *Derrida*. Paris: Flammarion.

Radcliff, Benjamin and Amy Radcliff. 1993. *Understanding Zen*. Boston: Charles E. Tuttle and Company.

Robin, Léon. 1966. "Notice." *Platon: Phèdre*. Paris: Société d'Edition <<Les Belles Lettres>>. vii–ccv. Original = 1933.

Suzuki, Shunryu. 1970. *Zen Mind, Beginner's Mind: Informal Talks on Zen Meditation and Practice*. Ed. Trudy Dixon. New York and Tokyo: Weatherhill.

Tanahashi, Kazuaki, ed. 1985. "Actualizing the Fundamental Point." Trans. Robert Aitken and Kazuaki Tanahashi. *Moon in a Dewdrop: Writings of Zen Master Dōgen*. New York: North Point Press. 69–73.

Thompson, W. H. 1973. *The Phaedrus of Plato with English Notes and Dissertations*. New York: Arno Press. Original = 1868.

Wellek, René. 1983. "Destroying Literary Studies." *New Criterion* 2: 1–8.

Zalloua, Zahi. 2018. *Theory's Autoimmunity*. Evanston: Northwestern University Press.

Zuckert, Catherine H. 1996. *Postmodern Platos: Nietzsche, Heidegger, Gadamer, Strauss, Derrida*. Chicago: University of Chicago Press.

# INDEX

**A**

abject, the xxiv, 117, 141, 166
Achebe, Chinua xxv
Adorno, Theodor 153
Althusser, Louis 106
Amador, Carlos 166n1
Anacreon 50, 176
Anderson, Benedict 90, 92–94
Antigone xxiii, 124–26, 129–34,
    159–60
    *Antigone* 3, 123–24, 131
Aquinas, Saint Thomas 15
Aristophanes 19, 41, 127, 167, 172n2
Aristotle xviiin2, xxi, 15, 32–33, 35–36,
    62, 72, 74, 128, 145, 167–68,
    170, 176
Arnold, Matthew 167
assessment xxiv, 150–53, 158, 161,
    163, 171
Atticus 76–82, 85
Augustine, Saint 15, 25, 55, 90

**B**

Bach, Johann Sebastian 5, 10
Bakhtin, Mikhail 13, 15, 29, 106, 137, 142
Barthes, Roland 14
Bataille, Georges 13, 16, 109n8
Baudelaire, Charles 16
beautiful, the 2, 12, 24–25, 47, 49, 109,
    123, 127, 131, 134, 149, 151, 161–62,
    166–67, 175
Beauvoir, Simone de 1
Bennett, William 170
Bergson, Henri 1
Blanchot, Maurice xxii, 14, 72, 76, 78
Bloom, Allan 170
Bloom, Harold 14
Bodhi Darhma 173
Brautigan, Richard 9
Brecht, Bertolt 14

Bronte, Charlotte 1
Buddhism ix, 172–74
*Bury My Heart at Wounded Knee* 8
Bush, George W. xxiv

**C**

Camus, Albert xi, xxii, 91, 98, 101
*Catch 22* 9
Catullus, Gaius Valerius xi, 10–11,
    15n6, 86
Cervantes, Miguel de 4
Césaire, Aimé 4
Cicero, Marcus Tullius xi, xix, xx–xxii,
    3, 7, 15, 26–29, 34–35, 42, 46–47,
    55, 71–87, 176
Cixous, Hélène 138, 142, 143n16
classics xi, 2, 9, 26, 27n1, 32–33, 43n3, 44
Clément, Cathérine 141
Copjec, Joan 63n18, 125, 133, 160
Culler, Jonathan 14
Cynic (philosophy) 167
Cyrenaic (philosophy) 167

**D**

Dante Alighieri 15
de Man, Paul 13, 14, 25, 28, 38, 51, 76,
    81, 106
debt xx, 1–7, 10–11, 17–18, 22, 41n1,
    167–68, 171, 177
deconstruction xi, xiii, xvi–xvii, xix, xxi,
    13–14, 19, 25, 28, 41–42, 47, 52,
    59, 63, 67, 107, 119, 144, 146,
    168, 174
Deleuze, Gilles 65, 150n3
democracy 76, 81–82, 103
Derrida, Jacques xi, xiii, xvi–xviii, xx–xxii,
    2, 7, 13–15, 17, 28, 41–51, 55–67,
    71–87, 89, 95–98, 102, 165, 167–70,
    172, 175–76
    *Différance* xvii–xviii, 13, 60, 155n11

Derrida, Jacques (*Continued*)
  *Khôra* xxi–xxii, 29n7, 46, 55, 58–62,
    71, 86
  *La Carte postale* 17–20, 22, 46, 59, 61,
    167–69
  "La Pharmacie de Platon" ("Plato's
    Pharmacy") xxi, 18n10, 41–42, 44–
    50, 59, 61, 65, 79n11
  *Les Adieux* 95–98
  *Politiques de l'amitié* (*Politics of Friendship*)
    xxii, 61, 71–87, 96
  *Positions xvii*
  *Spectres de Marx* (*Specters of Marx*) xxii,
    71–72, 76–77, 86, 95
Di Leo, Jeffrey 1
Dogen xi, 174
Dumézil, Georges 17

**E**
Eagleton, Terry 106, 109
Eco, Umberto 28
elegy 32
Eliot, T. S. xiii, 10
enjoyment (*jouissance*) xvi, xviii, xx, xxiii,
    102, 107–8, 118, 123, 128–34,
    139, 142, 144–45, 159, 172
enlightenment 165, 172–74
Epicureanism 80, 85, 167
epistemology (epistemic) xiv, xvi, 16, 22, 56,
    91, 95, 119, 140, 163, 169
ethics xxiv, 34, 72n5, 91, 96–97, 108–9,
    118, 123, 129–30, 134, 152,
    158–60, 166

**F**
feminism xxiii, 15, 16, 125–26, 134,
    137–46
Foucault, Michel xi, xiii–xiv, xviii, xixnn3–4,
    xx, xxii–xxiii, 7, 13, 16–17, 25, 28, 61,
    76, 78, 81, 102, 123–26, 128–29, 131,
    166, 170–71, 173–75
  *History of Sexuality,* volume one 16n8, 124
  *History of Sexuality,* volume two (*L'Usage
    de plaisirs*) xxiii, 66, 94, 123–28,
    134, 177
  *Il faut défendre la société* (*Society Must Be
    Defended*) 91–94, 169–71
Frank, Jill 33, 41n1, 47n6
Frankfurt School 14

freedom xxii, 9, 34, 91, 93, 96–98, 100–1,
    117, 119–20, 129, 131, 134, 153,
    157–62
Freud, Sigmund xi, xiv–xvi, xviii, xxiii, 1, 9,
    14, 17, 19–22, 47, 123, 125, 129–32,
    134, 137n1, 141, 142n12, 144–45, 160,
    167–69, 176–77
  death drive xvi–xvii, xxiii, 71, 123, 125,
    129–33, 153, 160–61, 177
  pleasure principle xvi, xxiii, 17–22, 63,
    110, 123–26, 128–34, 160, 167, 172
Friedman, Milton 5
friendship xxii, 2, 71–87, 125n6, 127

**G**
gender 12, 111, 137, 138n5, 140,
    144–45
Goethe, Johann Wolfgang von 3, 166n1
the good xii, 45, 62n11, 97, 101, 109, 126–27,
    130, 134, 161, 167, 175
Guattari, Félix 65

**H**
Halperin, David 125
Hartman, Geoffrey 14
hauntology (haunting, the spectral)
    xvii–xviii, xxiii, 47, 72, 76, 78, 81–82,
    86, 97–98
Hegel, G. W. F. xvii, 14, 25, 30, 38, 107, 112,
    115, 117–18, 132, 156, 171
Heidegger, Martin 107, 117
Herbert, Kevin 10–11
Hirsch, E. D. 170
Horace 1, 34
hospitality xxii, 90–91, 95–103
humanities xi–xiii, xx, xxii–xxiv, 2–3, 5, 7,
    31, 106, 108, 150–51, 153, 161–62,
    165, 171

**I**
Irigaray, Luce xi, xxiii, 64, 137–46, 165
irony xxi–xxii, 28n5, 31–37, 41–43, 47–52,
    58–61, 65–67, 82, 84, 86–87, 101,
    163, 165, 167, 176

**J**
Jameson, Fredric 119–20
Janan, Micaela 138n5
Julian of Norwich 124–26, 132–34

# INDEX

justice xxiv, 1, 25, 61, 76, 87, 89, 96–97, 99, 101, 161, 166–67, 175
Juvenal xi, 110–12, 116

**K**

Kant, Immanuel xxiii, 27–28, 109n7, 151n4, 154–56, 158, 173
Keats, John 13
*Khōra* (*chora, khôra*) xii, xxi, 1, 29n7, 55, 59–67, 71, 96
Kierkegaard, Søren xi, 41, 46, 167, 172
Kofman, Sarah 165
Kojève, Alexandre 14
Kristeva, Julia xi, xx, xxiii, 7, 13, 16–17, 71, 76, 80, 107–8, 123n4, 124–28, 134, 137n1, 138, 139n6, 165

**L**

La Boétie, Étienne de 76, 81
Lacan, Jacques xi, xiii–xvi, xviii, xx, xxiii, 3, 13–15, 17–22, 27–28, 96, 102, 106–10, 117–18, 123, 125–32, 137–46, 150n3, 156n12, 158–61, 165, 167–68, 170
Laelius, Gaius 73, 75–86
Lentricchia, Frank 14
Levinas, Emmanuel 91, 95n6, 96–98
liberalism 95, 170
  neoliberalism xiin1, xx, 95, 171
*libertas* (frankness) xxi, 34–35, 38
literature (the literary) xi–xii, xx–xxiii, 2, 9–10, 13–16, 22–23, 27–28, 31, 43n4, 44, 56, 77, 105–11, 115–16, 118, 120, 170, 172, 177
*logos* xii, xvii, xix, xxi, 1, 3, 7, 27–28, 38, 42, 44n3, 46, 48, 58–59, 62–63, 150, 167, 175
Lucilius 34–35
Lukács, Georg 14
Lysias 43–45, 50, 52, 175–76

**M**

Mallarmé, Stéphane xi, 110, 112–16
Marx, Karl xxiii, 1, 71–72, 107, 144, 151n6, 169
Marxism 14, 71, 93, 168
Maurras, Charles 167
Miller, J. Hillis 14, 15n6, 17

Montaigne, Michel de 72–73, 76, 81, 85, 171
Mowitt, John xiin1
Mozart, Wolfgang Amadeus xxiii, 137
music xxiii, 2–3, 5–6, 8–9, 16, 19
*muthos* xvii, xxi, 44n5, 58–59, 62–63

**N**

Nabokov, Vladimir 105
Neruda, Pablo 2
neuroscience xv, 13, 159
Nietzsche, Friedrich 19, 72–73, 93, 170, 172–73

**O**

Oedipus xvi, 130
  *Oedipus Rex* xv
Origen 171
Ovid 32, 168

**P**

philosophy xii, xviii–xxii, xxiv, 1–2, 11, 13–14, 16, 18, 22, 26–29, 31–32, 35, 41–42, 45, 47–48, 50, 52, 56, 59–61, 63–67, 72, 77n9, 78, 80–82, 85, 94–95, 106, 113–14, 120, 150, 152–53, 155, 158, 160, 162, 167, 169–73, 175–77
Plato xi, xvii, xxiv, xix, xxi–xxii, 1, 7, 14–20, 27–29, 33, 41–46, 48–50, 52, 55–60, 62, 64, 66–67, 71–72, 74, 80, 97, 123–24, 126–27, 145, 166–69, 172–75, 177
  *Apology* xxiv, 33, 35, 51, 58, 61, 64, 66–67, 78–80, 84, 150–51, 162, 167
  *Gorgias* xix, 29, 42, 46
  *Greater Alcibiades* 48–49, 79–80, 124n4
  *Phaedrus* xxi, 18n10, 16, 29, 41–47, 49–50, 63, 79n10–11, 80, 123–24, 126–27, 167, 175–76
  *Philebus* xvii, 17–22, 28, 58, 63, 97, 134, 154, 167–68
  *Republic* 27–28, 45–48, 51–52, 56–57, 62n11, 150, 167
  *Symposium* 16, 19, 51, 60, 64, 79–80, 123–24, 126–28, 134, 150–51, 153, 161, 167, 172, 174

*ntinued*)
*Theaetetus* xxiv, 28, 29n7, 31, 56n1, 62, 64, 149–50, 152–53, 155, 157, 162–63
*Timaeus* xxi–xxii, 29n7, 46, 55–65, 67, 71, 96
Platonism 22, 50, 55–56, 60, 63
neo-Platonism 16, 55
Plotinus 16
Proust 1, 3
psychiatry xiii–xiv, xvi
psychoanalysis xi, xiii–xvi, xix, xxii–xxiv, 7, 13n1, 14, 16–17, 19–22, 28, 107–10, 117, 120, 123–28, 134, 137–38, 141–43, 145–46, 150n3, 158, 161, 167–68, 171
psychology xiii–xiv, xvi, 34, 150, 158
Ego Psychology xiv, xvi
Puhvel, Jaan 17
Pythagoreanism 46, 51, 55, 80, 175

**Q**
queer theory 125
Quintilian xxi, xxviii, 32, 35–36

**R**
racism 89–95, 101–2, 107n5, 113, 141, 165, 169
repeatability xiv, xxiv, 150–52, 159, 161, 163
unrepeatability xiv, xxiv, 129, 151–52, 159
rhetoric xi–xiii, xv–xvi, xviii–xxiii, 14, 26–33, 35–38, 41–43, 45, 47, 50–52, 63, 74, 91, 106, 110–11, 151, 169, 175–77
Rorty, Richard 17, 38
Rousseau, Jean-Jacques 14, 28, 93

**S**
Sappho 50, 176
Sartre, Jean-Paul xi, xxii–xxiii, 7, 14, 105–10, 117–20, 157
Saussure, Fernand de 14, 26n2
Schmitt, Carl 72–73, 76, 80
science xiii–xiv, xvi, xviii, xxii, 14, 16, 25, 27, 31, 36, 44, 58, 106, 128, 138, 145, 151–52, 155–56, 158–59, 161, 165, 175

social science xiii–xiv, xvi, xxiv, 14, 25, 150, 151n4
Scipio Aemilianus Africanus, Publius Cornelius 75–86
Scott, Walter 169
*Ivanhoe* 4, 7
Seneca 15
Shakespeare, William xv, 3, 109
Sidney, Sir Philip 13
Socrates xi, xix, xxi, xxiv, 1, 18, 20–21, 28–29, 32–33, 34n11, 35, 37, 41–52, 55–58, 60–61, 64–67, 78–80, 83–85, 106, 123, 126–27, 134, 142, 149–55, 157, 159, 161–63, 166–69, 172, 174–77
sophists xi, xviii, xxi, 41–48, 51–52, 58, 84–85, 151
Sophocles xi, 3, 15n6, 129, 159
Stein, Gertrude xii
Sterne, Laurence 13
Stesichorus 51
Stoic philosophy 26–29, 33, 83–86, 167, 171, 173
sublime xxiv, 109–10, 118, 120, 123, 125, 130, 166
Surrealism 14

**T**
Thackeray, William 13
theory (literary and cultural) xi–xiii, xviii–xxv, 13–17, 22–23, 26, 28, 30–33, 35, 38, 71, 106–7, 110, 112–13, 118, 124–25, 156, 165, 168–72, 175–77
Tolkein, J. R. R. 9
*topos* 29n7, 60, 62
Trump, Donald xxiv, 89, 117
truth xii, xiv, xvii–xxiv, 15, 20, 25–31, 33–38, 41–42, 44, 46–50, 52, 62, 65–66, 94, 123, 126–28, 130, 134, 138, 143, 152–54, 156–62, 166, 170–77
post-truth xii

**V**
Vlastos, Gregory 36
Vonnegut, Kurt 9

**W**
Watkins, Calvert 17
Wellek, René 170
Wittgenstein, Ludwig 29
Wordsworth, William 2

**X**
Xenophon xxi, 32, 167

**Y**
Yaoshan 174, 177

**Z**
Zalloua, Zahi 149n1, 171–72, 174
Žižek, Slavoj xi, xxiii–xxiv, 90n1, 107, 109, 129–31, 141, 150n3, 152–62

Milton Keynes UK
Ingram Content Group UK Ltd.
UKHW041853171024
449616UK00002B/20